CONCORDE
A PHOTOGRAPHIC TRIBUTE

CONCORDE
A PHOTOGRAPHIC TRIBUTE

ADRIAN MEREDITH

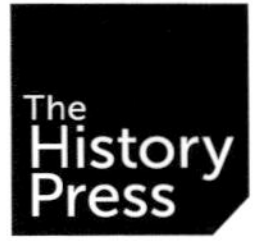

The History Press

Also by The History Press

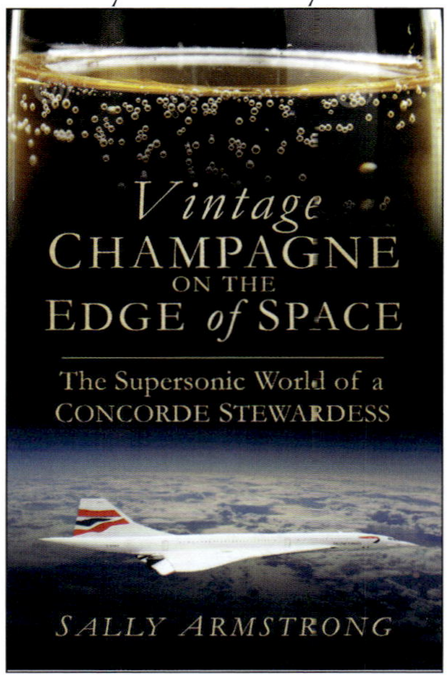

First published 2009
This paperback edition published 2013
Reprinted 2015, 2021, 2023

The History Press
97 St George's Place,
Cheltenham, Gloucestershire, GL50 3QB
www.thehistorypress.co.uk

© Adrian Meredith, 2009, 2013

The right of Adrian Meredith to be identified as the Author
of this work has been asserted in accordance with the
Copyrights, Designs and Patents Act 1988.

All rights reserved. No part of this book may be reprinted
or reproduced or utilised in any form or by any electronic,
mechanical or other means, now known or hereafter invented,
including photocopying and recording, or in any information
storage or retrieval system, without the permission in writing
from the Publishers.

British Library Cataloguing in Publication Data.
A catalogue record for this book is available from the British Library.

ISBN 978 0 7524 9324 4

Typesetting and origination by The History Press
Printed by Imak, Turkey

CONTENTS

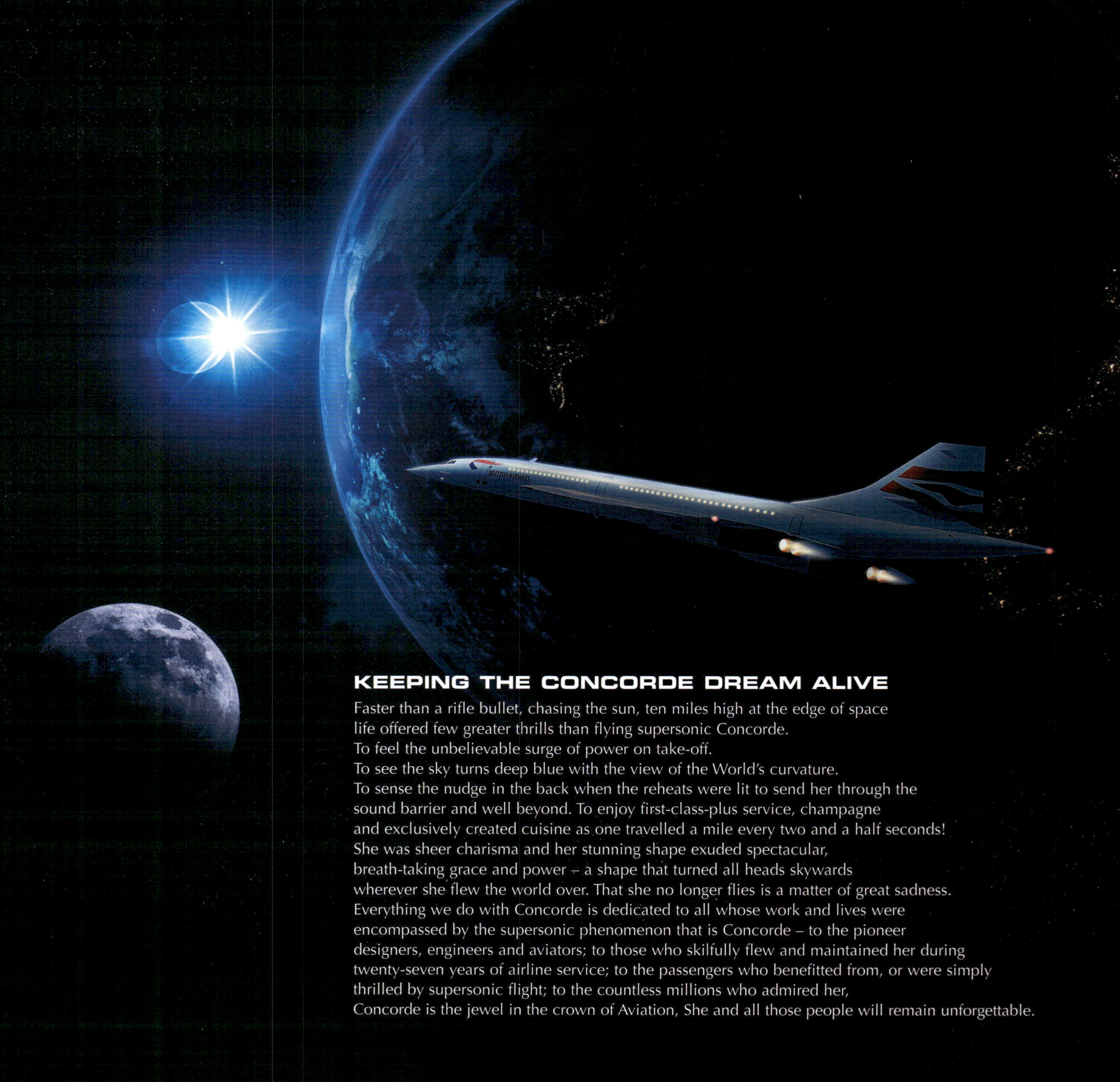

KEEPING THE CONCORDE DREAM ALIVE

Faster than a rifle bullet, chasing the sun, ten miles high at the edge of space
life offered few greater thrills than flying supersonic Concorde.
To feel the unbelievable surge of power on take-off.
To see the sky turns deep blue with the view of the World's curvature.
To sense the nudge in the back when the reheats were lit to send her through the
sound barrier and well beyond. To enjoy first-class-plus service, champagne
and exclusively created cuisine as one travelled a mile every two and a half seconds!
She was sheer charisma and her stunning shape exuded spectacular,
breath-taking grace and power – a shape that turned all heads skywards
wherever she flew the world over. That she no longer flies is a matter of great sadness.
Everything we do with Concorde is dedicated to all whose work and lives were
encompassed by the supersonic phenomenon that is Concorde – to the pioneer
designers, engineers and aviators; to those who skilfully flew and maintained her during
twenty-seven years of airline service; to the passengers who benefitted from, or were simply
thrilled by supersonic flight; to the countless millions who admired her,
Concorde is the jewel in the crown of Aviation, She and all those people will remain unforgettable.

ACKNOWLEDGEMENTS

First and foremost I would like to dedicate this second publication of my book to Lady Marshall, the wife of the late Lord Marshall who sadly passed away in 2012. Without the support of Lord Marshall, Concorde would not have survived her twenty-seven years of commercial flying with British Airways.

I would also like to thank friends and colleagues for their collaboration and help in producing this book, especially Concorde Senior Captain Mike Bannister, who, over the years, has spent many hours chatting with me about our experiences with Concorde.

A special thanks and acknowledgement to Gordon Roxburgh from Concorde SST, Captain Brian Walpole and Captain Jock Lowe for their support, especially with The Four Concordes tenth anniversary photography.

I would also like to thank sincerely Mike Blunt, previously the editor of *British Airways News*, for his assistance with many Concorde assignments, especially the Queen Mother's eighty-fifth birthday celebrations. In addition to British Airways, in particular the late Lord King for his support and encouragement during my freelance years with British Airways, and my dear friend Andy Patsalides, formerly of British Airways' Marketing Department.

Sincere thanks to the late Arthur Gibson, with whom I worked very closely in the 1980s and on various Concorde air-to-air assignments; his stunning artistry will be greatly missed in the aviation world.

Libbie Schmidt, from Australia: without Libbie this book would never have been published, as she was my introduction to The History Press. Thanks as well to Amy Rigg and her team, for all their efforts in designing and publishing this historic book.

Last but not least, a special thanks to my family: my dear wife Angela, for without her this book would not have been written; my beautiful daughter Emma; and Scott, a super, talented son, who is a graphic artist and helped me to restore many images for this book.

And finally, my photographic journey and experiences with Concorde and the crews, and all who flew in her, has been literally 'OUT OF THIS WORLD'!

All photographs taken by Adrian Meredith unless otherwise stated. For copies of the photographs in this book please visit www.concordephotos.com.

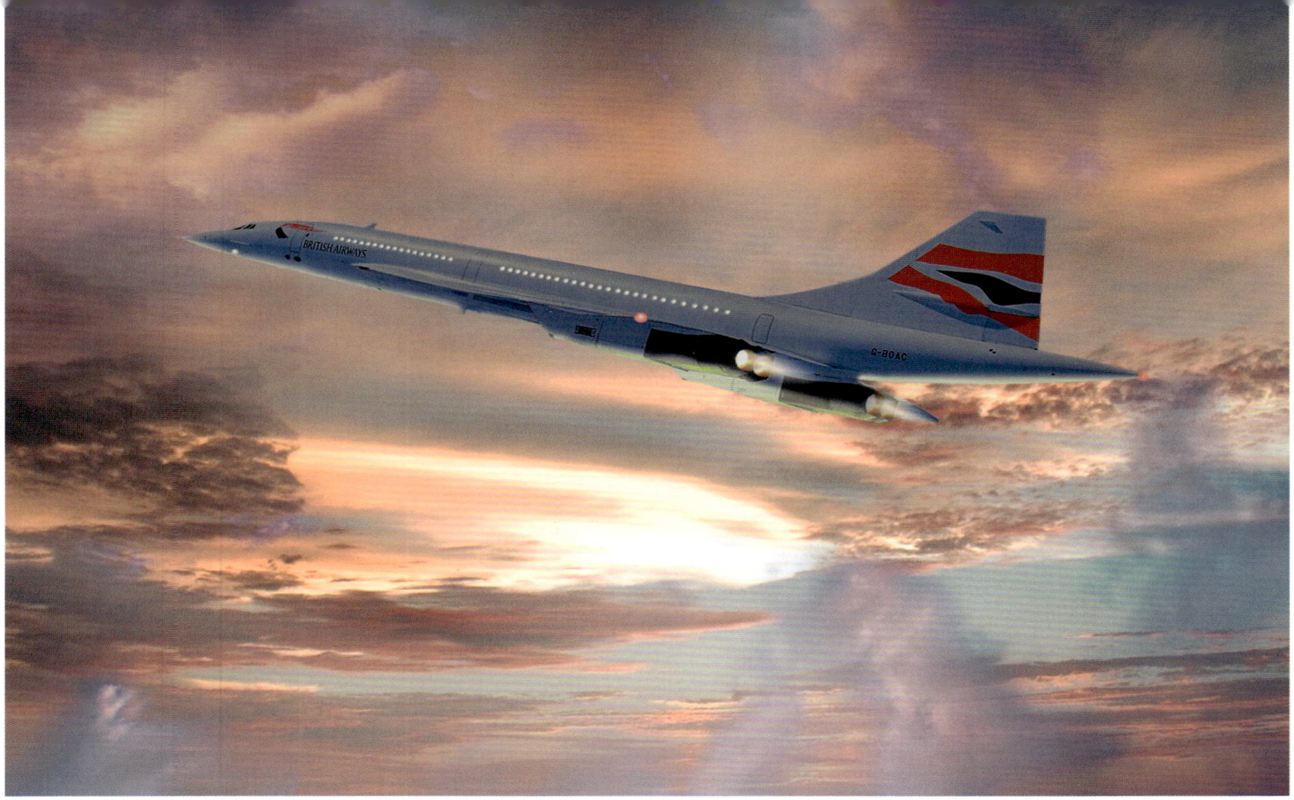

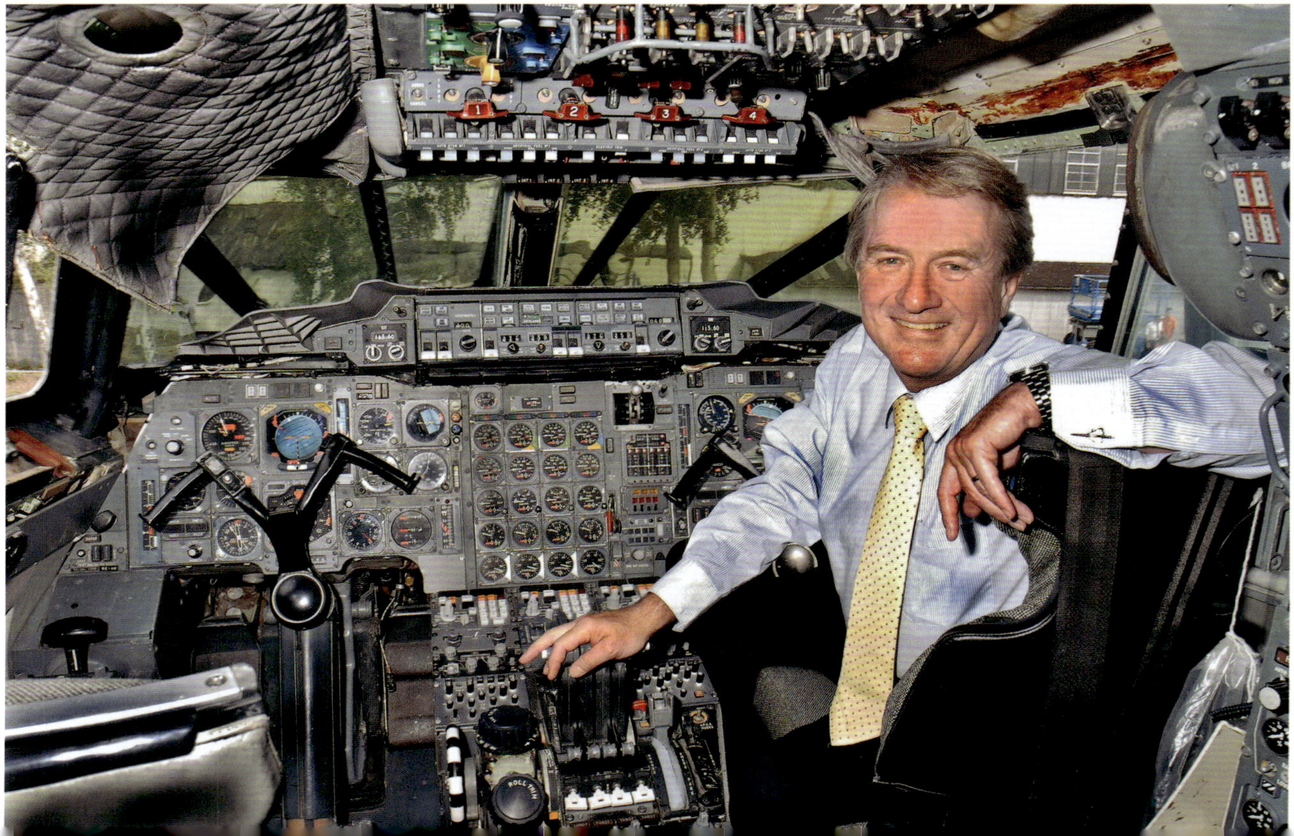

FOREWORD

Almost all seven-year-old children have pictures on their bedroom walls. Certainly, in 1956, I was no exception. Except it wasn't pop stars, actors or actresses that looked down upon me, it was aeroplanes. Famous fighters and bombers were joined by the new generation of jet aircraft and the most sophisticated airliners of the day. I have been fascinated with aviation ever since those mid-fifties days.

I can clearly recall sitting on a beach near Bournemouth in the heat of that summer and looking up to watch a small airliner on its way to France. With the precociousness of a seven-year-old, I worked out that flying the journey from our home to the seaside would have taken only twenty minutes as opposed to the awful five-and-a-half-hour coach journey we'd endured. I was sold! I wanted to be a pilot when I grew up.

I didn't think it through at the time but the path from there to joining BOAC as a VC10 pilot in 1969 involved a lot of hard work, study, sacrifice and not a little good luck. To keep me going and inspired, the pictures on the wall were joined by ones in the study, ones in books and ones in albums. They remained, however, all with one theme – aviation.

When I first saw Concorde 002 taking off from Filton on Wednesday 9 April 1969, I knew that I wanted to be a Concorde pilot. Then the pictures started changing but the inspiration they gave didn't.

To my eyes, and the eyes of countless others, an outstanding aviation photograph draws out the essence of it all: the designs that appeal to both sides of the brain – scientific and artistic; the beauty of the so many different colours that a sky can be; the way in which the same machine can appear so different through the lenses of different photographers. This book, by my good friend Adrian Meredith, draws together the very best of aviation-related photography over the forty-four-plus years since that first Concorde flight.

As well as Adrian's excellent work, there are pieces by other master practitioners of this elusive art, including Arthur Gibson, Mike Broomfield and John Dibbs – who I have seen in very close formation on a number of occasions. Believe me, it concentrates the mind enormously when you are flying at over 300mph and bringing a Concorde and a Jet Provost so close together that you can read the maker's name on John's camera!

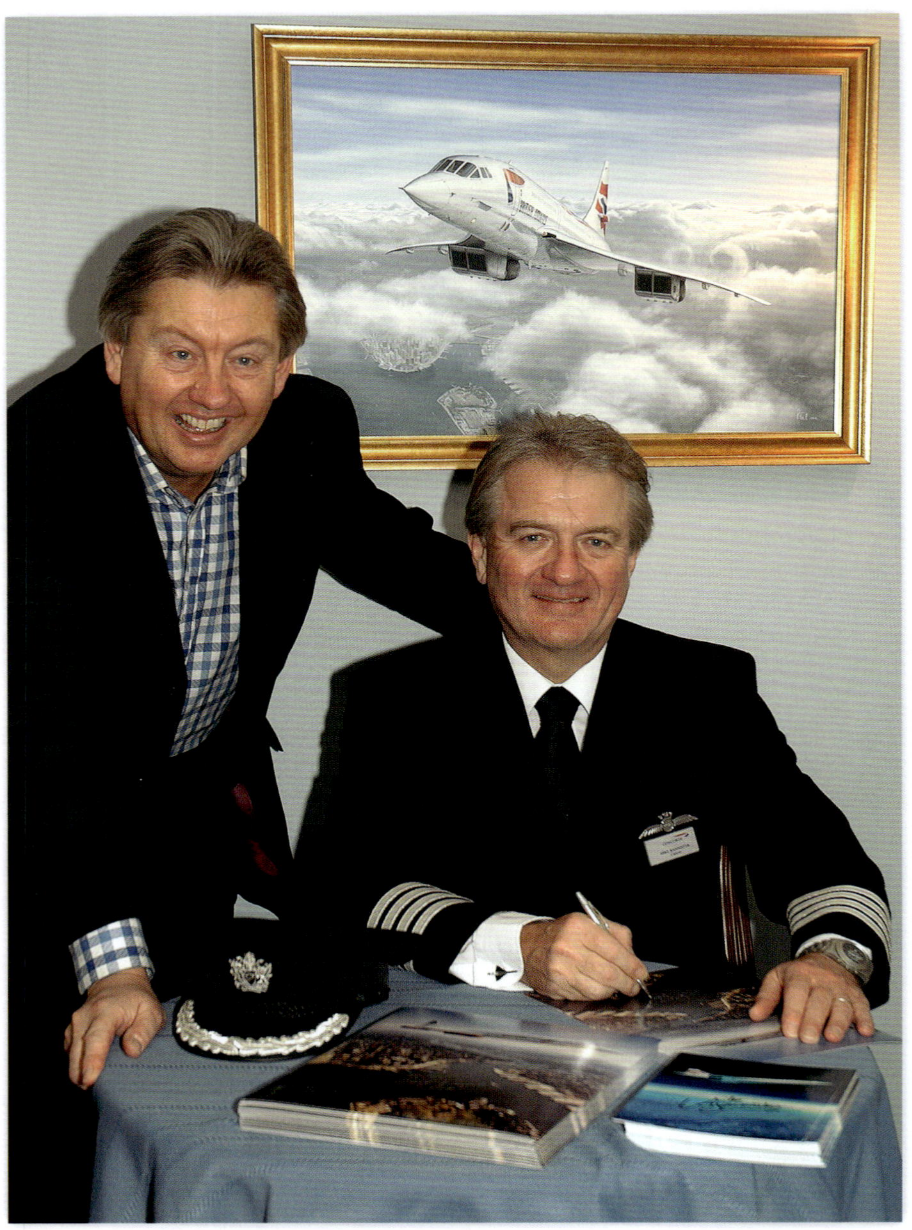

And then there was flying in close formation with the Red Arrows for HM the Queen's Golden Jubilee celebrations on 4 June 2002. I've never seen a million people before, but there we were, going down the Mall at just 300m above the ground. Believe me, seeing over a million people waving and cheering is very moving. Plus we could see Her Majesty clearly on Buckingham Palace balcony as she also waved – and smiled!

Just one year later, Concorde retired. So many say that it was surreal to say goodbye to such an aircraft when there is nothing to replace her. But the dream lives on, with both British Airways and Air France aircraft being key exhibits at sites across the globe, and none more so than at Brooklands Museum in Weybridge, UK. There lives the largest Concorde collection in the world: an aircraft, G-BBDG; the world's largest Concorde spares holding; the very simulator that I and my colleagues learned on; and, to welcome them all, the 40 per cent Concorde model that used to be at Heathrow now stands as proud 'Gate Guardian' at the entrance. It still stops the traffic.

Since their arrival 'DG has attracted over 300,000 visitors taking a virtual flight and the simulator has actually been flown by 3,000 lucky pilots. I regularly go back to Brooklands Museum to fly that simulator – but now just for the fun of it. With progress in computing since the simulator first entered service, it is now more realistic than ever before. To watch the excitement in the eyes of members of the public, young and old, as they fly the simulator, which effectively was the twenty-first Concorde, for themselves is truly refreshing and invigorating. It keeps the Concorde dream alive.

The pictures in this book trigger wonderful memories of my forty-six years in aviation and of the twenty-two years that I spent flying the most beautiful aircraft in the world. If you were fortunate enough to fly on Concorde then they will bring back an unrepeatable experience. If you wished you'd flown on Concorde then stimulate your imagination with the images in these pages. Not only does every one tell a story, they are a tribute to the one thing that makes all aviation so successful. No, it's not the aircraft, however beautiful; it's the people who make aviation – people worldwide who have been inspired, thrilled and motivated by the art of the air, just like that seven-year-old all those years ago.

Captain Mike Bannister
Former Chief Concorde Pilot ~ British Airways

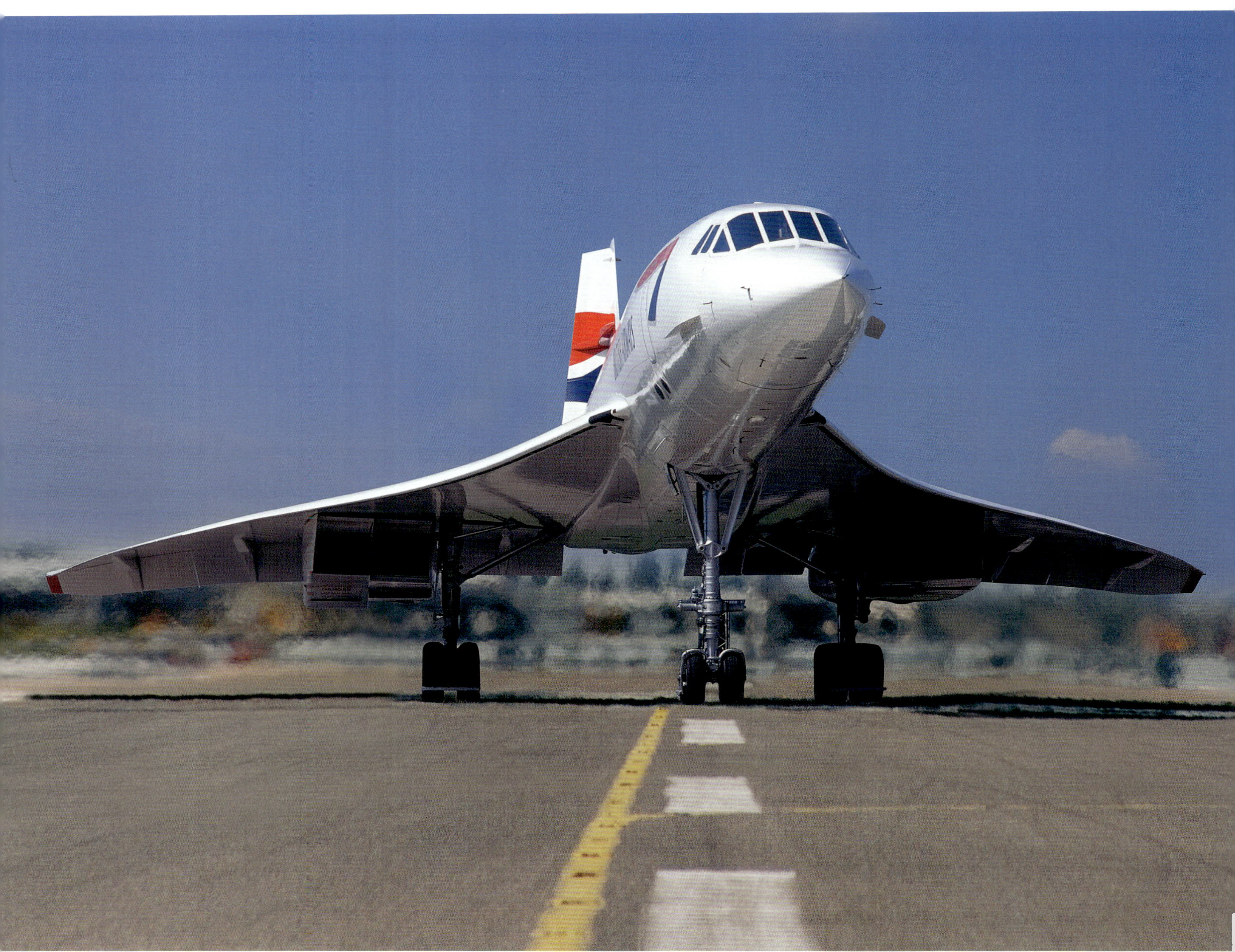

INTRODUCTION

I was born on 2 April 1952. My upbringing was not so different from many a working-class family living on the outskirts of London, in Merton; the days when all my cousins and friends played football in the street, and, when we got bored, would all travel up to town on the Tube for a day out. My father worked night shift as a G.P.O. engineer, and my mother worked as a telephonist for the Ministry of Defence. I had a basic education: being dyslexic, which was unheard of in those days, meant my school days were pretty hellish, but when I was a young boy, for treats, my father used to take me to the Toy Fairs in Olympia, London.

One particular year at Olympia was etched into my memory. A very large crowd had gathered in the centre of the main hall; being about nine or ten, I recall quite vividly pushing my way through a sea of legs, and sneakily edging to the front, to see what all the fuss was about. Displayed before me, and mounted on a low plinth, was an enormous glossy white model, at least 10ft long. It was shaped like a paper model aeroplane; we kids were always making them in class – they used to whiz through the air. The crowds and myself gazed in awe; no one had ever seen anything like this before. 'What's that Dad?' I asked in eagerness. 'That's Concorde son, a futuristic plane,' he replied. This was my first glimpse of what my future had in store for me; little did I know then that my career path would be so closely connected with this fantastic vision.

I left school with no formal training, and started working in a photographic agency in Fleet Street in 1967 as a tea and messenger boy. After a few years I progressed into the darkroom, and finally I left to take up a position as a trainee commercial photographer in a studio in the famous Windmill Street, London.

1976 was a good year: in June I married my wonderful wife, Angela, who was a model, and patiently sat for many tedious hours being my test guinea pig for numerous photographic shoots. That same year I won the coveted Ilford Photographer of the Year Award, and, later on, I also secured the position of senior in-house photographer for British Airways. This was the start of my thirty-year career in aviation photography, during which time I covered a vast portfolio of assignments and travelled to exotic locations all over the world, shooting not just British Airways aircraft but also the locations for their holiday brochures. This was also the year Concorde entered service.

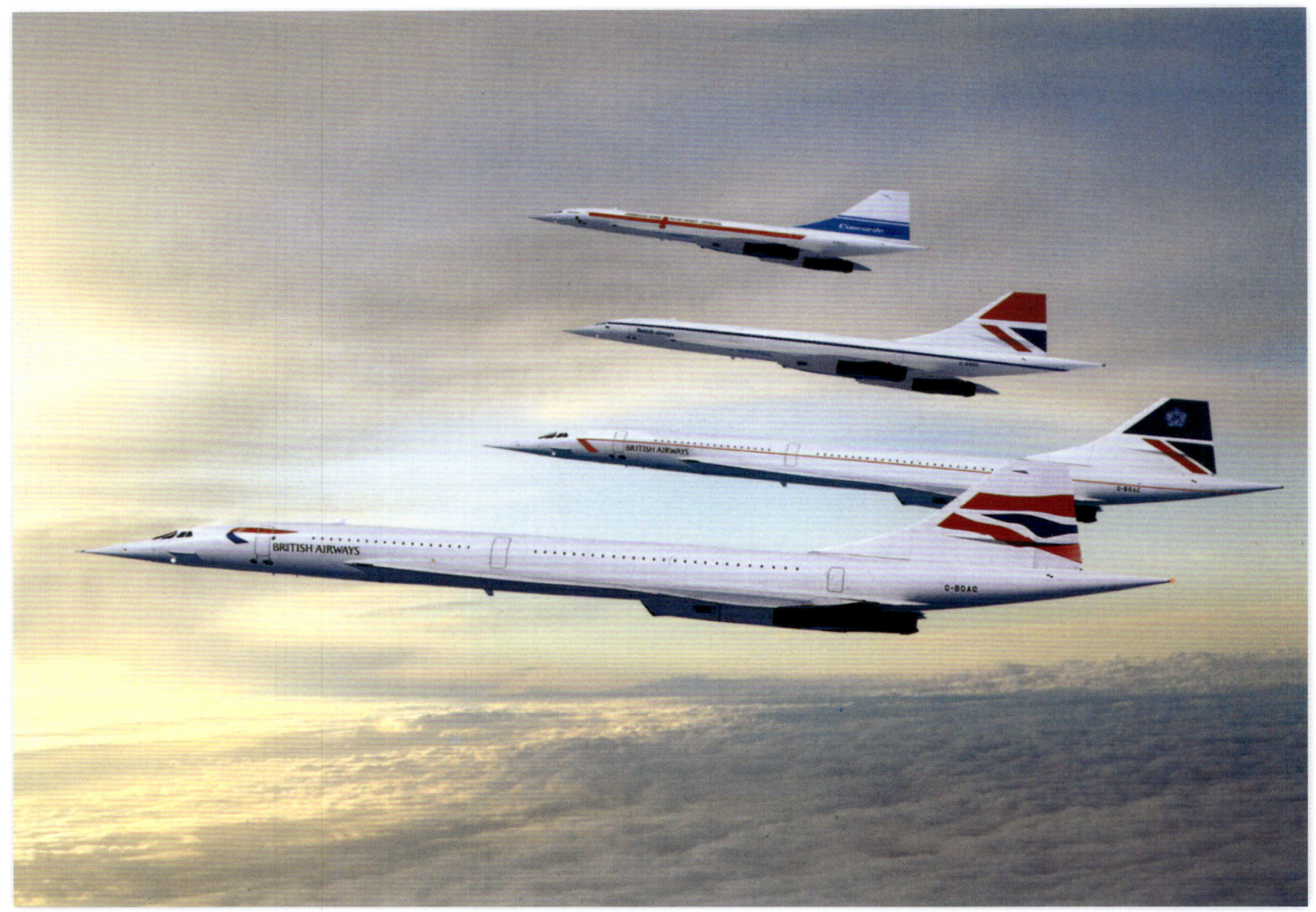

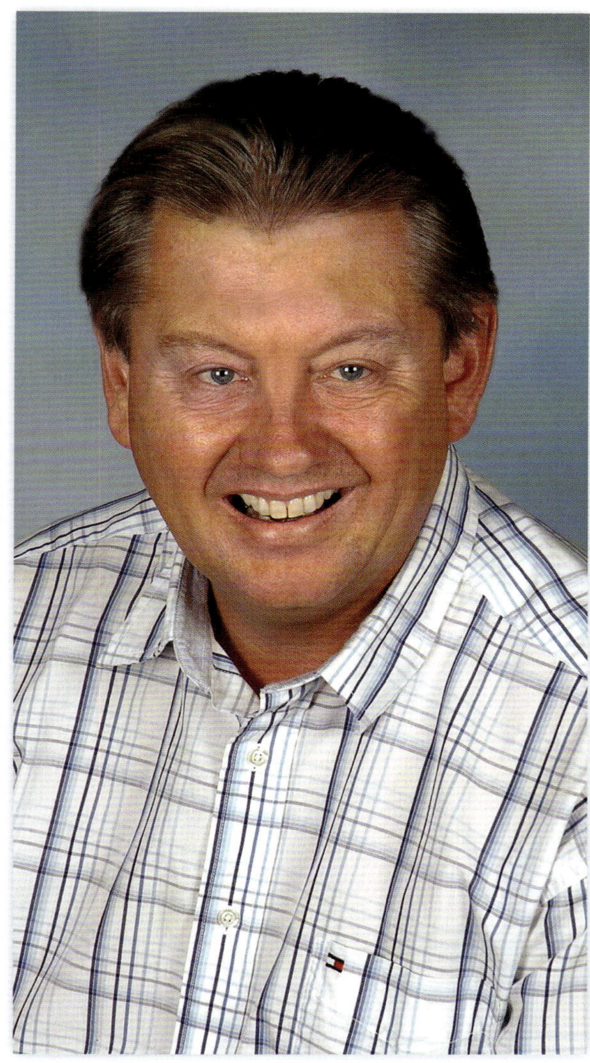

On my first day my boss at the Photographic Department correctly predicted that photographers would still be taking pictures of Concorde for years to come: 'From underneath she looks like a rocket, and if you look down, she's like a swan.' That same day I was taken to the Concorde hangar. At the time I did not realise that this would be the start of my love affair with the world's favourite aircraft, an icon so very photogenic it can look totally different from various angles. Concorde is undoubtedly the most inspiring aircraft ever to fly, one of the wonders of the modern world, flying at supersonic speeds of 1,350mph, at an altitude of 60,000ft.

Take-offs and landings can look fantastic if shot with a really long tele-photo lens – this can make the aircraft look like a bird of prey – but the most enjoyable part of photographing Concorde is taking air-to-air photography, especially when the chase aircraft is a Lear jet! My most prestigious assignment was the celebration of Concorde's tenth anniversary and I was very honoured to be given this assignment. The only day when the four commercial Concordes were available, and not in service, was Christmas Eve 1985. This involved the launching of four Concordes in succession, to create a variety of formation images. This alone was a technical feat in itself and nothing like this had ever been attempted using commercial planes before.

I have been very fortunate to have been the official Concorde photographer for her twenty-seven years of commercial service, and have travelled all over the world photographing this unique aircraft. I was also given the prestigious assignment of photographing the Queen Mother on Concorde to celebrate her eighty-fifth birthday.

There have been many books published on Concorde, some technical, others telling the history, but this book, which tells the story of the Concorde journey, also includes some of the best photographic imagery, plus many unpublished images, as well as some famous images from some of the world's leading aviation photographers, including Arthur Gibson and John Dibbs.

I hope you enjoy reading this wonderful pictorial tribute as much as I have enjoyed writing it.

CHAPTER ONE

EARLY DAYS OF CONCORDE

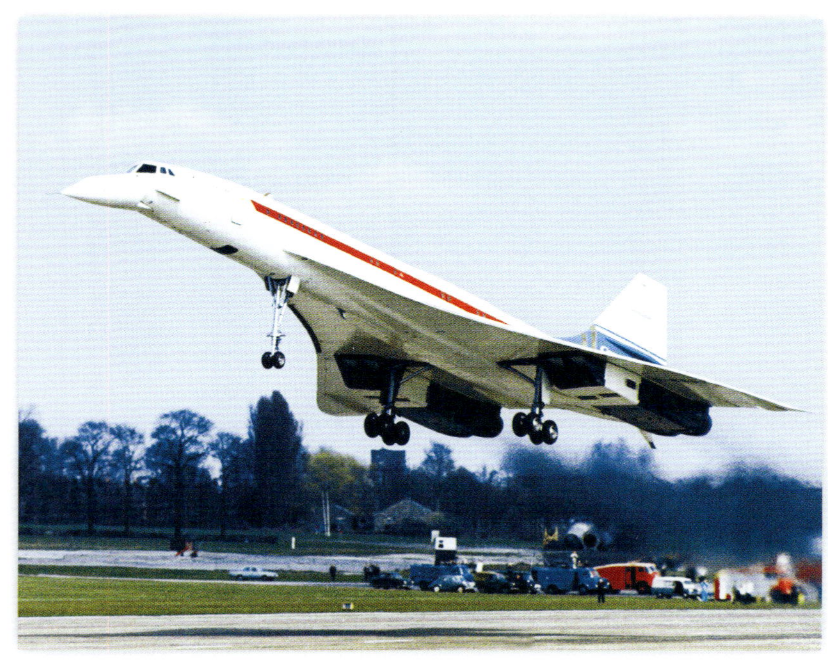

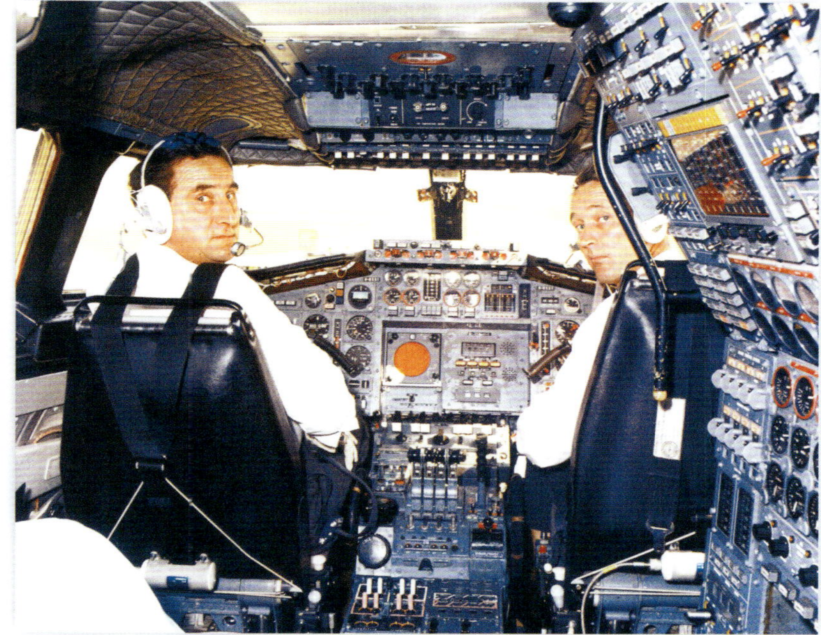

Filton, Bristol, 9 April 1969

The world's press assembled to capture the British-made Concorde 002 (G-BSST) take-off on her first ever maiden flight. The crew on that flight included chief test pilot Brian Trubshaw, co-pilot John Cochrane and flight engineer Brian Watt. The 9,000ft runway at Filton had previously been lengthened for the Brabazon airliner, but it was still too short to test the full range of flight for Concorde.

FIRST HISTORIC FLIGHT

Sunday 2 March 1969 was a very historic day: the sun was shining and the Anglo-French supersonic aircraft, Concorde prototype 001 (F-WTSS), got ready to take to the skies for the first time. At Toulouse Airport, journalists and TV crews from around the world gathered to witness and record aviation history for millions of viewers worldwide.

Final pre-flight checks were being made aboard the aircraft by the crew, comprising Andre Turcat, Jacques Guignard, Michel Retif and Henri Perrier, and the world held its breath!

Surrounded by emergency vehicles, Concorde 001 rolled forward and slowly taxied to the line at the end of the runway. There was a crescendo of sound from the four huge Olympus 593 engines as they were fired into life.

After what seemed an eternity of time, with the world's press and media waiting, the final take-off checks were carried out, the engines were opened up to full power, and brakes released. She slowly picked up power, then, quickly gathering speed and with a tremendous roar from the engines, she lifted her distinctive nose into the air to the excited shouts of British BBC commentator Raymond Baxter: *'She flies, she flies!'*

Concorde 001 approached for landing just a short twenty-nine minutes later, and was brought safely back onto the Toulouse runway to tremendous applause as she taxied to a halt in front of the airport building.

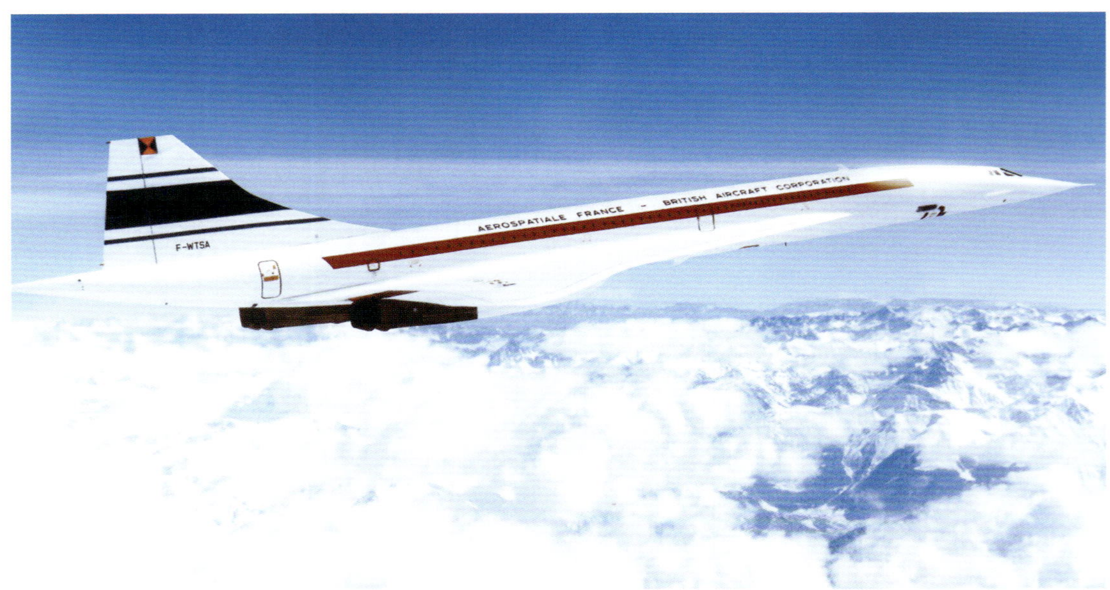

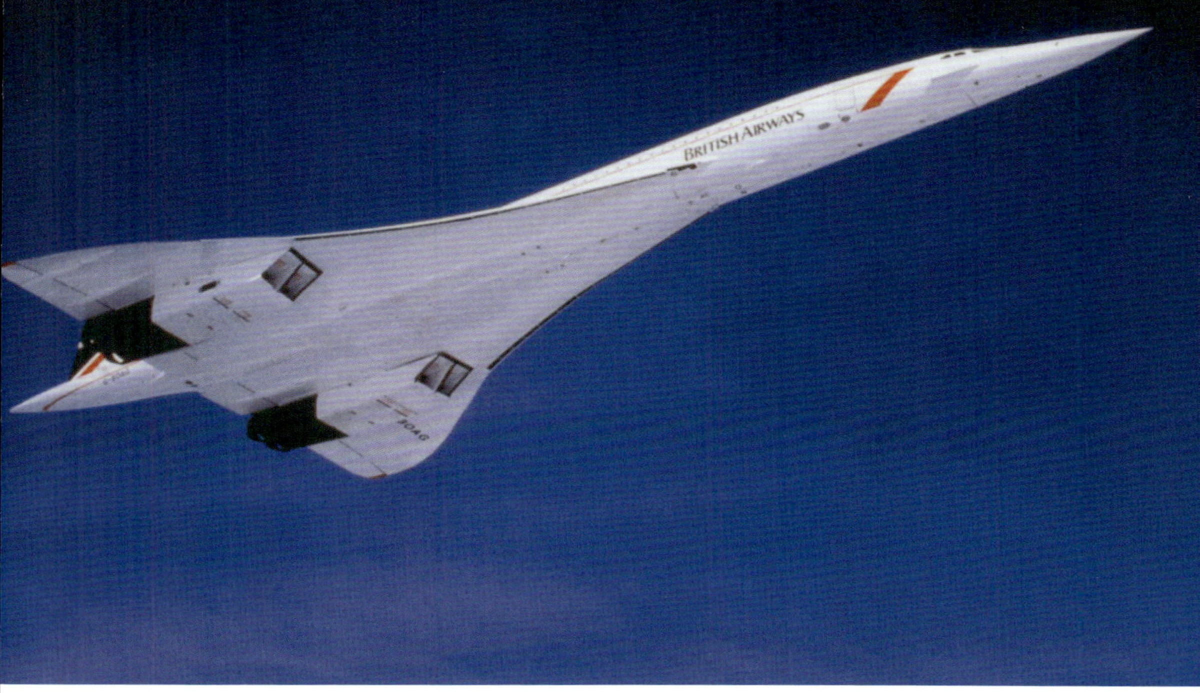

1969

This is one of my favourite air-to-air photographs of Concorde as it shows that wonderful delta wing and long, sleek fuselage.

This book is a tribute to celebrate forty years of Concorde; a photographic journey from her first flight to her final landing.

1969 was a memorable year in aviation history: the very first Boeing 747 jumbo jet took off from Seattle, and the world also witnessed the launch of Apollo 11 and Neil Armstrong taking his first steps on the Moon; in the same year supersonic aviation travel began with Concorde.

SOME MEMORABLE FACTS FROM 1969

1 APRIL	France withdrew from Nato
21 JULY	US Apollo 11 lands on the Moon
15 AUGUST	The famous Woodstock music festival starts
3 SEPTEMBER	The President of North Vietnam, Ho Chi Minh, dies
12 SEPTEMBER	President Nixon, the newly elected President of the United States, orders the resumed bombing of North Vietnam
20 OCTOBER	The birth of the ARPAnet – messages between two computers
FAMOUS TUNES:	Elvis released *In The Ghetto*, and Simon & Garfunkel were top of the charts with *The Boxer*

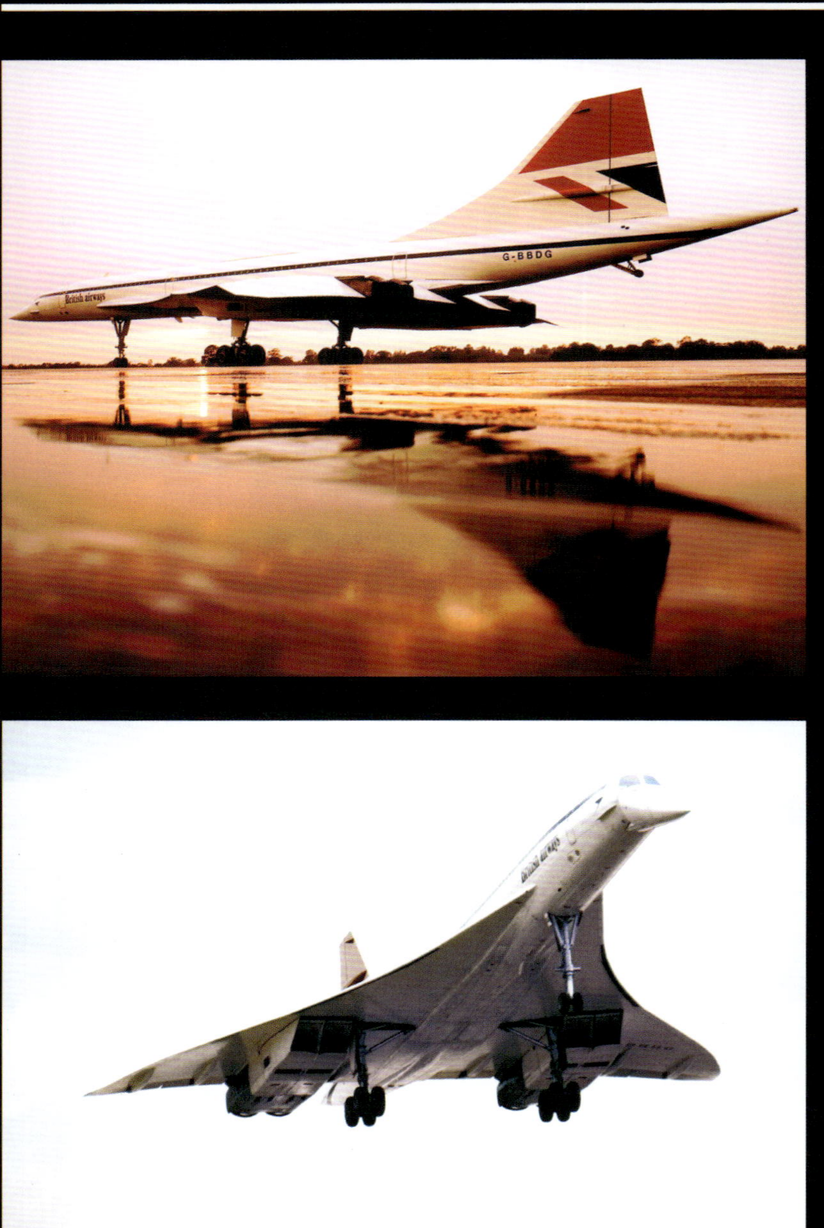

G-BBDG test aircraft 202

Taken at dusk after her first flight into Fairford, this was the first photograph of Concorde in British Airways colours. We had the runway hosed down by the Airport Fire Service to give us that wonderful mirror reflection.

First take-off from Filton, Bristol, 13 February 1974

Concorde test aircraft 202 G-BBDG takes off for the first time from Filton with test pilot Peter Baker at the controls. She landed afterwards at RAF Fairford, Gloucestershire, which was considered to be a more suitable airfield for Concorde's test programme as the runway was longer than Filton. This aircraft never went into commercial service, but was used for future development. Flying 1,282 testing hours, her last flight into Filton was on 24 December 1984. She is now at Brooklands Museum, Weybridge, Surrey.

An artist's impression of a future supersonic aircraft in the 1950s.

1968: A stunning, early visualisation of Concorde in BOAC livery, although she never actually flew in these colours.

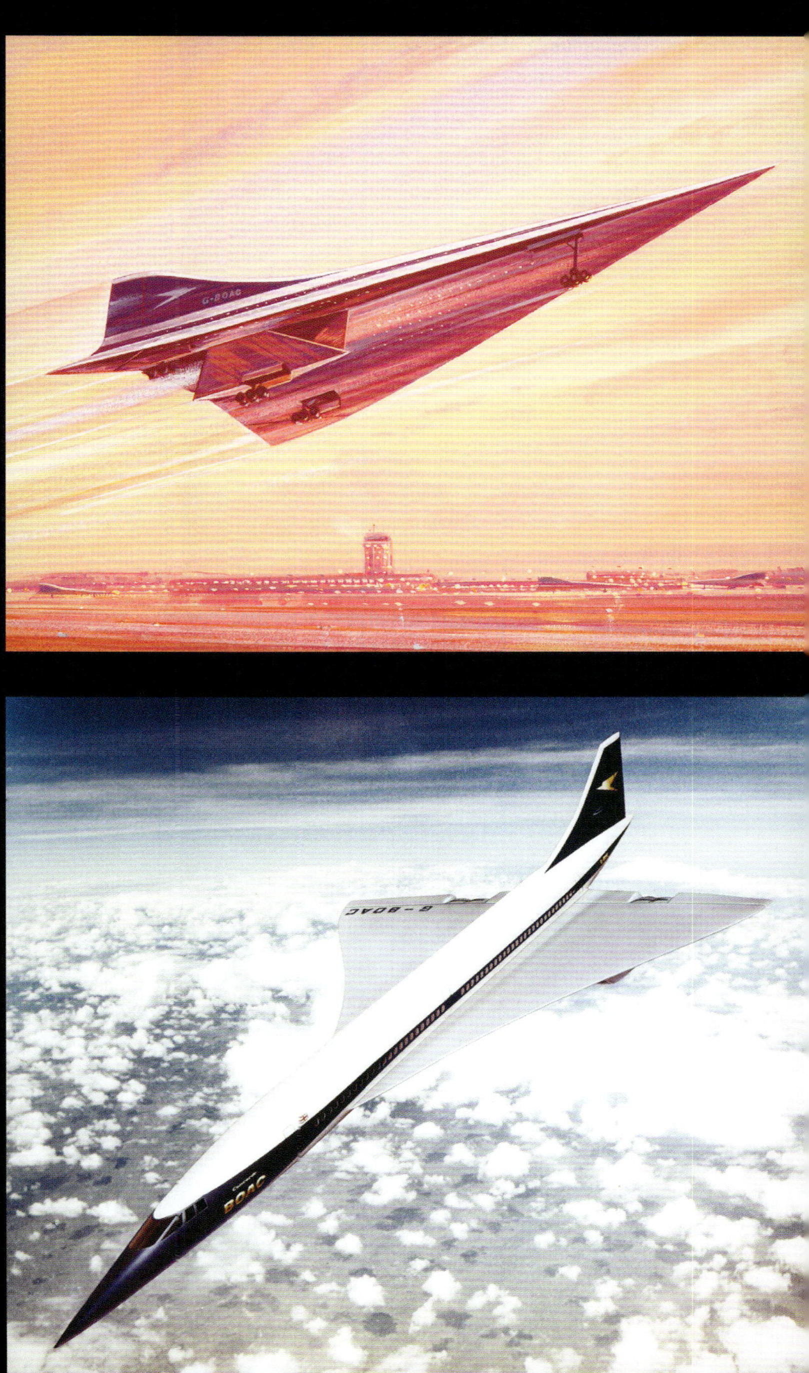

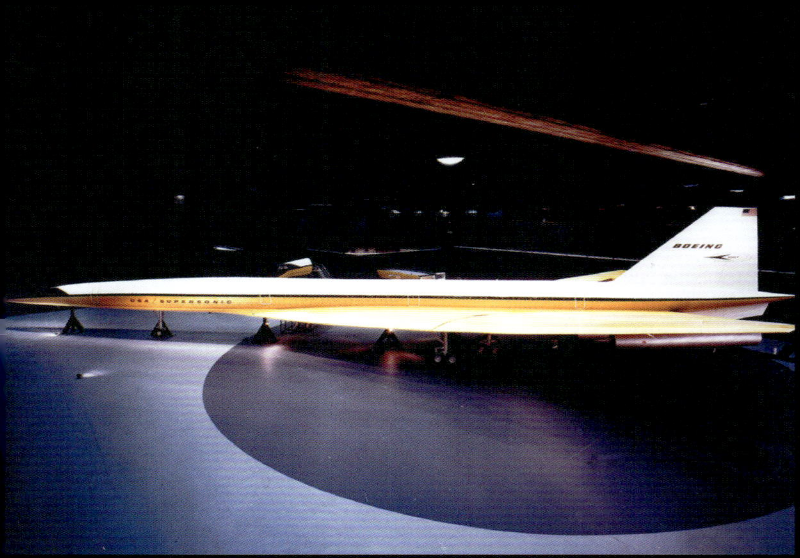

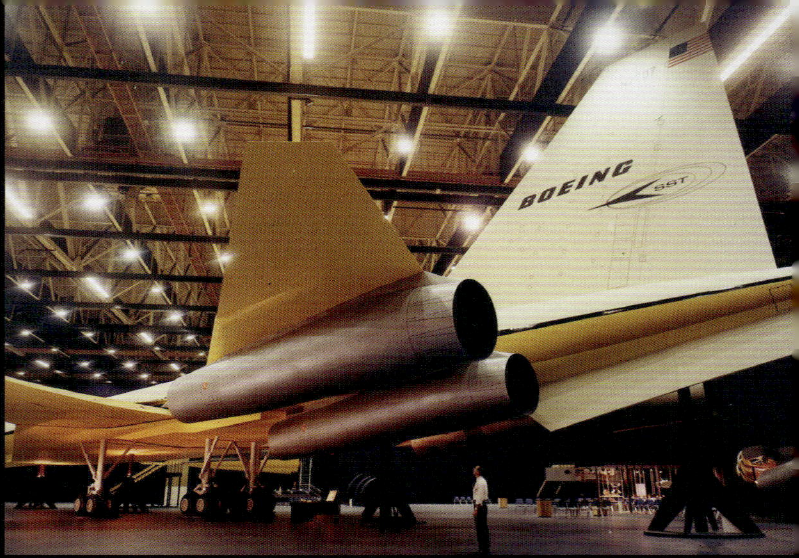

BOEING
USA SUPERSONIC

BOEING
SST

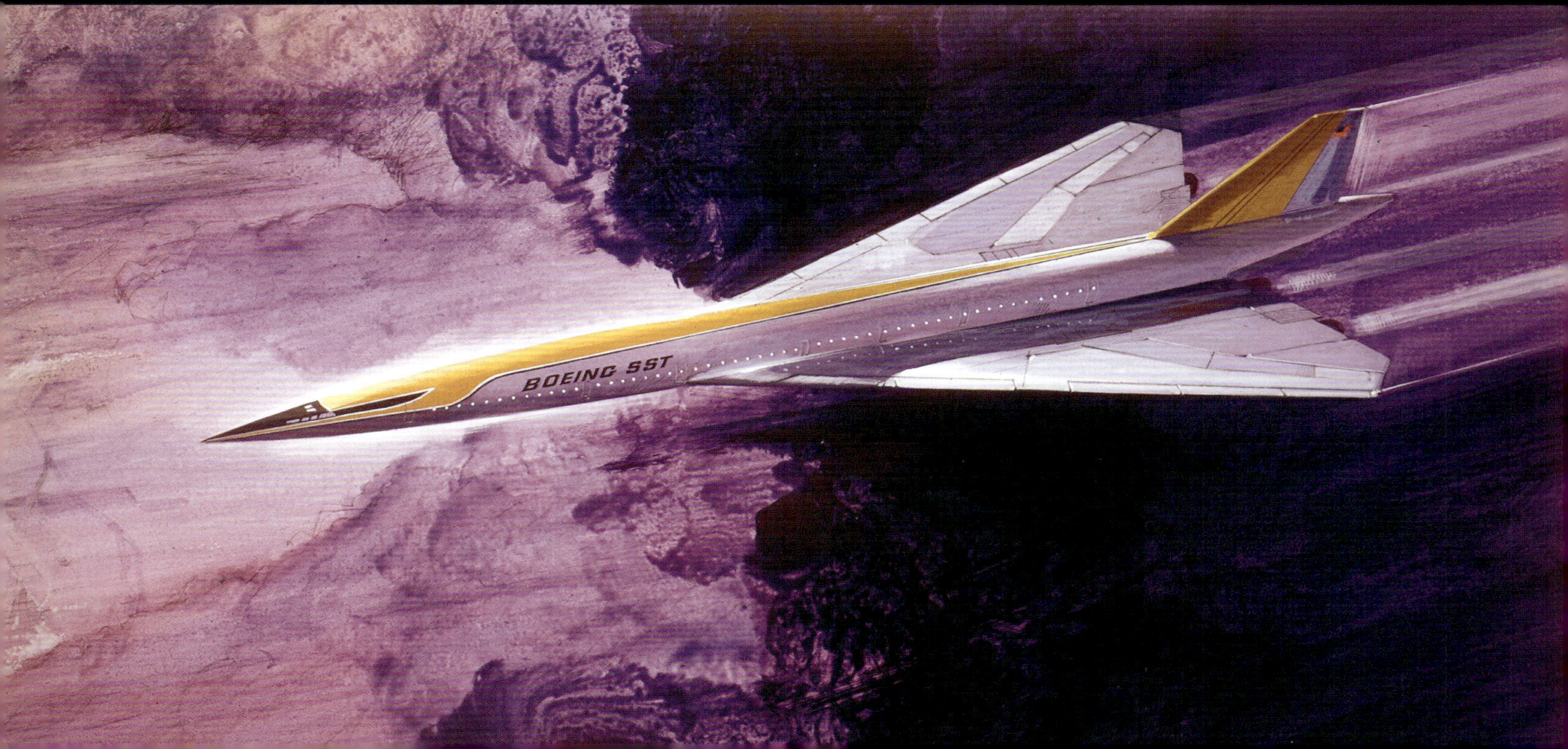

BOEING SST

A mock-up of the Boeing supersonic flight deck.

Interior mock-up of the Boeing SST B2707. The psychedelic futuristic uniform was designed by Pucci and modelled by the famous 'Braniff Babes'.

Opposite: 1966: A mock-up of the giant B2707, Boeing Corporation's answer to supersonic travel. It stretched an incredible 318ft long and would have been the largest supersonic passenger aircraft ever to be built, carrying 300 passengers at a speed in excess of Mach 3 (2,000mph).

J.F. Kennedy decided to support the supersonic monster machine to demonstrate American superiority – it could cross the Atlantic in 100 minutes – but unfortunately it never got off the ground.

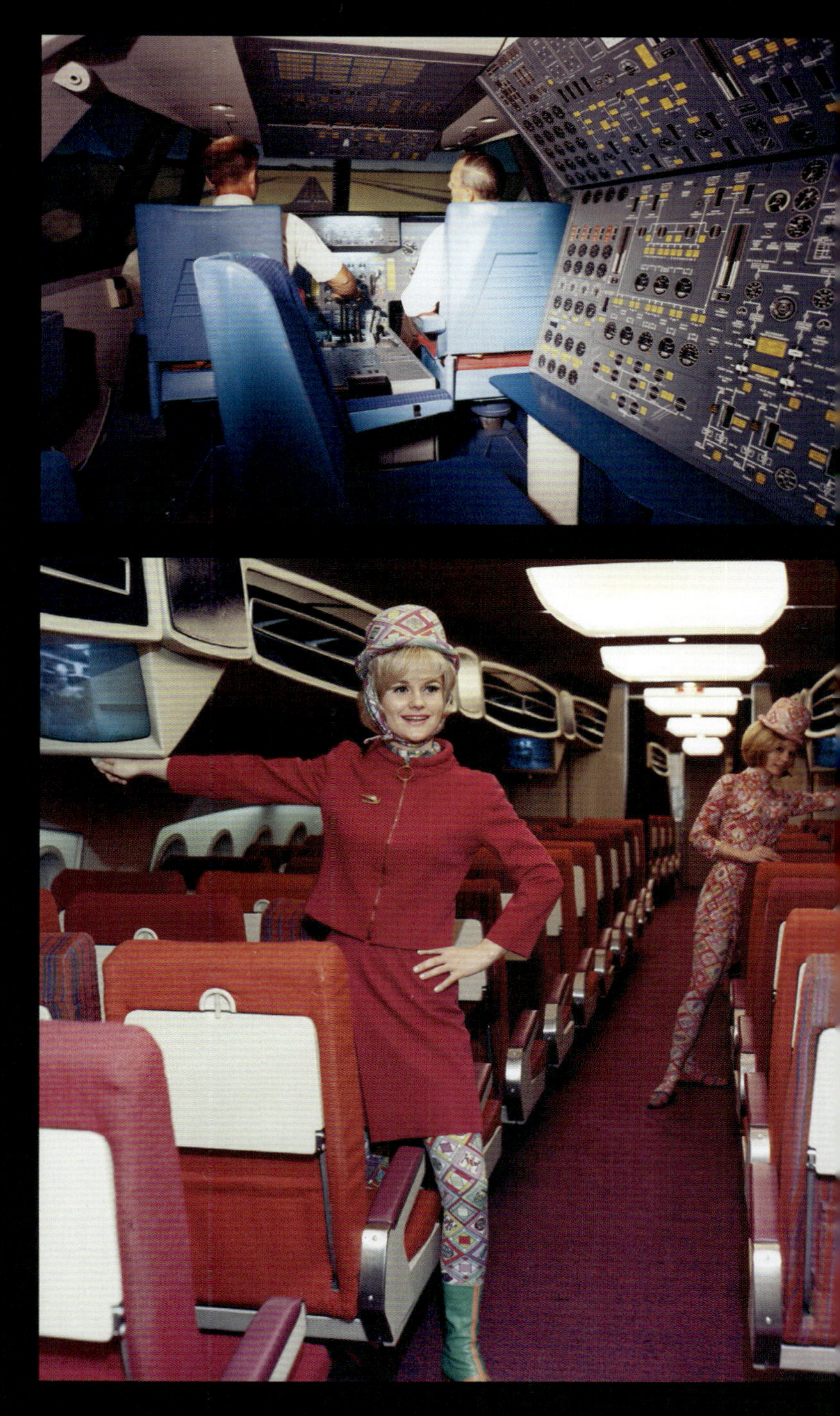

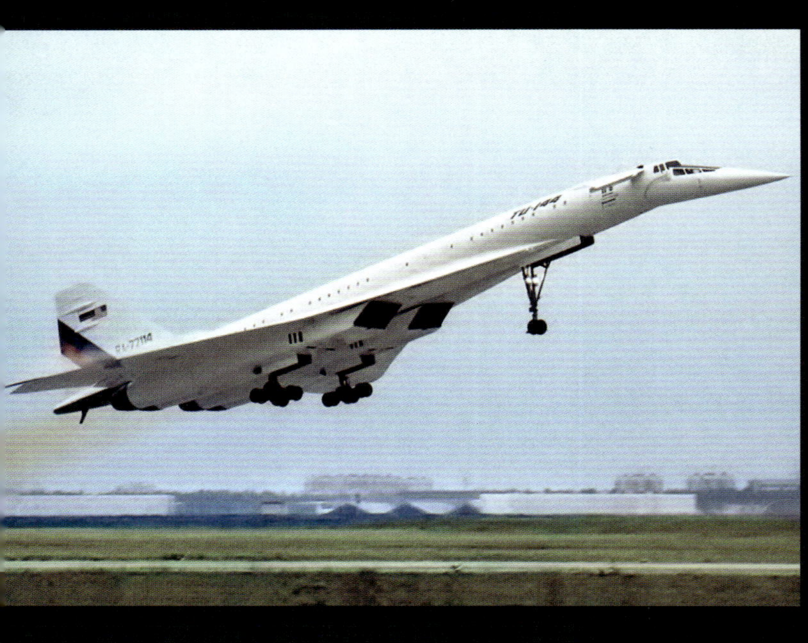

The Russian Konkordski, December 1968

Beating Concorde 001 by just three months, the Russian-built SST Tupolev TU-144 takes to the skies. Looking 'suspiciously' like its rival Concorde, it was aptly nicknamed 'Konkordski', was planned to fly at Mach 2.36 and carried 120 passengers.

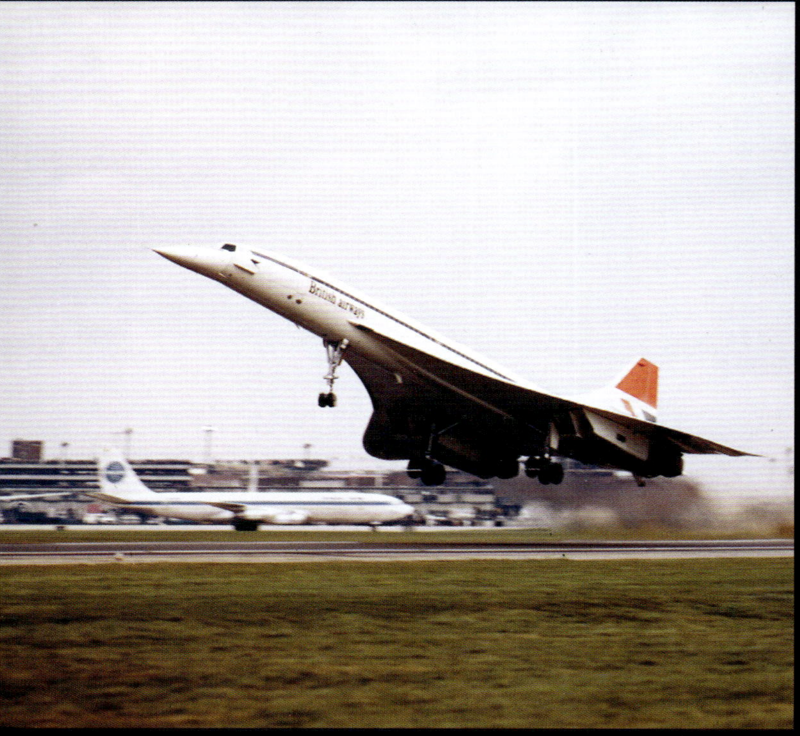

First British Airways commercial Concorde G-BOAA flight

The first commercial flights of Concorde took place on 21 January 1976. British Airways flew their Concorde from Heathrow Airport to Bahrain, whilst Air France took off from Paris to Rio de Janeiro simultaneously. British Airways Concorde flights from London to New York and back used the flight numbers BA 001 to BA 004. Flight numbers BA 001 and BA 004 are now used from London City to JFK Airport.

Concorde G-BOAA first flight crew Captain Norman Todd, Captain Brian Calvert and Senior Flight Engineer John Lidiard on the inaugural service to Bahrain. The flight included such guests as Sir George Edwards (Chairman BAC) and Sir Stanley Hooker.

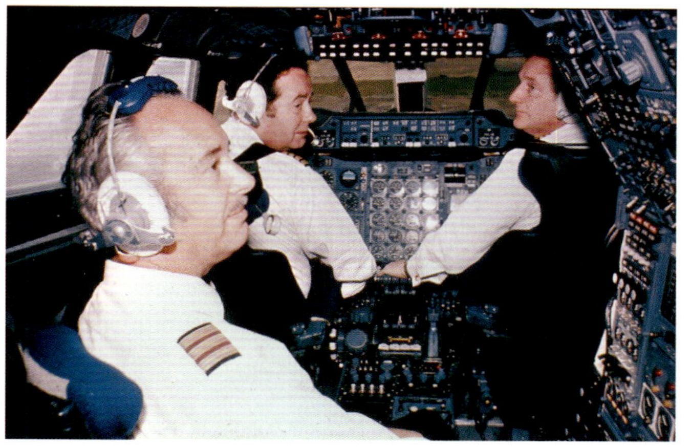

Concorde over the Earth, 1976

One of the first air-to-air photographs of Concorde G-BOAA flying at 60,000ft. Now in the stratosphere, flying on the edge of space and burning 5 gallons of fuel per mile (5,650 gallons per hour), you can clearly see the curvature of the Earth.

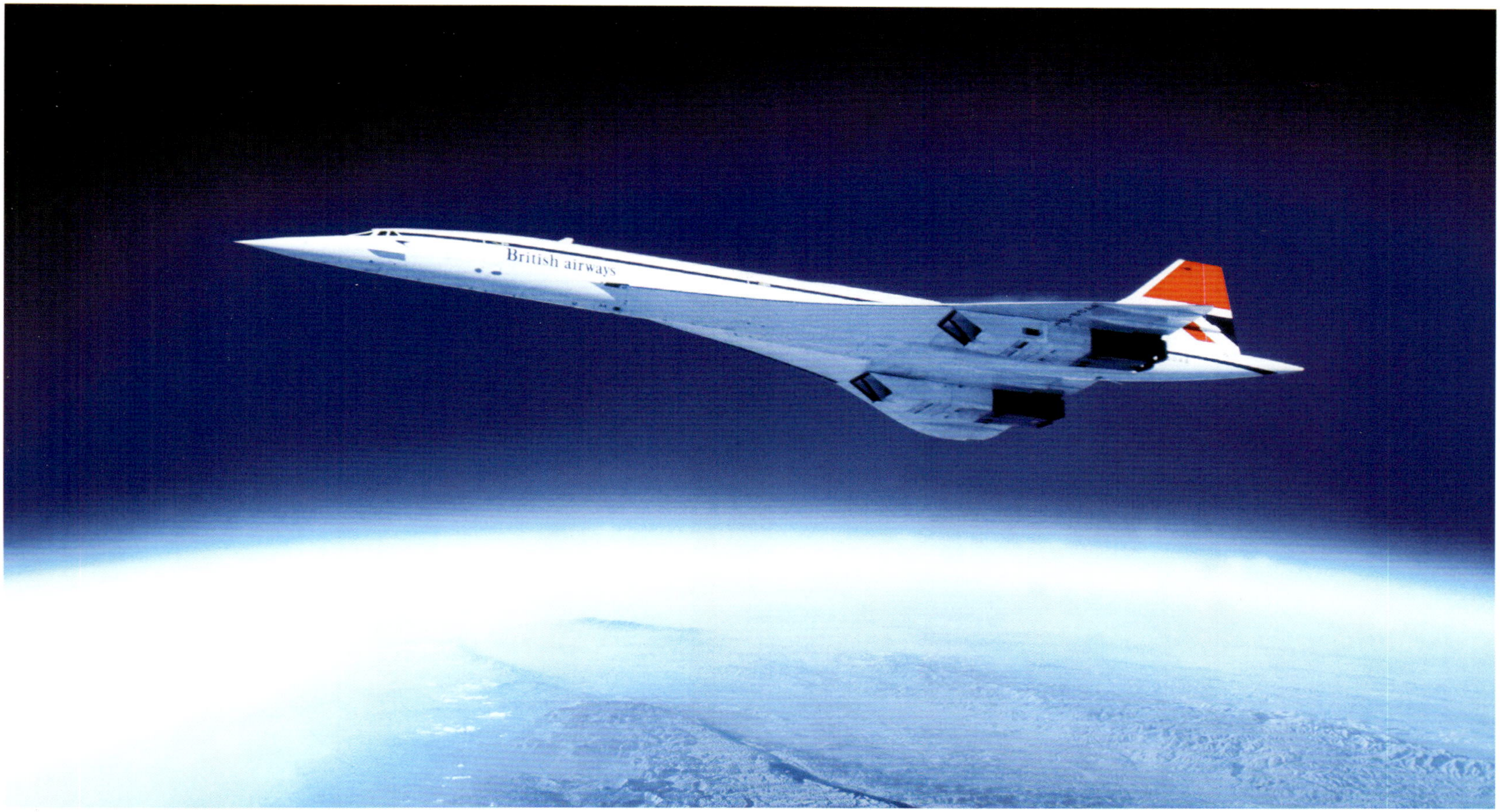

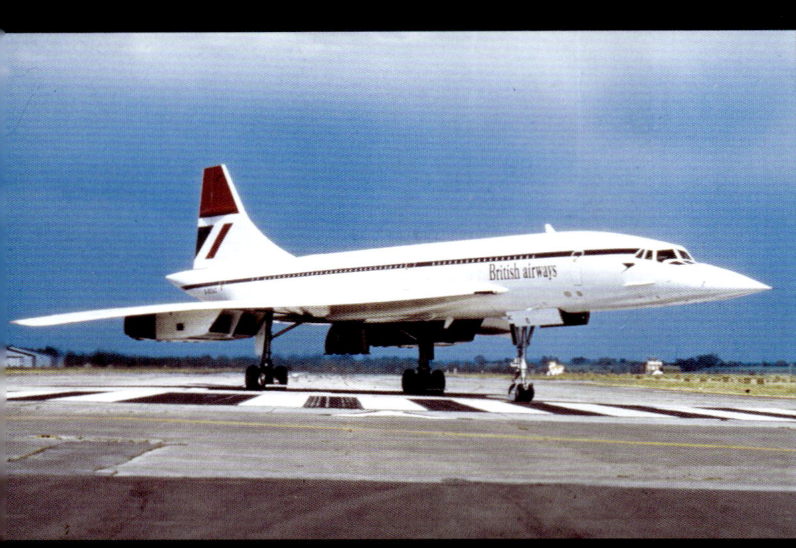

Concorde G-BOAA at Bahrain
in 1976.

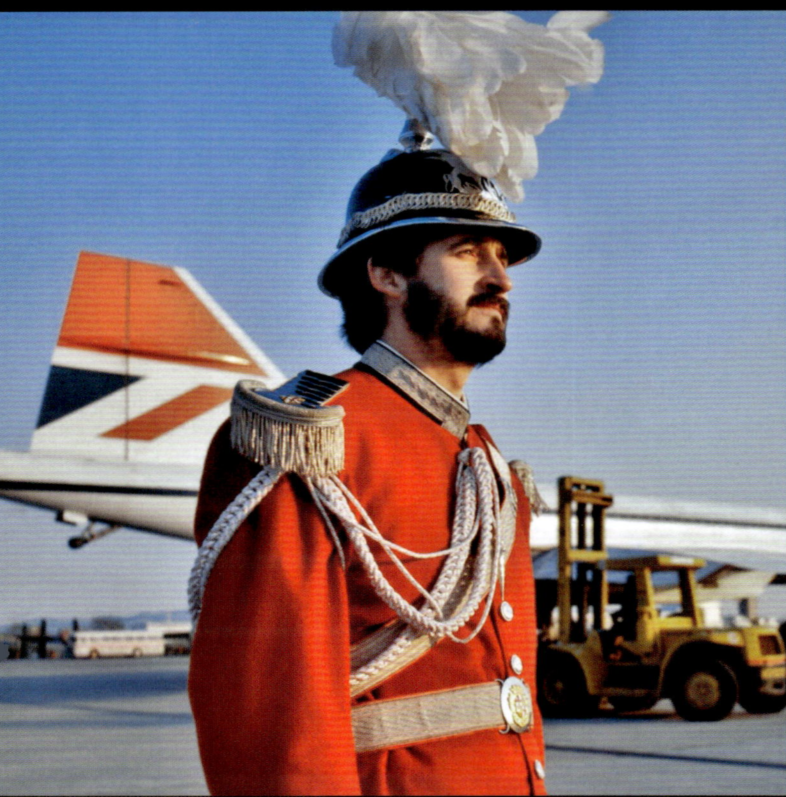

The inaugural Concorde flight to Barcelona brought
the main airport road to a grinding halt as 25,000
Spanish locals and aviation enthusiasts came to
witness Concorde's first visit to Spain.

Being sent to Barcelona for the first time to
get that important PR shot for the press, as a
photographer one has to have a bit of luck. I found
a Spanish National Guard in full regalia, which
was just perfect for this shot.

British Airways and Air France inaugural flights meet at Dulles International Airport, Washington on 24 May 1976.

The weather was perfect as I took this photograph of the two Concordes together. It was a good shot, but I needed a good *press* shot, and just by chance a US cop stood right in front of me with his right hand on his gun. I had to use a fisheye lens to capture the whole image, but I think this photograph says it all.

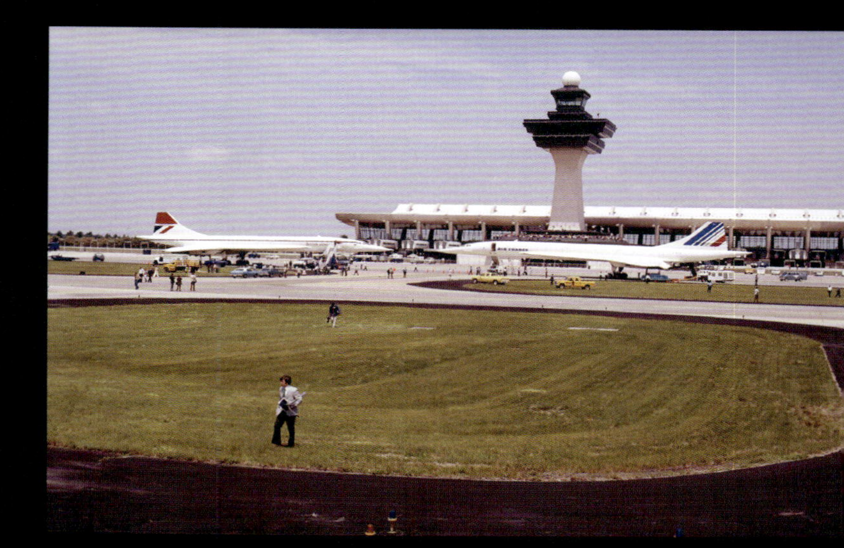

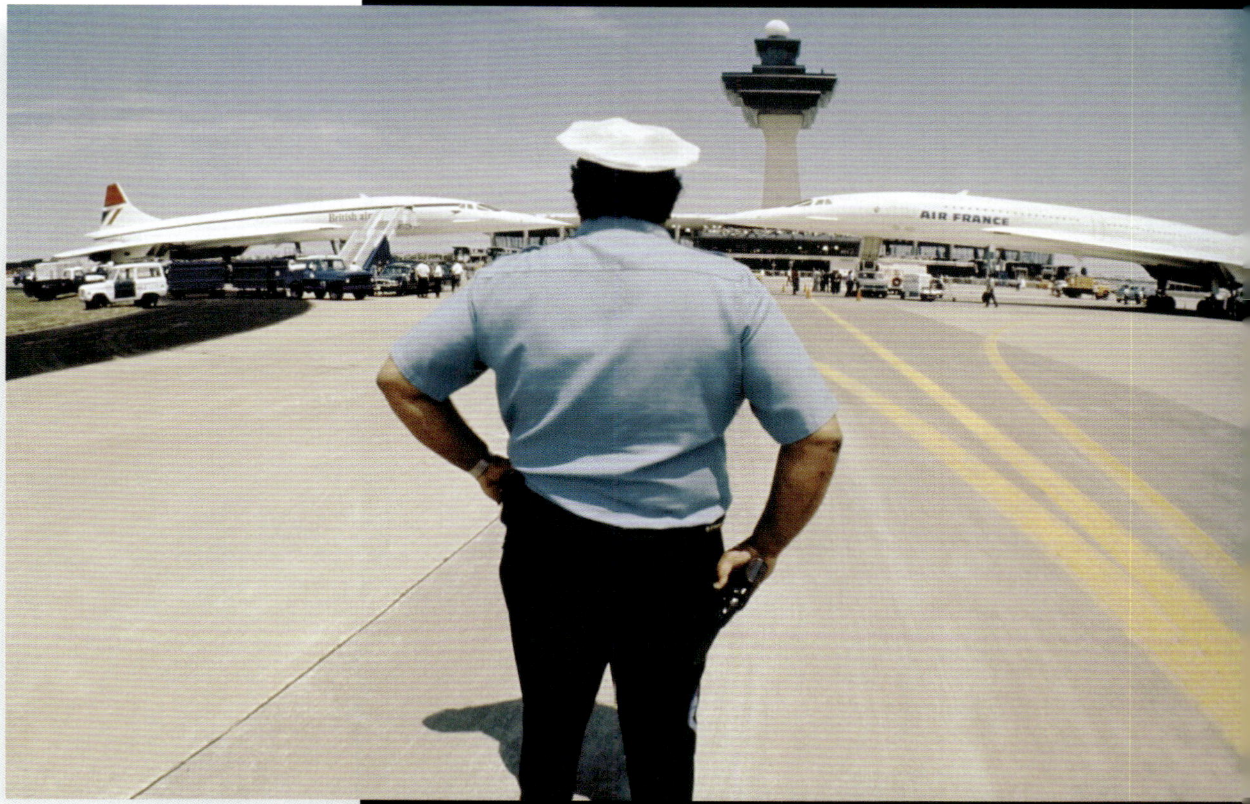

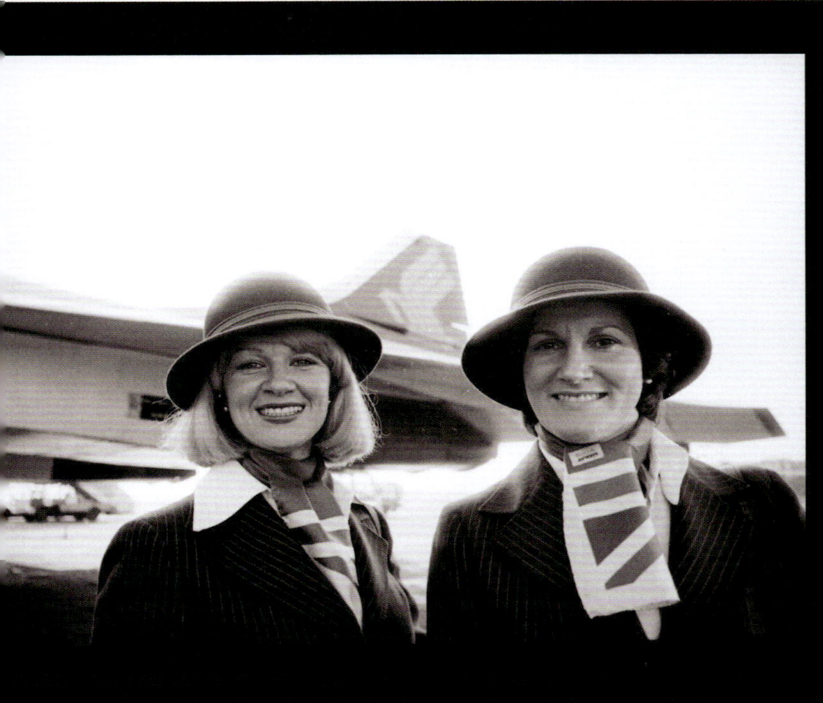

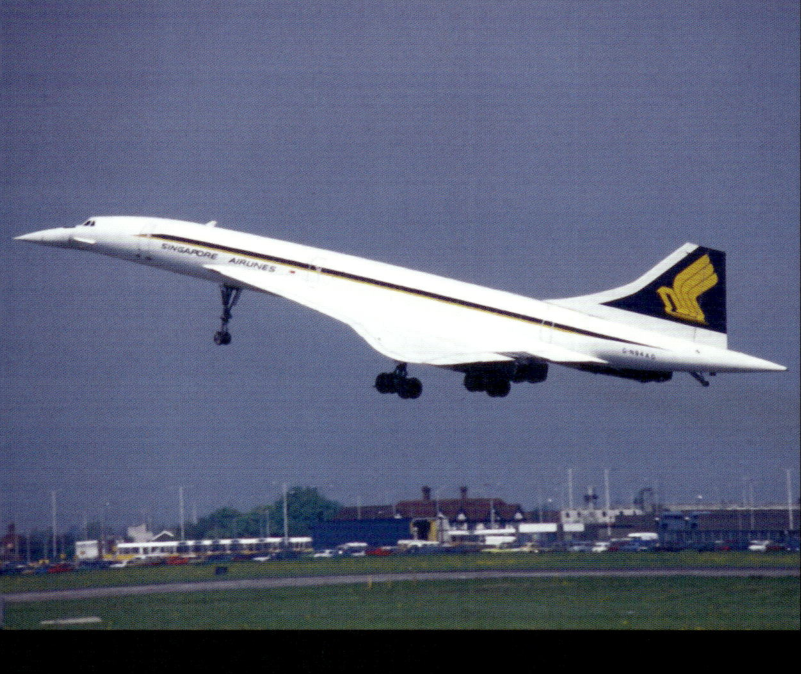

December 1977: British Airways and Singapore Airlines started a joint service to Singapore, via an existing route from Bahrain, which had a shared British Airways and Singapore cabin crew.

British Airways Concorde – G-BOAD – is seen leaving Heathrow for the nine-hour journey to Singapore. The brief was to get a shot of the aircraft showing the Singapore colours. This aircraft was painted in two liveries; on the other side was the British Airways colours!

A subsonic service was inaugurated by Braniff Airways between Washington and Dallas (Fort Worth) on 12 January 1979. First registered as G-BOAA on 3 March 1974 to the British Aircraft Corporation Ltd, this aircraft was re-registered as G-N94AA / N94AA by British Airways / Braniff Airways.

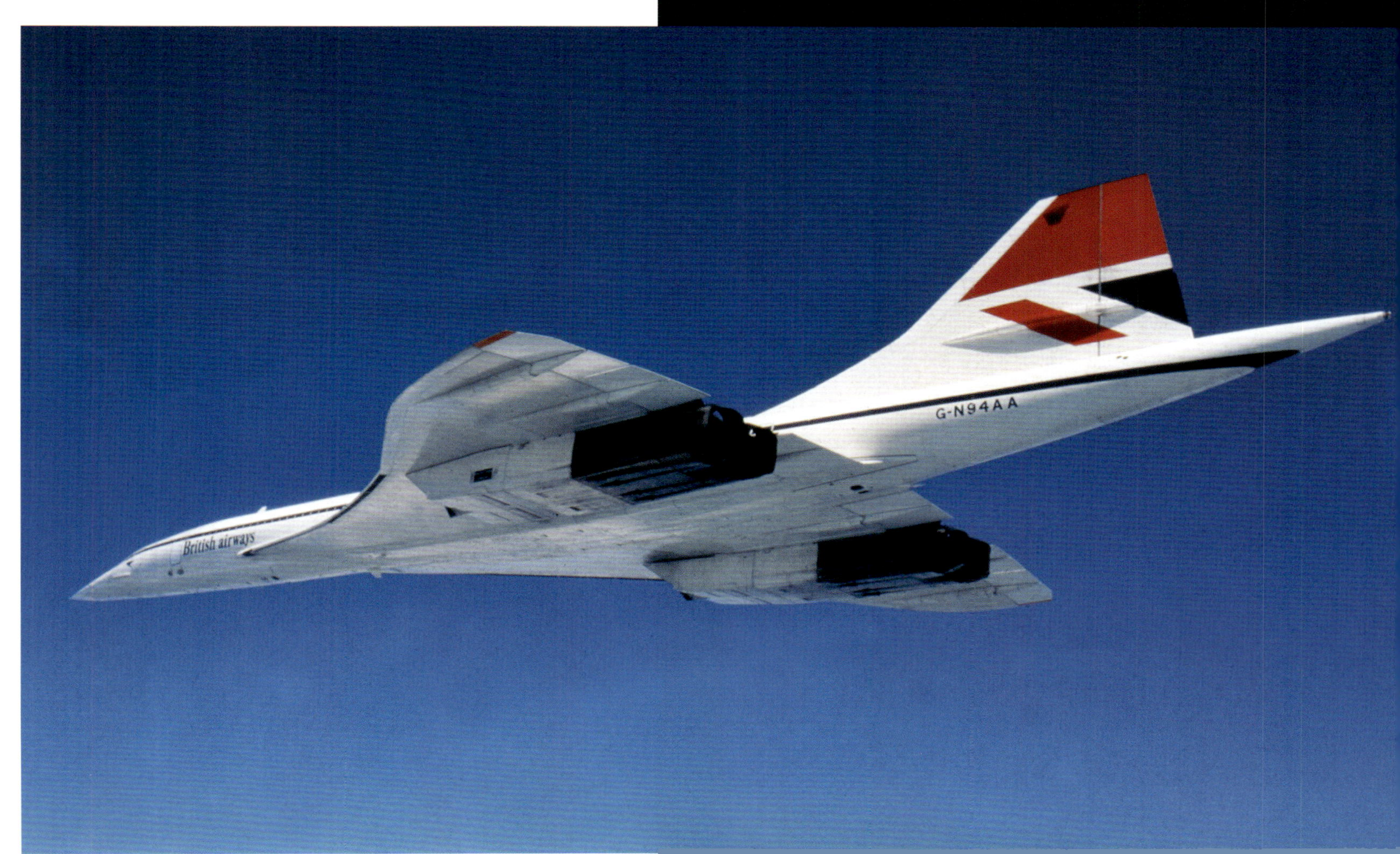

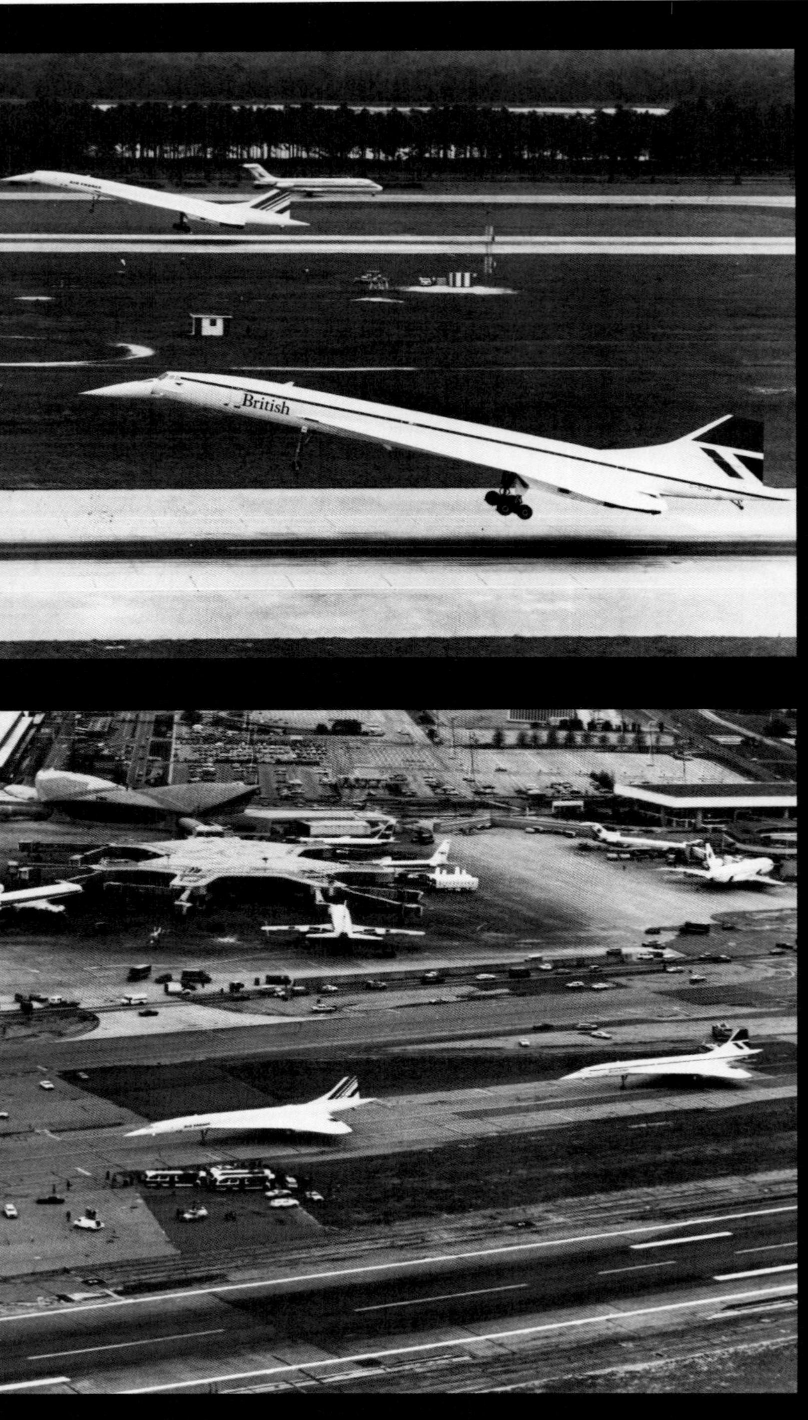

27 March 1984: British Airways opened a Concorde route to Orlando via Washington. This photograph was shot from a helicopter to show the first landing of BA and Air France Concordes into Orlando Airport for the opening of the new Epcot Center at Disney World.

The inaugural flight to JFK Airport, New York. 22 November 1977: After a long delay due to protests over local noise, British Airways and Air France began services to New York from London and Paris.

12 January 1979: A subsonic service was inaugurated by Braniff Airways between Washington and Dallas (Fort Worth).

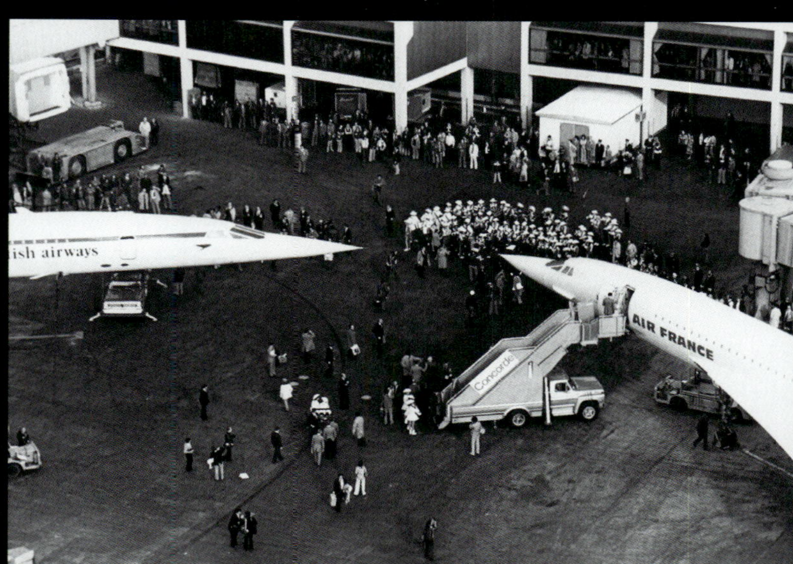

This early Concorde air-to-air shot was taken from a specially modified Lear jet, which has been designed to incorporate a unique periscope visual system pioneered by a company called Astrovision – literally a hole is cut in the top and bottom of the aircraft to allow the periscope to go through. It works in the same way as a periscope, with a monitor in the cabin to record the images, and enables the stills and film cameraman to capture unusual shots and angles that would not normally be possible by shooting through the aircraft windows.

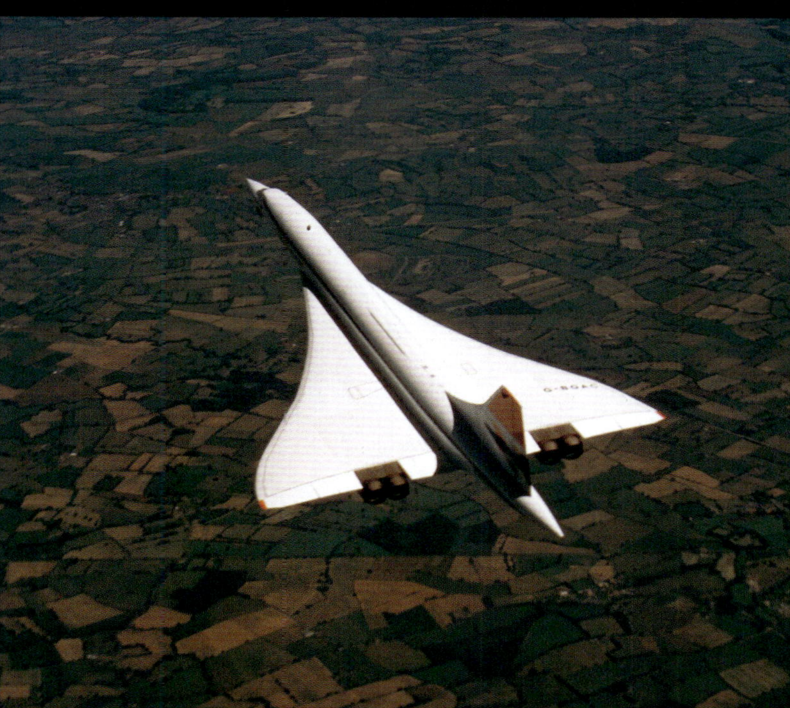

Livery

These air-to-air shots taken in 1976 from the windows of a Lear jet were the first to show the new British Airways livery designed by leading British designer Dick Negus of Negus and Negus. The design was a combination of the two liveries of the former two airlines BEA and BOAC, which merged in 1973.

British Airways altered the livery and dropped the word 'Airways' in 1980. Only a few shots exist in this design due to the new Landor livery which was introduced in 1984.

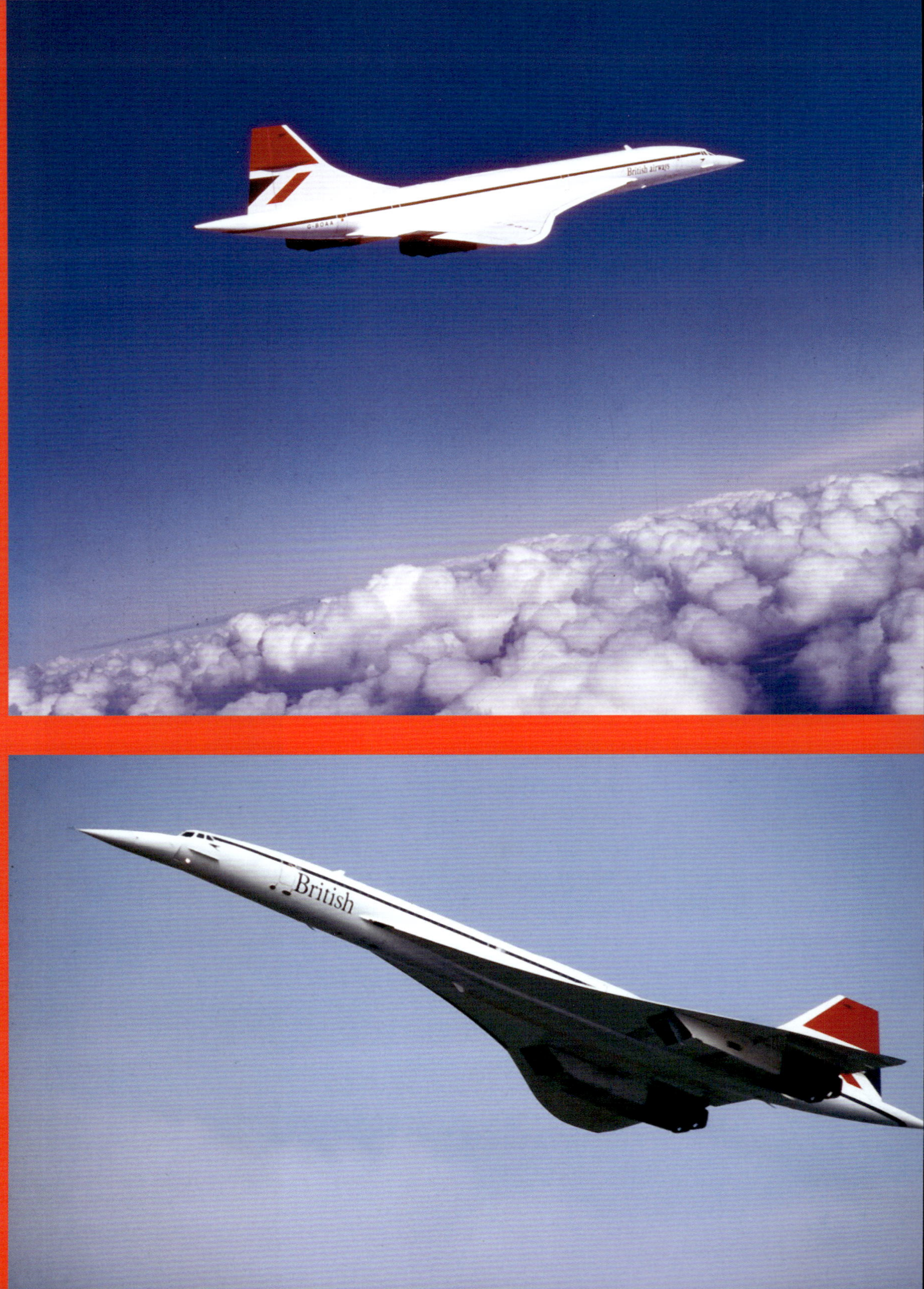

ARRIVALS

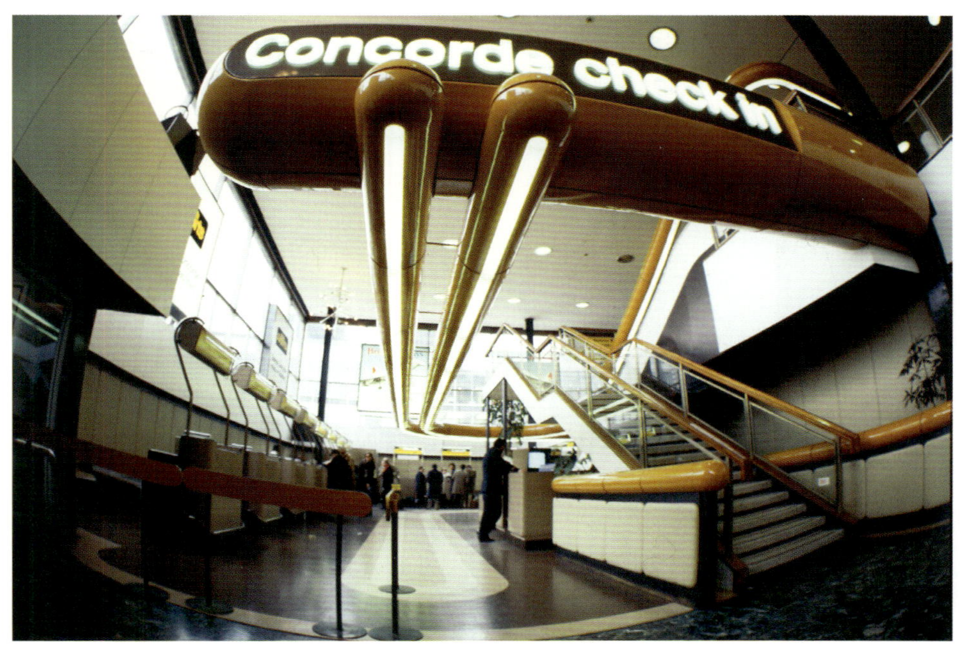

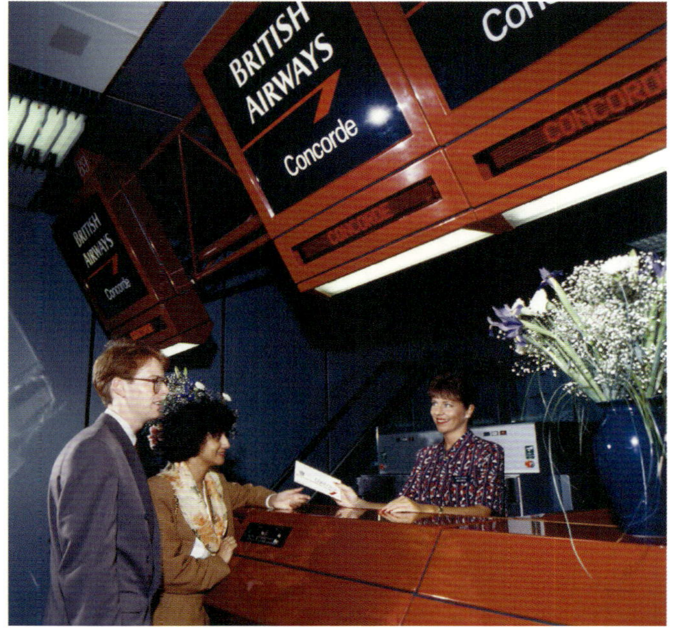

The first Concorde check-in desk opened in Terminal 3 on 21 January 1976. This prestigious check-in area was cordoned off and specifically designed so that celebrities could check in without the resident press pestering them. High-profile celebrity flyers were afforded a private status at check-in.

In 1984 the Concorde check-in desk at the new modern Terminal 4 building opened in glorious technicolour red, with the new Landor Speedwing livery colours displayed.

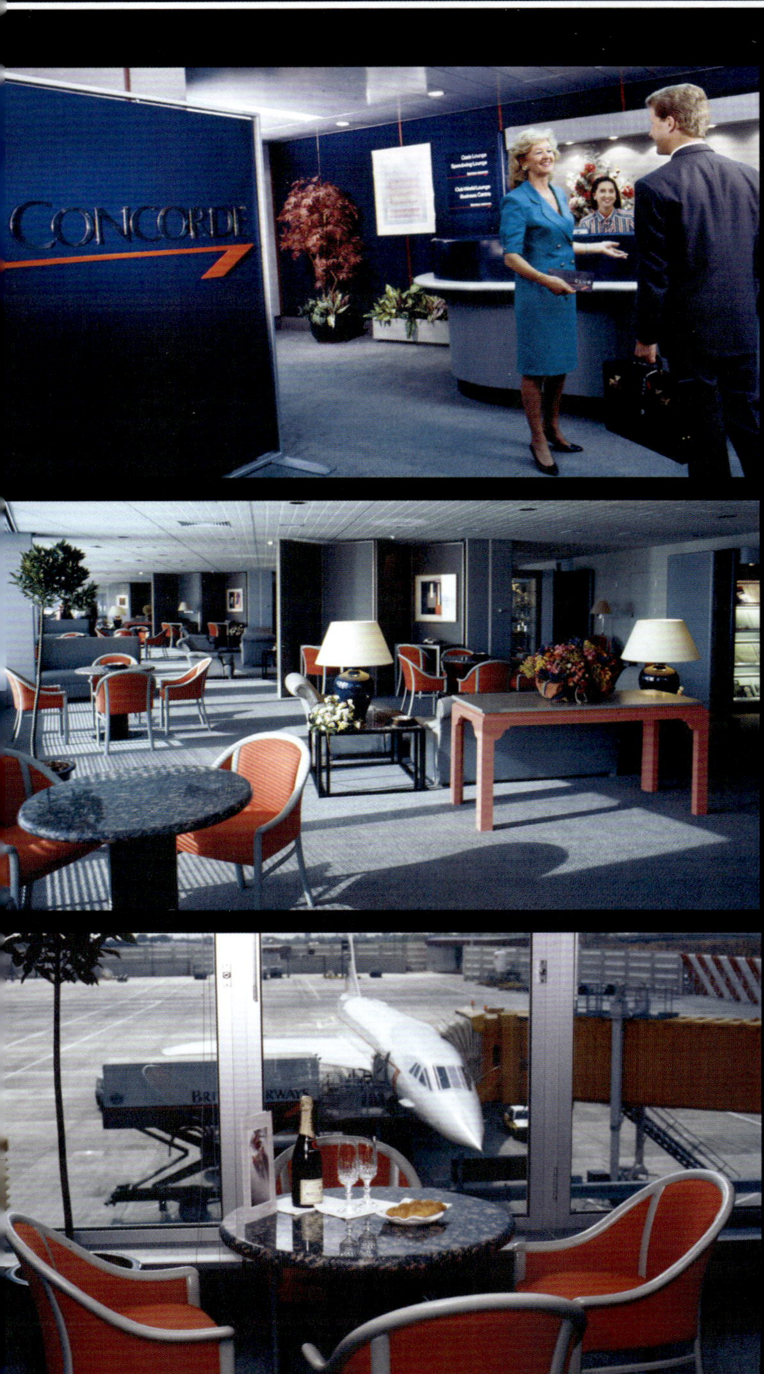

As a VIP-status Concorde passenger, you would be fast-tracked through Security and Immigration and often greeted by the British Airways Special Facilities Staff at the Concorde Speedwing Lounge.

The luxurious surrounds of the Concorde Speedwing Lounge at Terminal 4. Plush fittings and colour co-ordinated upholstery in red and grey reflected the Concorde colours.

A Concorde flight begins at the luxurious Speedwing Lounge under the magnificent, watchful eyes of the white bird. Efficient lounge staff would offer passengers champagne, sandwiches and a selection of handmade canapés. Twenty minutes before take-off a polite announcement is made to invite passengers to board the aircraft. 'Captain John Hutchinson will fly this Concorde flight on G-BOAB to New York JFK Airport. Flight time in just three hours twenty minutes.'

After arriving on Concorde BA 001 at JFK Airport, New York, in 1999, I only had a few hours to photograph the new Concorde VIP lounge designed by Sir Terence Conran. The area had a different feel to the London Concorde lounge, with a more contemporary, minimalist design to suit the American passengers. Once the shots were taken, I was back on Concorde for the return evening flight to London. There and back in one day!

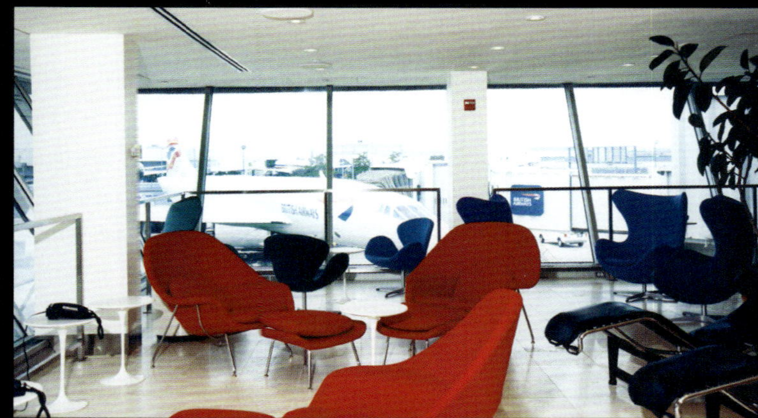

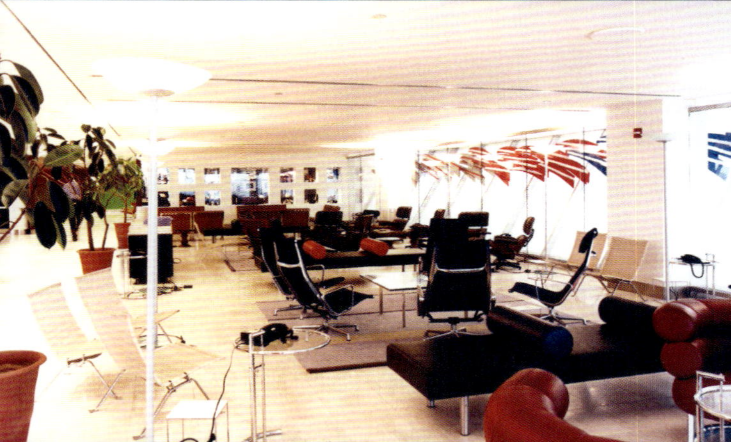

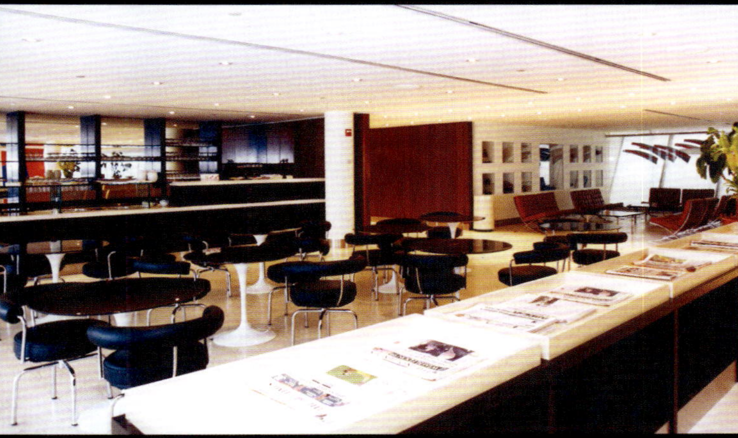

But when does the Concorde experience actually start? Is it as you enter the new dedicated Concorde lounge, to be served a salmon and cucumber sandwich, a sponge cake or a glass of champagne, the tea in bone china cups, or is it when you experience a full three-course meal in the dedicated VIP room in the Concorde lounge prior to boarding the aircraft? Maybe it is when you walk through the glass doors at the dedicated Concorde boarding gate, which looks like the grand entrance of a top executive boardroom, with subtle lighting, smooth clean lines exuding an ambiance of wood and soft textile furnishings, all creating a luxurious

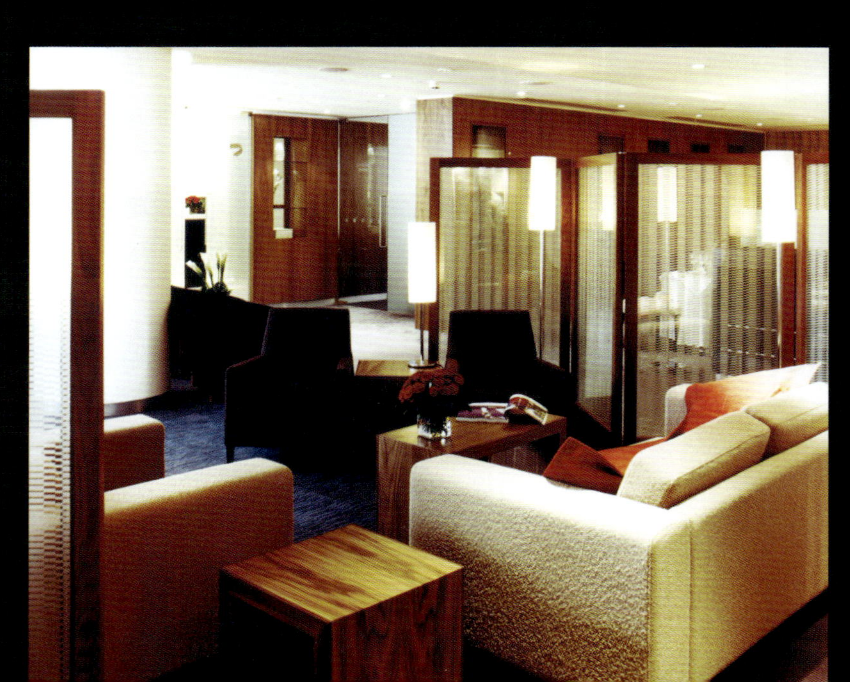
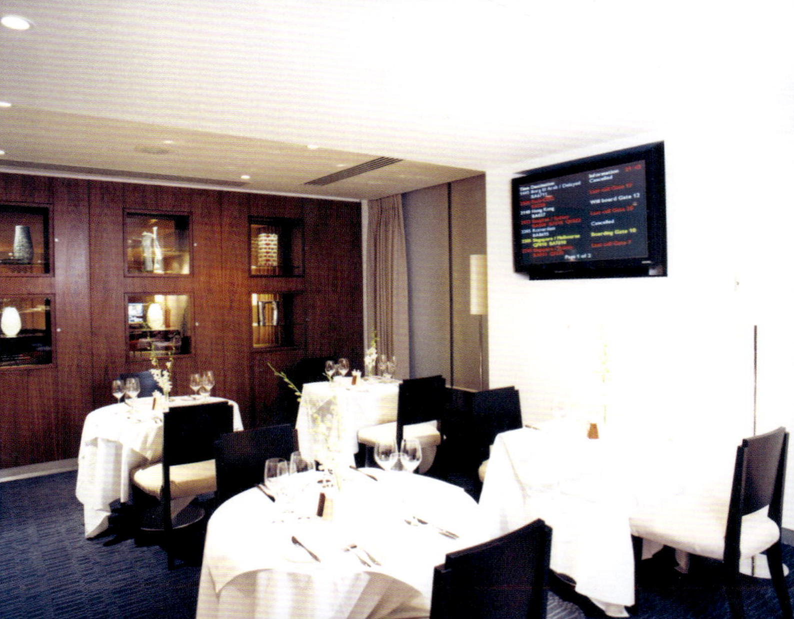

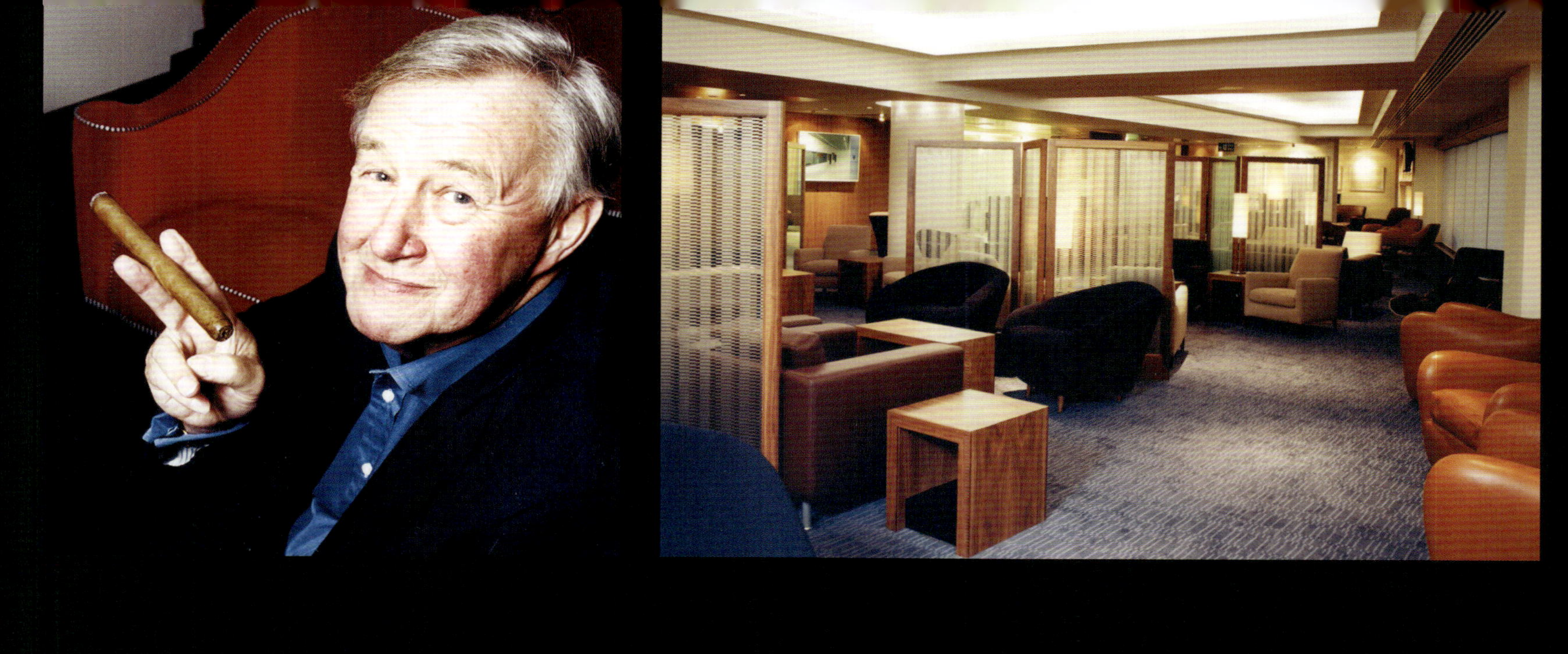

calmness, yet tantalising the senses to prepare you for what is to come: The Concorde Experience.

After taking many pictures of the lounges over late-night sessions, when the areas are passenger free, we thought it would be a good PR opportunity to photograph Sir Terence Conran as he designed parts of the lounges and furnishings. Here Sir Terence is sitting in the specifically designed Concorde smoking room, quite keen to pose with one of his favourite Havana cigars.

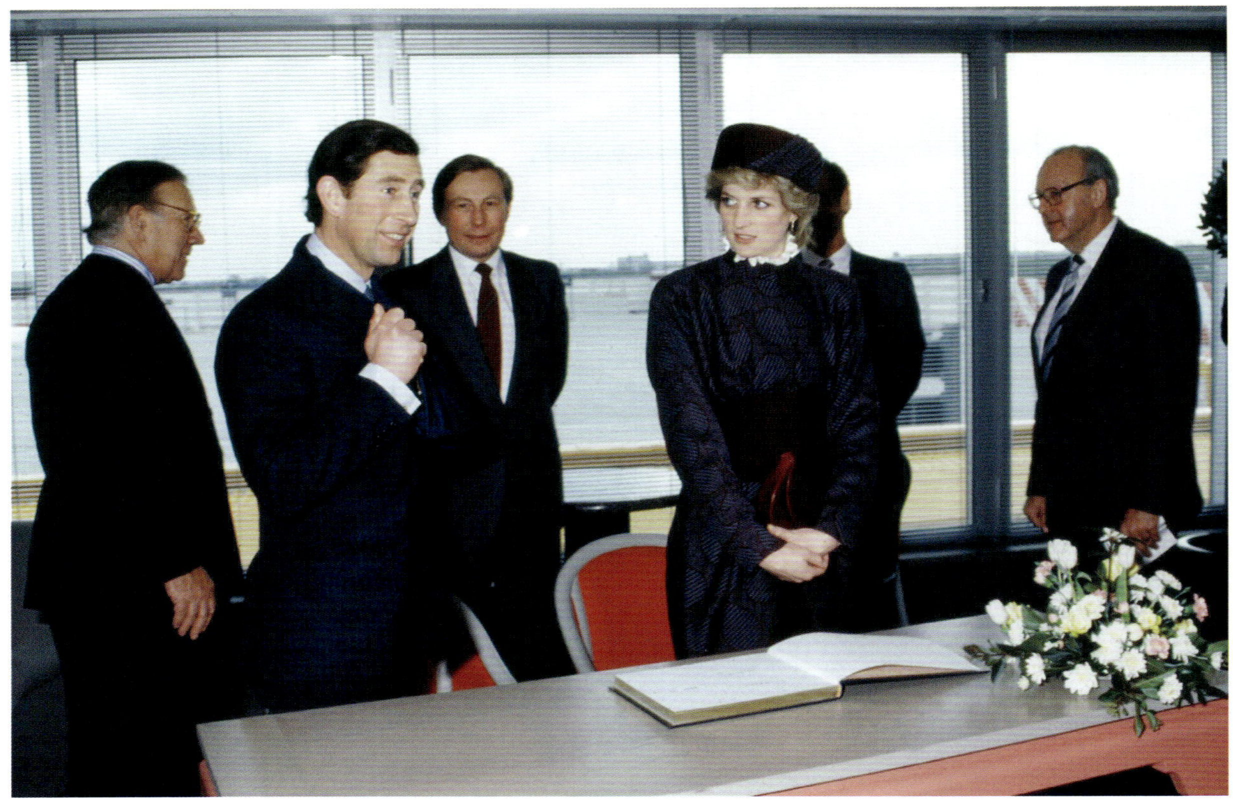

Prince Charles and Princess Diana officially opened the first Concorde lounge at Terminal 4 on 1 April 1986. After the press photographers had got their shots they were quickly ushered out of the lounge, leaving me to take some more informal shots. As soon as they were gone, Princess Diana took off her shoes and started to jump on the sofas and seats just like a little girl – it was great to see her so relaxed and having so much fun.

CHAPTER THREE

CONCORDE

INTERIORS/SEATING

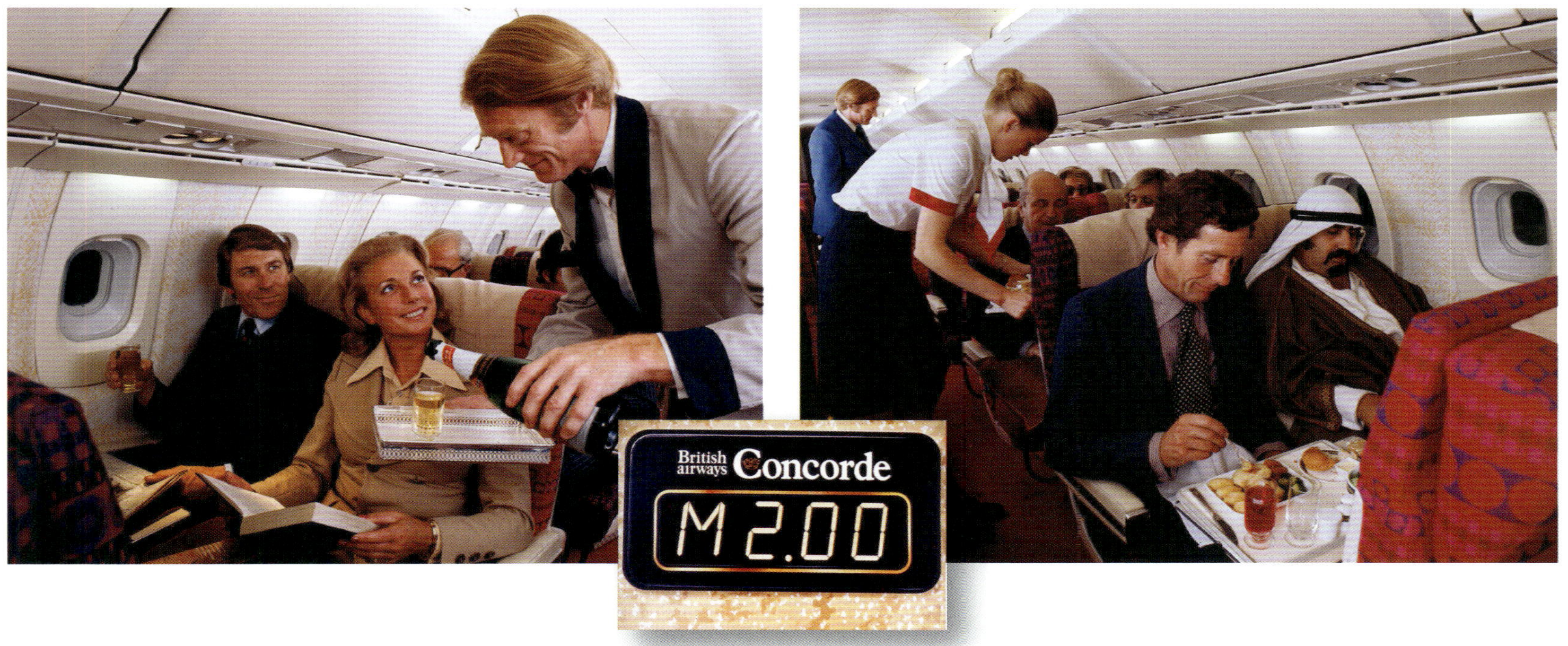

Concorde interiors 1976–1984

The first early seats in Concorde used multicoloured fabric coverings – a choice of pink pattern and purple print. Armrests were covered in cream leather. As you can see from these images, in the early days, especially when flying to Bahrain, one could find oneself sitting next to a royal prince, or sheik, throughout the journey. One interior shot also shows the original Mach meter.

New leather seats and interiors, 1980s

Boarding the aircraft from the departure lounge at London's Heathrow Airport, you are welcomed on board by one of the six cabin crew. Departure time is 10.30 a.m. and you are ready to start your supersonic journey of a lifetime. The new seats have now been changed from the old multicoloured fabrics and, sitting in a plush grey leather reclining seat, you are offered your first glass of Dom Perignon vintage champagne. The engines are now fully fired, and Concorde starts her taxi to runway 27 right. Despite having many fantastic flights on Concorde, the experience is always very exciting.

The first announcement is made by Captain John Hutchinson; he welcomes us on board the BA 001 to New York and informs us that our flight time will be three hours twenty-three minutes to JFK, cruising up to a height of 58,000ft and reaching Mach 2, which is a speed of 1,350mph.

At 10.45 a.m. Concorde's engines burst into life and, with full reheat, the aircraft is now roaring down the runway. With an enormous surge of power from the rear, one is forced back into the seat; it's a feeling of being in a very fast sports car. The roaring sounds of the engines are like no other aircraft, and at a speed of 250mph the aircraft soars into the air. After a few minutes of leaving Heathrow, the reheats are turned off and the noise level reduces; we catch a glimpse of Windsor Castle to our right-hand side. The cabin crew now start their in-flight service; senior cabin crew member Jack Stevenson will offer you the famous Concorde Cocktail comprising gin, Noilly Prat, orange curaçao, lemon juice and a dash of egg whites, shaken and not stirred. On the menu today is fresh prawn niçoise, canapés of Caspian Osetra caviar, roasted quail or baked lemon chicken with spring onion mashed potato, and rhubarb granulate tart for dessert. Your Concorde journey is well under way.

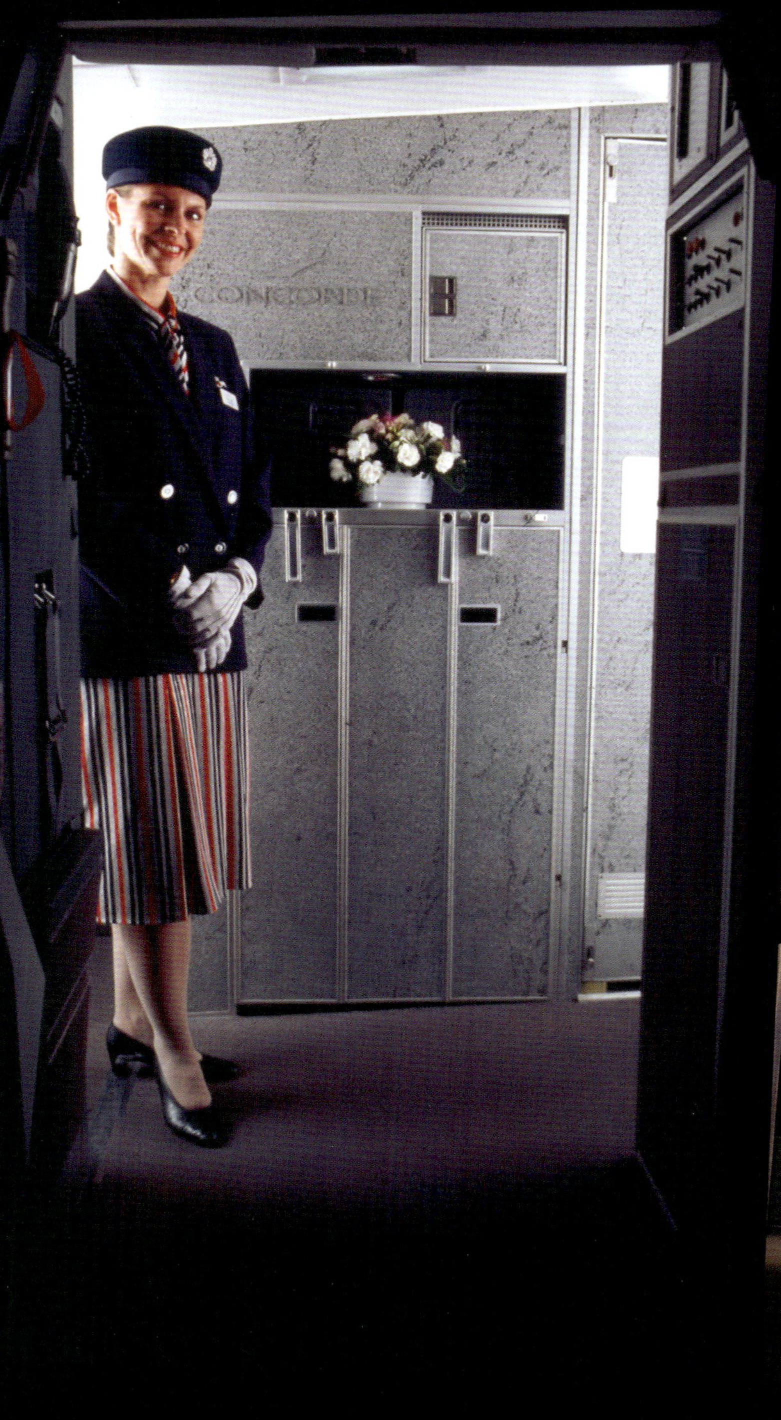

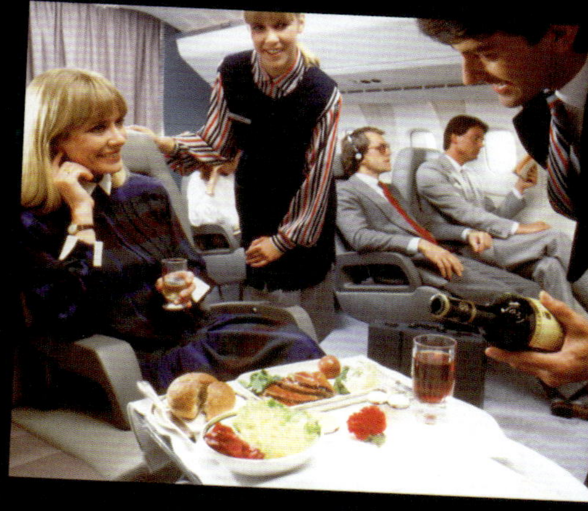

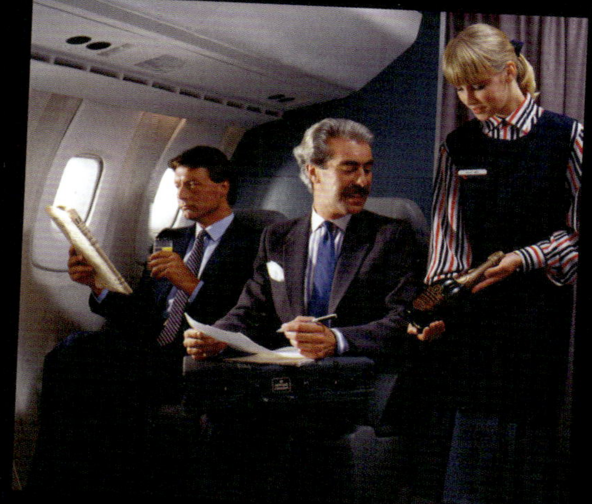

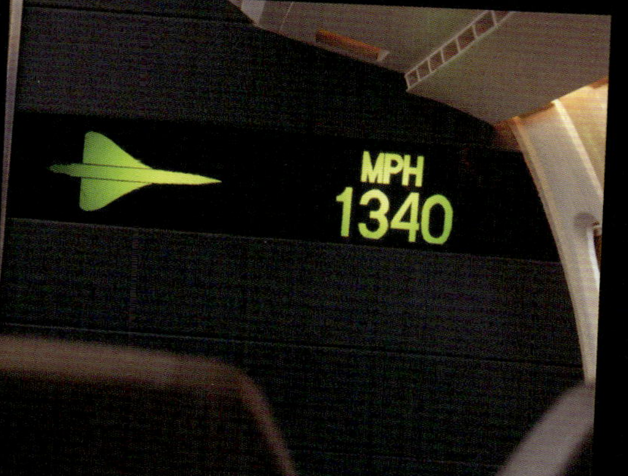
MPH
1340

'Concorde has the magic of the truly special and is a design icon of our times. It was way ahead of its time and gave us a glimpse into the future.'

Sir Terence Conran, designer

Creating space, 1990s

This new generation of leather seat was introduced in the 1990s (right). As the original seat armrest was fixed, the new seat would allow the armrest to be raised and give the passenger more room. As Luciano Pavarotti was a frequent flyer, who acknowledged his proportions by paying for two seats, this was a great improvement.

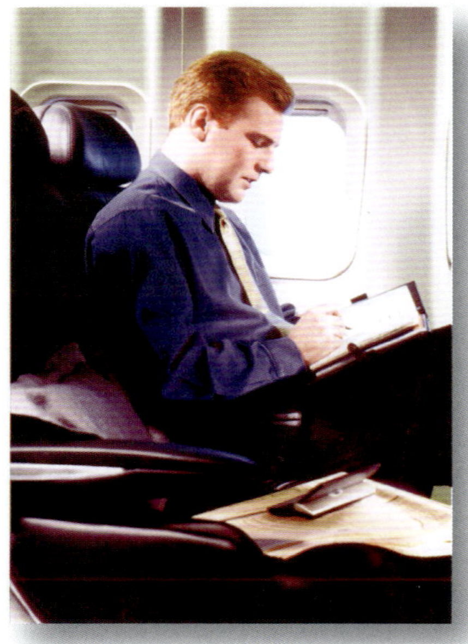

New interiors, 2001

Concorde went through a huge make-over and Sir Terrence Conran was responsible for redesigning the seats and some of the interior. The new indigo leather seats reflected a seat from an Aston Martin car, and the interior was designed to give an atmosphere similar to that of the Ivy Restaurant in London.

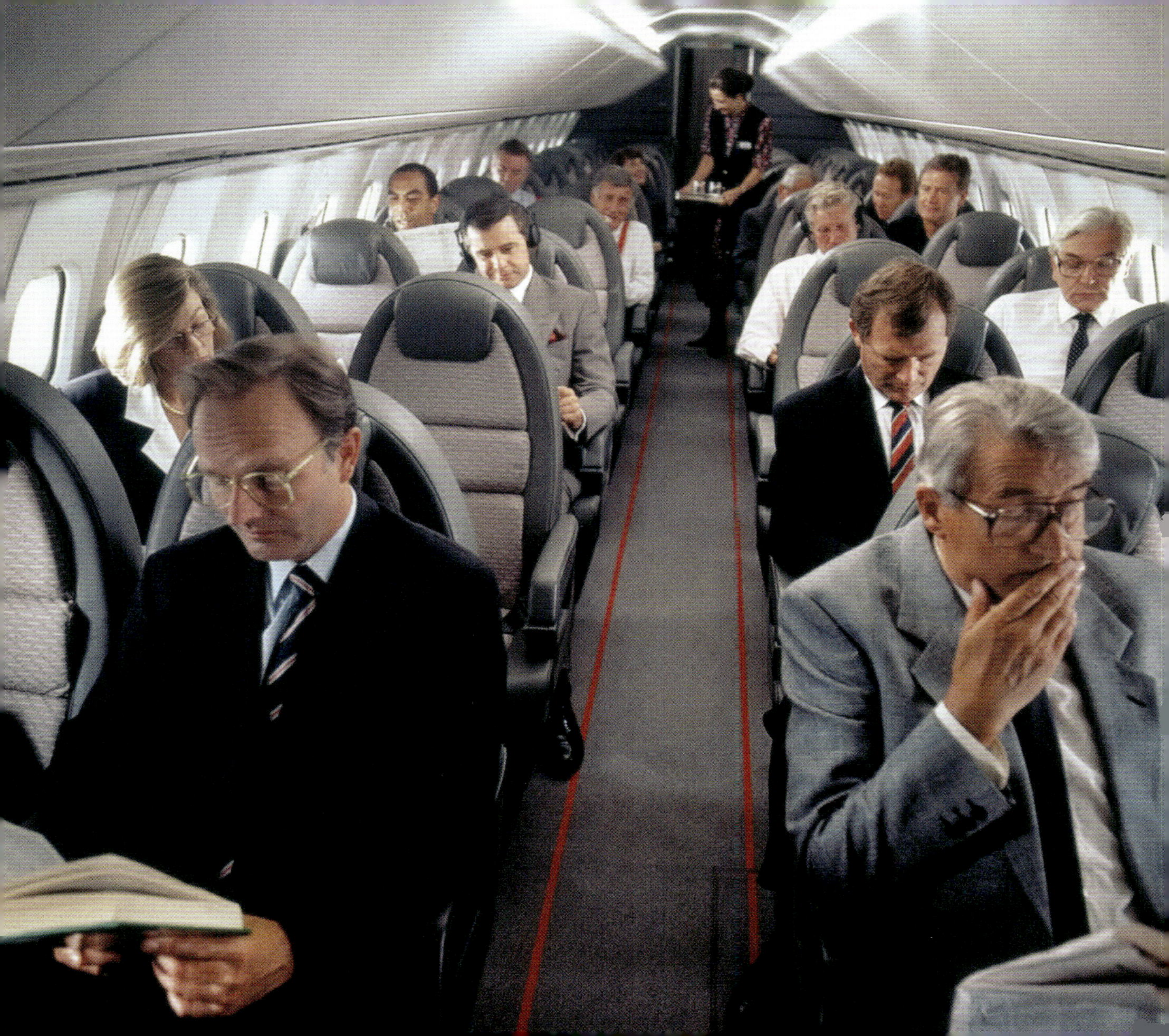

CATERING

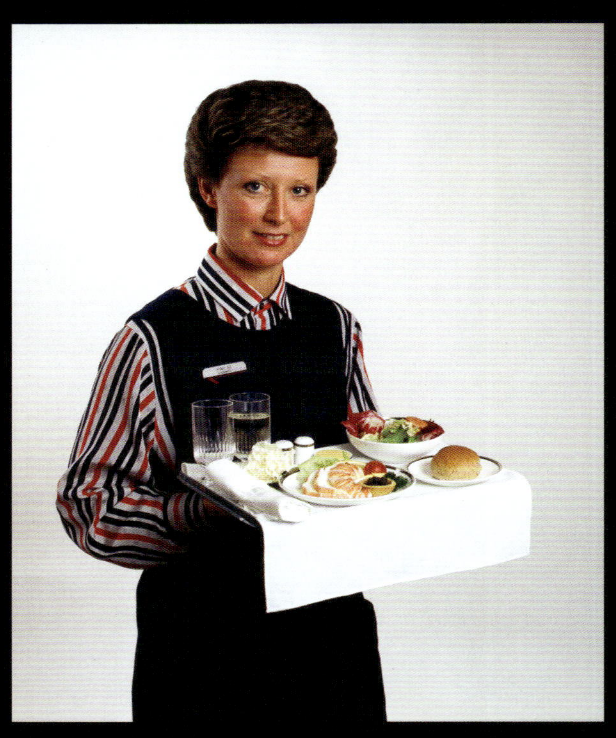

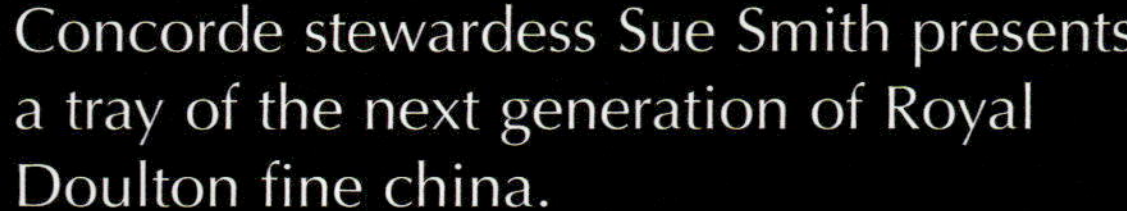

Concorde stewardess Sue Smith presents a tray of the next generation of Royal Doulton fine china.

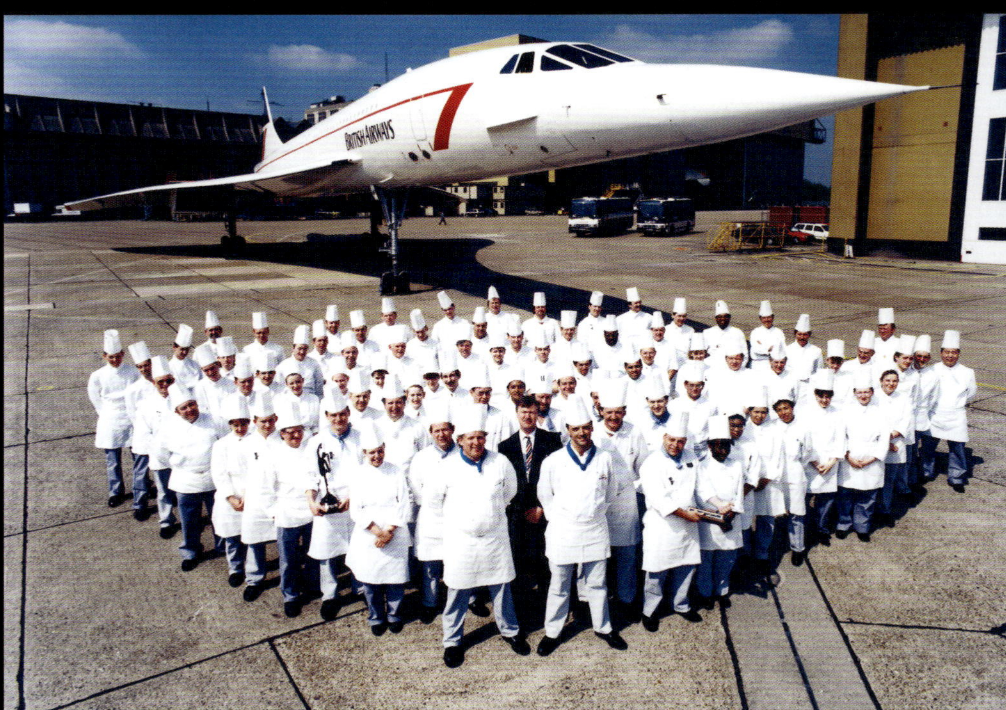

This PR picture was taken in 1991 and shows the dedicated chefs that helped to prepare and create the first-class food for Concorde. The gathering was to celebrate a prestigious catering award, and was shot from the aircraft steps.

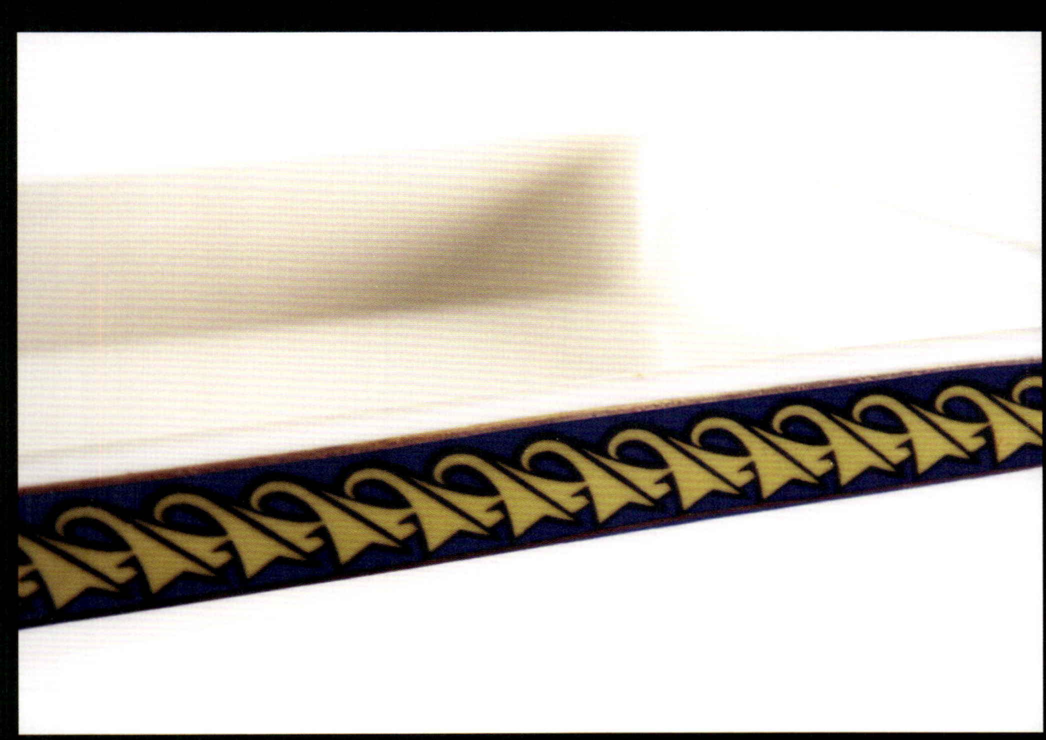

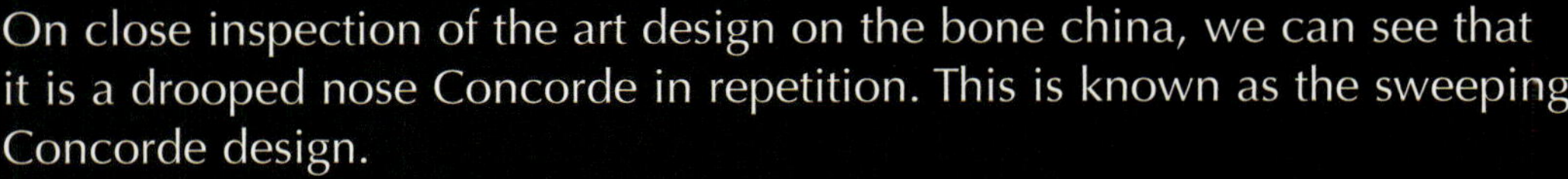

On close inspection of the art design on the bone china, we can see that it is a drooped nose Concorde in repetition. This is known as the sweeping Concorde design.

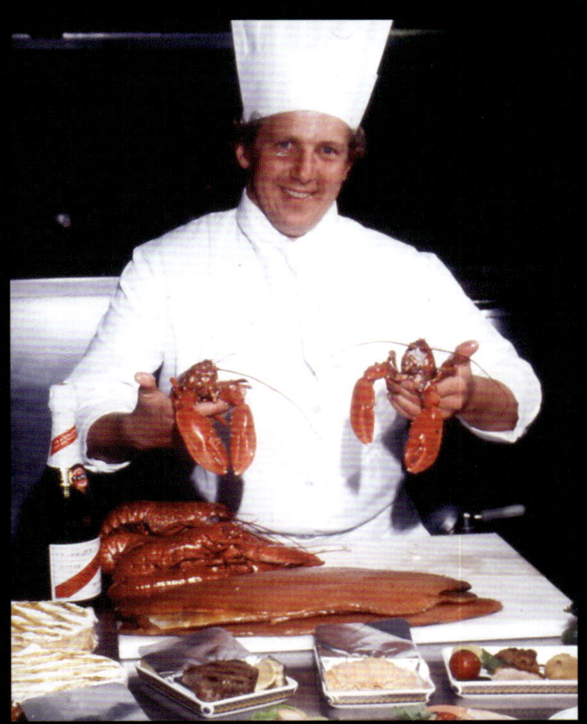

Chef Tubby Grey preparing a fine selection of sumptuous dishes carefully displayed on the very first Royal Doulton-designed chinaware in the 1970s.

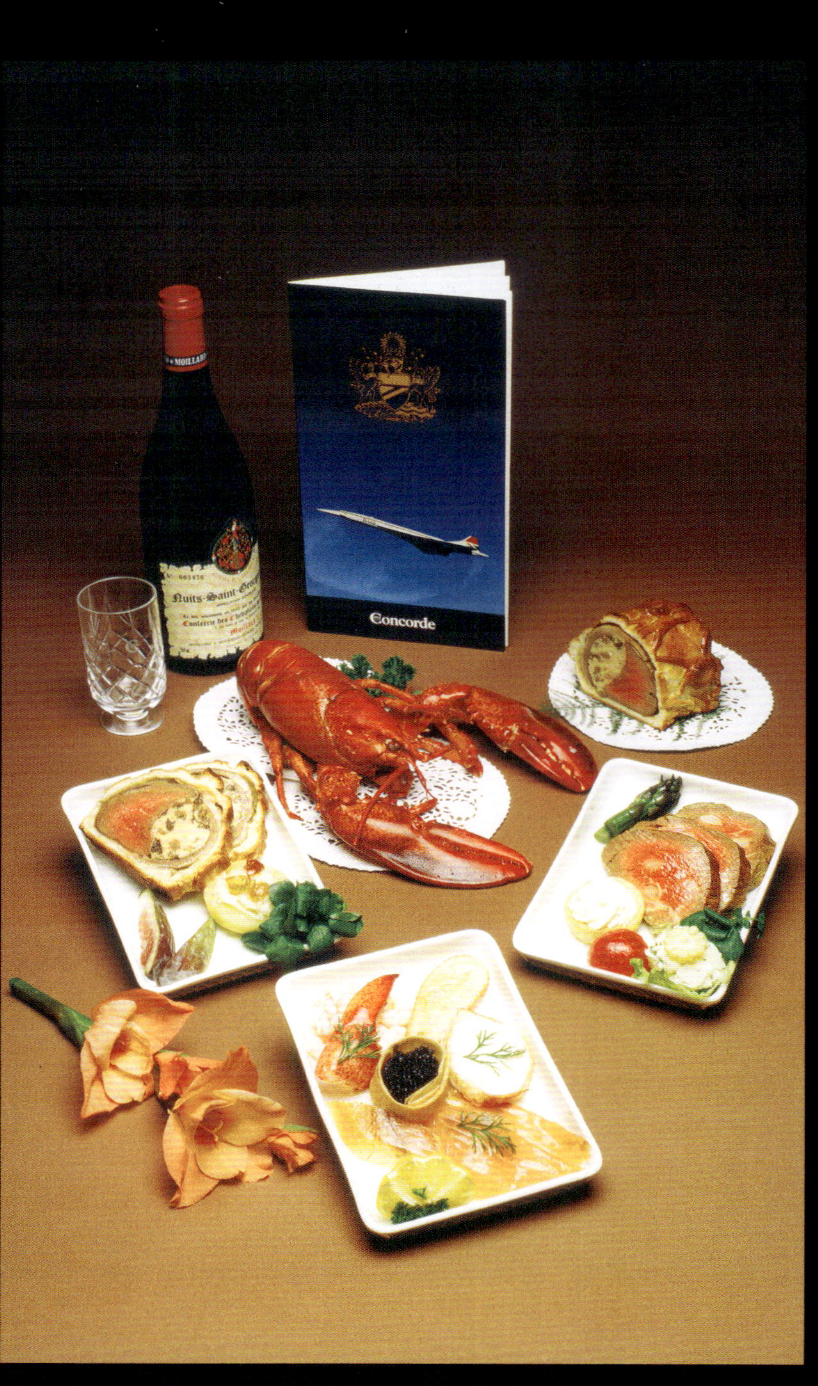

I spent many hours in the studio photographing different Concorde dishes. The very best in airline catering produced fresh lobster, smoked salmon, beef Wellington, the finest fresh fruits, a variety of fine cheese and a myriad of other mouth-watering dishes from around the world. This photograph shows the very first design, the blue Concorde menu.

One of the many delights of dining aboard Concorde was that you could always be assured of the superb quality of the food and the freshness of the produce used in the preparation of the dishes.

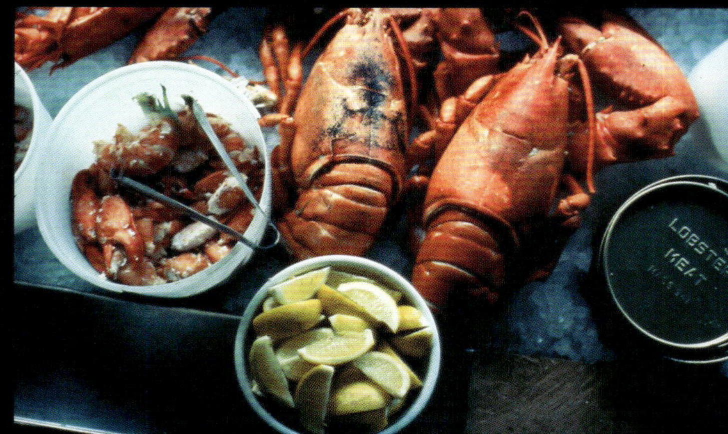

Express meals, healthy options and light bites were also among the choices provided. These were presented on a dressed linen tray, with Royal Doulton china.

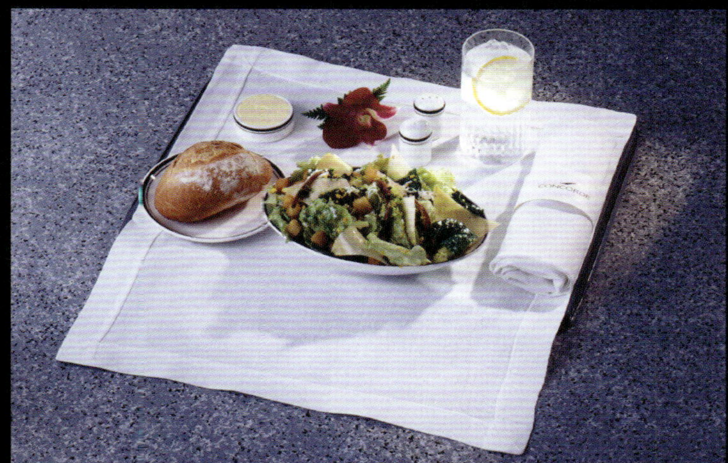

Afternoon tea.

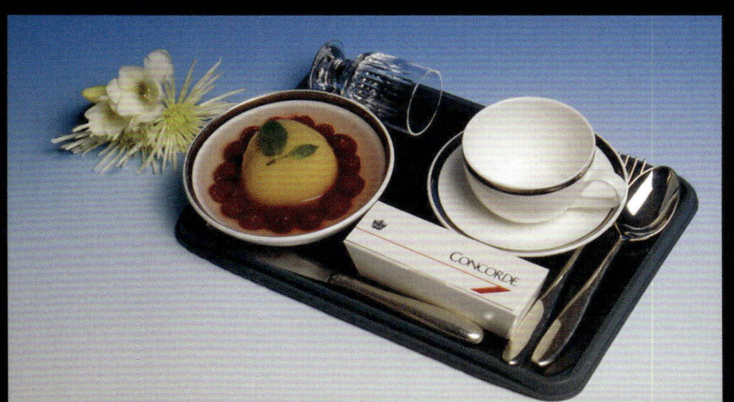

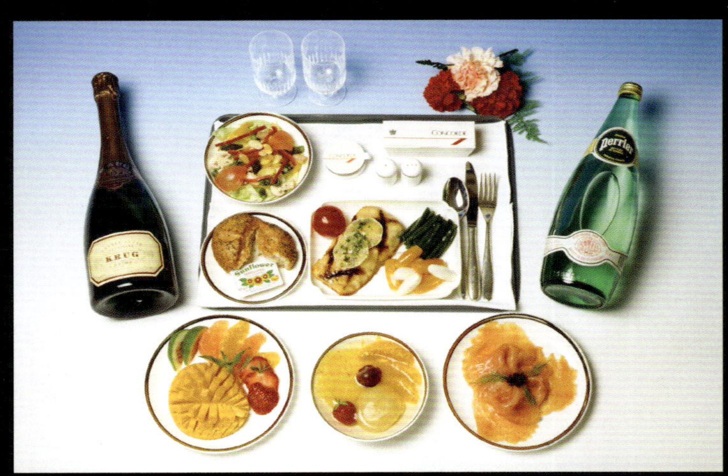

Concorde passengers were in for a real treat in the 1980s and '90s as celebrity chefs Michel and Albert Roux and Anton Mossimannas were asked by British Airways to create the innovative Concorde menus. Over 583,000 bottles of champagne have been served on Concorde since 1976, the most popular brand being Krug. £33 was the amount per passenger that BA allocated for food and wine. The average economy class long-haul passenger gets only £3.50 worth of food and drink.

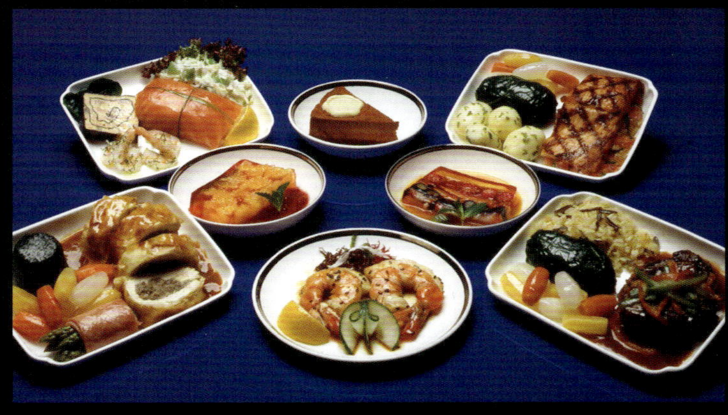

A selection of stunning meal options served on Concorde – from a three-course meal to a choice of light snacks, all beautifully presented.

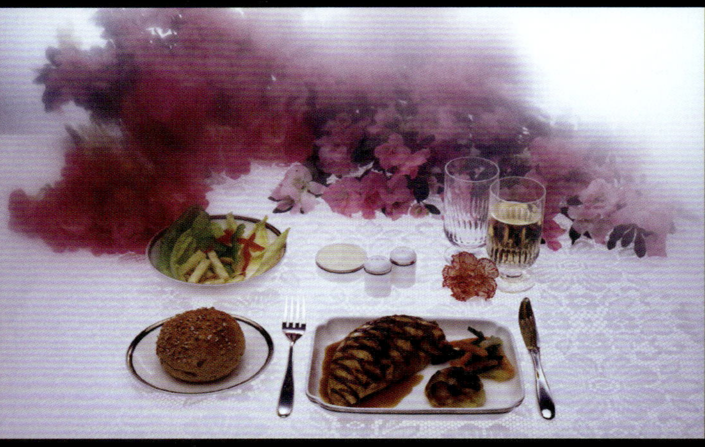

CHAPTER FOUR

SHOOTING CONCORDE

PHOTOGRAPHY 1

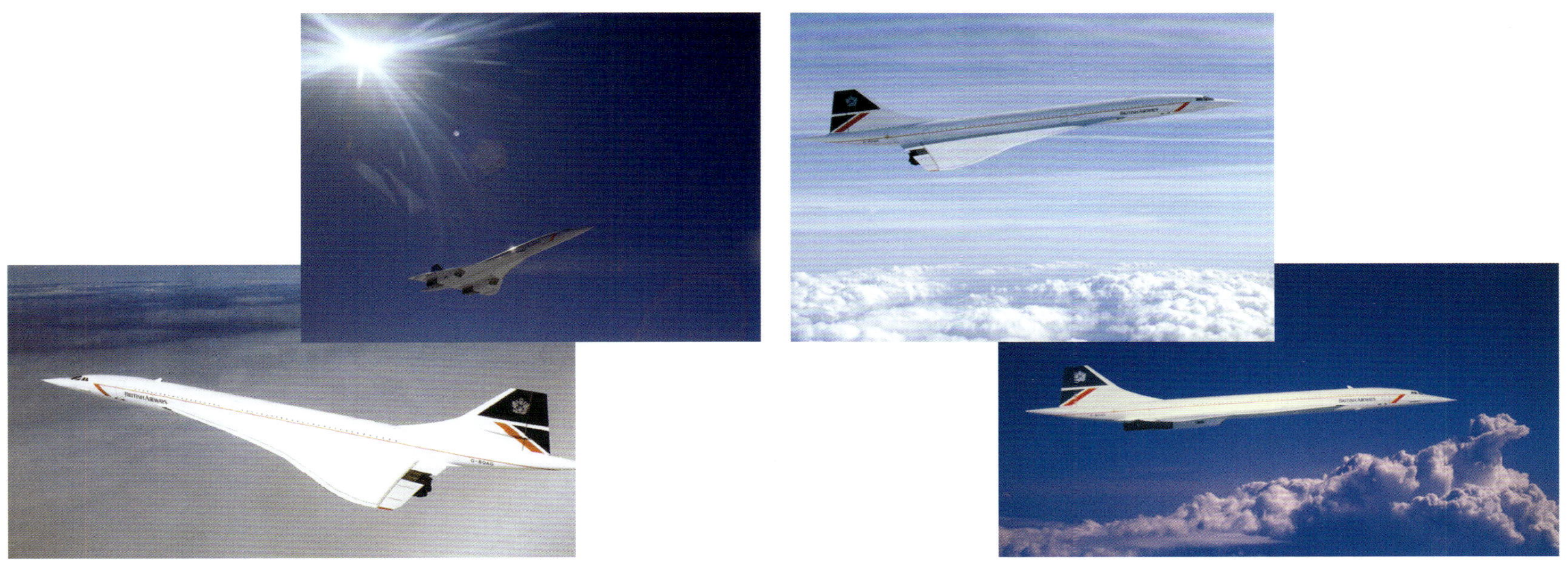

In 1985 British Airways introduced the new Landor livery and a film crew and I were despatched to Prestwick, Scotland, for a week to undertake new photography of the flagship Concorde.

We hired our usual Lear jet as the chase aircraft for the air-to-air photography, estimating that it would take over two days with the right weather conditions to produce the iconic images that we were after. Our brief was to show the new livery in full but also to try and achieve some exciting new angles to show Concorde at her best. The Lear jet that we used had special optically corrected glass which enabled us to take clear photographs. We relied, of course, on the expertise of the pilots to get as close as possible in order to get these stunning shots at various angles.

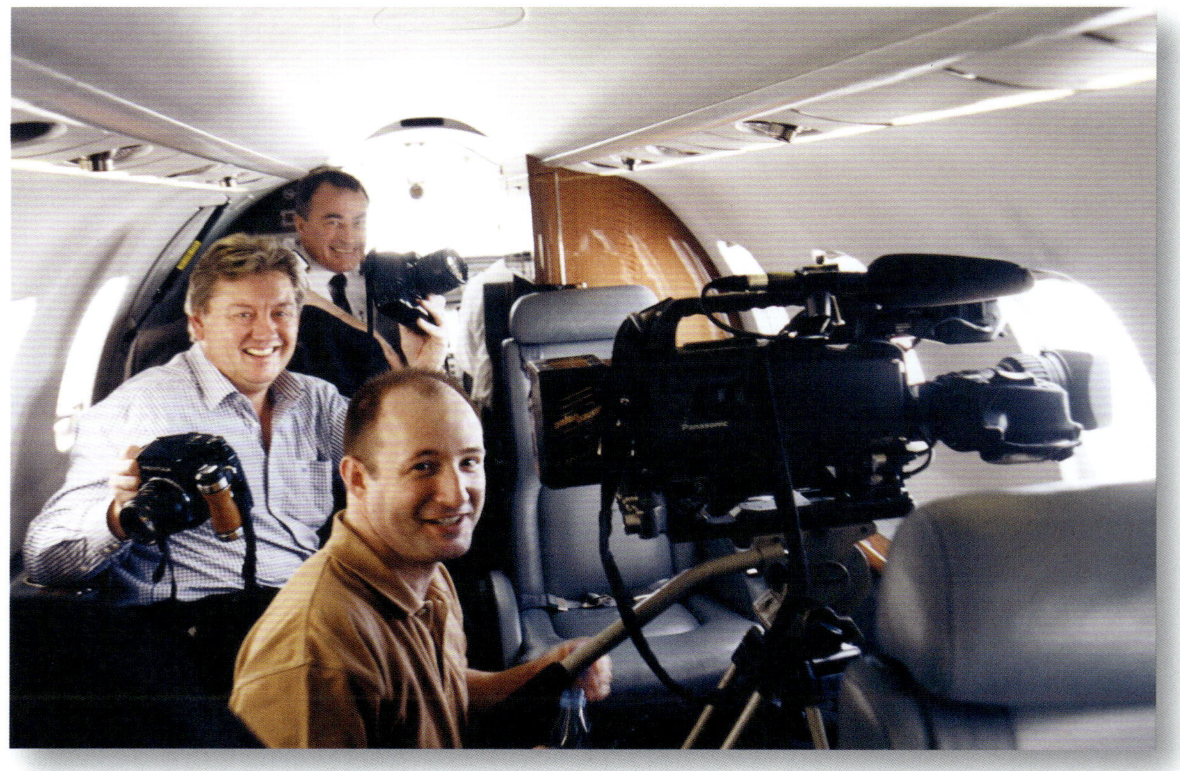

The interior of the Lear jet aircraft, with myself and the film crew on a typical
air-to-air shoot; notice how crammed the cabin is!

Opposite: This was one of my last shots of the day, as the sun was disappearing
over the Scottish Isles, showing Concorde looking very graceful in full silhouette.

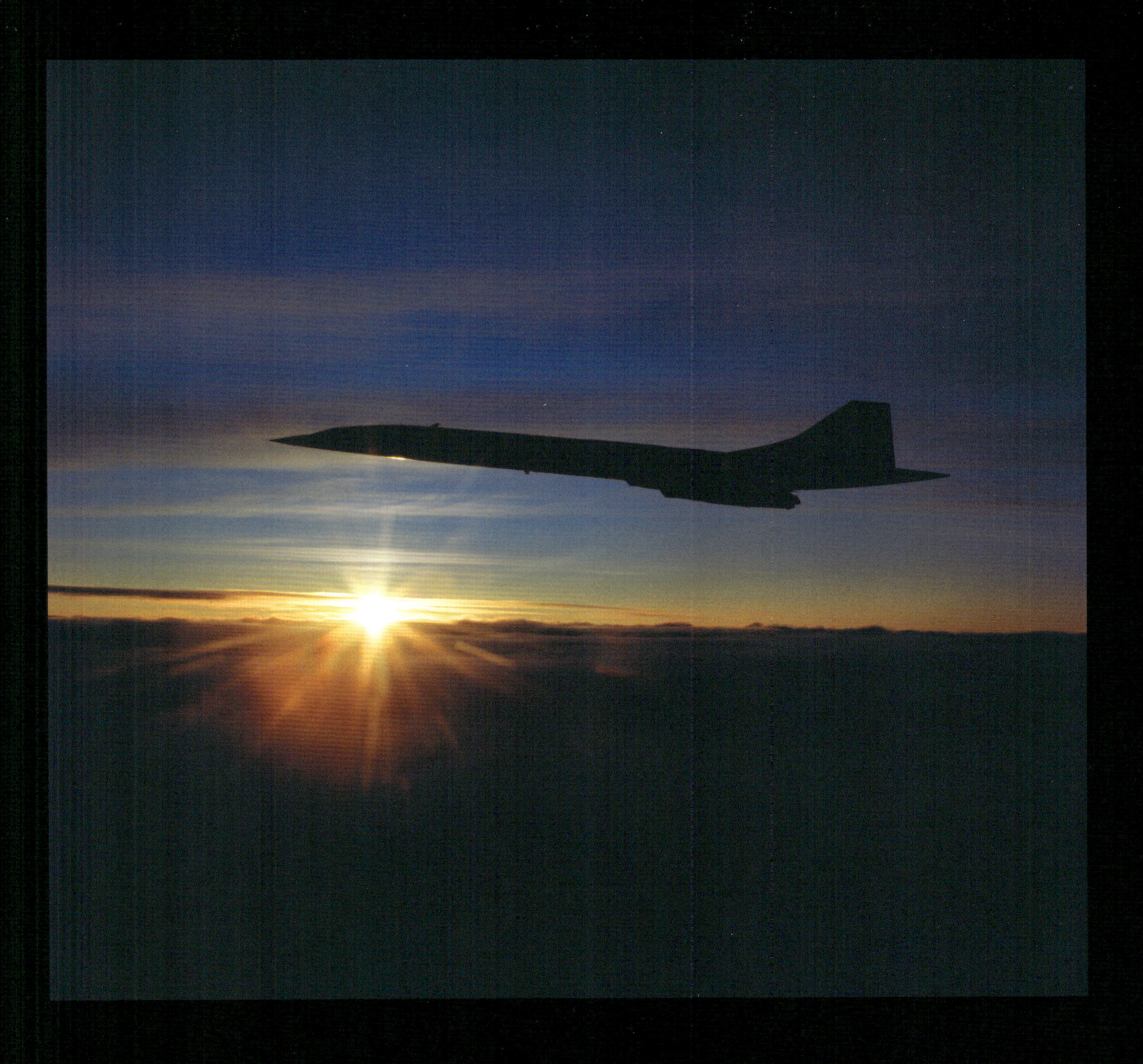

'I've never been closer to God.'
Lord Coggan, former Archbishop of Canterbury

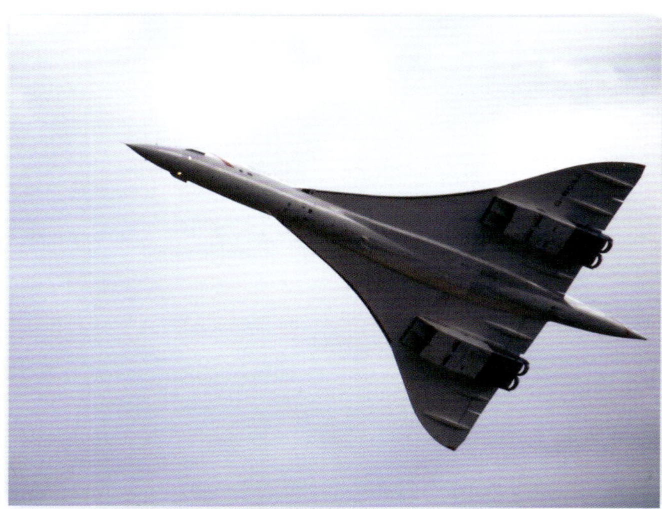

As part of our brief we had been requested to take some dramatic ground shots, plus take-offs and landings. The flight crew based themselves at Prestwick for the week, training new pilots for take-offs and landings, and this was very convenient for us as it enabled us to have a constant flow of aircraft movements, so we had plenty of opportunities to take hundreds of shots.

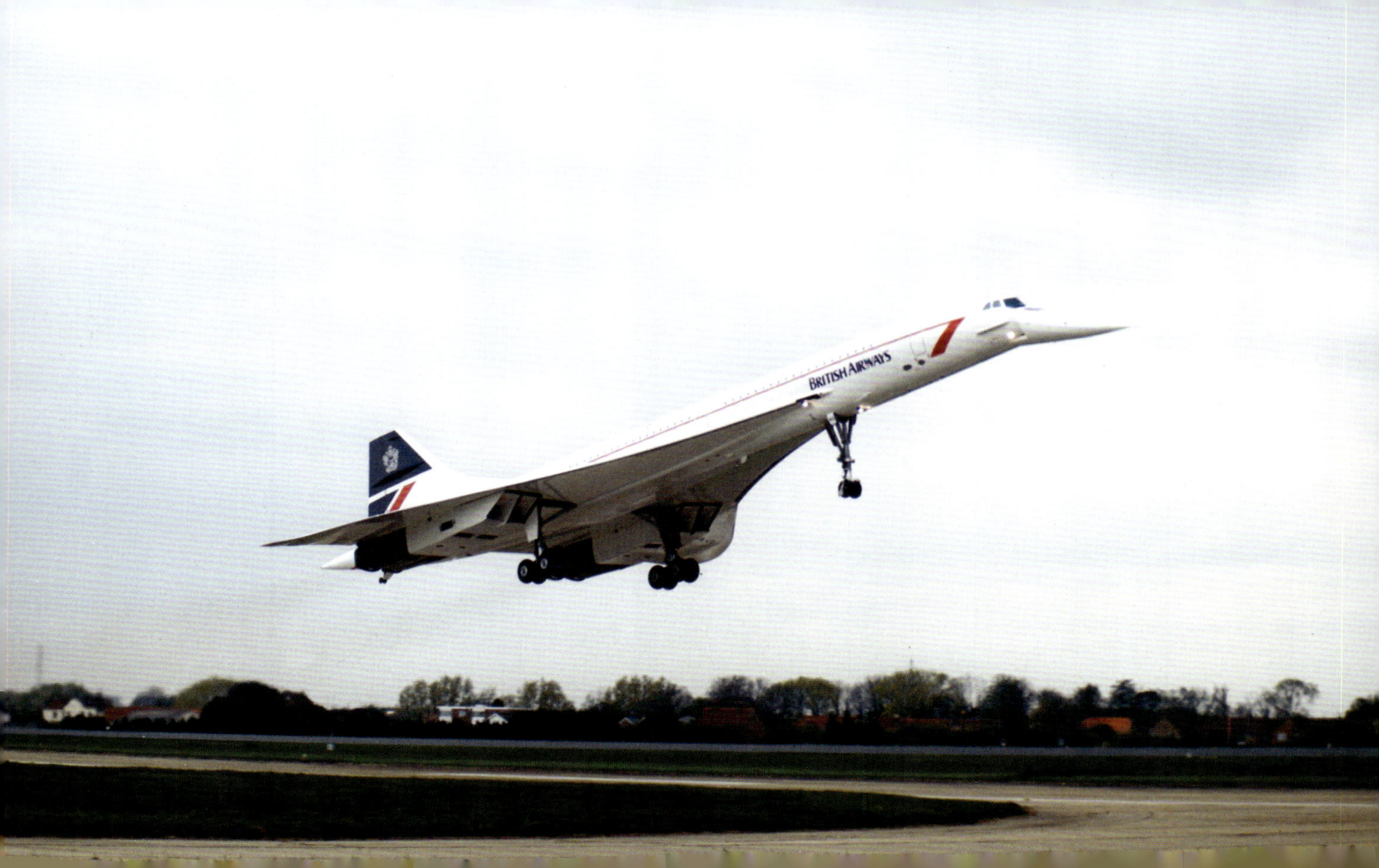
BRITISH AIRWAYS

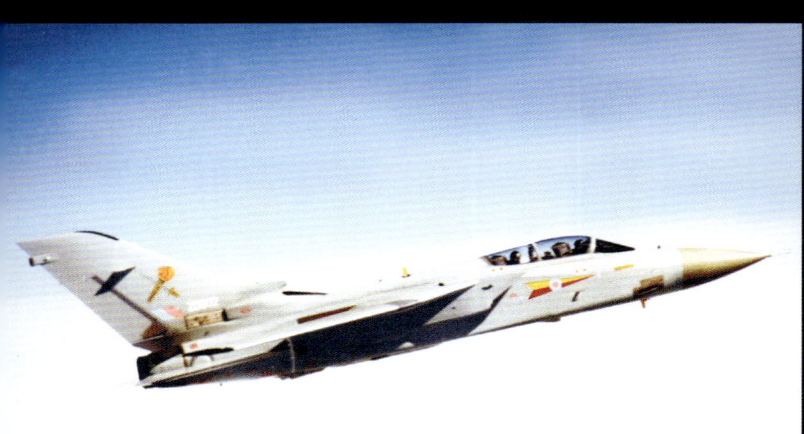

The RAF Tornado was rapidly running out of fuel, and was struggling to keep up with Concorde at Mach 2.

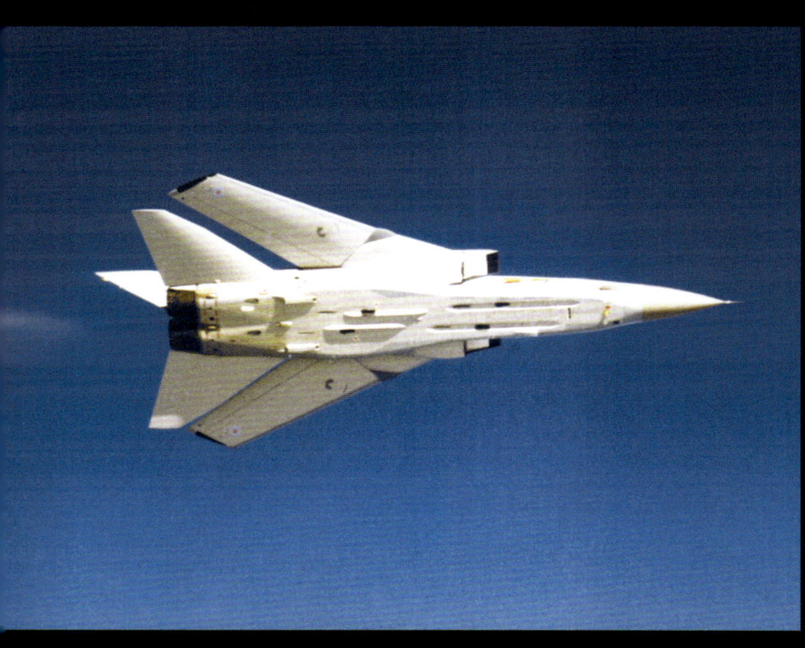

Opposite: A dramatic photograph of Concorde flying at supersonic speed – the only picture ever taken of Concorde flying at Mach 2, 1,350mph. This unique picture was taken from a Tornado fighter jet which rendezvoused with Concorde for just four minutes over the Irish Sea.

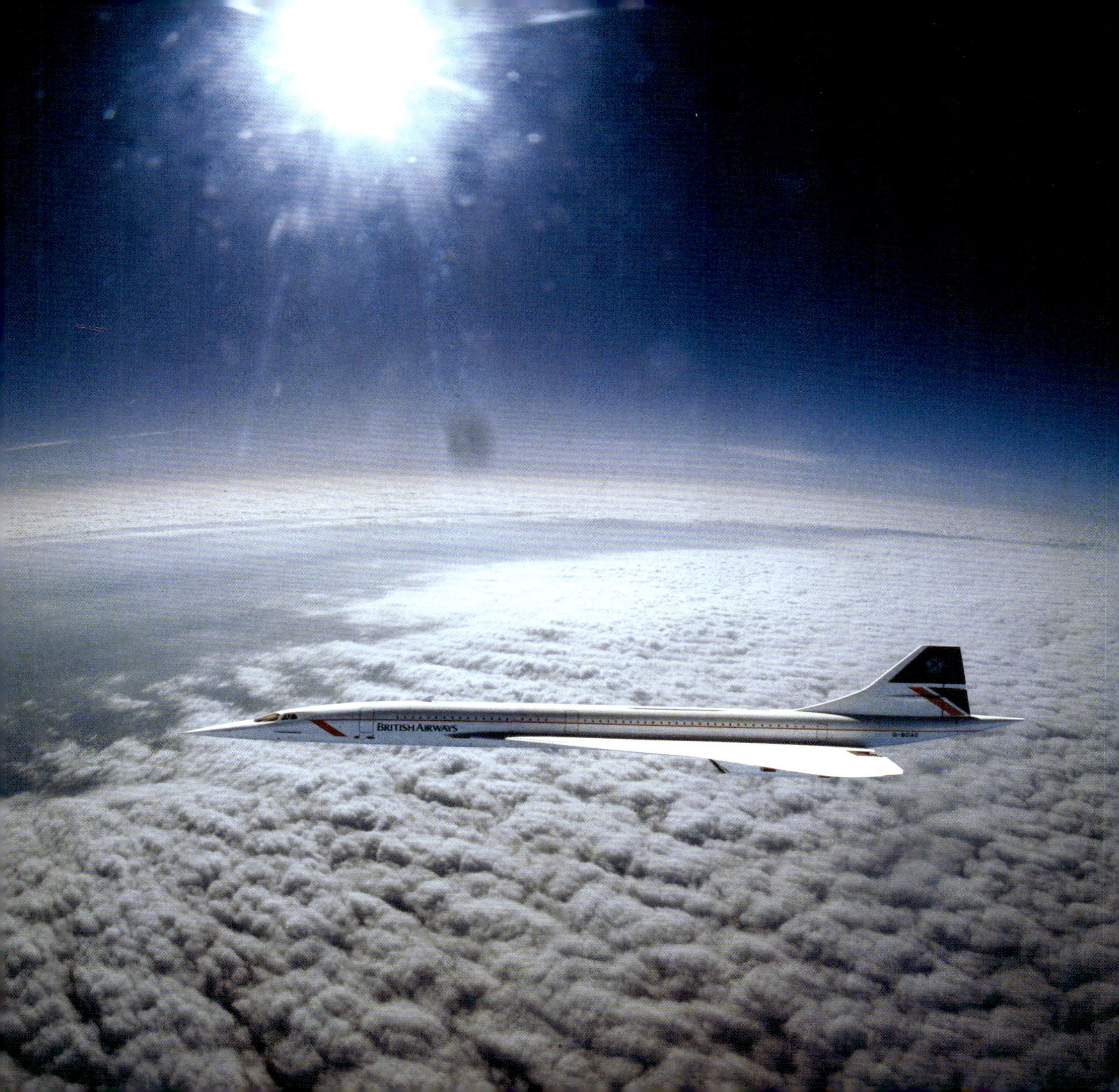

Concorde epitomises all that is associated with supersonic transatlantic travel and is also echoed in the famous song *Breakfast in America* by the group Supertramp. Concorde is the only aircraft in which you can arrive in the US *before* your departure time from London. You can leave at 10.30 a.m. at London time and land at JFK and still be down town for breakfast local time. Great for the business traveller.

This photograph has captured two infamous icons of the twenty-first century: Concorde flying out of JFK with the Twin Towers in the background. We had to get special permission from the FAA to fly over New York City. We hired a suitable Lear jet, and only had a small window of opportunity to capture this image, as time was very limited due to the fast speed of Concorde after take-off.

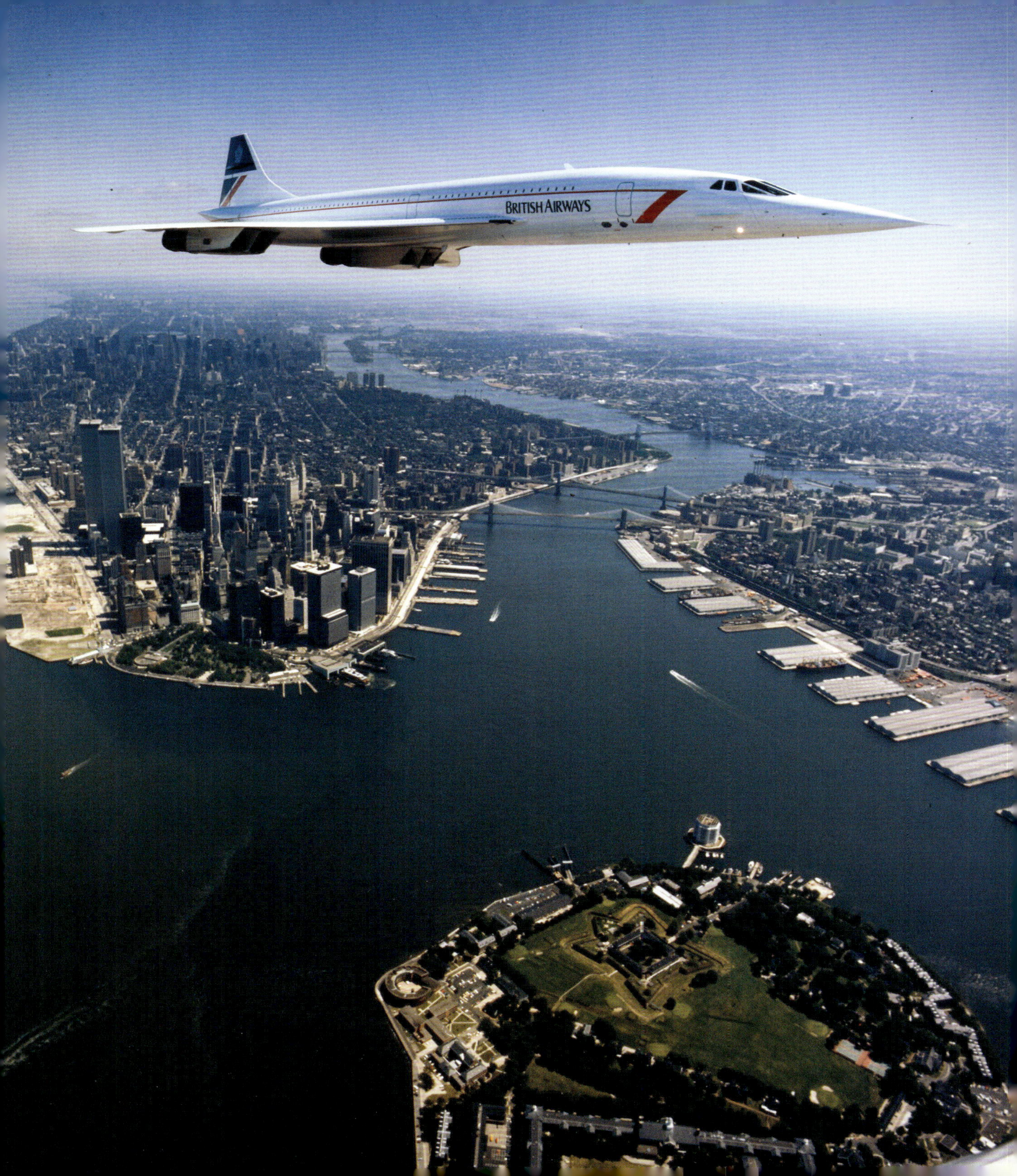

BRITISH AIRWAYS

Concorde went through various livery changes during her life, and as a result I had many assignments. One of my duties as a photographer would be to capture some dramatic take-offs and landings and obviously we had to show the livery design of the airline, but we were also trying to get dramatic visual shots of Concorde with long telephoto lenses. On one memorable occasion I was sent to Prestwick in 1985 to shoot the new Landor livery. During the last few days of that week I focused on trying to get that ultimate Concorde take-off shot. My friend and work colleague John Cook, the training captain, was flying the aircraft at the time and he knew I would be waiting at the end of the runway to try and achieve a head-on shot. Concorde had been circling, doing what we call touch and goes, all day long, and I found myself on my belly on the runway waiting for Concorde to take off for the last time at the end of the day. As the aircraft was rapidly coming towards me at a speed of 250mph I focused my lens to roughly where I thought the aircraft would lift off the runway, but to my surprise John Cook decided to bring the aircraft right to the end of the runway, where I was laying prone on the ground, at which point I thought my days were numbered. The noise and the heat and the fumes hit me and I felt like I was in an incinerator. Not realising that I had been pressing my motor drive through the whole sequence, to my surprise I had inadvertently managed to get this stunning photograph. I think I had kept my finger on the trigger in fear of death!

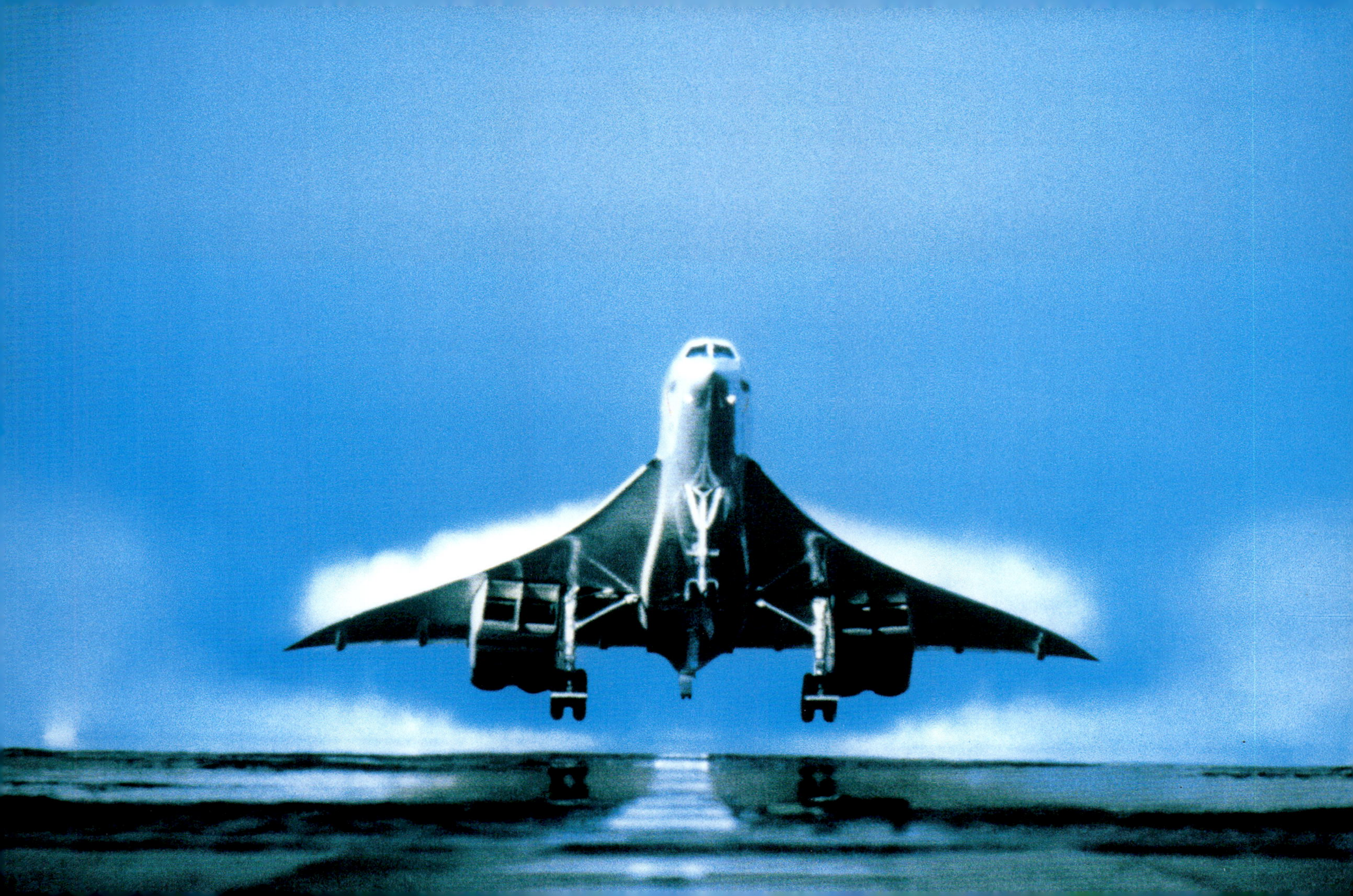

'There's the view of New York from the Triborough Bridge, there's the Sydney Opera House and there's Concorde – arguably the three most beautiful man-made sights in the world.'
Sir David Frost, TV journalist and frequent Concorde flier

Concorde, in the new Chatham livery, flying at twice the speed of sound in 1997. No other machine can fly at Mach 2, or 1,350mph, for four hours while carrying 100 passengers. At Concorde's cruising altitude you can see the horizon for up to 300 miles, a fabulous view for the passengers. She flies 300mph faster than the Earth's rotating orbit. According to NASA, when flying at 55,000ft you have now become an astronaut.

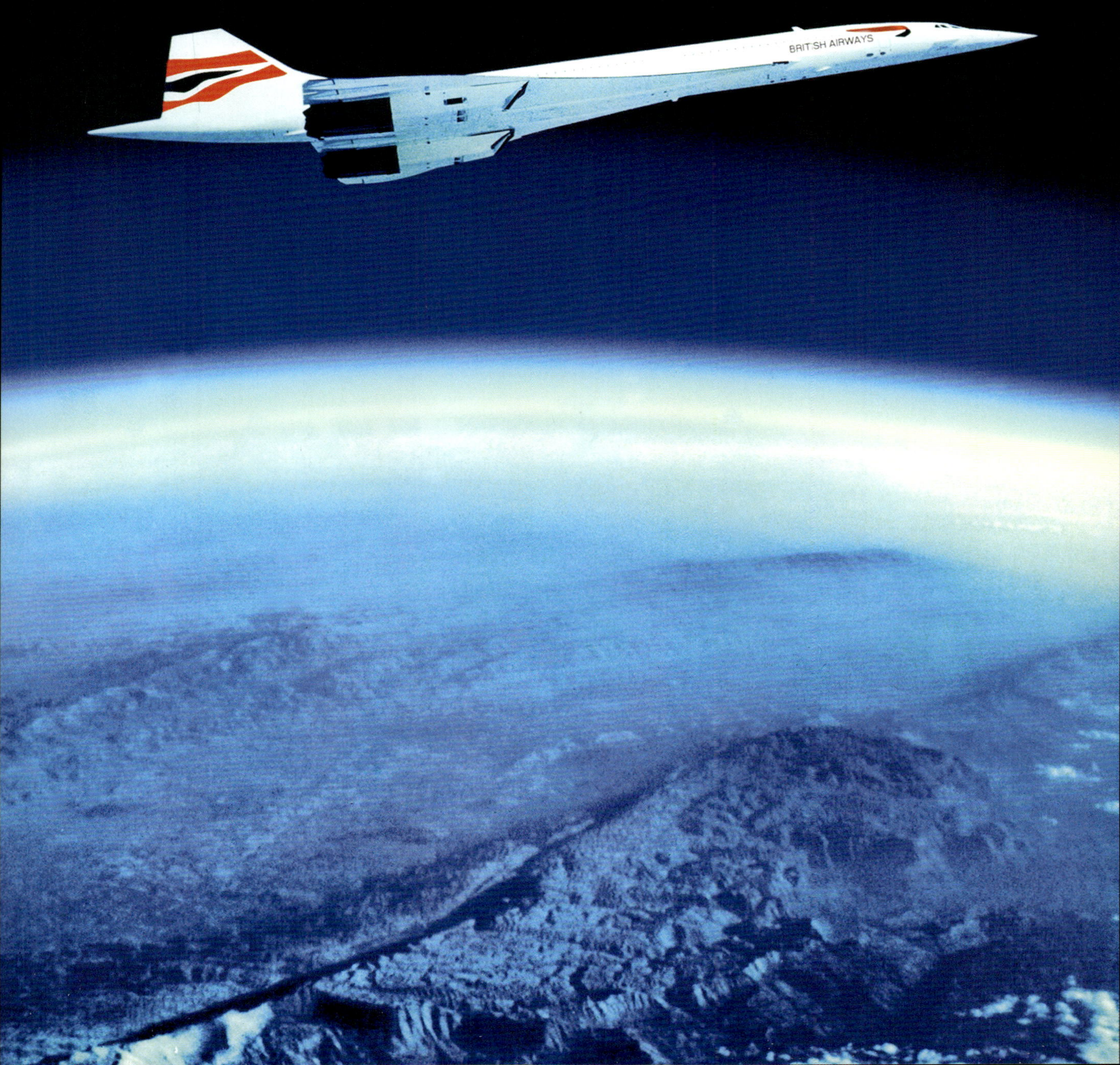
BRITISH AIRWAYS

THE QUEEN MOTHER'S BIRTHDAY

One of the most prestigious photographic assignments I have ever undertaken was to be asked by British Airways to be the official photographer at the Queen Mother's eighty-fifth birthday on board Concorde on 6 August 1985. She looked beautiful that day, dressed in canary yellow. With a radiant smile she climbed up the sparkling clean steps and into an even cleaner aircraft. I was very privileged to be in the front cabin with the royal guests, who included Viscount Linley and Lady Sarah Armstrong Jones. Lord King, the current chairman, hosted the celebrations. British Airways had also selected a number of personnel with similar birthdays to the Queen Mother to accompany the flight.

After take-off the Queen Mother spoke with all the crew and staff, but to my surprise came up to me first and asked, 'Does flying at supersonic speed affect the film in your camera?' to which I replied, 'No ma'am, it has no effect on the film.' She was exuberant, and very well informed, and knew all the roles of the staff, chatting with excitement in a very informal way. For the next few hours we were whisked across the heartland of the country, crossing Manchester, Carlisle, Glasgow and Aberdeen, culminating in a supersonic dash down the North Sea.

I had a few photographic opportunities; the first was to capture the Queen Mother on the flight deck with Captain Brian Walpole OBE as Concorde was flying supersonic. The second was the cutting of the official birthday cake with the royal guests. The Queen Mother had always wanted to fly Concorde, and was ecstatic that British Airways had arranged such a special treat; she enjoyed the event with much enthusiasm.

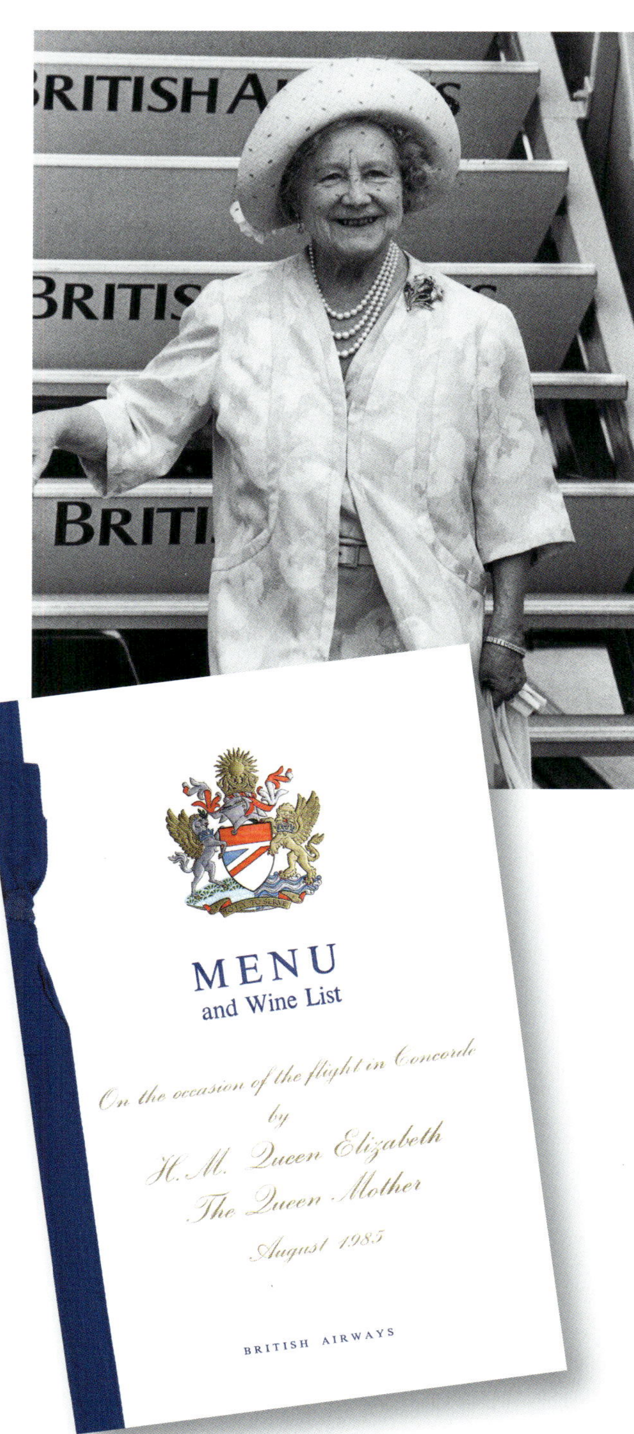

MENU
and Wine List

On the occasion of the flight in Concorde
by
H.M. Queen Elizabeth
The Queen Mother
August 1985

BRITISH AIRWAYS

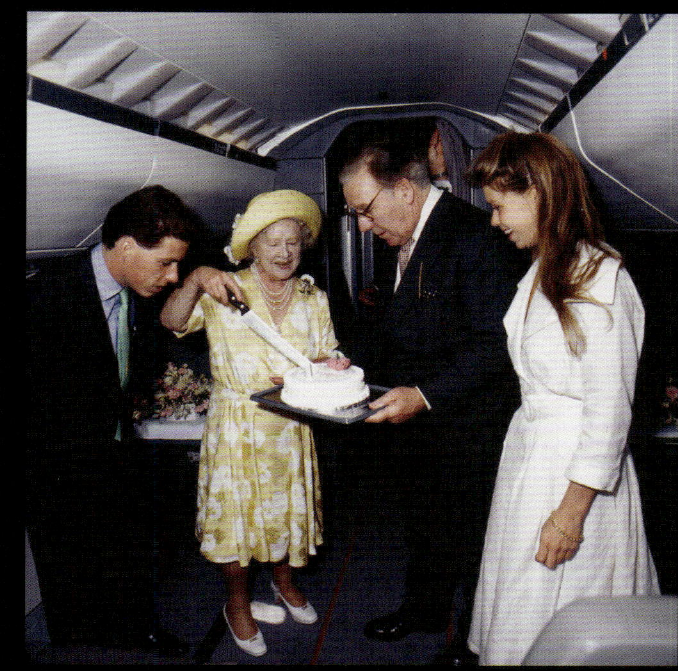

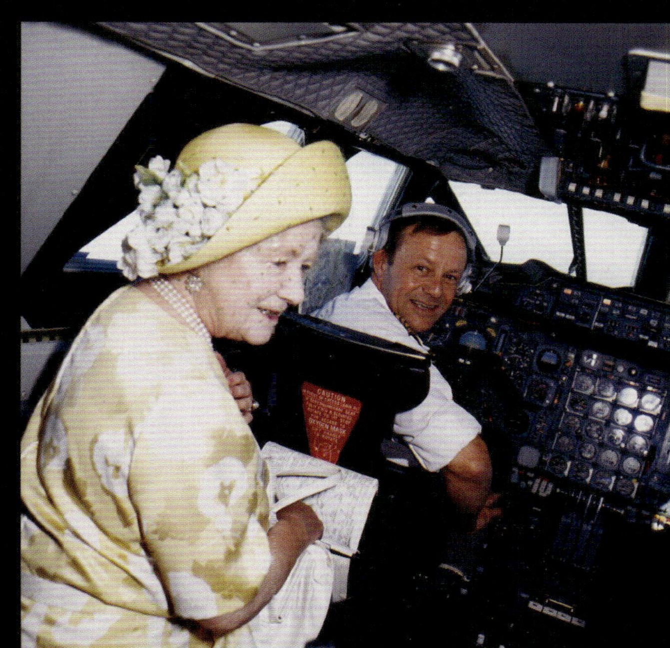

PHOTOGRAPHY 2

Concorde base training at Prestwick, 1985

Prestwick in Scotland was an ideal airport for Concorde and the training crews. Being remote, they could practise take-offs and landings up to twenty times a day without any complaints about noise levels from the locals. Prestwick Airport is also famous for the King of Rock and Roll, Elvis Presley, landing here on 3 March 1960. Elvis was finishing his American national service and stopped off in Ayrshire for a precious two hours. It was the only time Elvis was on British soil mingling with his fans.

The weather in Scotland was very changeable and we had to quickly spring into action as soon as we had a few hours of clear skies. Captain John Cook was very helpful; at breakfast we would discuss the best positioning for the photography. The aircraft were always sited near the general aerodrome buildings, which were not the best backdrops for the pictures, so John would take Concorde to the very end of the runway where the skyline was clear. The runway surface was not at all photogenic, so to soften this I spent many hours on my knees and stomach, placing the camera on the ground, which helps to blur out some of the tarmac foreground.

We always had good fun at Prestwick, and John on numerous occasions would put an L-plate on the front wheel leg of Concorde for his new trainee captains.

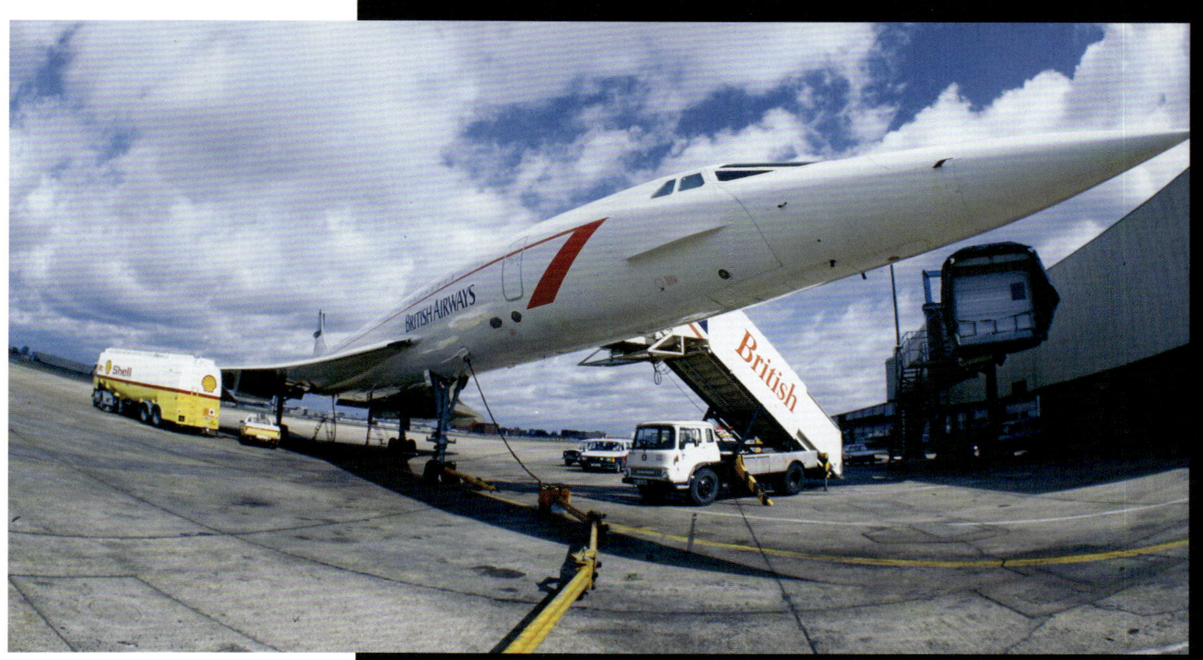

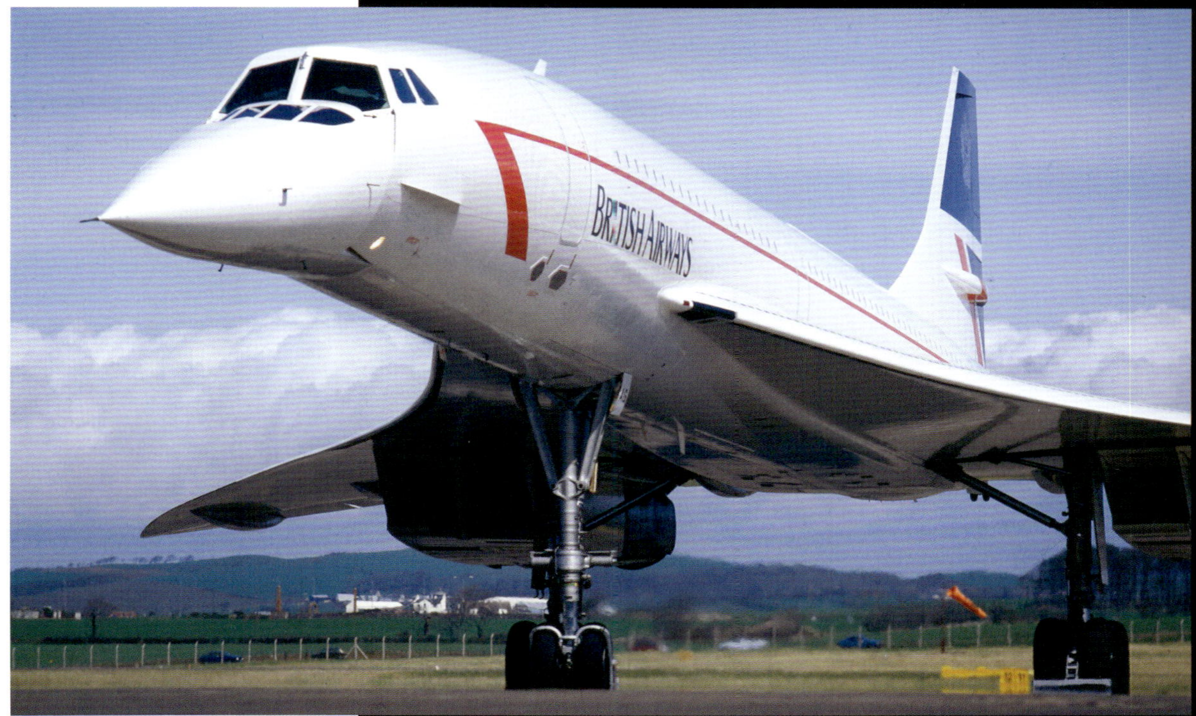

In great secrecy, I was asked by BA Public Relations to capture the new British Airways Landor colours. My brief was to take as many pictures as possible in just one hour in a remote area of Heathrow Airport. We did not want to alert the press, or give them any knowledge before the initial big press launch, which was to follow a few weeks later.

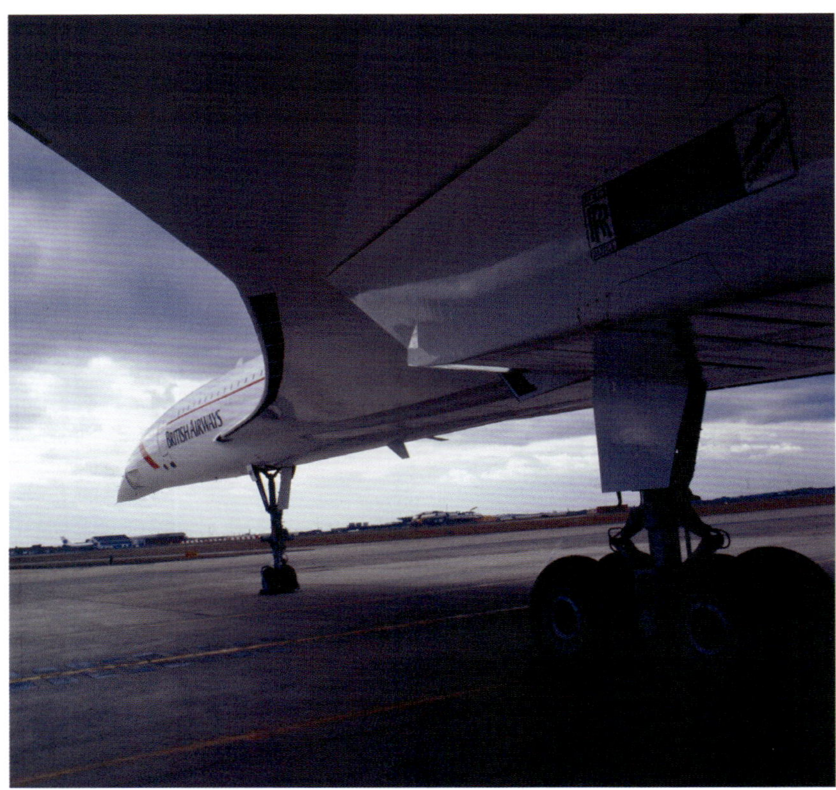

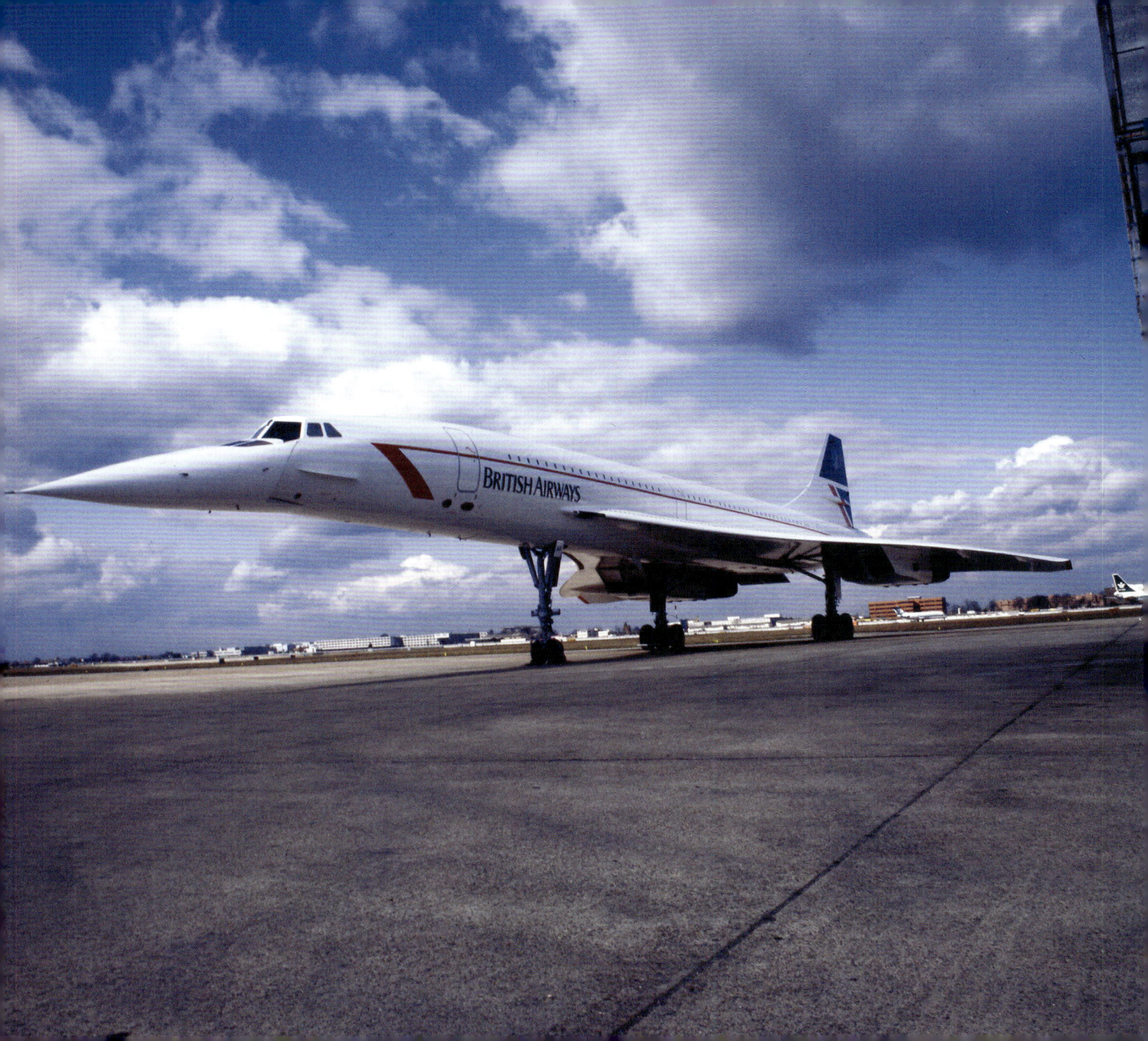
BRITISH AIRWAYS

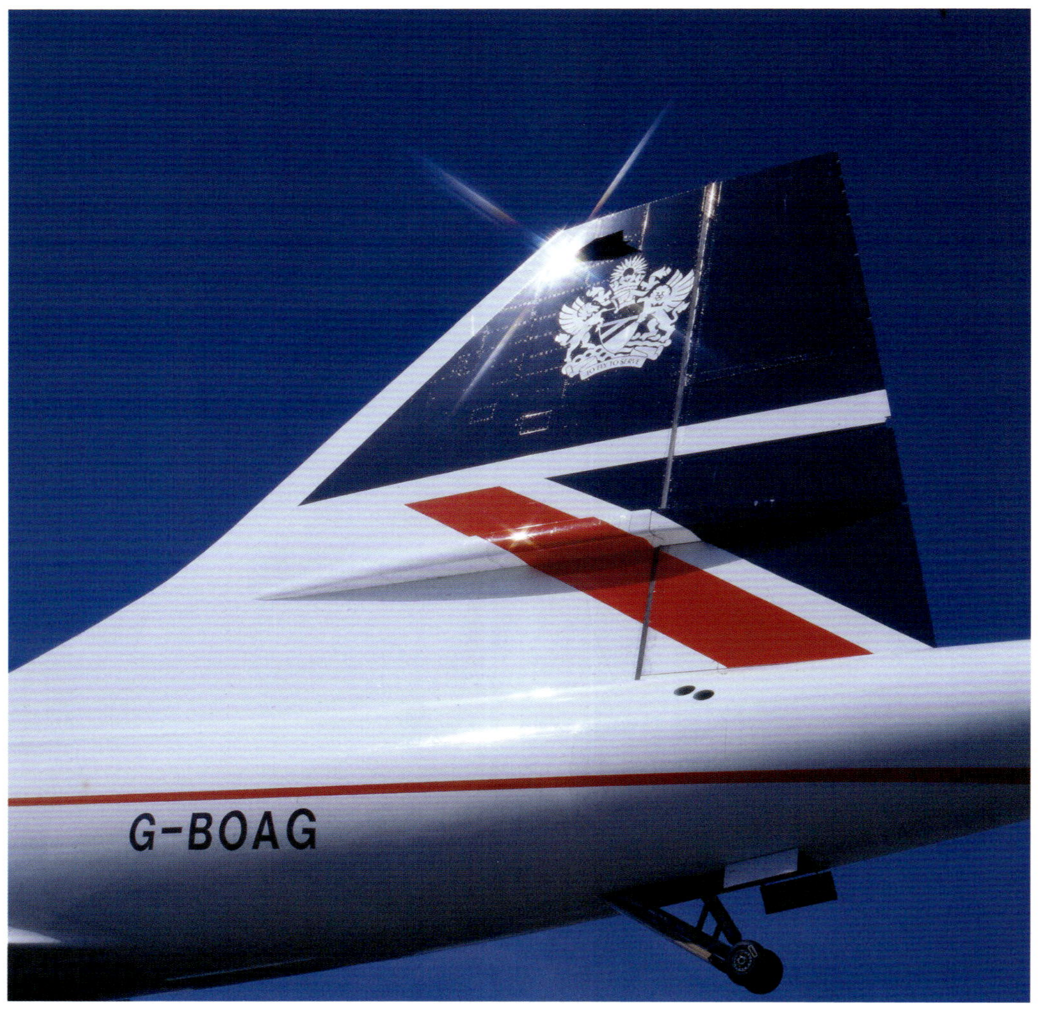

In January 1975 British Airways was granted a coat of arms in recognition of their importance to the nation. The motto read 'To Fly To Serve'. One had not been used on aircraft livery before. Coats of arms date back to the twelfth century when they were used by warriors who needed some means of identifying friend from foe on the battlefield. This was first time that the British Airways crest was used on the tail fin of Concorde and it became an iconic symbol of British Airways, being used from this time on for all BA aircraft in the Landor livery.

Opposite: The British Airways Pipe Band officially roll out the first Concorde in the new Landor colours. That same day Chairman Lord King and Chief Executive Lord Marshall took selected guests on a supersonic trip around the Bay of Biscay.

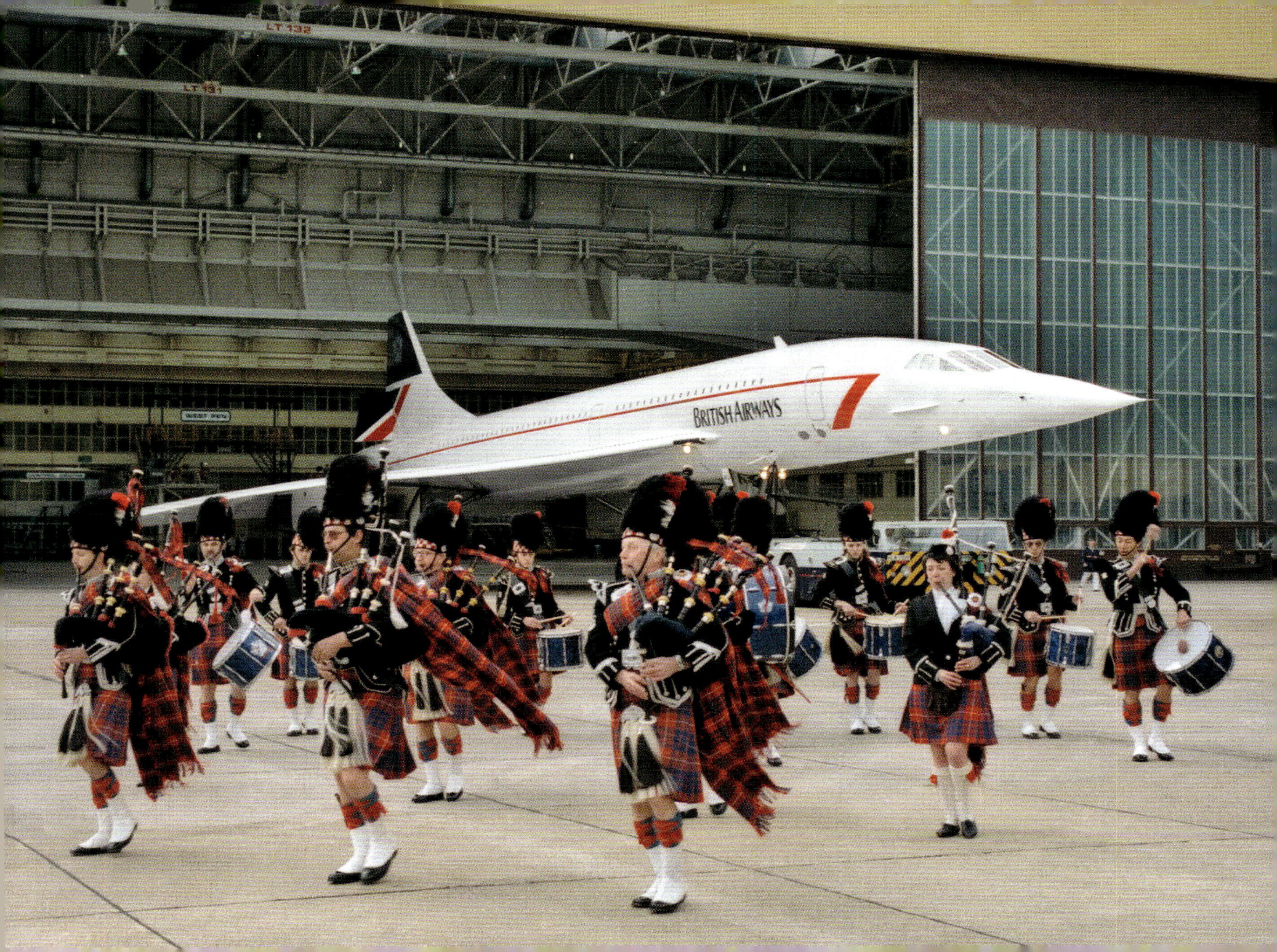
LT 132
LT 131
WEST PEN
BRITISH AIRWAYS

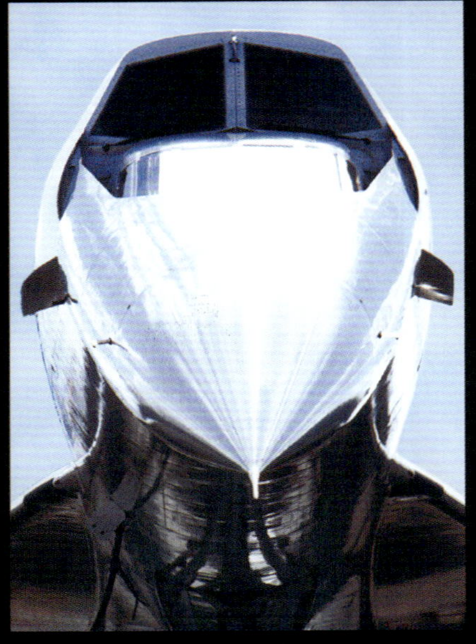 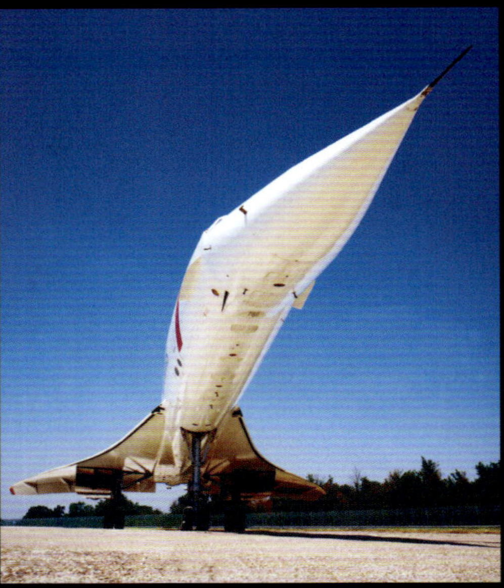 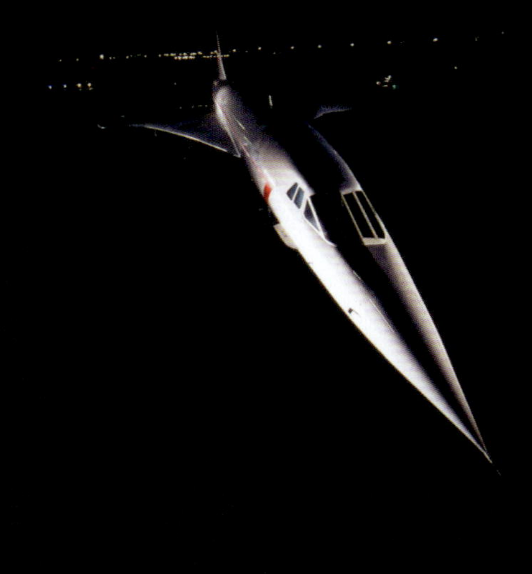

On many occasions I have been asked by training crews to photograph detailed shots of Concorde's famous drooping nose, which is very different from other aircraft. The flight crew has to drop the nose for take-off and landing, as it has been specially designed to give the pilots much better visibility. The nose also has a heat-resistant windshield which is brought into position after take-off, before entering supersonic speeds, to protect the main cockpit windows from heat. The heat on the end of the nose reaches an incredible 127°C (260°F).

The glamorous American singer Barbara Streisand once memorably claimed that the shape of her splendid nose was the inspiration for the Concorde designers. She said it should have been called the Streisand, and not the Concorde.

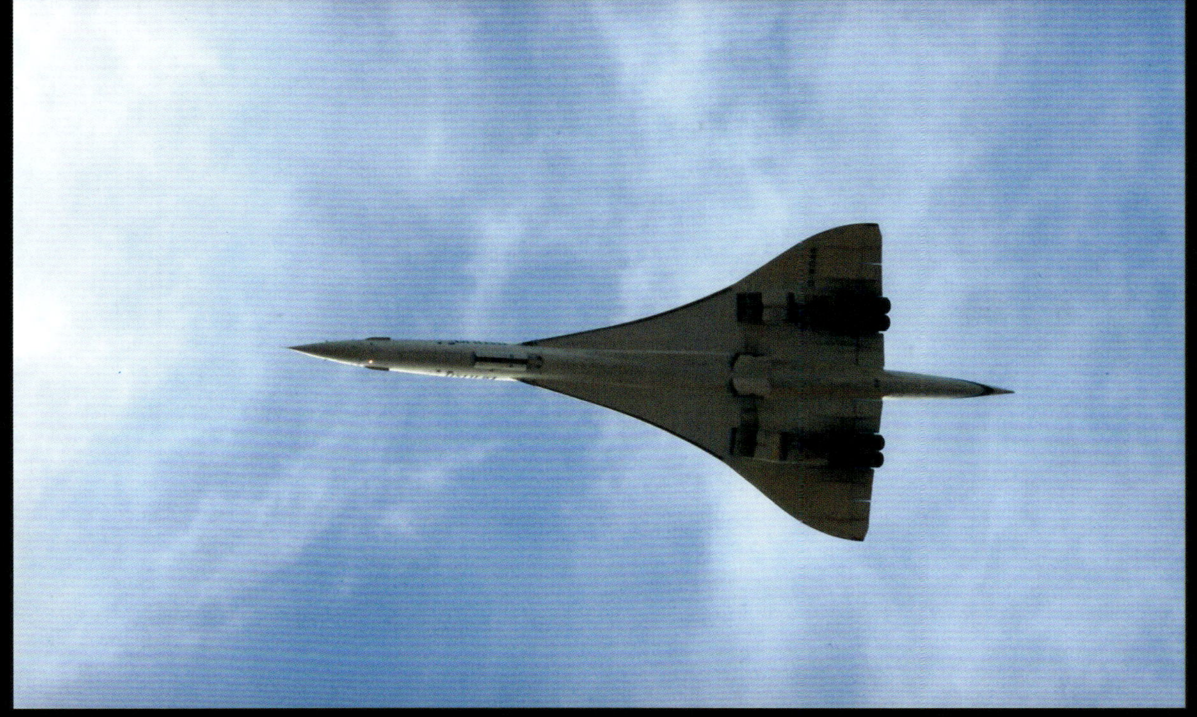

On many a sunny day at London Heathrow I would pack up my sandwiches, take a flask of coffee and drive my car through airside, and go out to the apron roads. I would always position myself in readiness for the 10.30 a.m. BA 001 Concorde London to New York flight, and get as near as possible to the runway. In those days we didn't have the strict security that we have now. After working at Heathrow for many years, the security personnel at BAA where very helpful and would often escort me to remote parts of the airfield, but usually I was able go off on my own, my aim being to capture as many dramatic aircraft images as possible in one day.

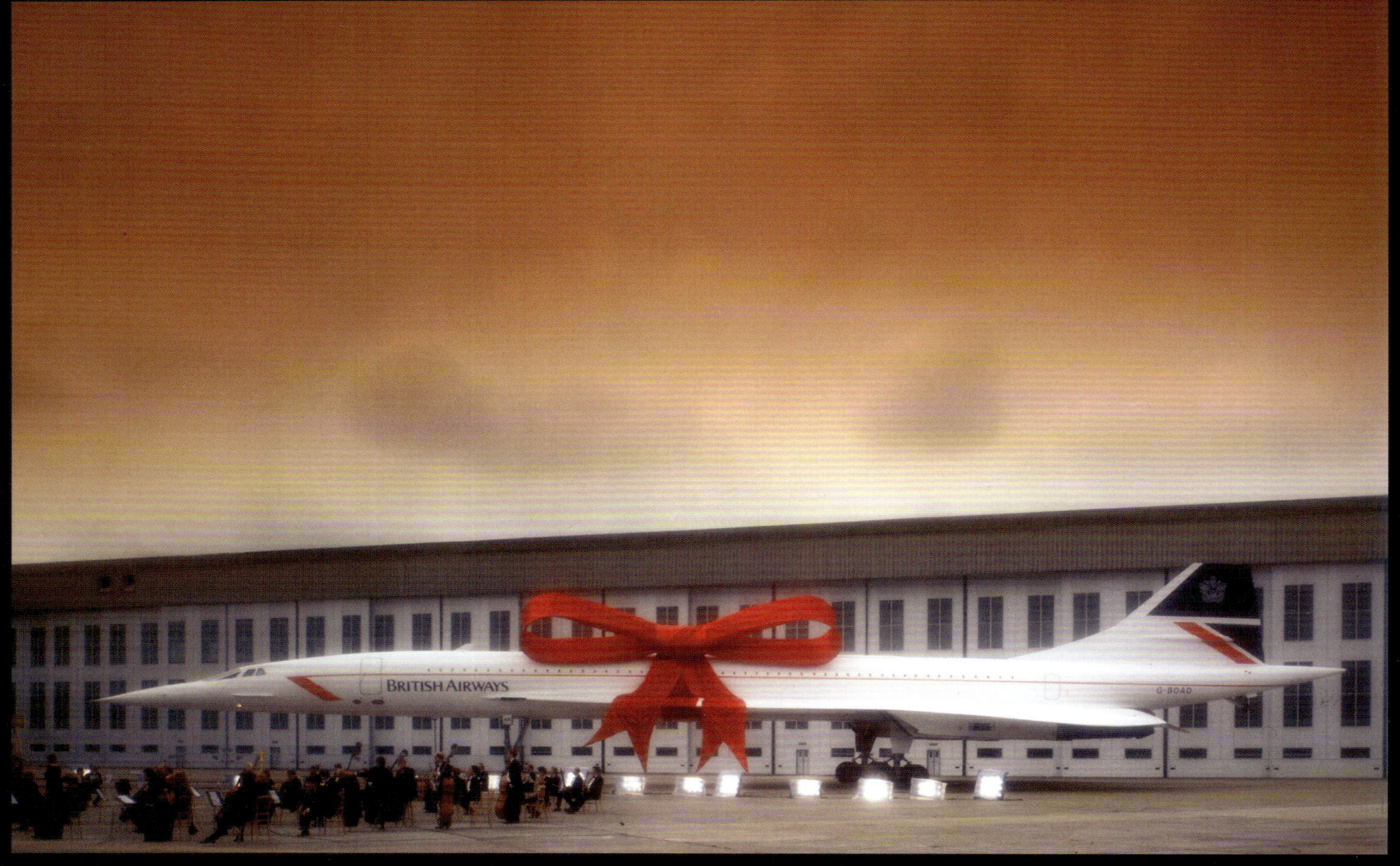

First public filming appearance of Concorde
G-BOAD, 1991

This TV and photograph shot was put together to promote a new TV commercial, which was staged and filmed at the British Airways Engineering Base at London Heathrow. Concorde was encased in a huge chocolate box-style red bow, with the London Philharmonic Orchestra in the foreground. This was a big British Airways promotion called 'The World's Biggest Offer'.

CHAPTER FIVE

THE HEIGHT OF AIRLINE FASHION

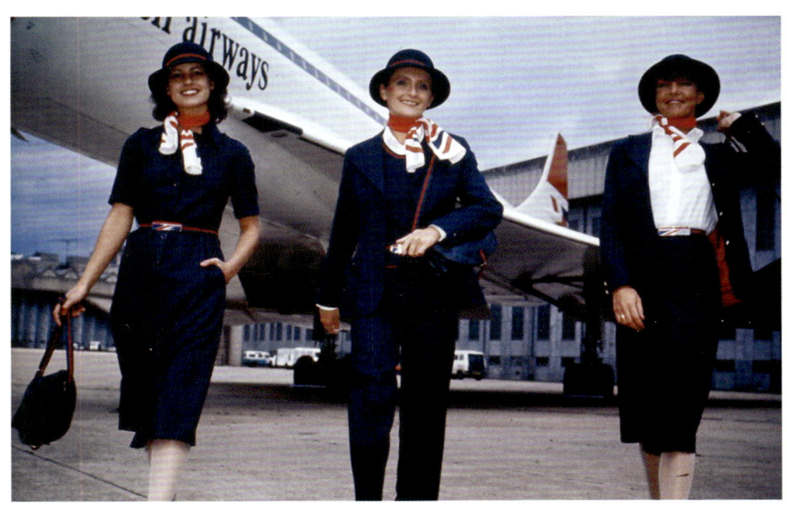
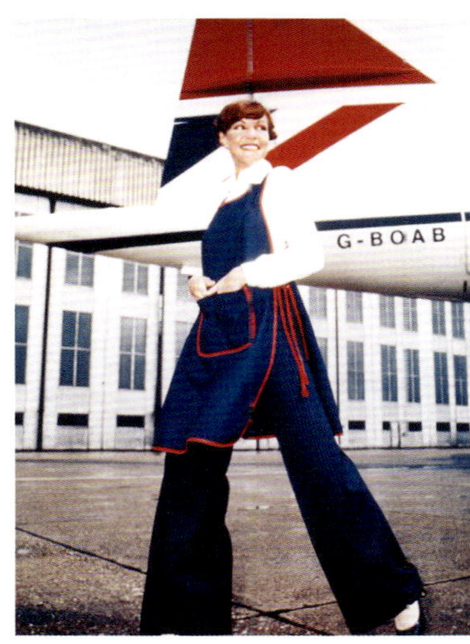
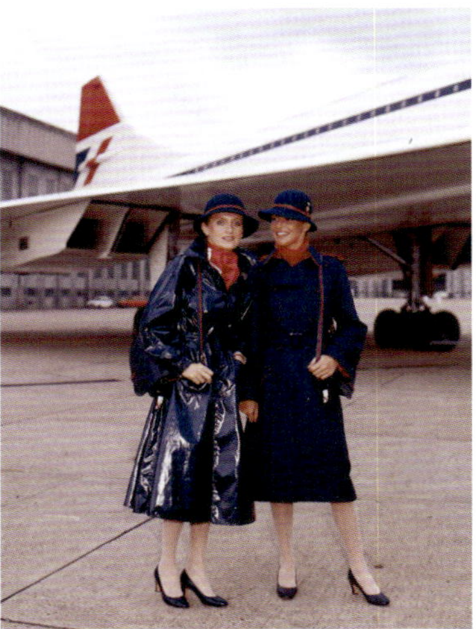

Concorde was often used as the backdrop for new uniform fashion photography. British Airways had many designers create different looks over the years, including the royal designer Hardy Amis in the early '60s. In 1977 Baccarat & Weatheral designed the city slicker pinstriped suit with the famous bowler hat design. For the first time stewardesses were given trousers, culottes and the new PVC wet-look rain macs. Other designers included Clive in the early years, Roland Klein in the 1980s and Paul Costello in the 1990s.

'Concorde is a commemoration of Britain's manufacturing skill.'
Tony Benn, Minister for Technology, 1969

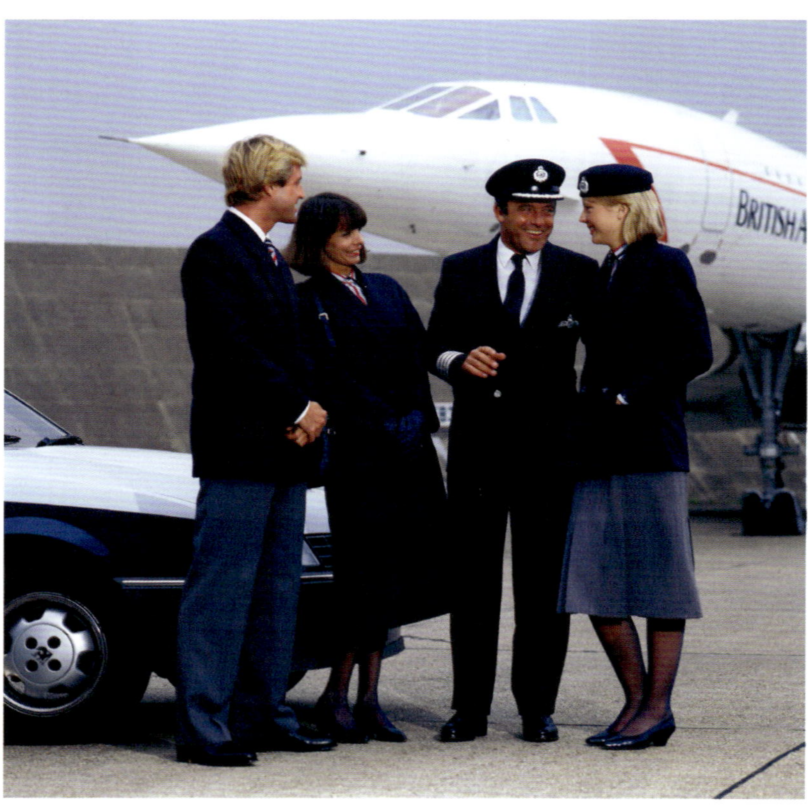

Uniforms designed in 1985 by Roland Klein, nicknamed the Stripe Tease

Once again Concorde was used as the photographic prop against which to highlight the elegance of the new British Airways uniform. The designs were more informal and reflected the casual style of the '80s, complete with bulky shoulder pads and a beret-style hat for the girls.

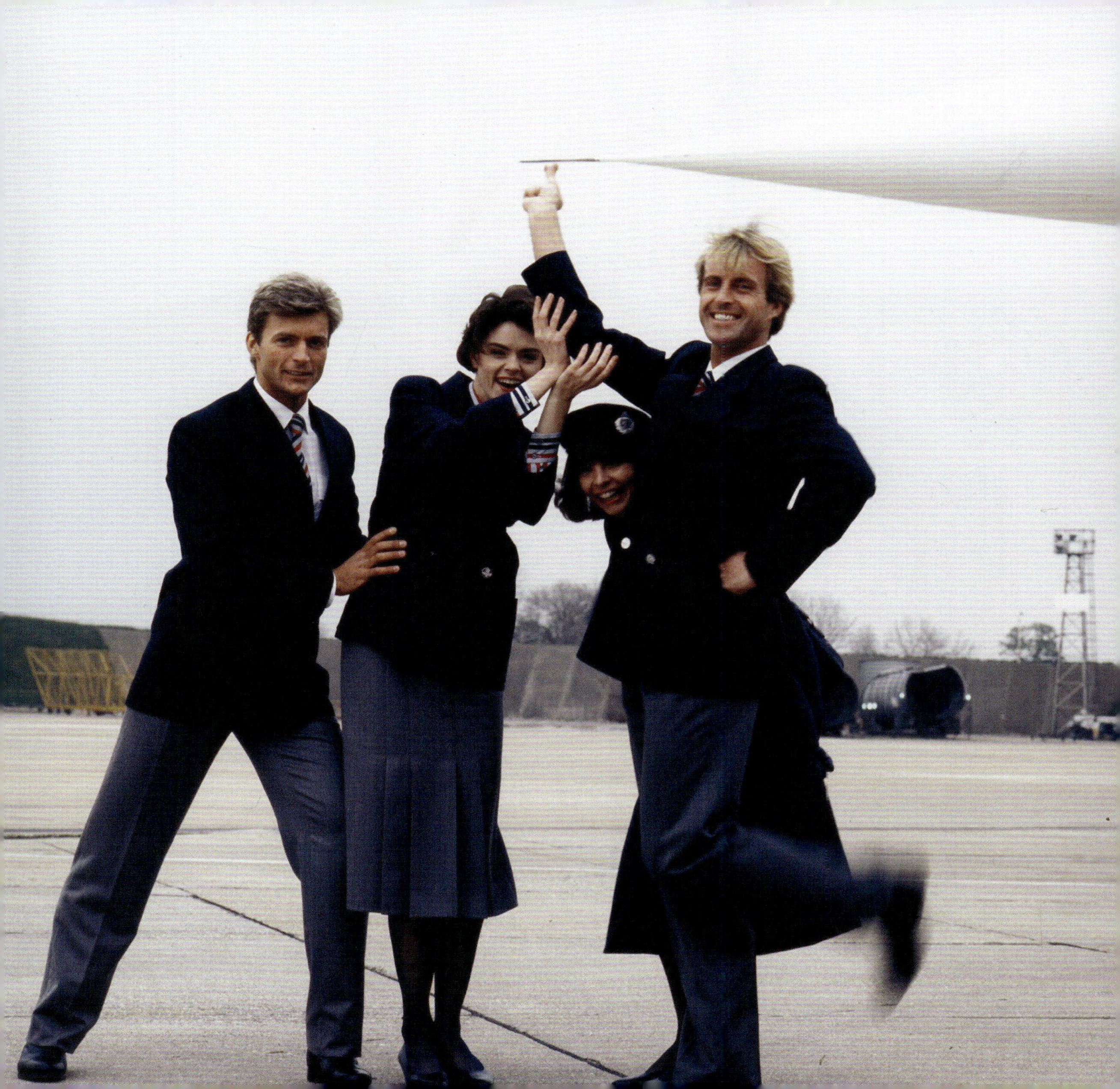

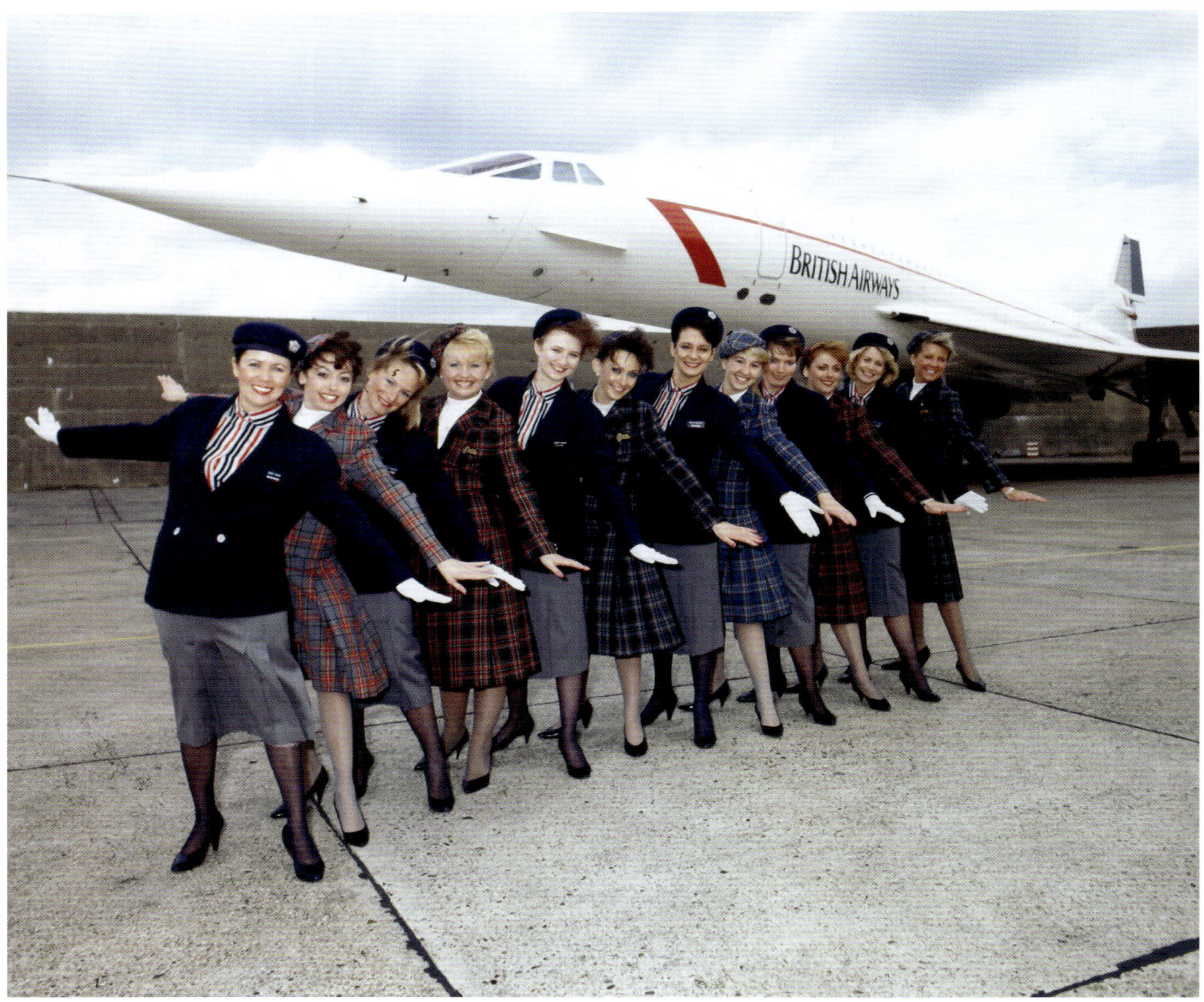

Jenny Owen, far left, heads up the new BA promotional team in April 1986. This PR shot was taken after the merger of British Airways and British Caledonian Airways to show the two different uniforms that both airlines were wearing at the time. 'B-Cal' girls had a selection of five different tartan styles to choose from.

CHAPTER SIX

FAMOUS TRAVELLERS

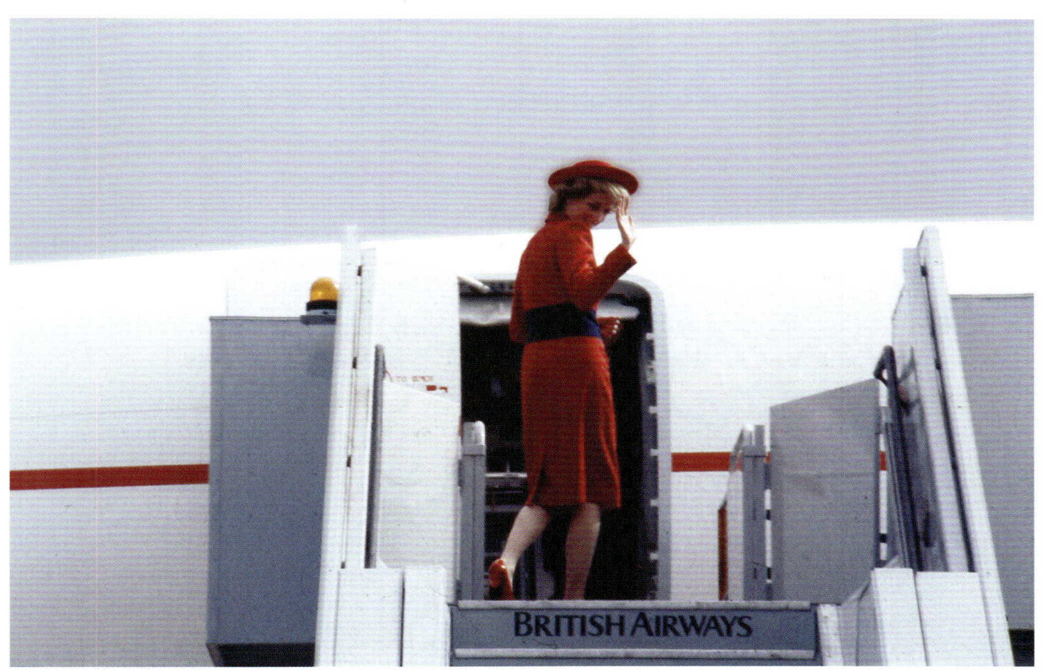

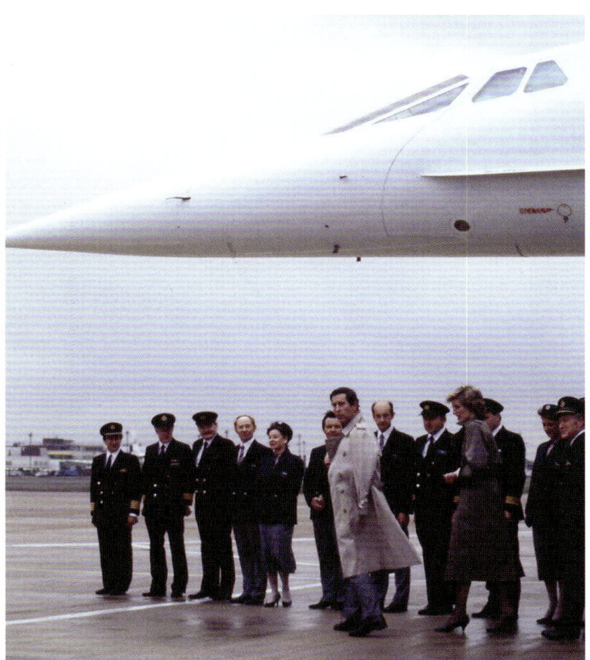

For twenty-seven years I covered all the royal departures from Heathrow Airport, plus the Prime Minister's official flights. Concorde also saw many famous travellers. These shots capture the late Princess Diana boarding her flight to Vienna in April 1986, looking very shy and demure in her stunning red outfit; she flew out to meet Prince Charles, who accompanied her on the return flight home.

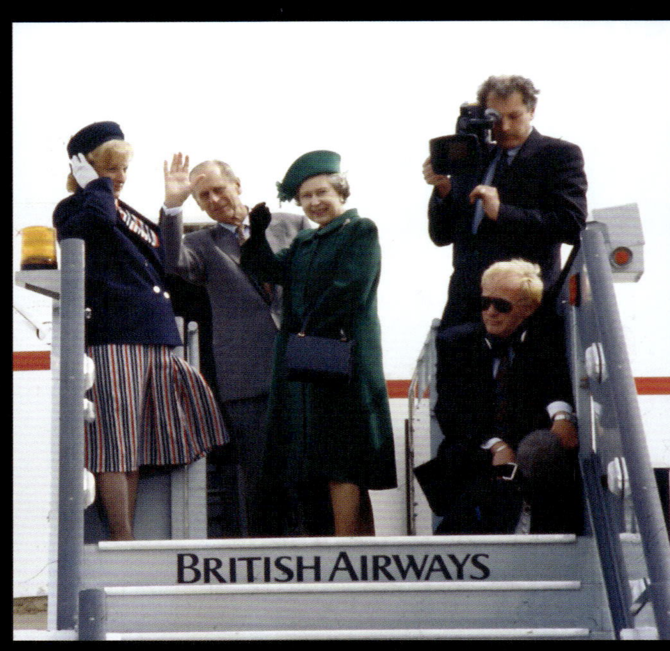

I can remember spending many hours, in all weather conditions, waiting on the tarmac airside at Heathrow for the royal entourage. In May 1991 the Queen jetted off to Washington for the start of her state visit to the United States. Here she is pictured on the steps of Concorde with HRH Prince Philip. Concorde left Heathrow at 11.05 a.m. and touched down at Edwards Air Force Base exactly on schedule at 10.10 a.m. local time.

The Queen flew many times on Concorde. The black and white photograph captures the Queen on the Barbados flight in 1977 and in 1979 with Prince Philip to Kuwait.

A stunning photograph of Concorde departing on the new route to the Caribbean island of Barbados.

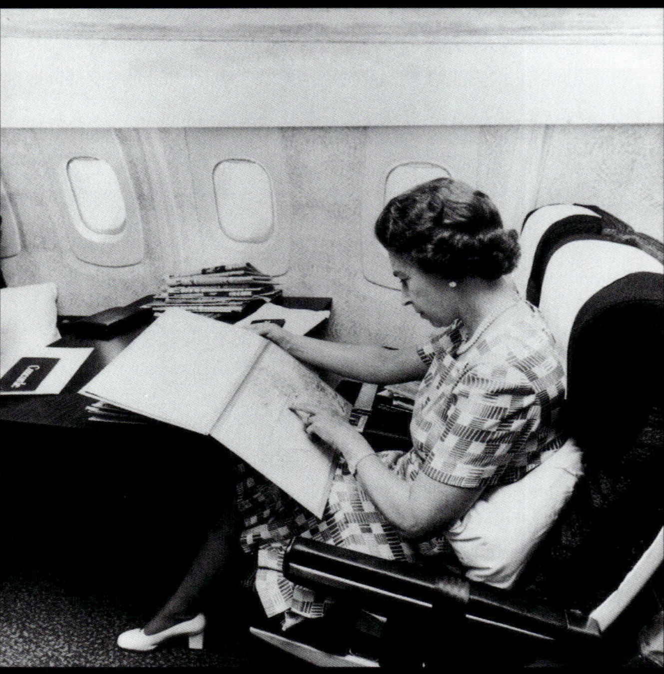

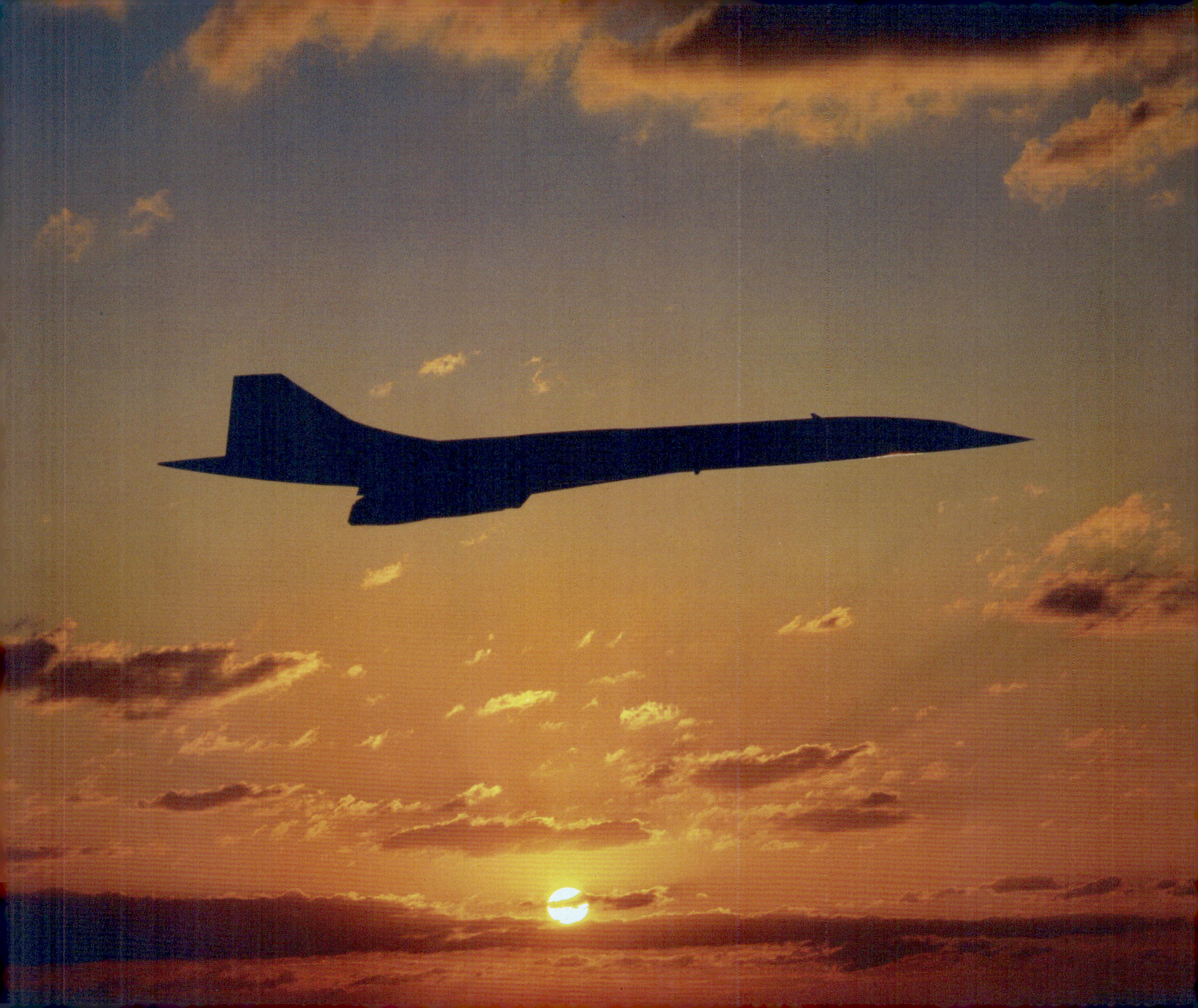

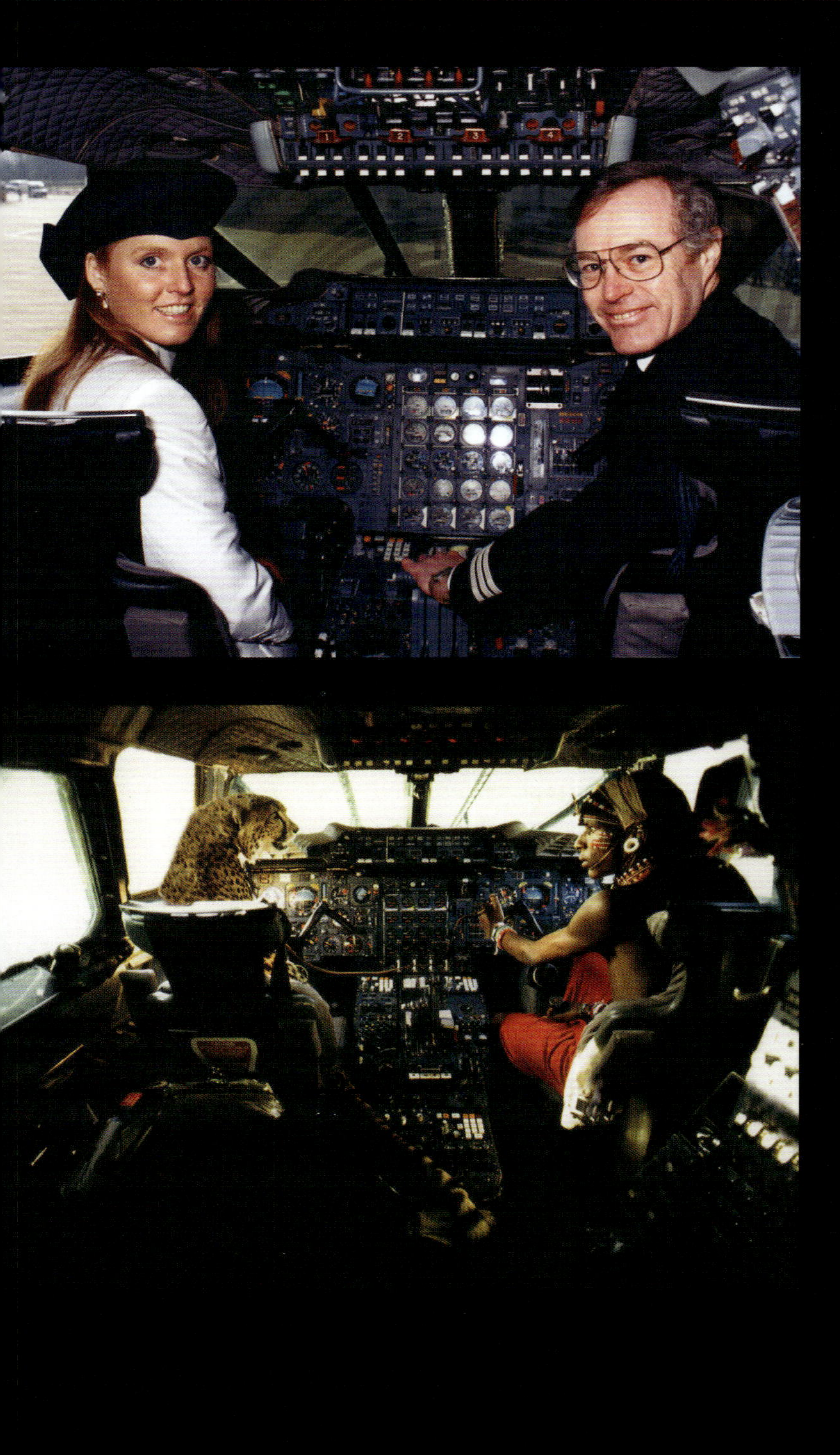

The Duchess of York with Captain Jock Lowe

In 1987 the Duchess of York was on a royal visit to Heathrow Airport and requested to go on board Concorde. The Duchess was extremely interested in the flight deck as she had just taken her private flying licence exam.

The local Kenyan press came up with this publicity shot as a fantastic idea to promote Kenya Africa: a Masai warrior in full dress sitting next to a cheetah on the flight deck.

CELEBRITIES

Joan Collins with a British Airways Special Service Agent.

The late Margaret Thatcher on board Concorde with Captain Brian Walpole.

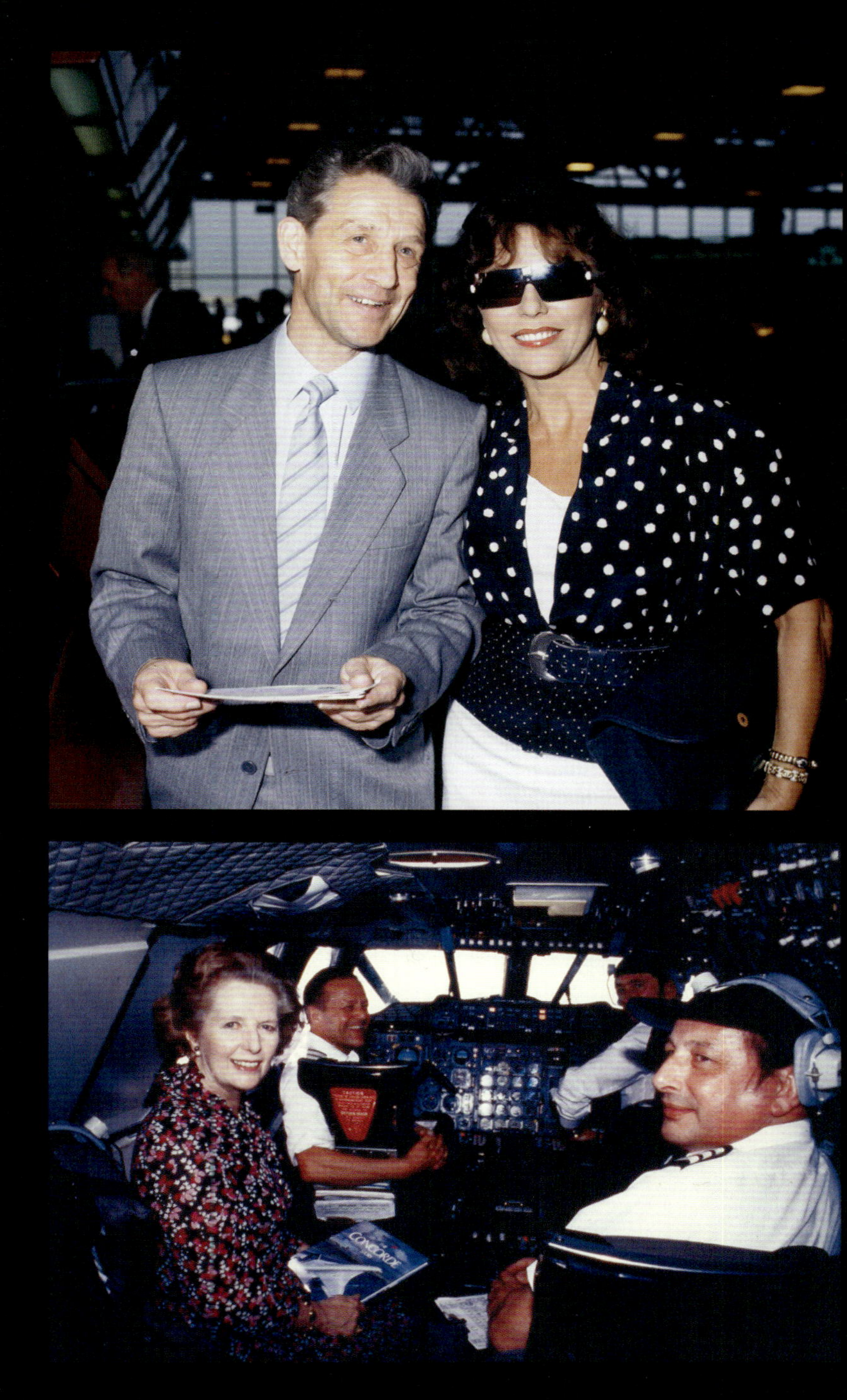

Sir David Frost was the best-known regular user of Concorde, and his favourite seat was 23D, towards the rear of the front cabin.

It's a record no one can ever beat – the world's most-travelled Concorde passenger. Fred Finn was on the first and last Concorde flights and holds the Guinness World Record for the most Concorde flights as a passenger. He is pictured here on the left, with Captain Brian Walpole centre and David Springbat – who also flew over 300 times on Concorde – on the right. In total, Fred Finn flew 718 times on the Queen of the Skies between 1976 and 2003 – all of them in the same seat, 9A.

The regular flyers vie for the first row window seats 1D or 1A, the most famous being 1A which the Queen Mother sat in.

Celebrities such as Michael Winner, Cilla Black and Lord Lloyd Webber all started their winter vacations in Barbados on Concorde, and this was the only way to travel. Concorde was also a firm favourite with Joan Collins, Robert Redford, Sir Sean Connery and many music artists such as Sting, Mike Jagger, Sir Elton John and Luciano Pavarotti, who in the early days of Concorde always purchased two seats to sit in.

Politician James Callaghan became the first British premier to go supersonic, and subsequently Prime Ministers Margaret Thatcher, John Major and Tony Blair have all graced the seats.

Concorde has enjoyed her moments of sporting history too: she flew the England World Cup football team home in 1998, and Suggs, the lead singer from the group Madness, claimed a record with the world's longest putt; he hit a ball down Concorde's aisle; by calculation it travelled 5 miles in twelve seconds. Concorde also flew home the victorious Ryder Cup golf team in 1995, being welcomed back into Dublin by 5,000 fans.

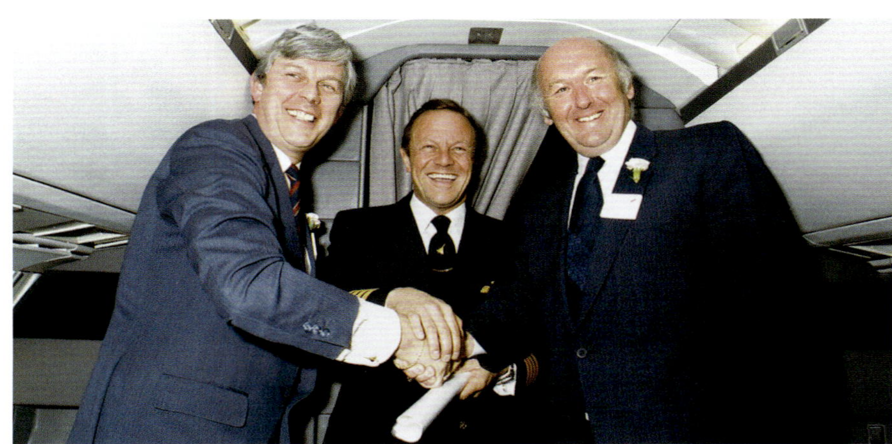

CHAPTER SEVEN

PR & PROMOTIONAL PICTURES

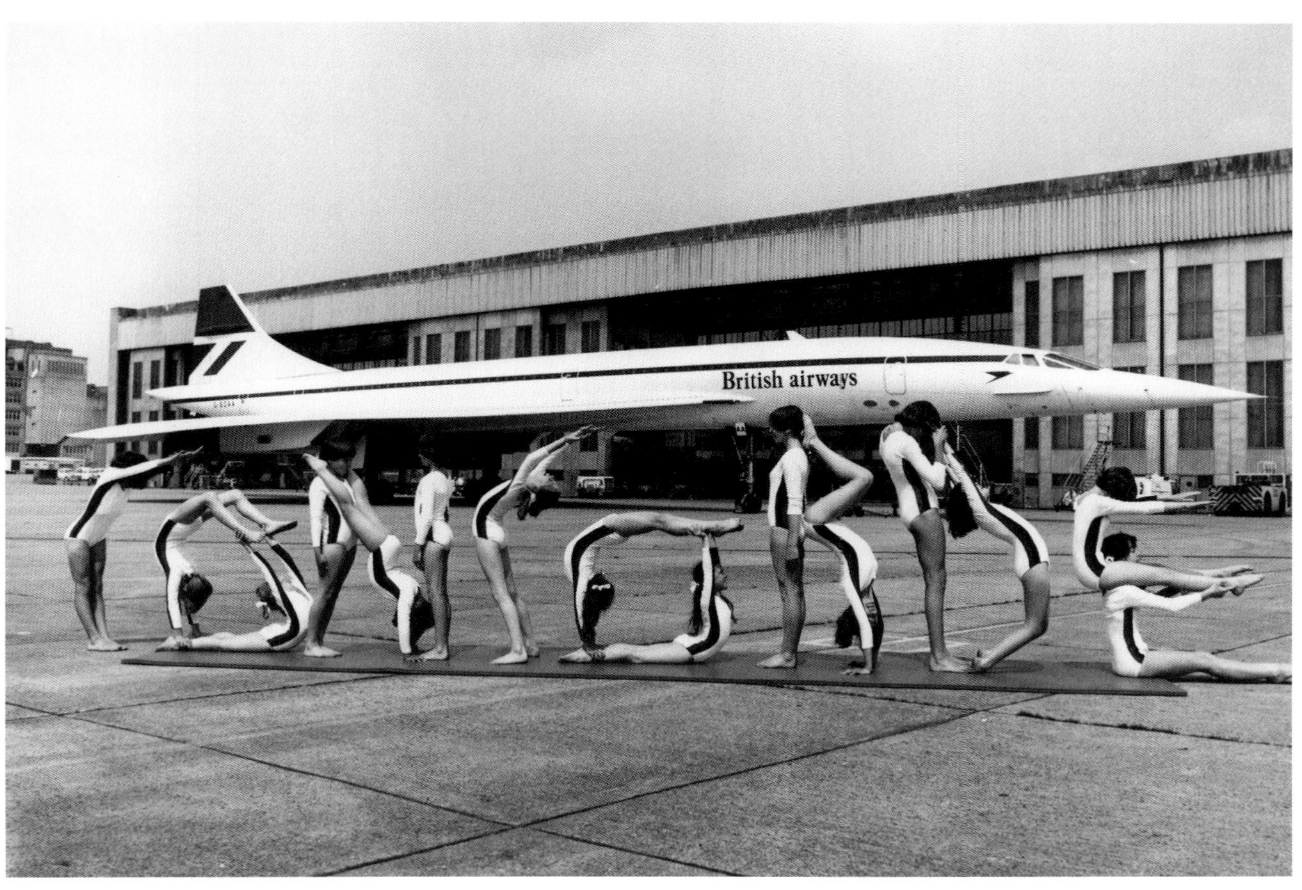

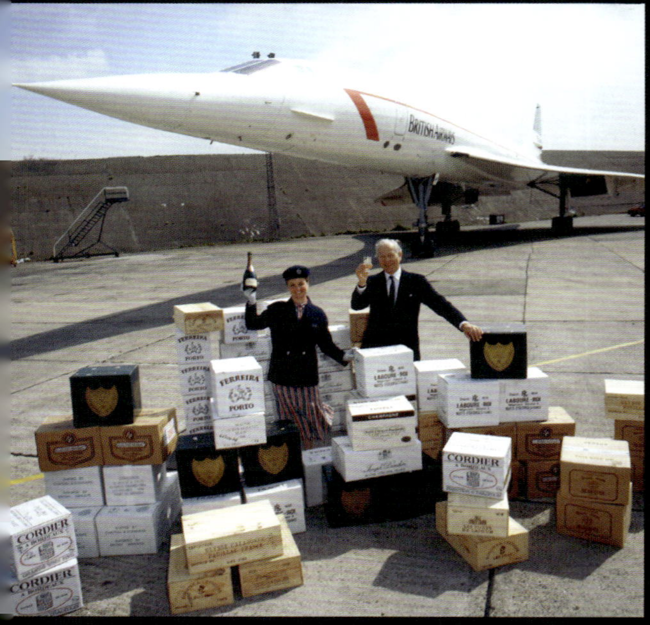

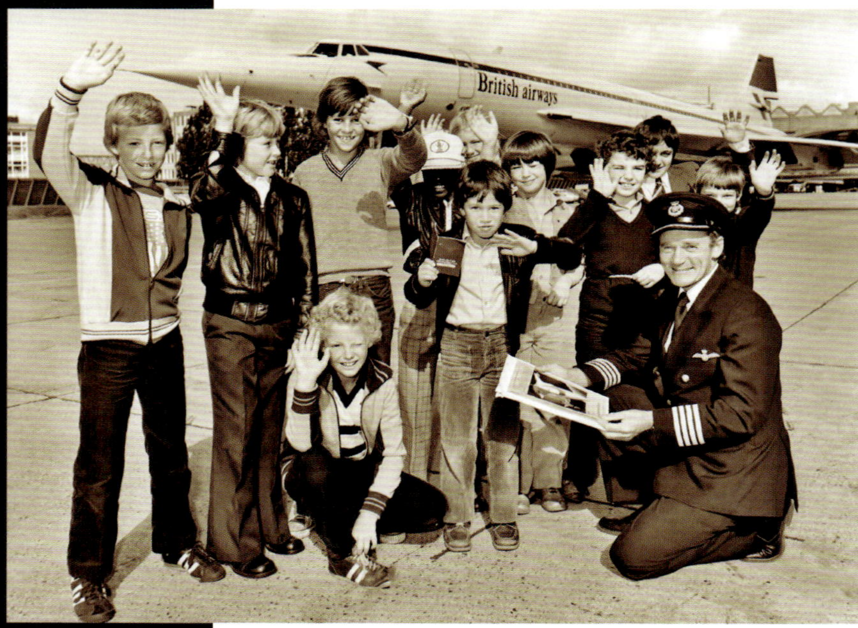

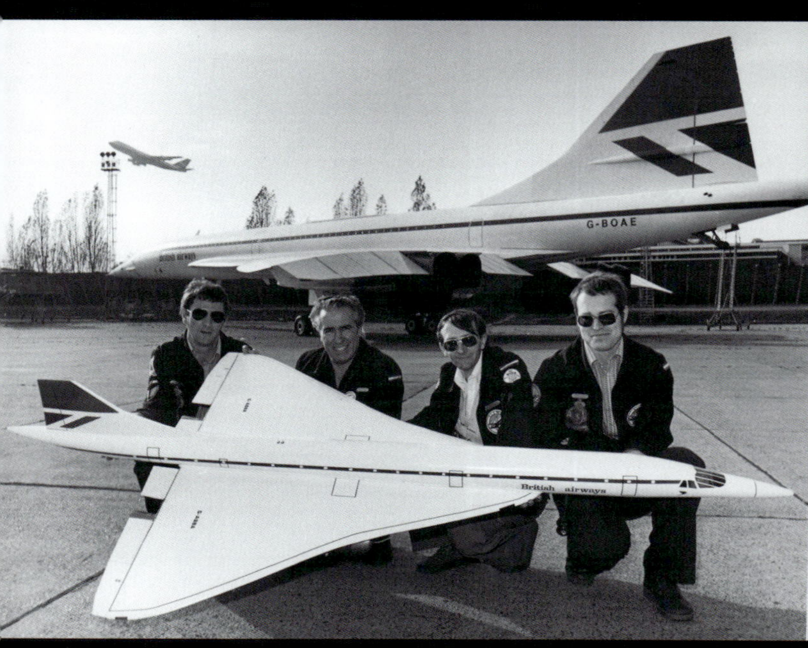

The airlines used to use Concorde in many different ways for promotional and PR purposes and were always coming up with innovative ideas. Here, and on the previous page, we can see a selection of various assignments. In 1988 top wine expert Michael Broadbent, who selected the fine wines for Concorde; the local gymnastic team in 1979 spelling out the word Concorde; the local Junior Jet Club pictured with the late Captain Leo Budd; the Amsterdam model-making team who made the largest flying Concorde model in 1978, as well as many vintage cars.

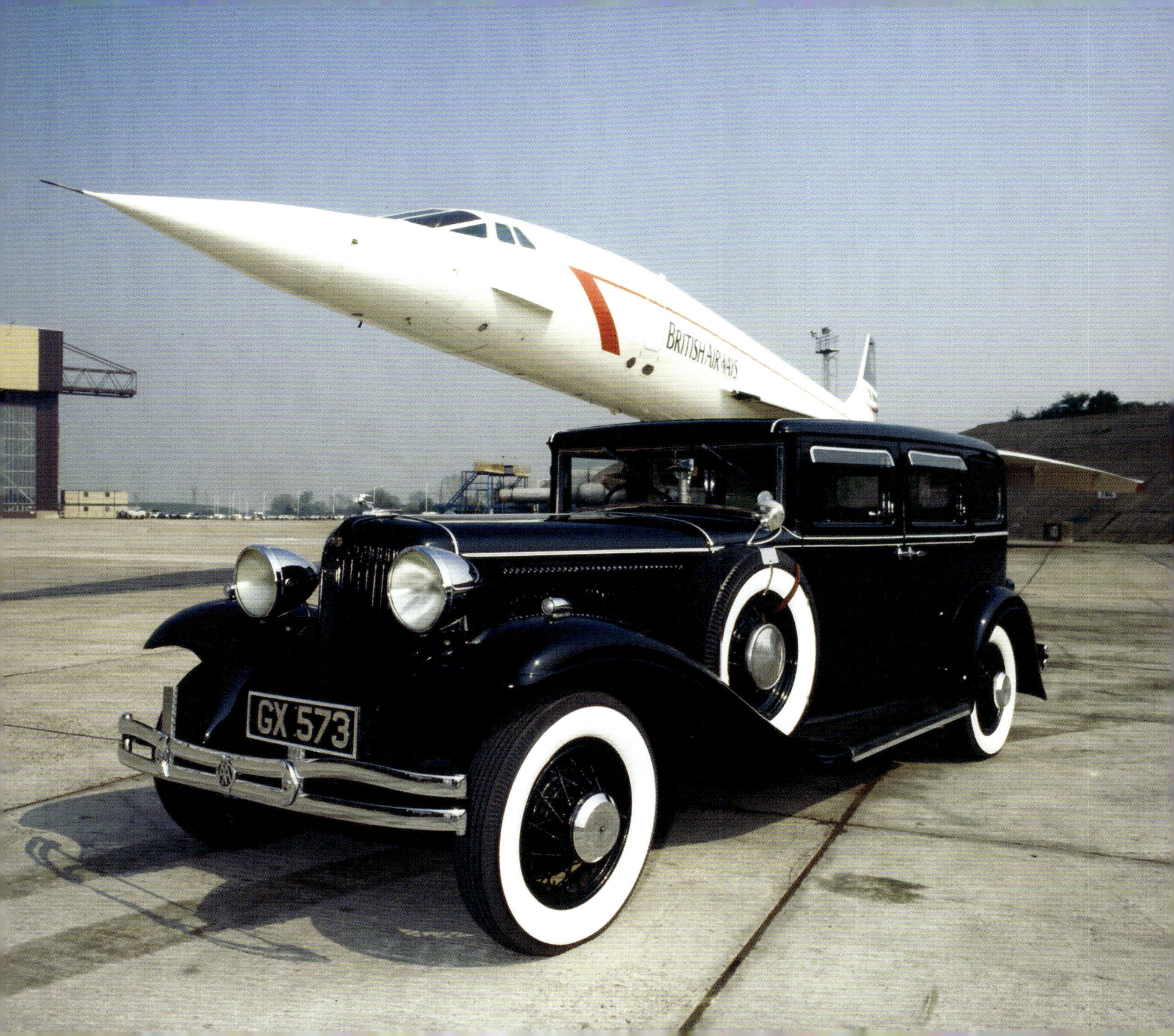

BRITISH AIRWAYS
GX 573

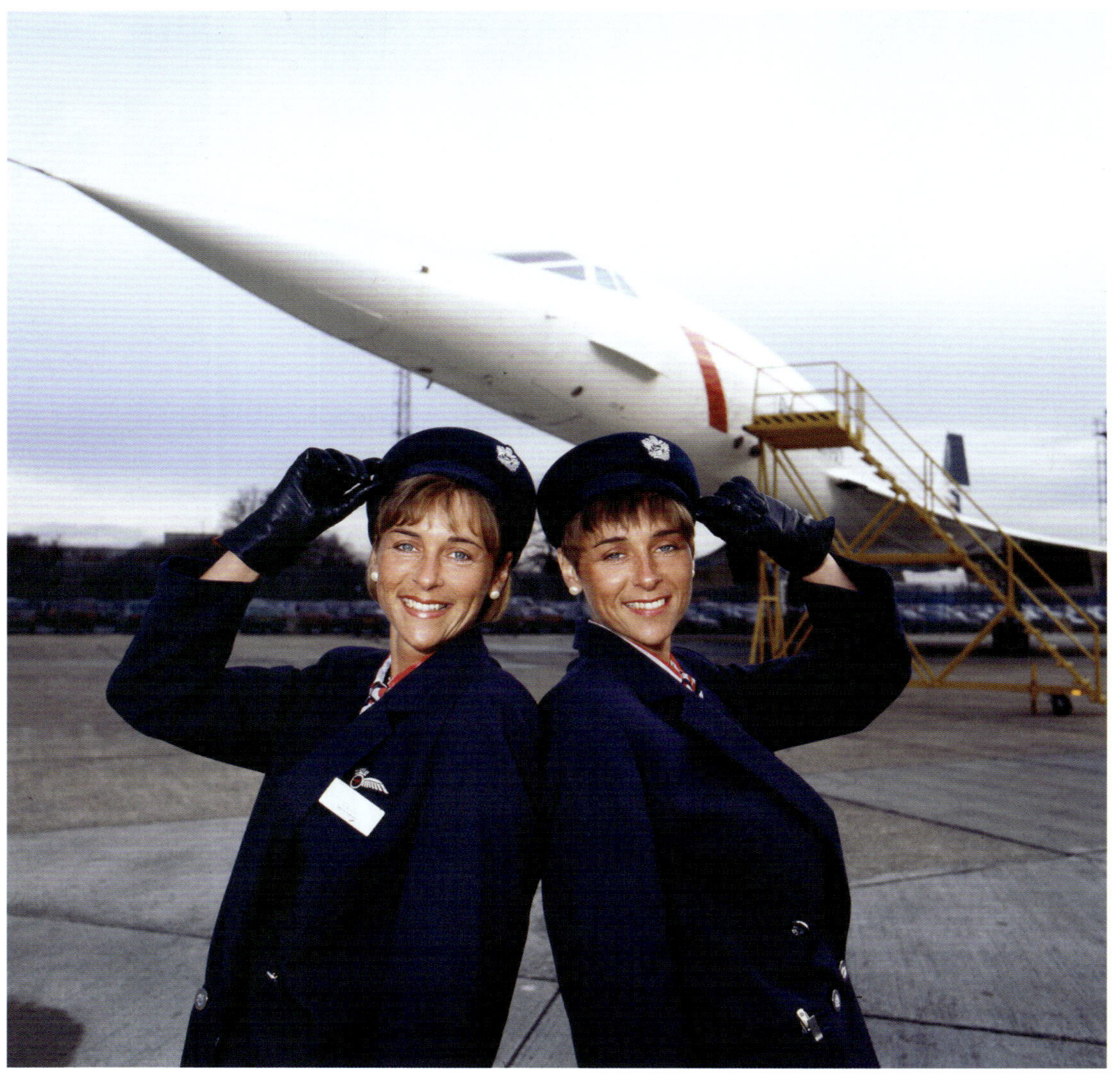

In 1993 Concorde was graced with the first set of twins to fly on board. Estelle and Elaine Moffatt were amongst the latest intake of new Concorde cabin crew. The identical twins delighted and surprised the Concorde passengers. They would stand side by side doing the safety demonstrations and you could see the startled expressions on the passengers' faces. The twins flew on scheduled flights to New York, Washington and Barbados, and on special charters to Lapland and Paris.

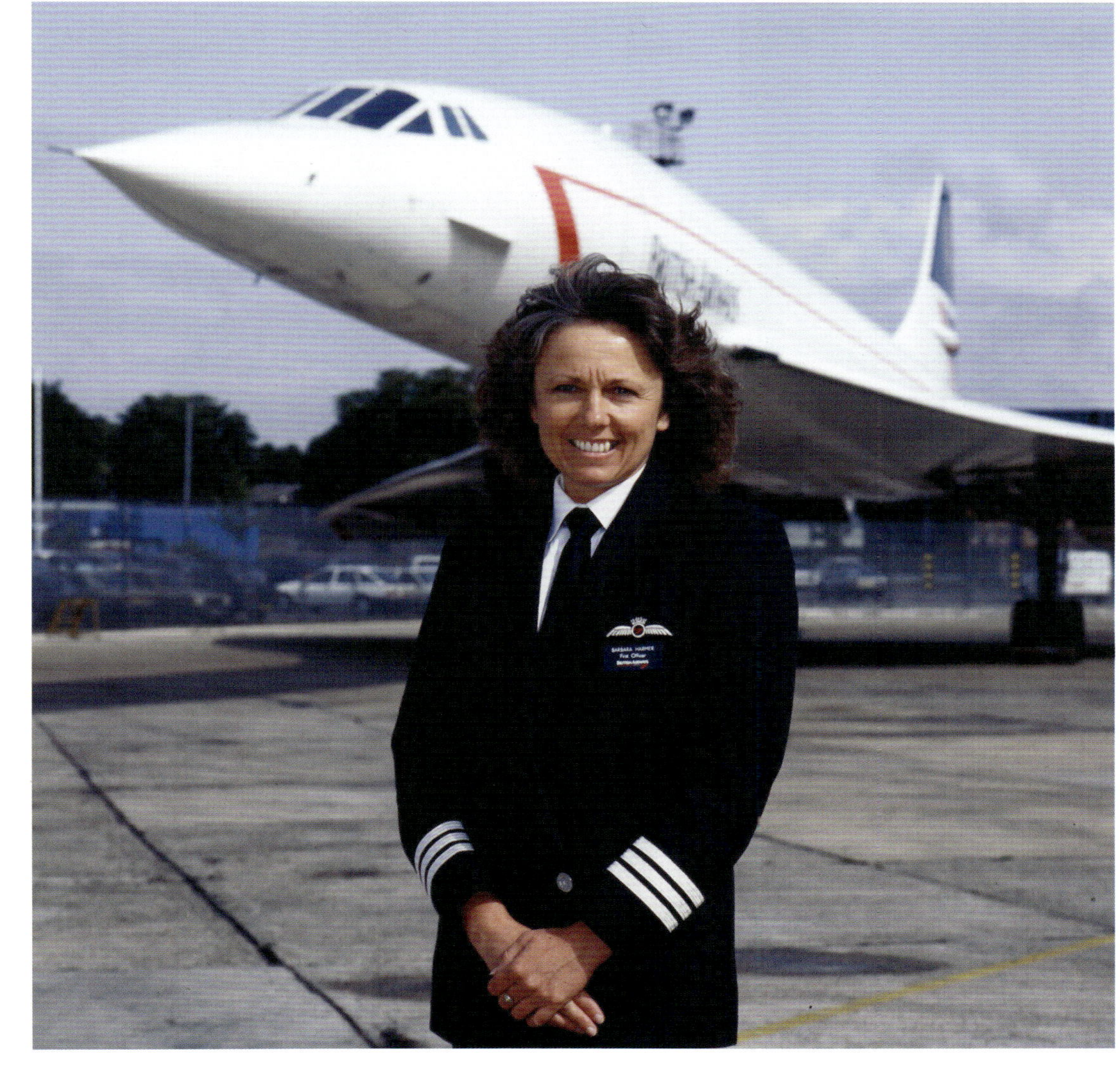

British Airways pilot the late Barbara Harmer was the first woman to fly a supersonic airliner. Here she is in 1993 in front of Concorde.

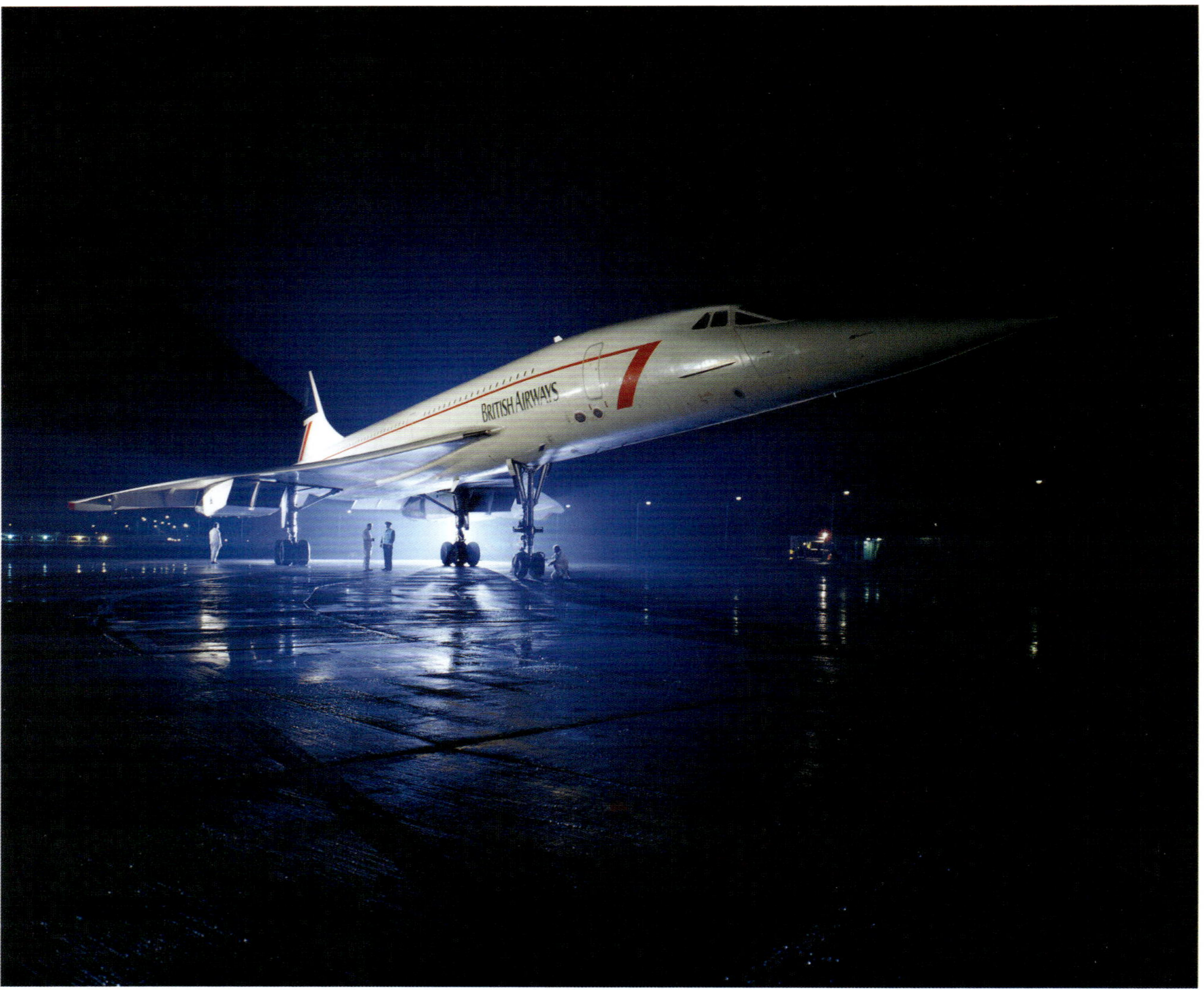

One particular evening publicity shot in 1986 took hours to set up at the Engineering Base. The night was dark and wet, and we had to bring in special exterior film set lighting hired from Shepperton Film Studios to illuminate the aircraft in order to capture the engineers carrying out their general maintenance.

Two hundred and fifty dedicated engineering staff looked after Concorde. Some of the most enjoyable photographs that I have taken have been at Concorde Engineering Base, Hangar TBB, at Heathrow. This hangar could hold up to six Concordes. Every time Concorde returned from a flight she would be taken into the hangar for checks and maintenance due to her advanced, high-tech specification. Here Concorde engineer Carl Percy is using a boroscope to carry out an internal inspection of one of the Olympus engines.

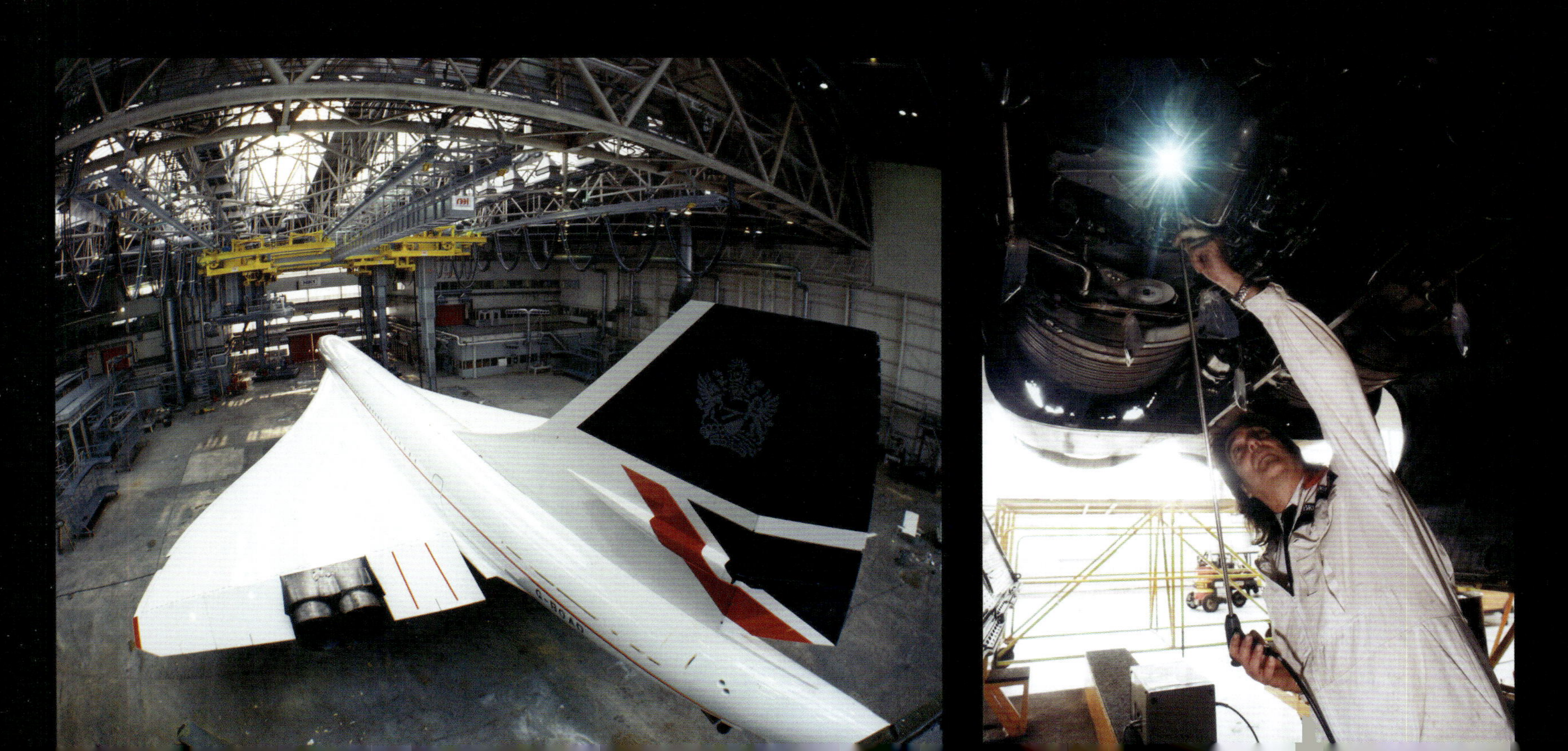

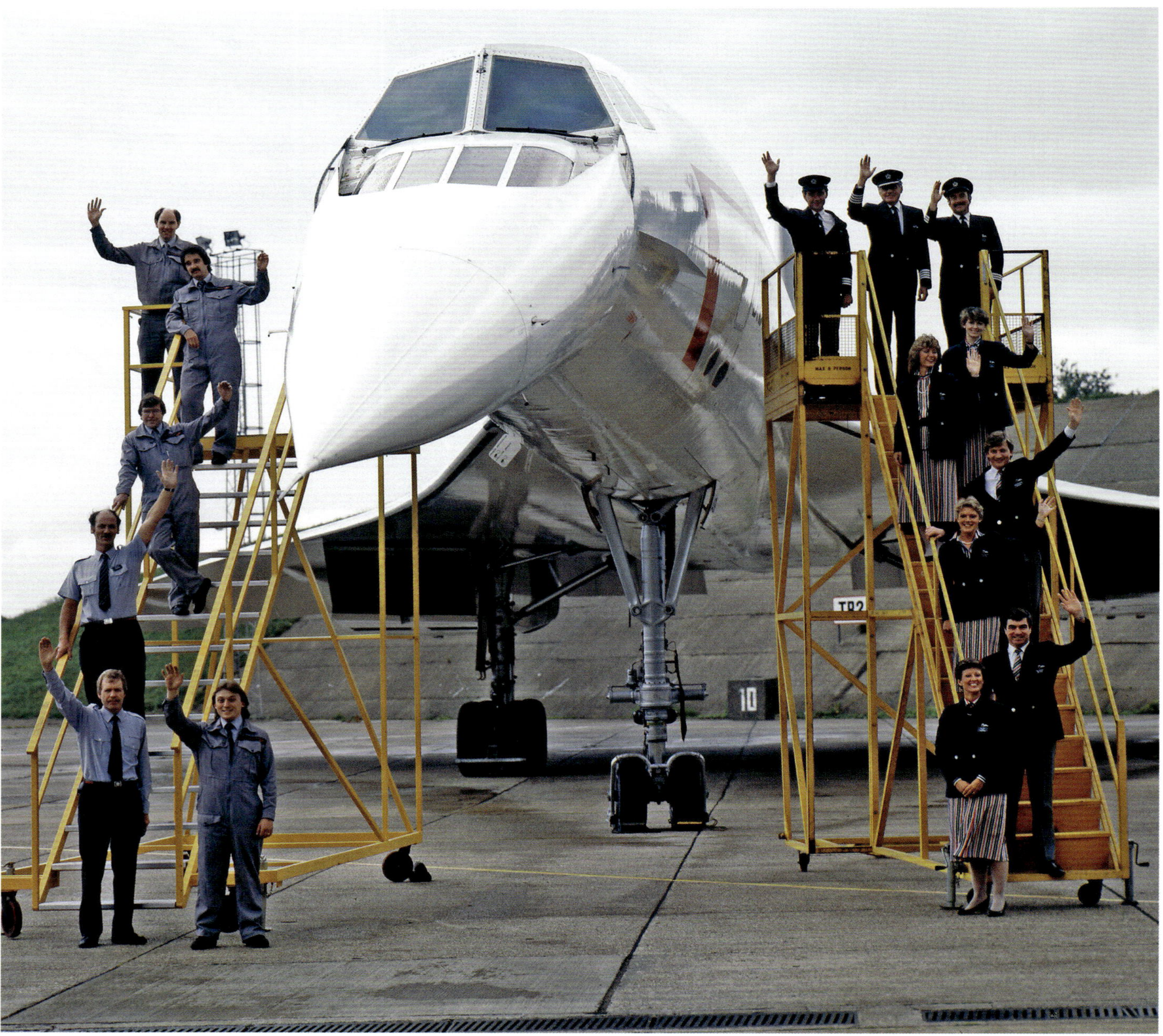

Three elements necessary to get every Concorde flight in the air pose for the camera: to the right of Concorde the flight and cabin crew, and to the left, on ladders, the engineering crew.

CHAPTER EIGHT

CHATHAM DOCKYARD
LIVERY

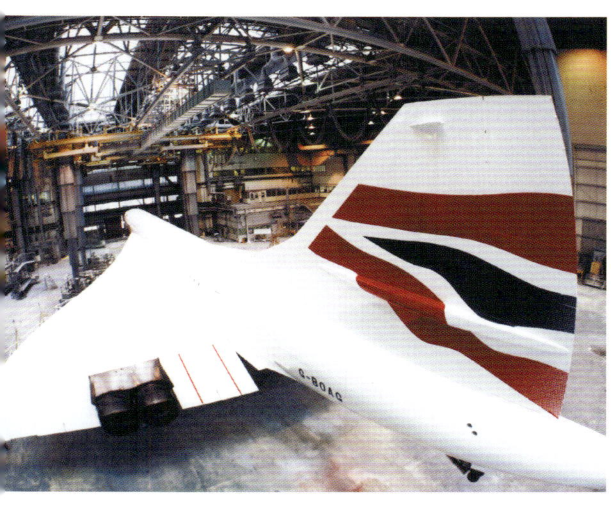

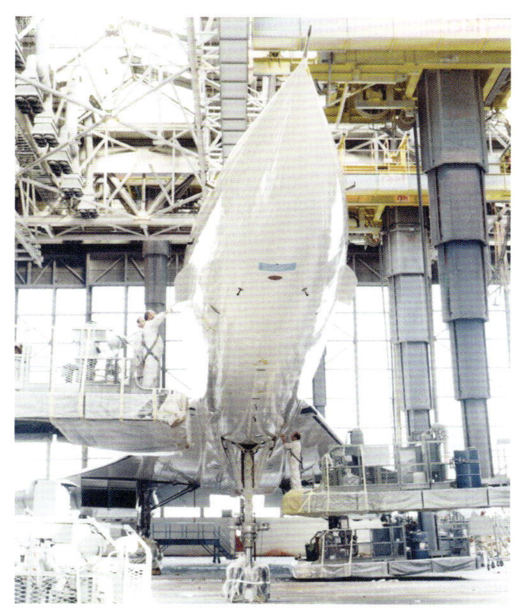

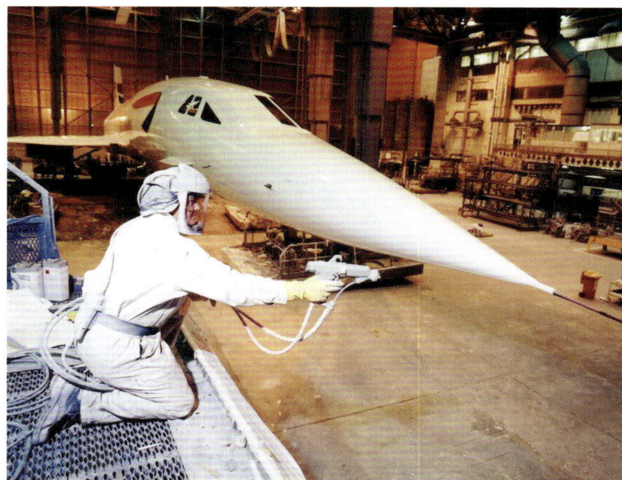

We always had great fun at Engineering; the crews were always very helpful in supporting us to set up the shots. The photographs show Concorde in the BA Paintshop in 1997 being masked-up for a new paint spray in preparation for Concorce's final colours – the new Chatham Dockyard livery – in 1997. To get the tail shot was very hazardous as I was harnessed into a lifting cradle – basically a huge standing platform – which would raise me above the top of the tail section of Concorde, approximately 50ft high. I do not have a very good head for heights! This dramatic shot was taken with a fisheye lens to capture the entire tail and the length of the aircraft.

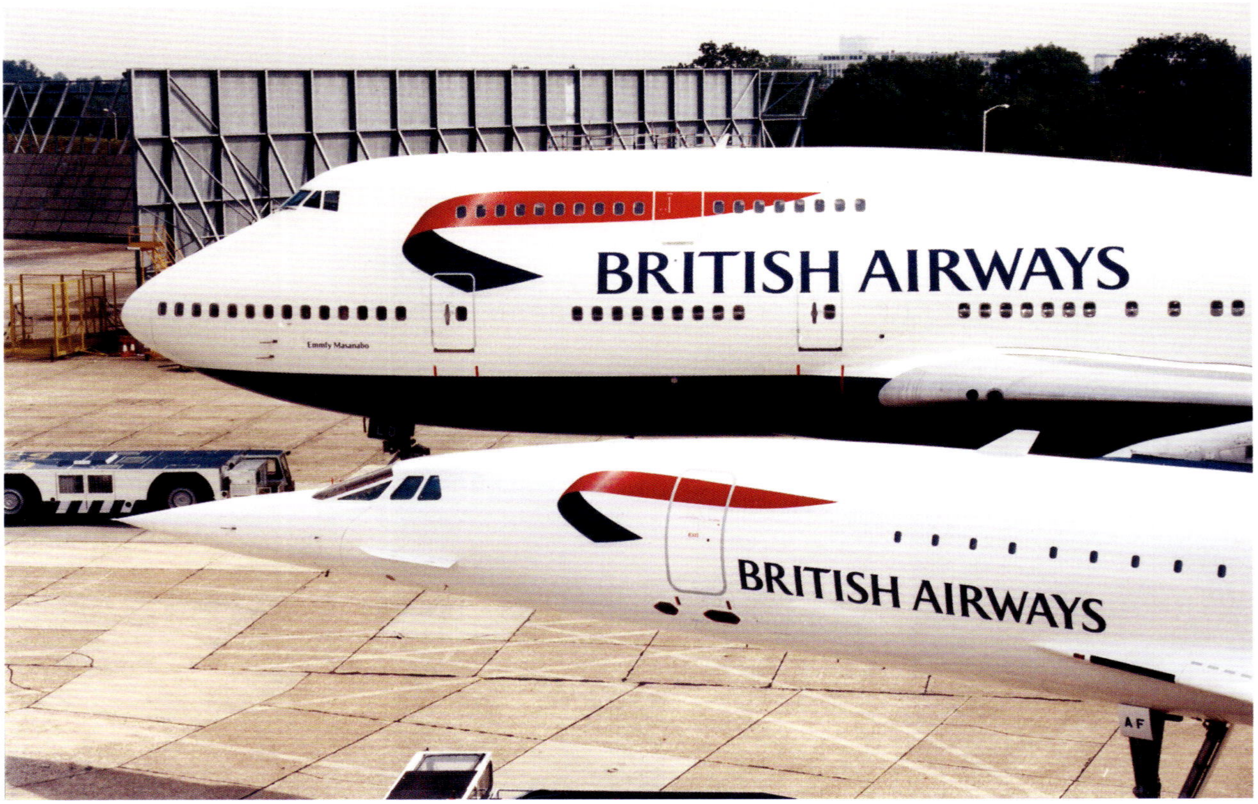

The first PR photograph to show Concorde in her new colours, twinned with a 747 jumbo in the background. My chief photographer, Mike Bromfield, who worked for me for eighteen years, took this shot from the top of a cherry picker outside the main Concorde hangar.

The new Chatham Dockyard livery was so called because the tail flag design was taken from Nelson's famous flagship HMS *Victory*; it was derived from the admiral's original flag loft which is preserved and on display in the Greenwich Museum at Chatham in Kent, England. London-based Newell and Sorrell designed the original Chatham Dockyard livery.

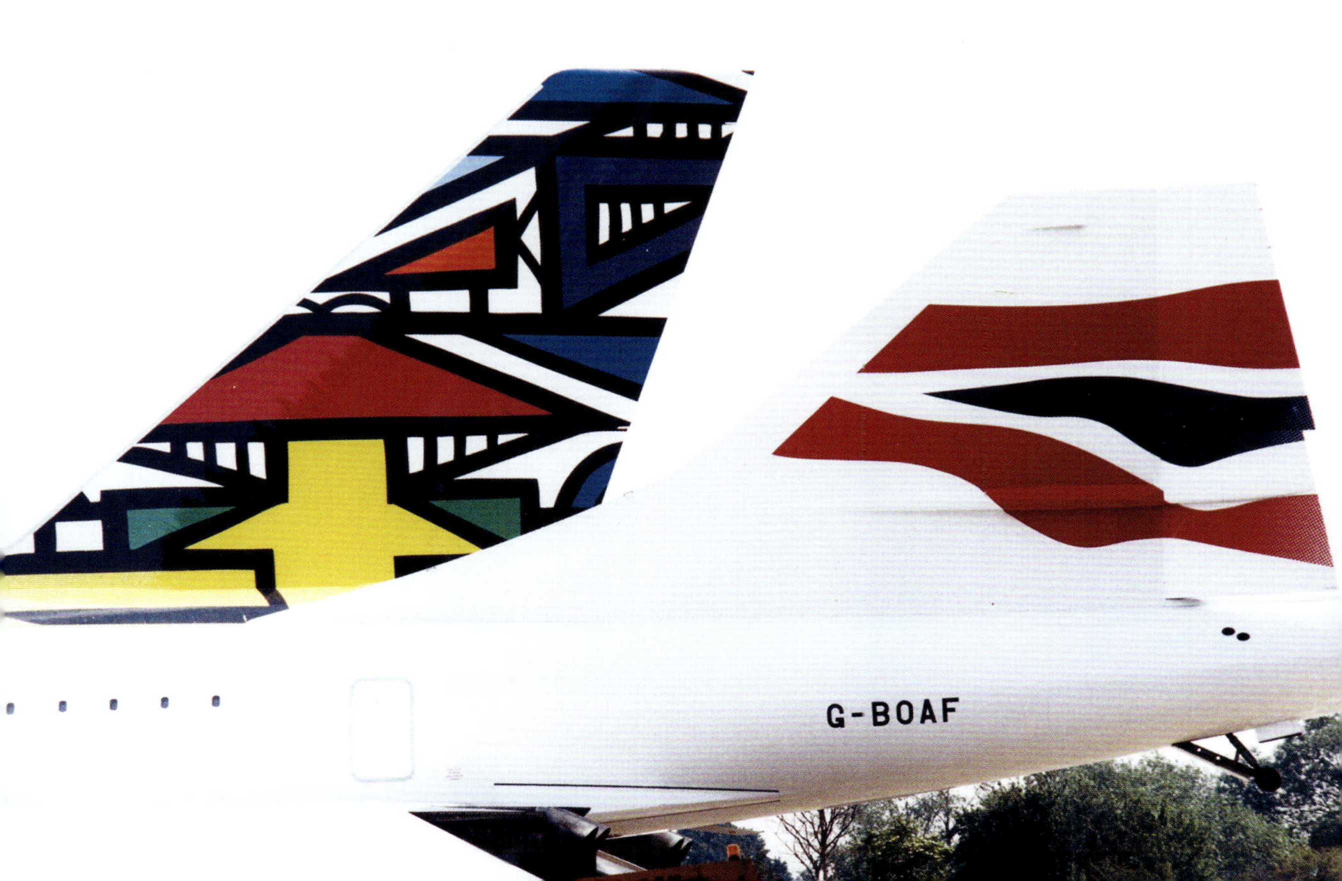

G-BOAF

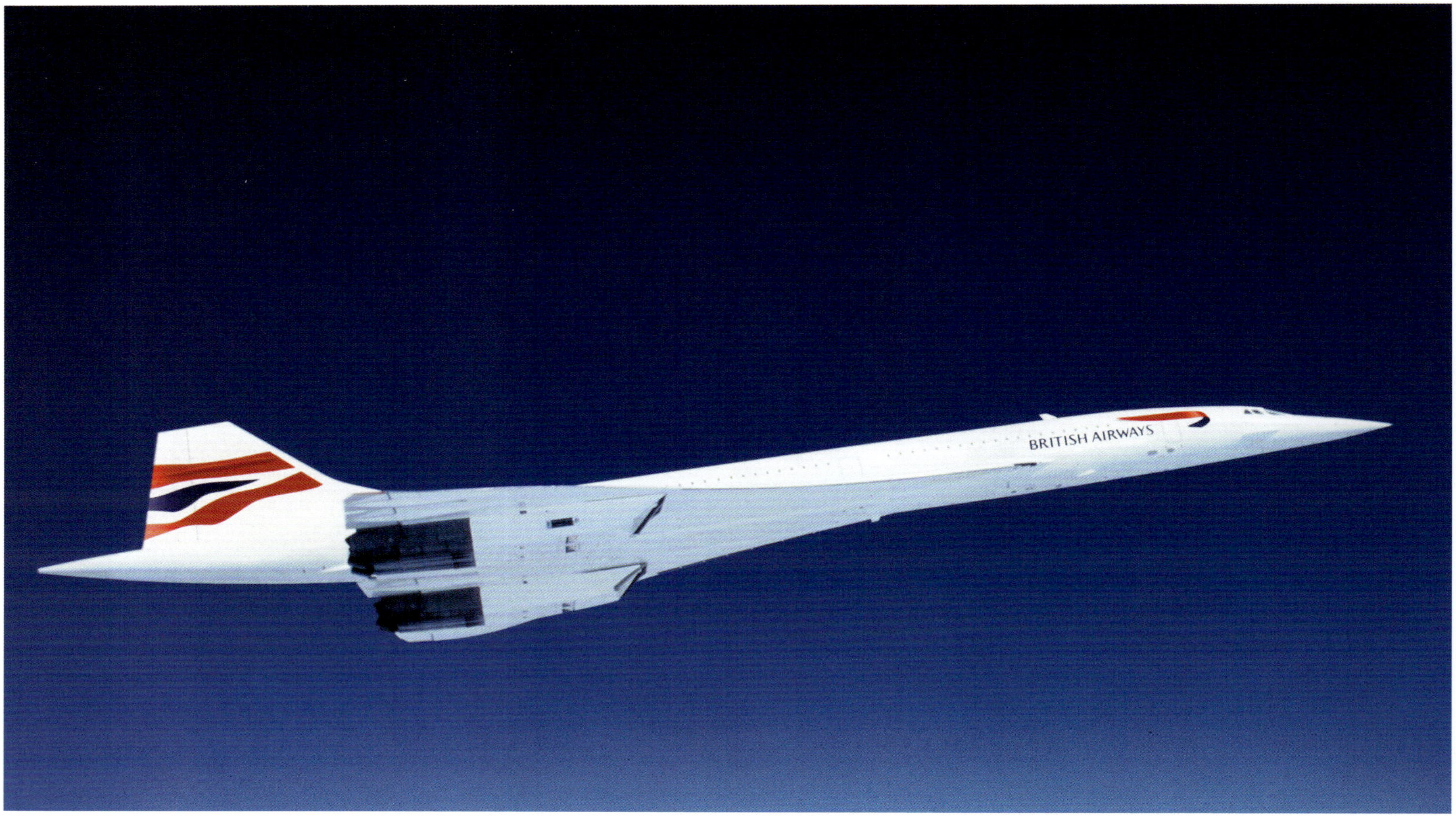

The Concorde model at the entrance of London Heathrow Airport showing the new Chatham livery.

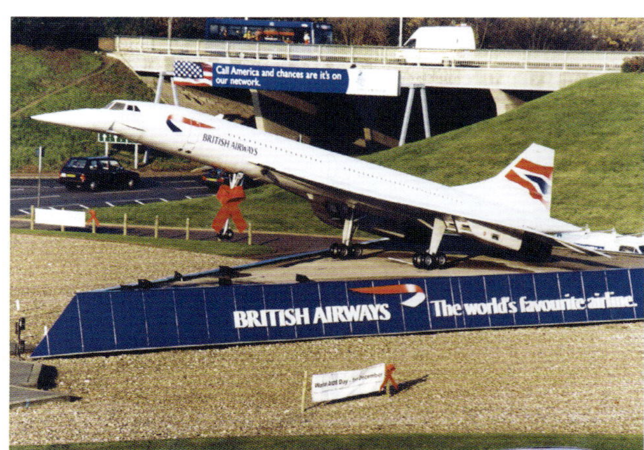

CHAPTER NINE

DISASTER STRIKES

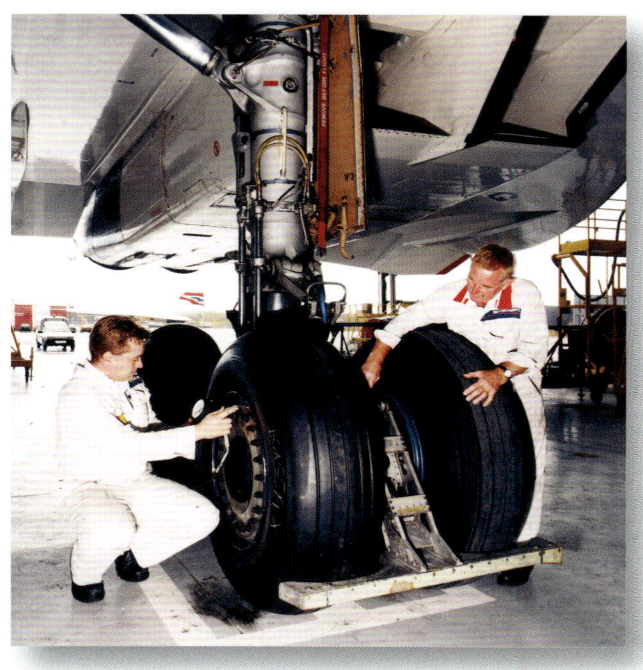

On 25 July 2000 an Air France Concorde took off from Charles De Gaulle Airport and crashed ninety seconds later, just 1 mile from Paris, coming down onto a hotel. All crew and passengers were lost. She was just a mile away from a potential safe landing site at Le Bourget. All Concordes were grounded shortly after the accident.

British Airways and Air France took the option to modify the aircraft and get the Airworthiness Licence back. This process took nearly a year of painstaking modifications, and technical engineering was scrutinised. It has to be said that Concorde's engineering record was second to none in the aviation industry. The main modifications were to line the fuel tanks with Kevlar to prevent any fire outbreak in the wings if there was any damage. The engineers also fitted new Michelin tyres, the same as used on the new Airbus A380, as these would not break up when punctured.

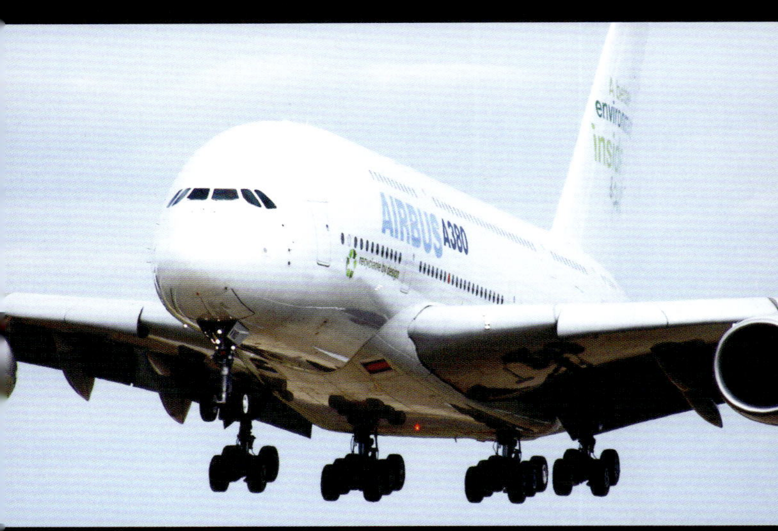

The new Airbus A380.

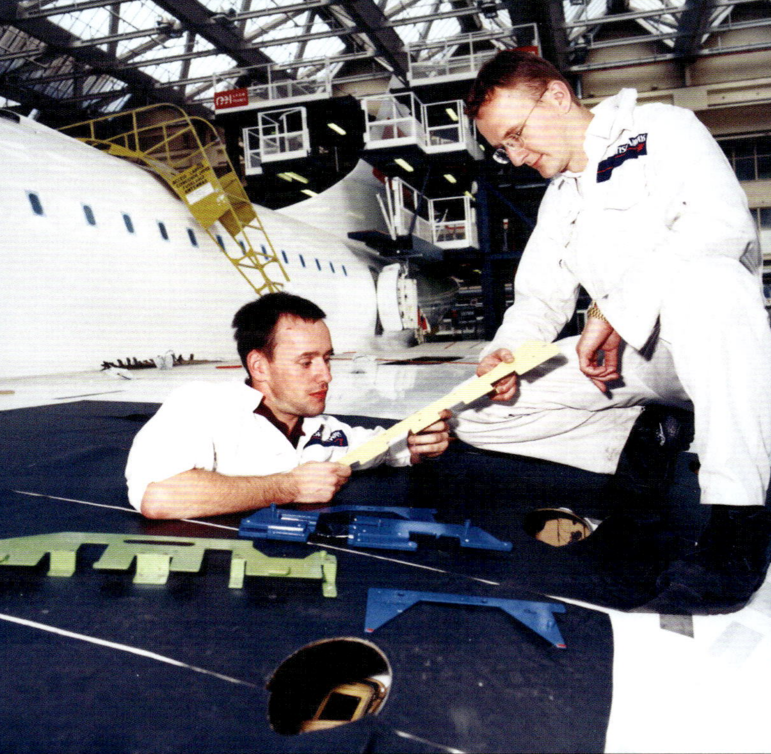

This photograph shows engineers actually inside the fuel tank of the wing. The area was so restricted that only the smallest engineers could crawl in and carry out the Kevlar modifications in the limited space available.

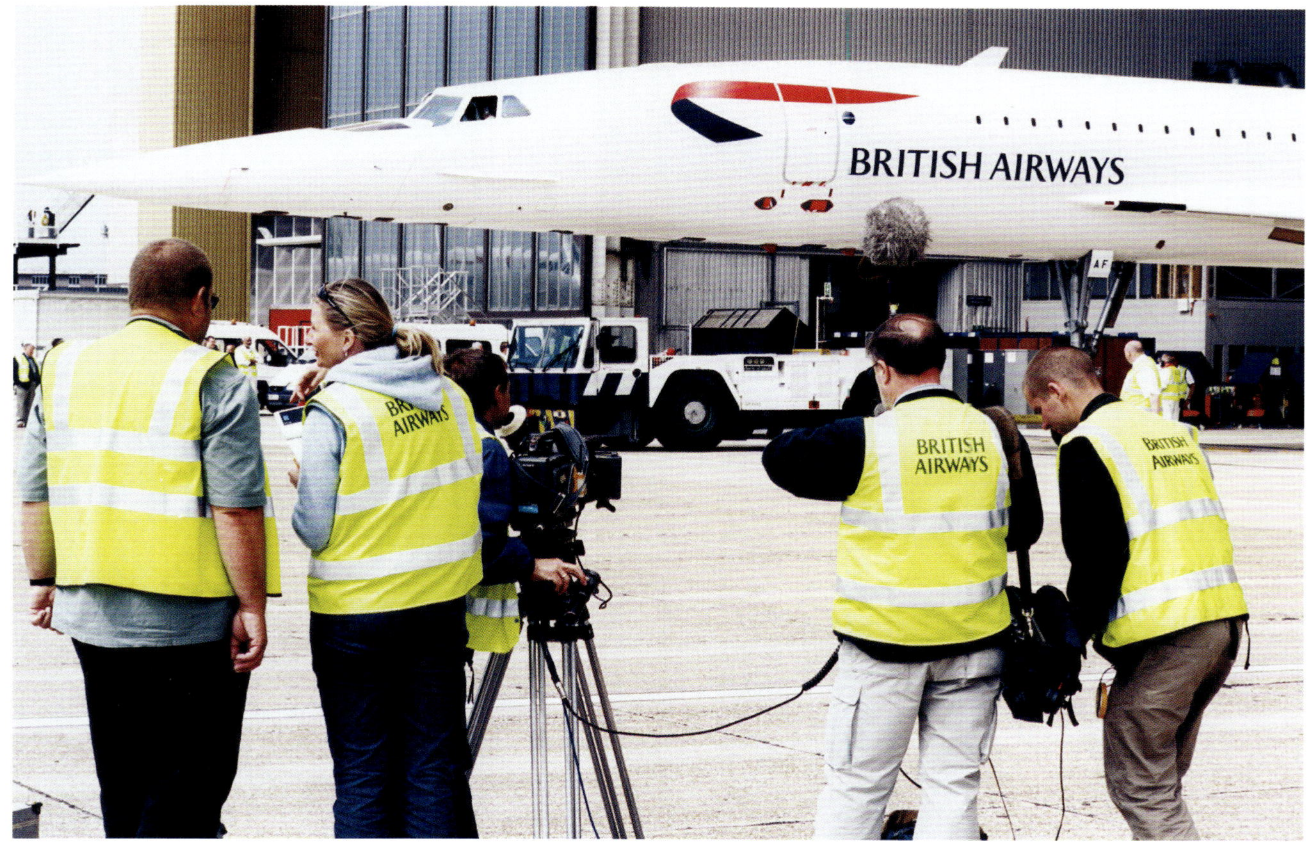

Concorde is towed out for the first time on 19 June 2001 after the engineering modifications in preparation for her first test flight later that year. The waiting world's press eagerly stood by to record this historic moment.

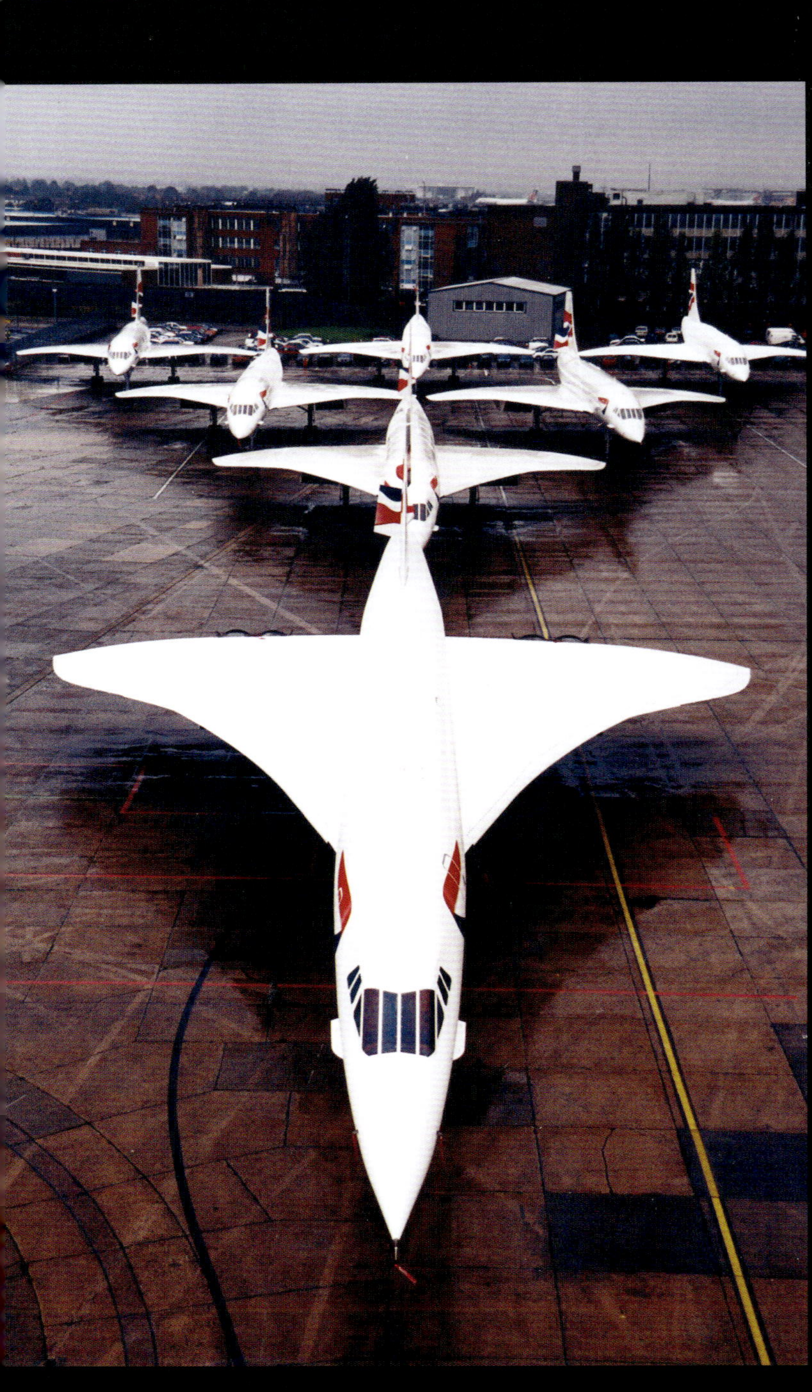

The fact that all seven Concordes were grounded for one year following the Paris air crash actually gave us the opportunity to photograph the whole fleet together in one shot for the first time. On a cold, bleak day with torrential rain in October 2000 – far from ideal conditions – we mounted a high-lift cherry picker to over 100ft. In the gusting wind we hung on for dear life to get these shots, but we managed to capture the seven wonders of aviation history. Several attempts were made with a variety of wide-angle shots and this is one of my favourites.

BACK IN BUSINESS

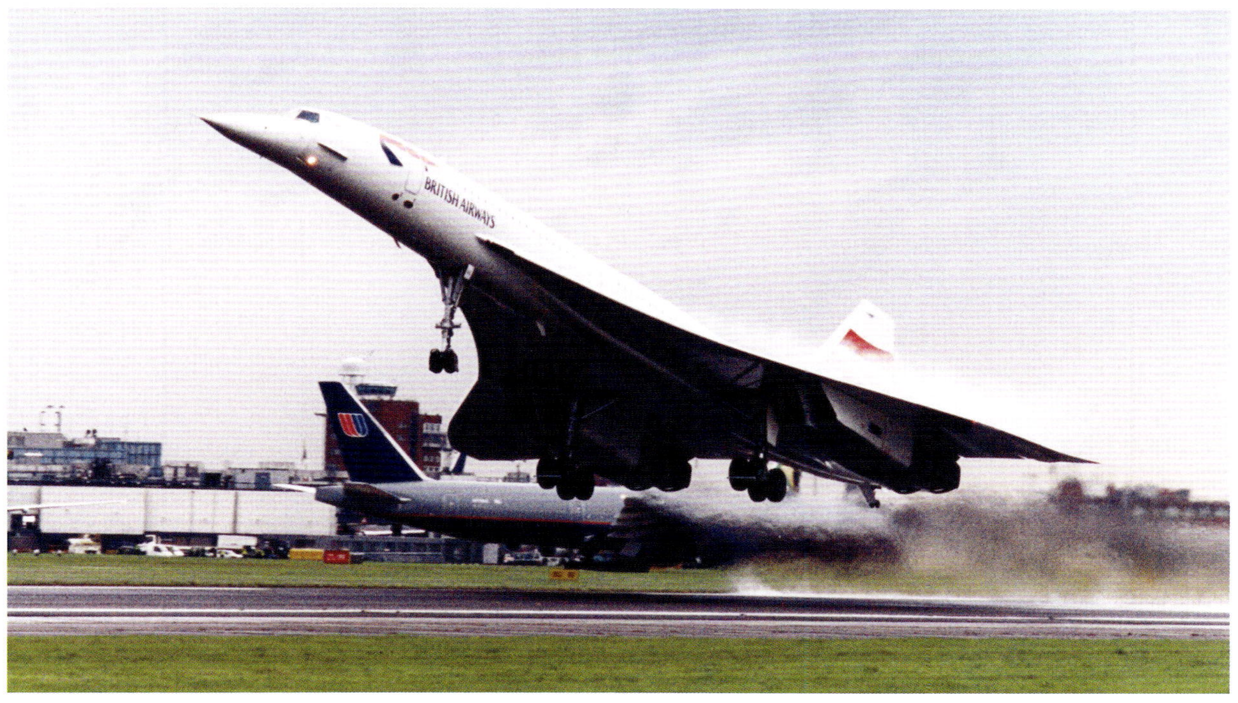

On 7 November 2001, Chief BA Concorde captain Mike Bannister and SFO Andy Barnwell taxied the first newly modified Concorde out onto the runway at London's Heathrow Airport. With the world's media watching keenly, at 10.44 a.m. Alpha Echo took to the skies with Captain Mike Bannister at the controls. Again the weather conditions were not that great, but we managed to get an impressive photograph.

(Photograph by Mike Bromfield, Adrian Meredith Photography)

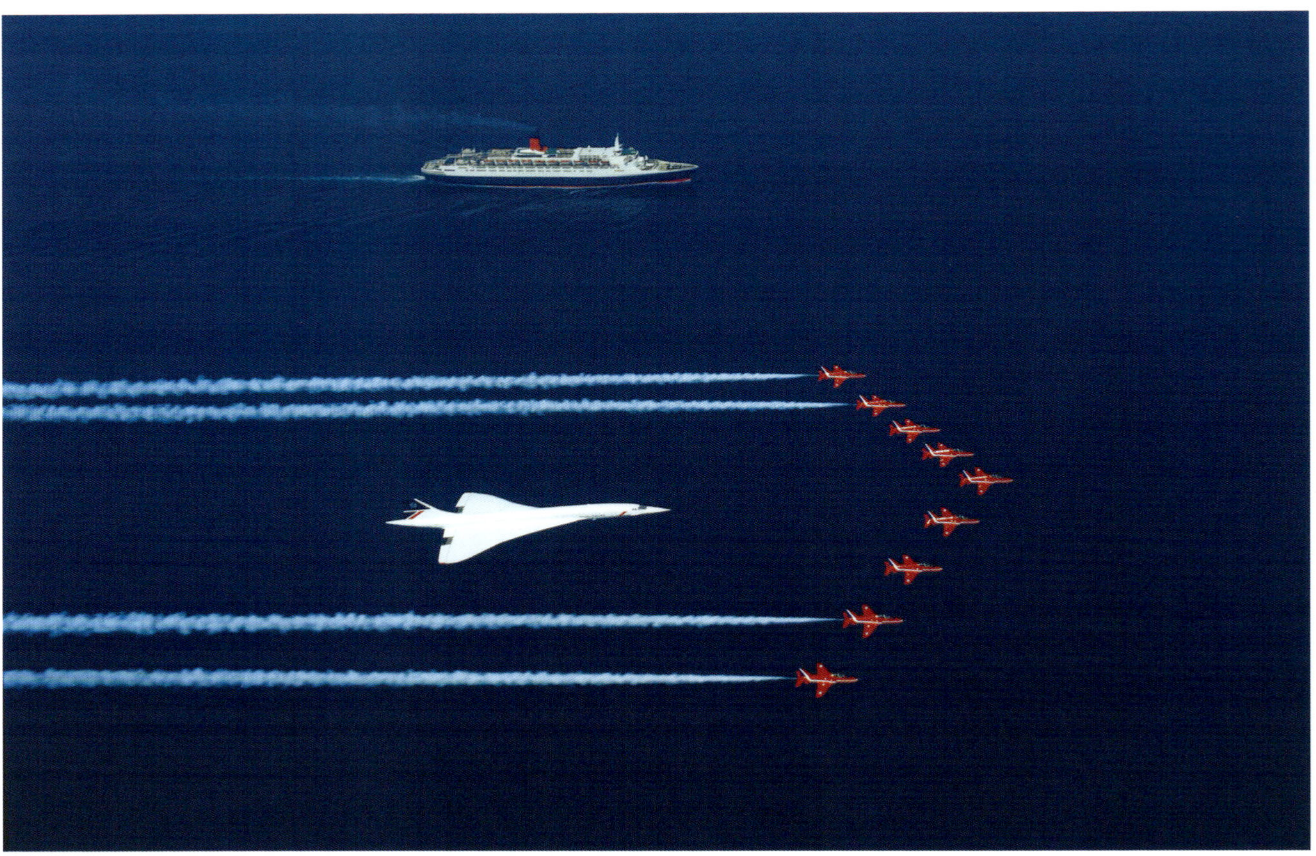

Concorde with the Red Arrows and the *QE2* in the summer of 1985

The late Arthur Gibson was an ex-RAF pilot well renowned for photographing the Red Arrows. The *QE2* was in the English Channel, having just left Southampton. There were only two fly-pasts allowed. Arthur Gibson was in the tenth Red Arrow, flying upside down, and looking down on Concorde, the Red Arrows and the *QE2* when this memorable photograph was taken. At the controls of Concorde G-BOAG were Captain Dave Leney and CFO Jock Lowe.

(Photograph by Arthur Gibson/Adrian Meredith Collection)

Concorde with the Red Arrows in 1996

Concorde would on occasion be escorted by the Red Arrows, especially for royal and aviation celebrations.

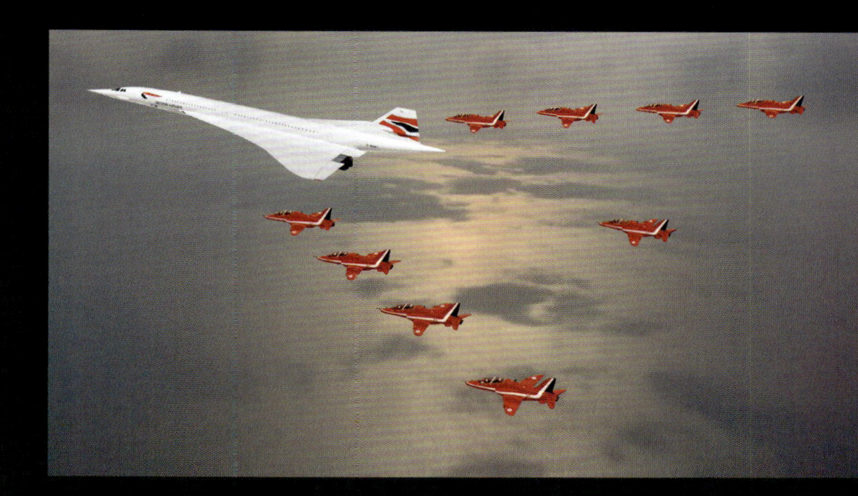

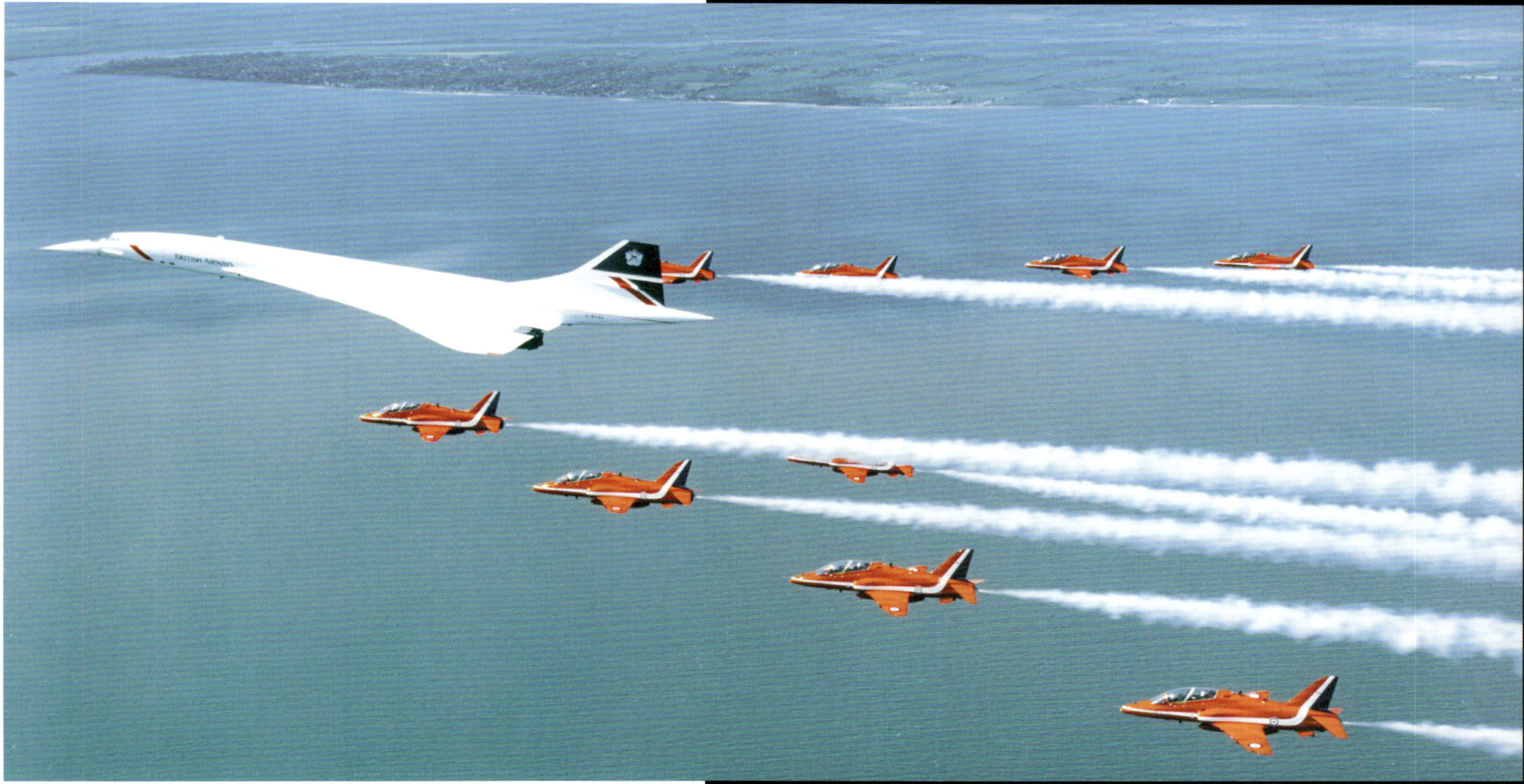

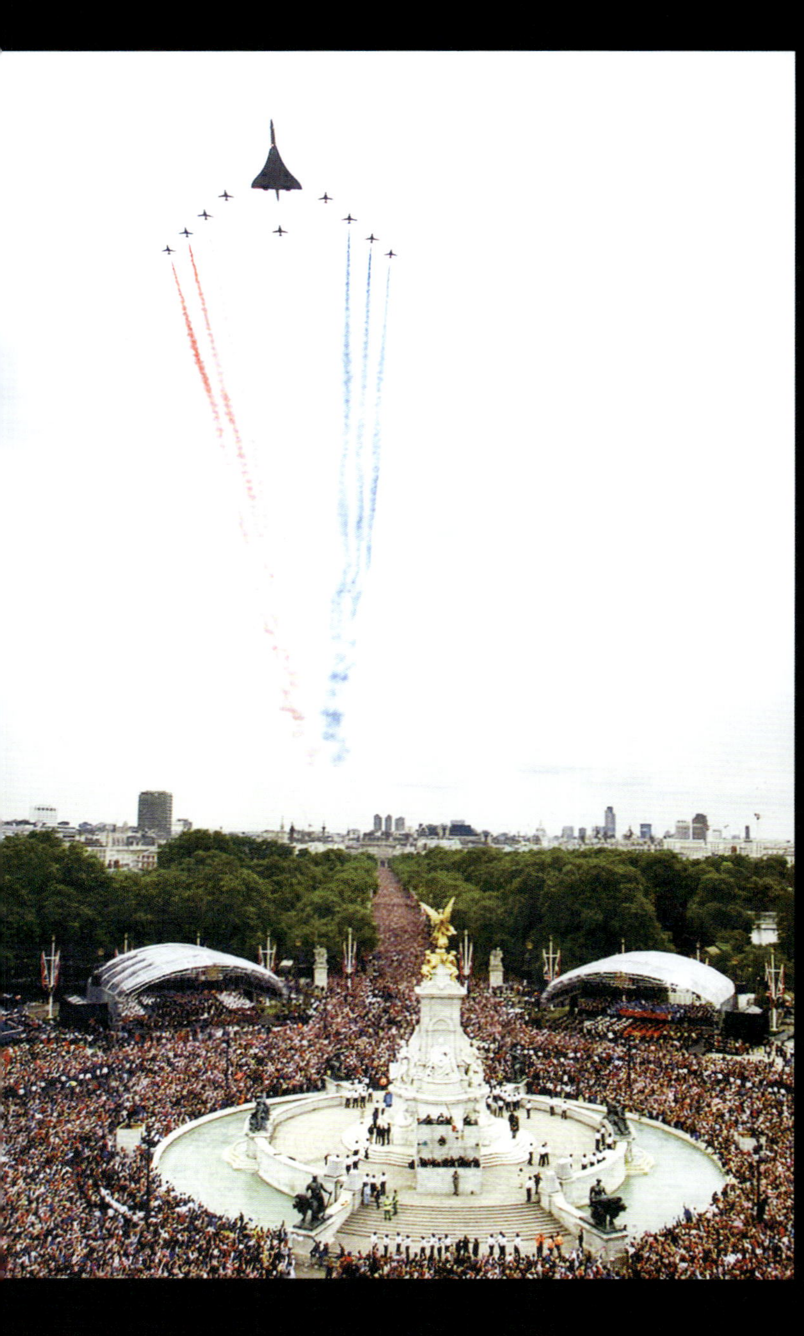

Another memorable occasion to celebrate the Queen's Golden Jubilee was a fly-past over Buckingham Palace on 4 June 2002. These photographs were shot from the ground, with Concorde and the Red Arrows on a low-level flight path down the famous Royal Mall leading to Buckingham Palace.

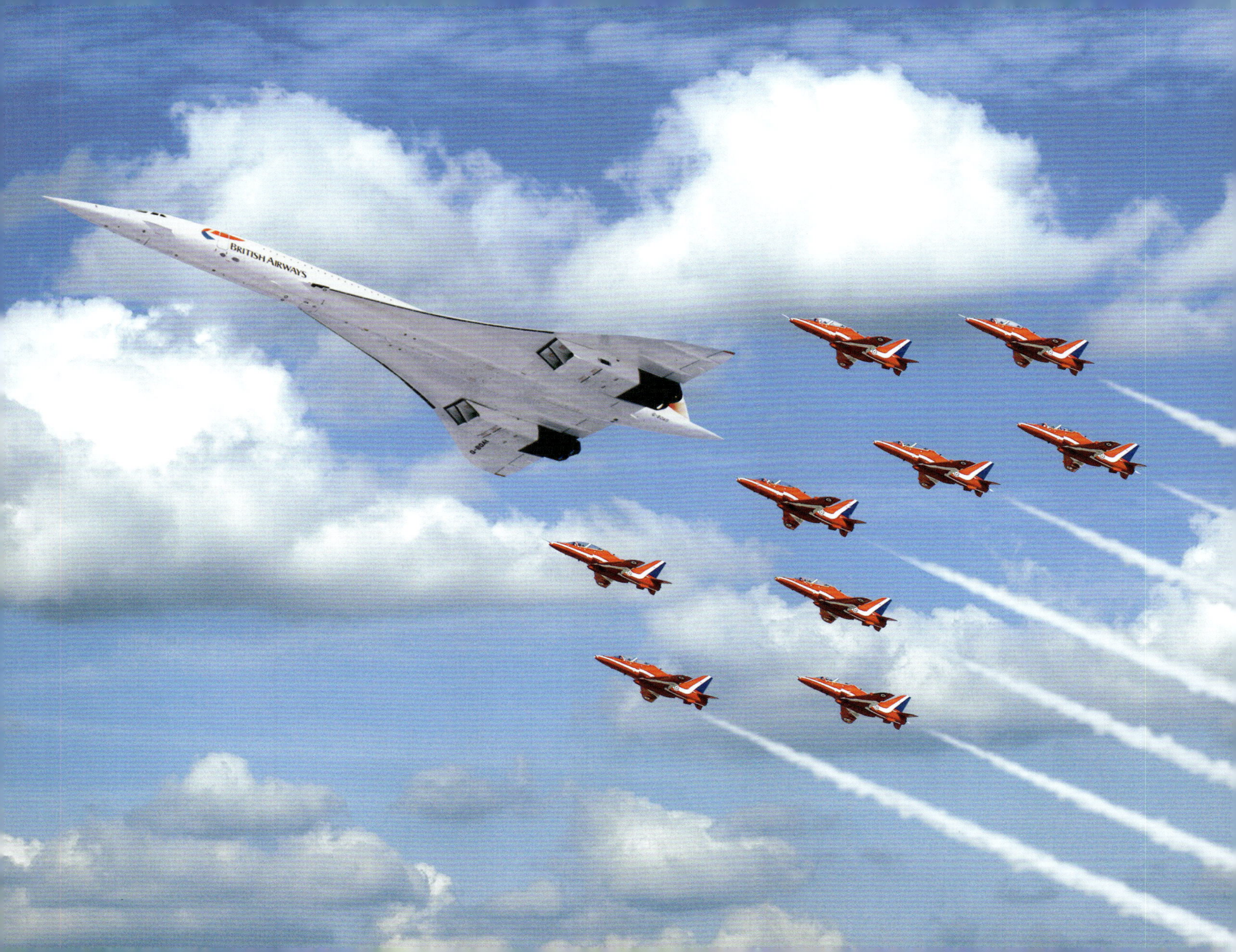

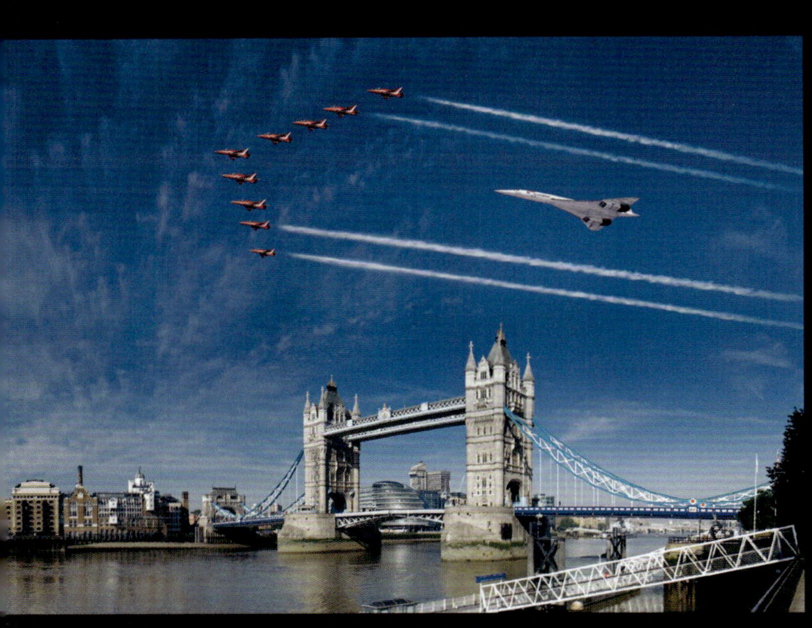

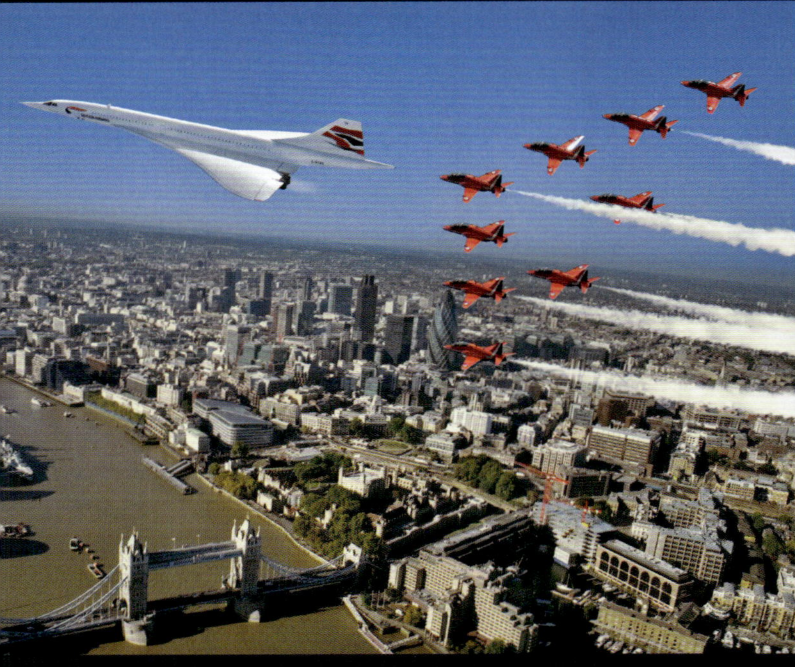

Concorde & Red Arrows

British Airways Concorde G-BOAD and the Red Arrows flying into Central London at 6.25 p.m. on 4 June 2002 for the Queen's Jubilee fly-past down the Mall then over Buckingham Place at a height of 1,500ft and a speed of 280 knots. On the Concorde flight deck were chief pilots Mike Bannister and Les Brodie, and Senior First Officer Peter Carrigan.

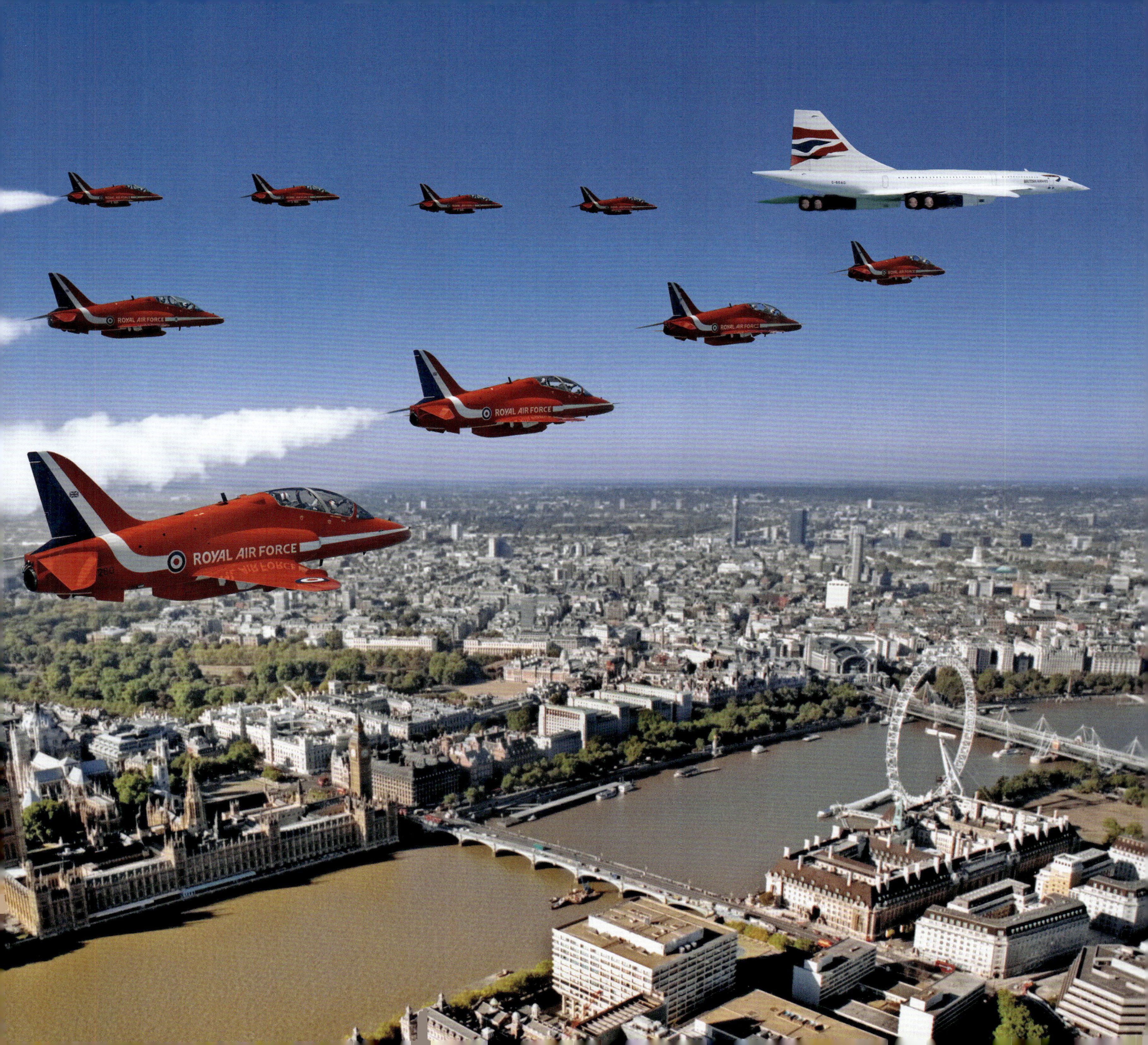

This stunning photograph was taken by Captain Mike Bannister through the pilot's cockpit window in Concorde. It captures the Red Arrows flying in formation alongside in celebration of the Queen's Jubilee.

(Photograph by Captain Mike Bannister)

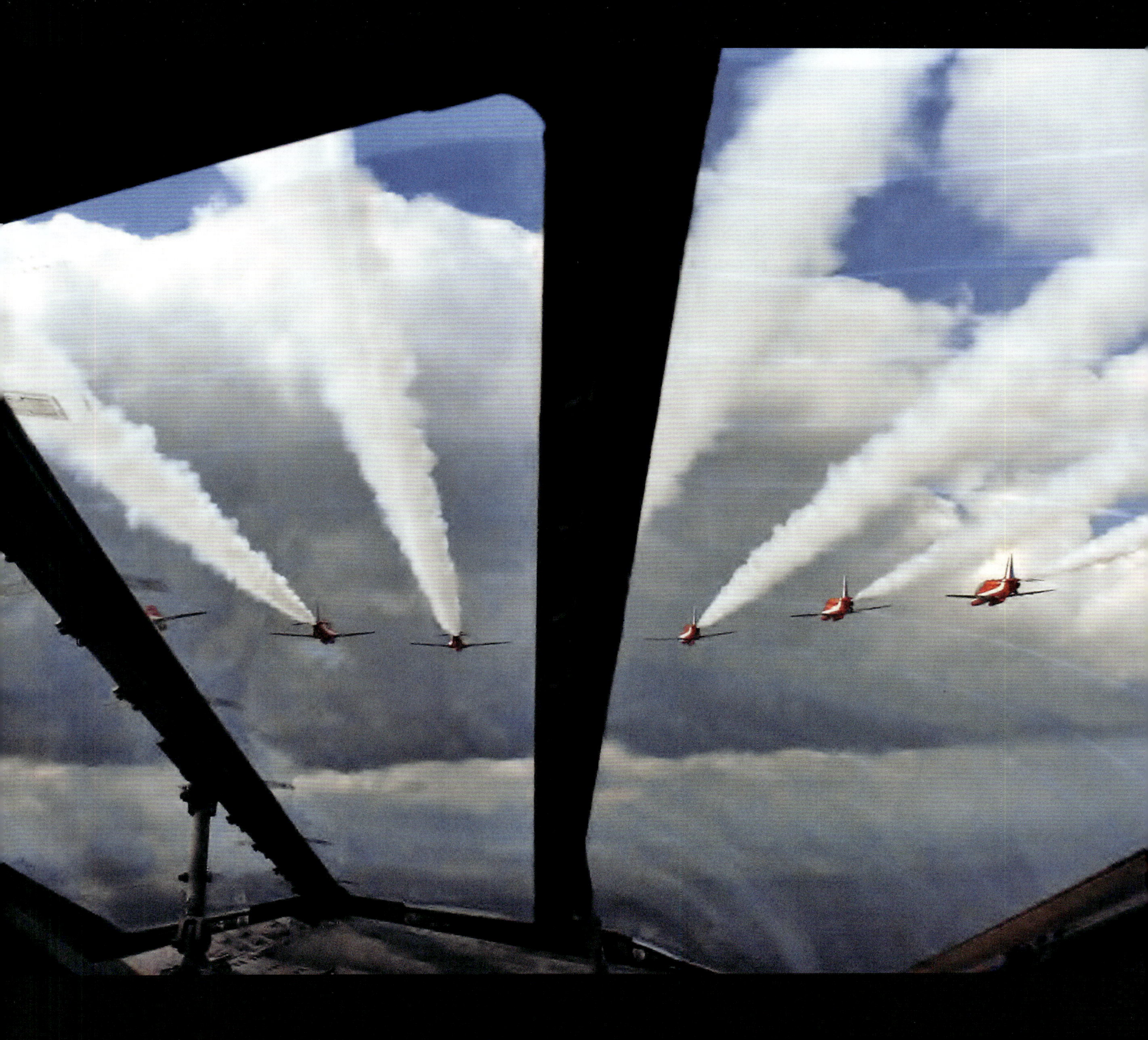

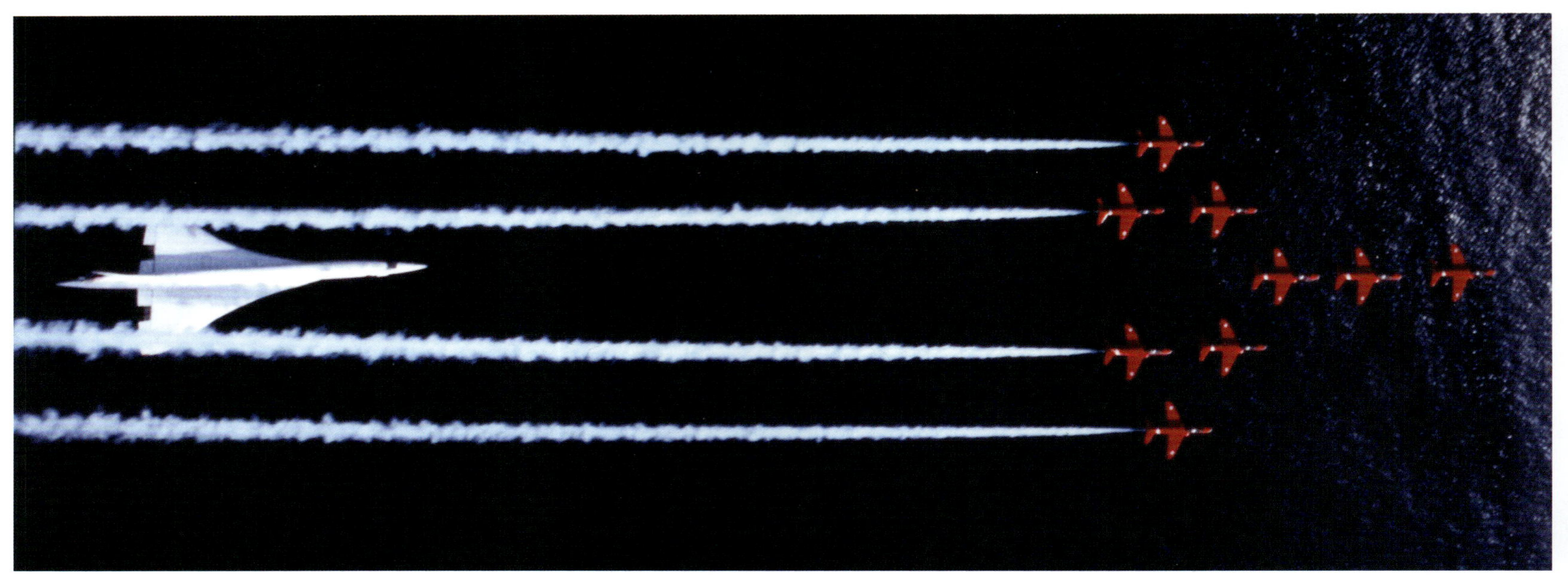

In 1983, BAC test aircraft G-BBDG receives a flying salute from the Red Arrows before her retirement later that year. This aircraft is now sited at Brooklands Museum, Weybridge, England.

'Why would anyone want to travel any other way? So what if our ears are ringing 'til Kingdom Come with sonic booms to match Gabriel's horn?'

Joan Collins, actress

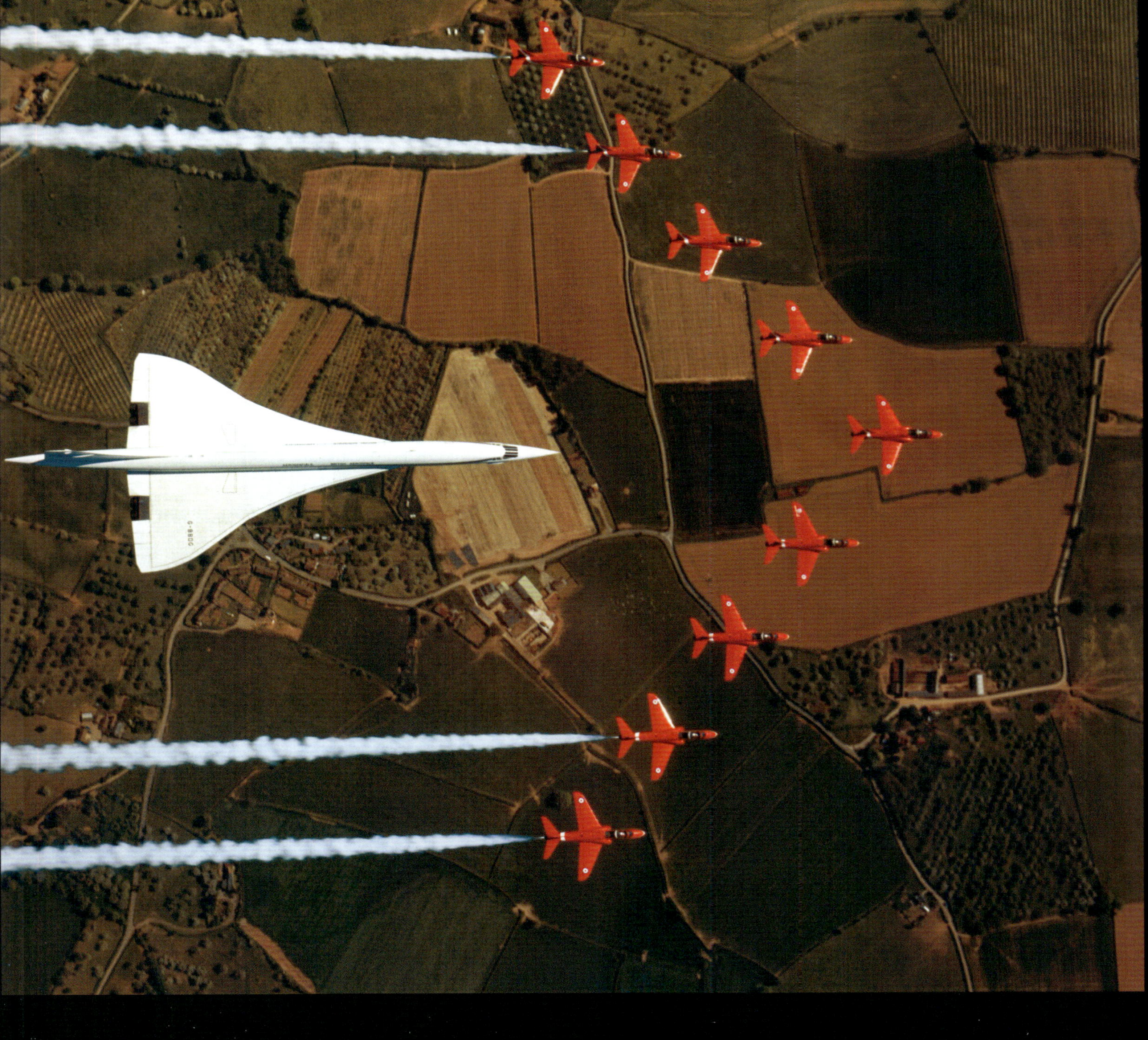

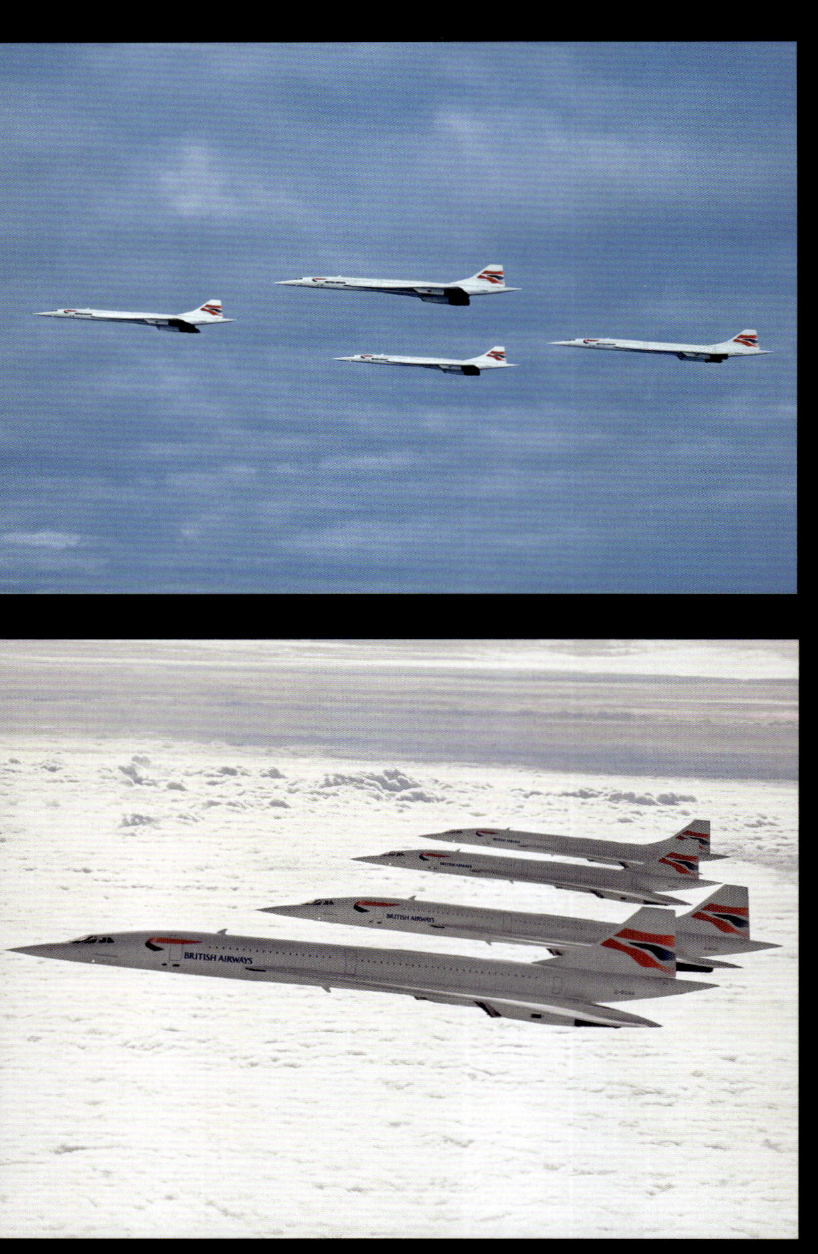

Concorde's tenth anniversary celebrations

This was one of the most important and exciting photographic assignments I have ever undertaken, and very prestigious for Concorde: the ten-year anniversary of Concorde's commercial service. The date was Christmas Eve 1985; this was actually the only day possible that we could photograph four of the Concordes together as they were not flying commercially that day.

Many hours were spent at the briefing sessions to ensure the formations were military precision perfect. Different formations were discussed – the swan, the diamond, the echelon – and decided upon to ensure all went to plan. Nothing like this had ever been done before commercially. Concorde senior captains Brian Walpole and John Cook both had a wealth of experience of flying in formation from their days in the RAF. My task was to capture in essence the group formations. The flight plan was to take off from Heathrow, fly to Filton in Bristol, the home of Concorde, down the Bristol Channel, and return to London.

The Lear jet had to be fitted with optically corrective glass in the windows, which wouldn't distort the camera's image. We were to take off first in the Lear jet from London Heathrow, and special permission had to be granted for each Concorde to take off every thirty seconds, in succession. This had never been done before.

The weather was very dark and gloomy as it was December and the sun was low and watery. We rose above, and circled over, the clouds to brighter skies, and as we looked down, we saw each Concorde pop through the clouds like a firing bullet. After the fourth aircraft had emerged we quickly descended and took chase at full throttle to try and catch them up. They started to manoeuvre and steadily flew into position for the first formation, flying in diamond, then echelon and then swan formation.

The weather was very poor unfortunately, and every time they set up for a different formation a bank of cloud would roll in and the Concordes would have to break off their positioning for safety. This gave me the briefest of opportunities to liaise with the pilots in between the shooting. As soon as they were back in another formation I knew the photography had to be very quick; on one occasion

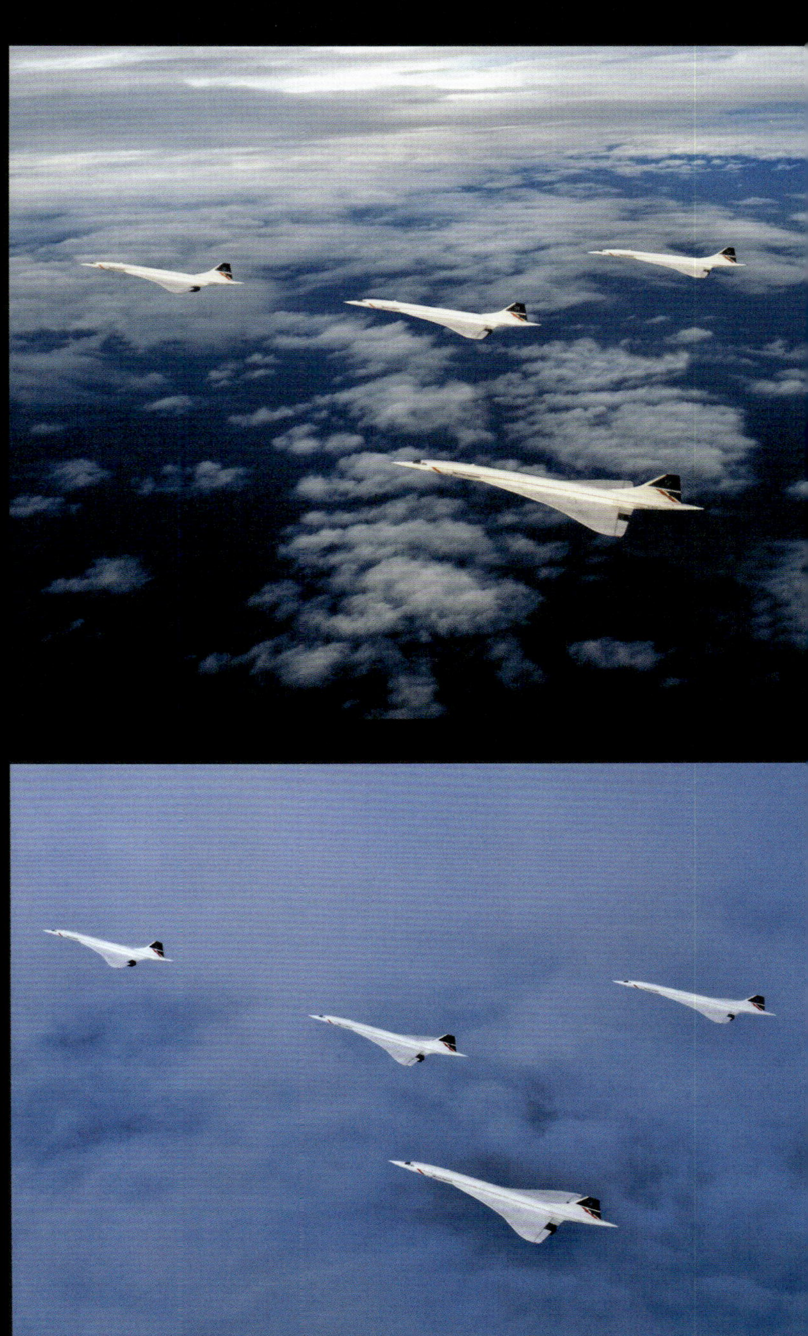

we banked steeply, sweeping over the top of the formation to get the perfect overhead shots. Other photography was taken side-on. During one stage of a particular formation the Concorde wing tips were only 70ft apart. The entire exercise took one hour and forty-five minutes and all the Concordes returned safely home, and thankfully I had all the shots in the can.

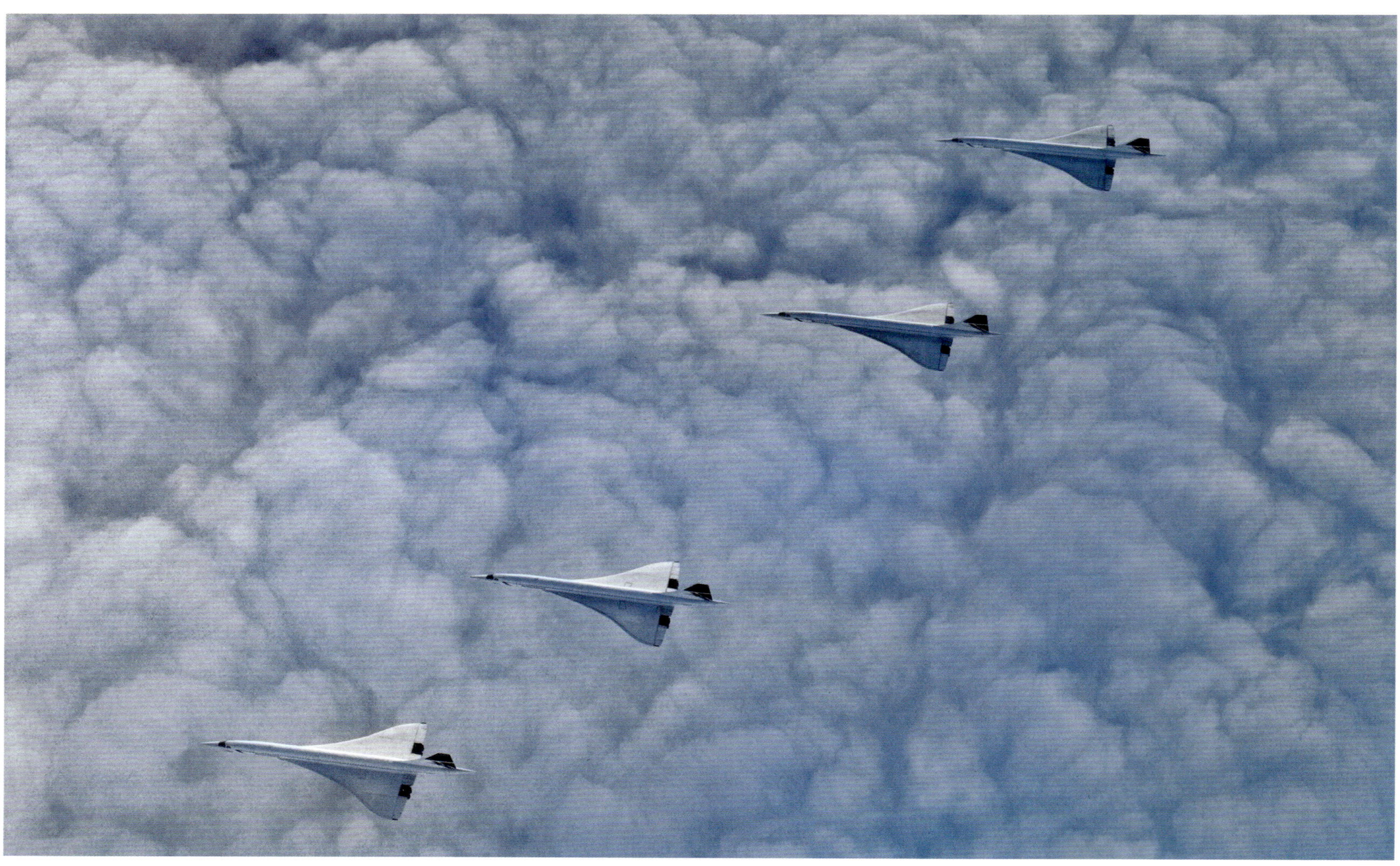

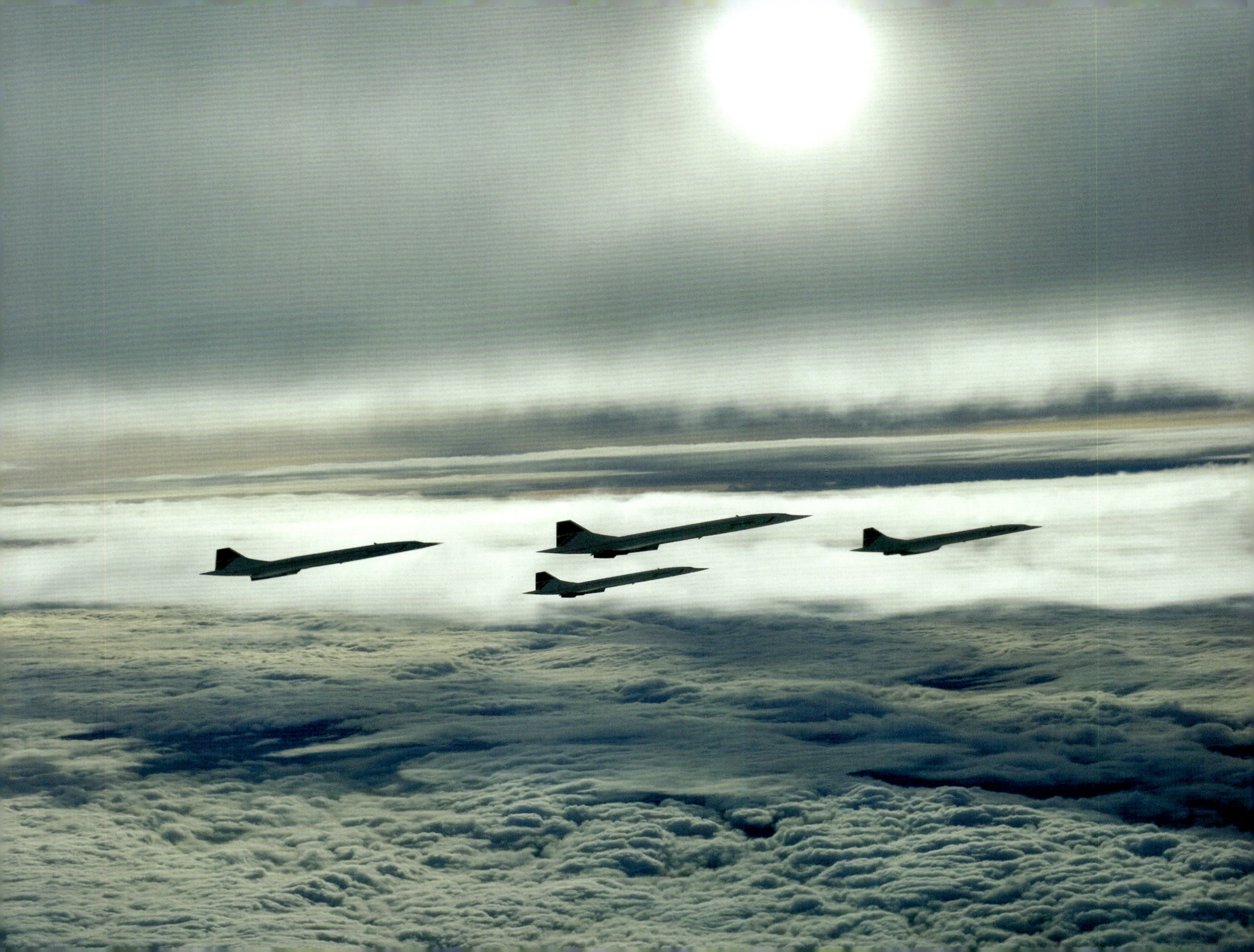

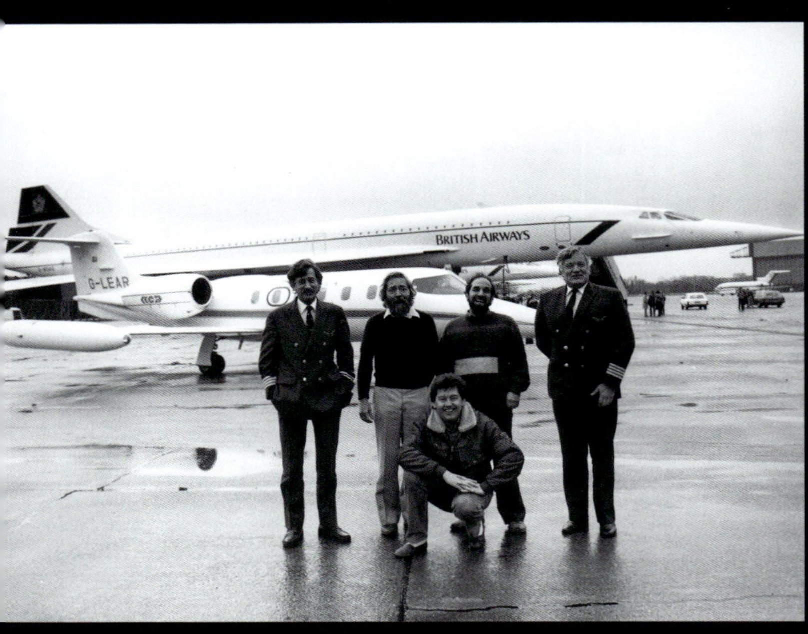

The Lear jet crew: two captains, two cameramen and myself kneeling in the foreground. The specially chartered jet was from Northern Executive.

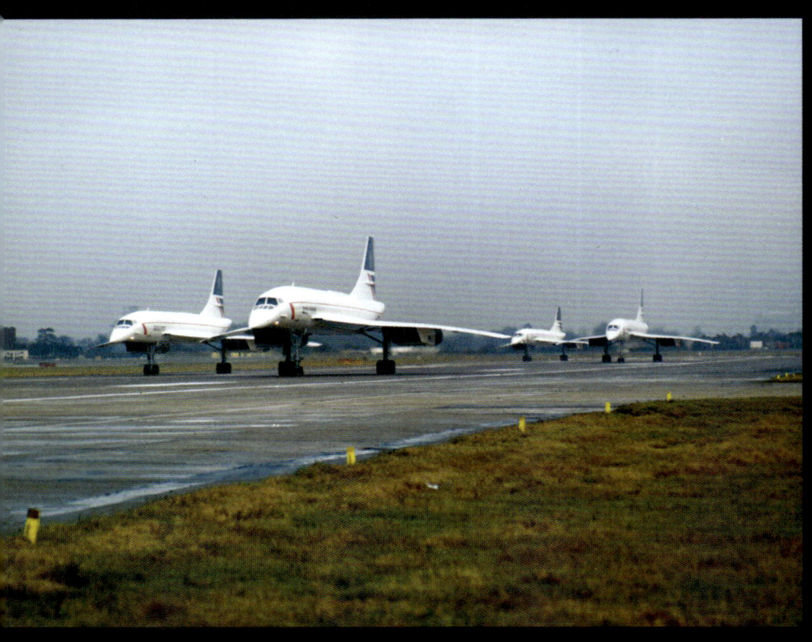

The four Concordes taxi out from the Engineering Base onto the runway; events were now in place for this historic flight. The whole of London Heathrow came to a complete halt to watch the simultaneous take-offs of all four Concordes.

Richard Noble broke another record by flying three Atlantic crossings in one day to celebrate Concorde's tenth birthday: London to New York, New York to London, and finally London back to New York.

Richard Noble OBE, project director and driver of Thrust 2, set a new land speed record on 4 October 1983 when his record-breaking car Thrust 2, which then held the current speed record, travelled at 633.468mph. His record was later broken on 15 October 1997 by Andy Green in the new Thrust SSC which travelled at 763.035mph in the Black Rock Desert, Nevada.

All the passengers were in for a special treat on this day; surprise surprise, champagne and a celebration tenth anniversay cake were distributed to all those on board. Celebrations began in the Concorde Lounge, with BA Chairman Lord King and British Concorde test pilot Brian Trubshaw.

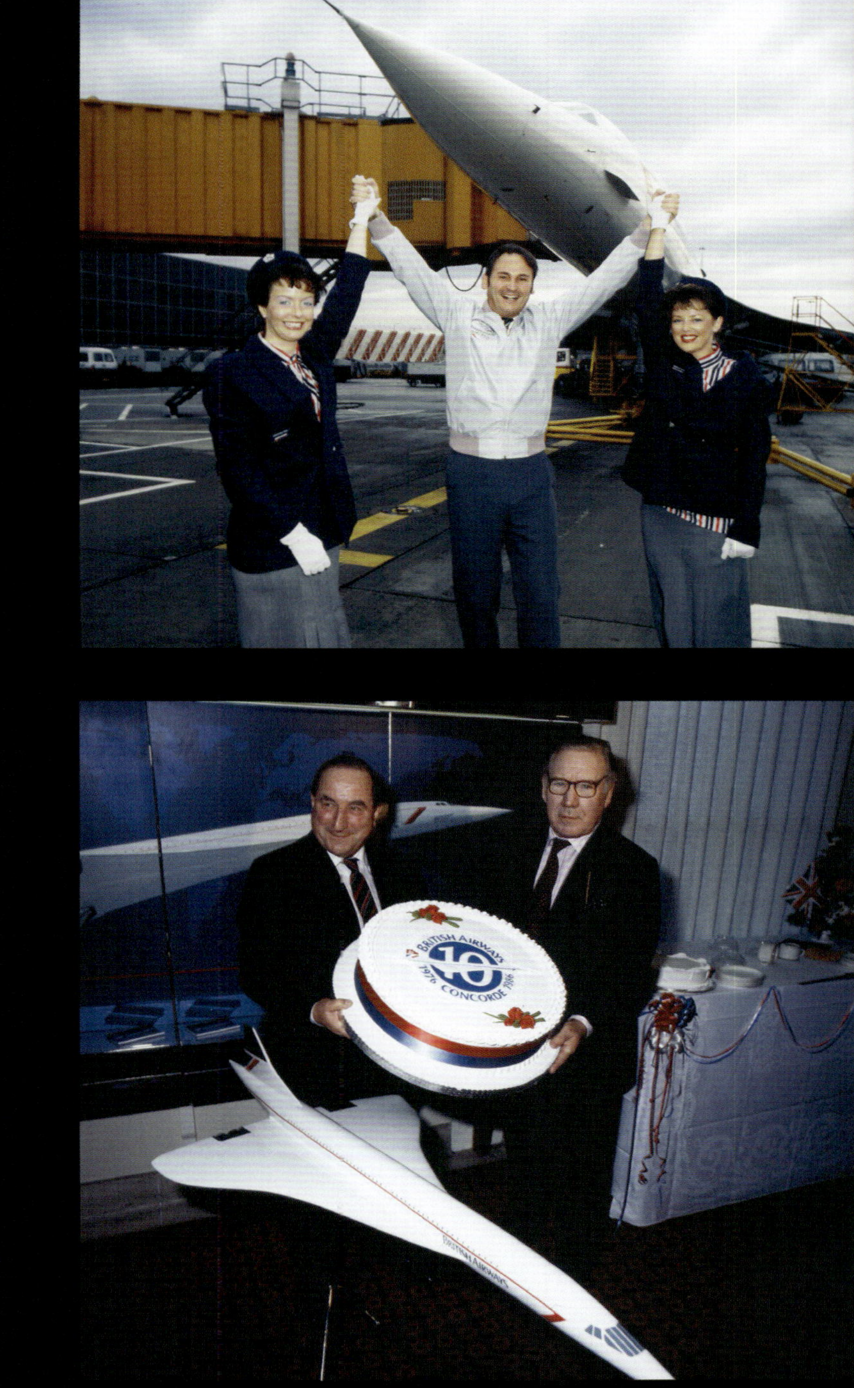

To follow on from the air-to-air photography, this shoot was set up on Boxing Day 1985 as a fall-back option in case the air-to-air photography wasn't sufficient. We arranged for six out of the seven Concordes to be towed into a fan formation outside the Concorde hangar. It took the ground engineers six hours to position the aircraft into this tight formation. We demonstrated the formation with small Concorde models beforehand to show the engineers the placements.

A helicopter had been hired for the air-to-ground shoot. Unfortunately the wind was gusting over 50mph, rain was lashing down, and although the helicopter landed safely next to the six Concordes, air traffic control were not happy for us to do the photography in these bad weather conditions. However, I was strapped into a safety harness and hung out of the side of the helicopter. The conditions were so precarious that Captain Brian Walpole insisted we could not shoot directly overhead of the six Concordes because, if we crashed, we could potentially have wiped out the entire Concorde fleet. The helicopter pilot finally agreed to take me up for just ten minutes and I shot this photograph from the side.

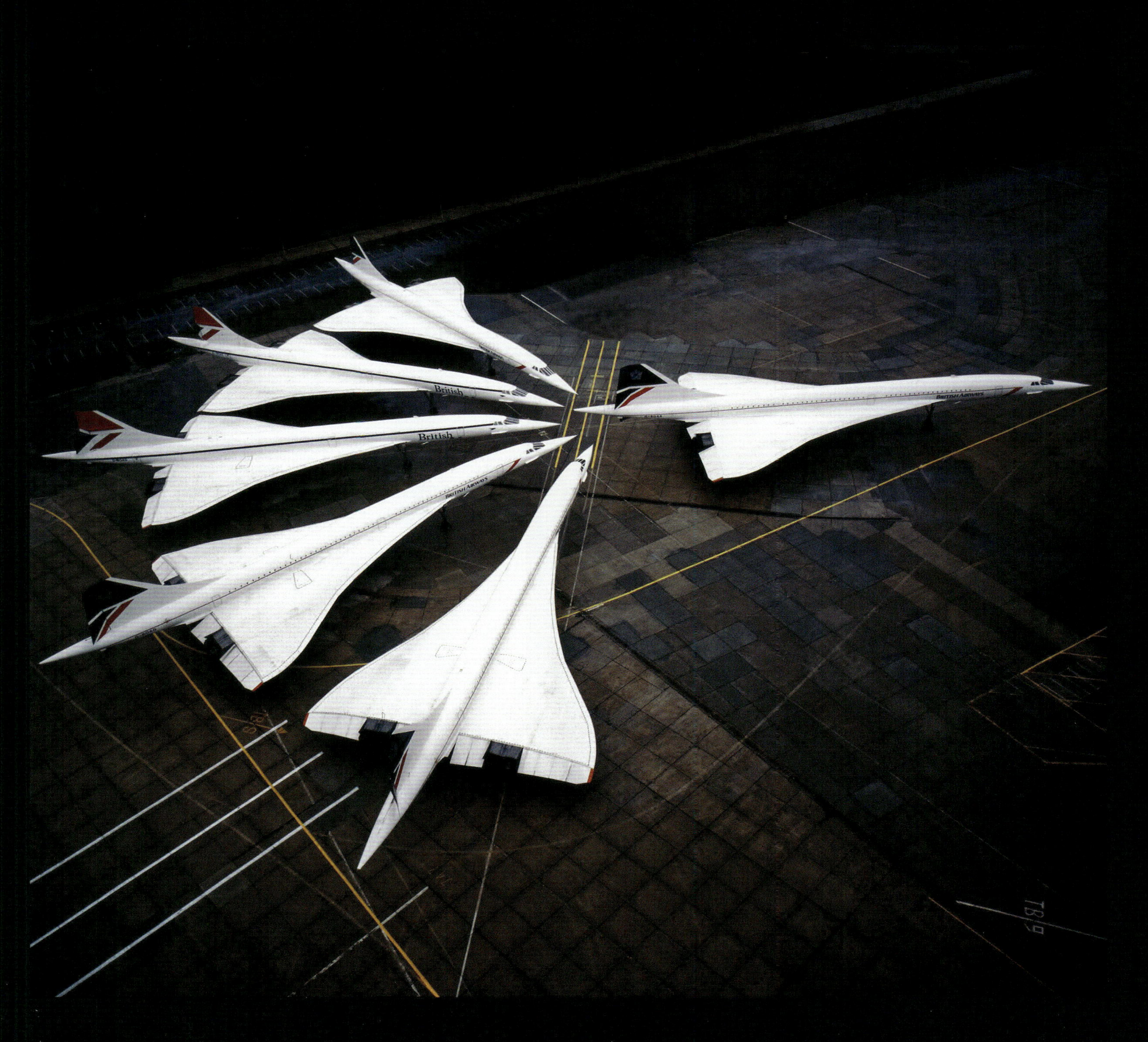

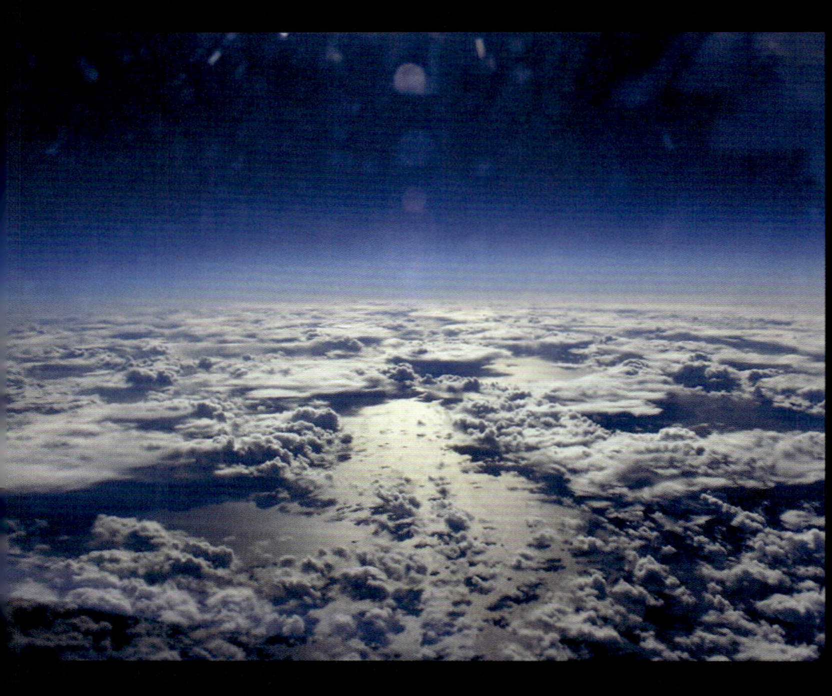

'Curvature of the Earth' – taken from the flight deck of Concorde G-BOAF on Tuesday 17 July 2001 over the South-West Approaches at 58,000ft as we returned from the first 'Operational Assessment Flight' post the incorporation of the design modifications.

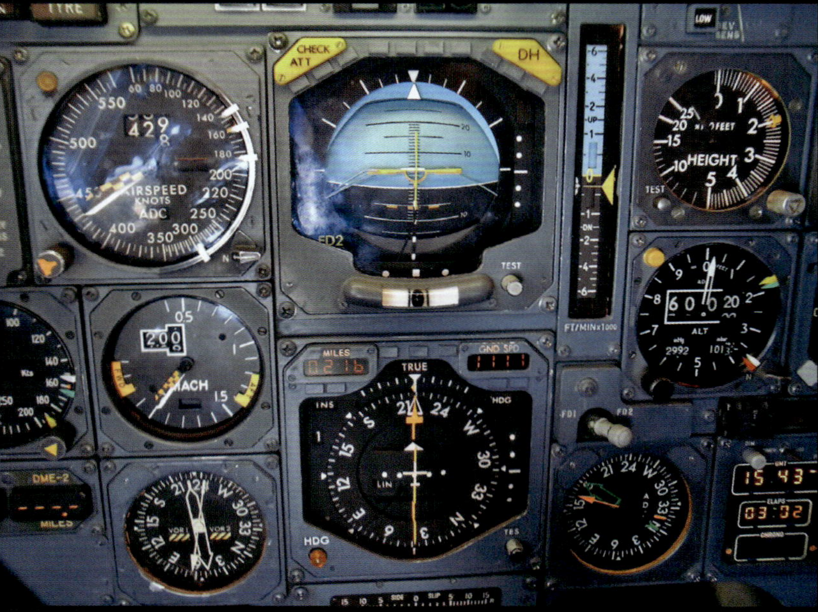

'The last time Concorde ever reached 60,000ft' – the pilots' panel of Concorde G-BOAE at 15.43 GMT on Monday 17 November 2003 just before starting the deceleration and descent into Barbados. The instruments show a speed of Mach 2, an altitude of 60,000ft, and that the aircraft had been airborne for just three hours and two minutes before reaching this point.

(Photographs by Captain Mike Bannister)

'The famous visor – the captain's view' – the view from a Concorde captain's 'office window' whilst flying supersonically towards some large transatlantic storms.

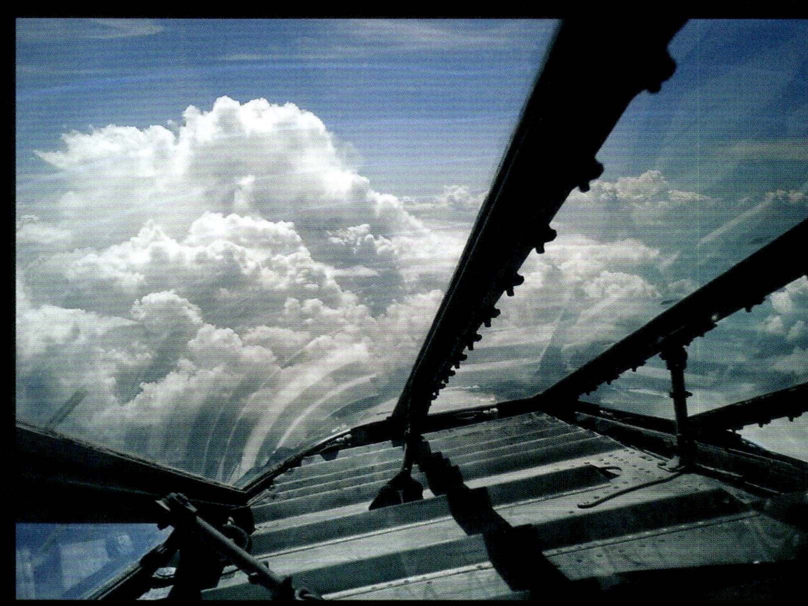

'Concorde grew 8-10 inches in flight' – but the only place where it could easily be seen was on the flight deck where a gap appeared between the systems panel and the adjacent bulkhead. On the final flights the crew put the flight engineer's cap into the gap, which closes completely when Concorde is on the ground. The cap is jammed solidly until the next time that Concorde flies supersonically again!

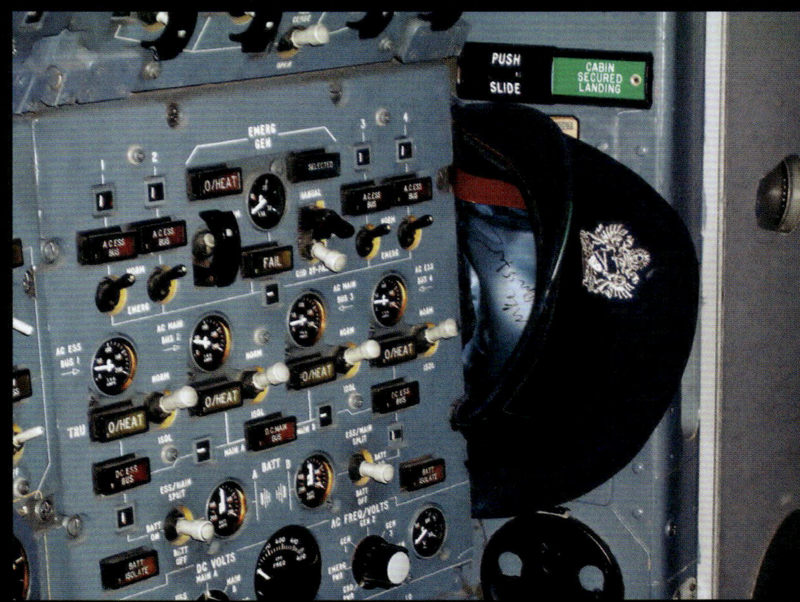

(Photographs by Captain Mike Bannister)

Crew Perspective

Concorde flight deck training

Senior Training Captain Les Brodie, on the left, is seen here going through technical checks with his first officer and flight engineer on the flight simulator – an exact replica of the interior of the flight deck – at Filton, Bristol.

There were a total of 189 flight crew that flew the British Airways Concorde during 1976–2002: this consisted of sixty-nine captains, sixty-four first officers and fifty-six flight engineers.

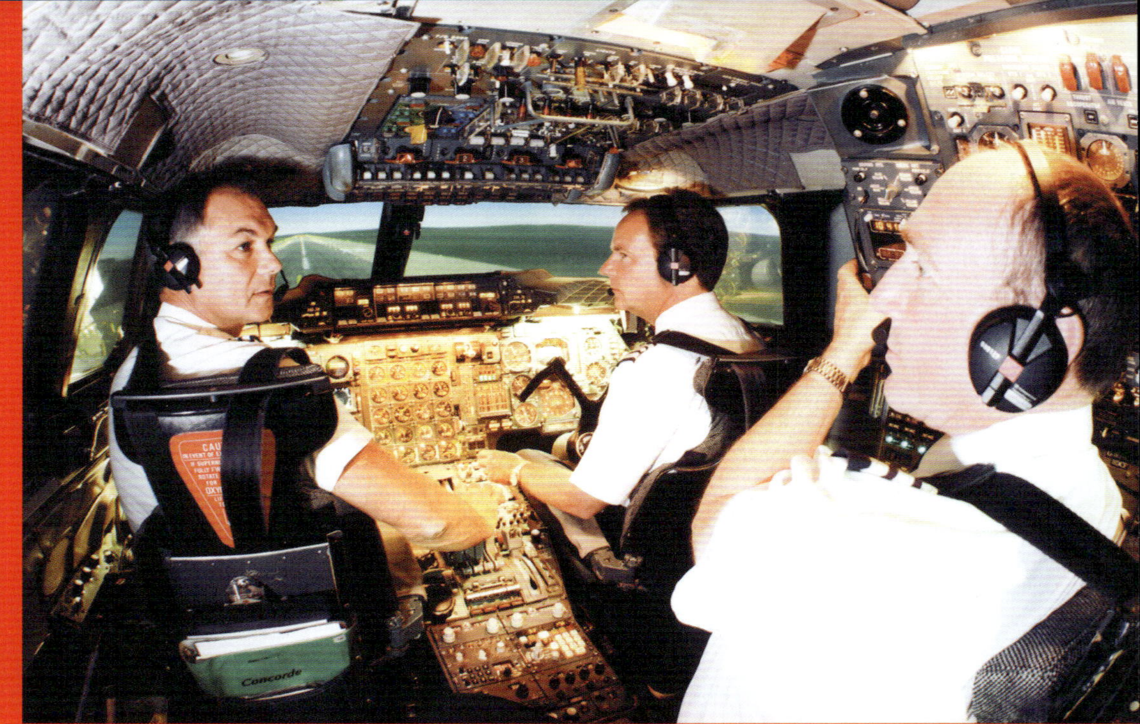

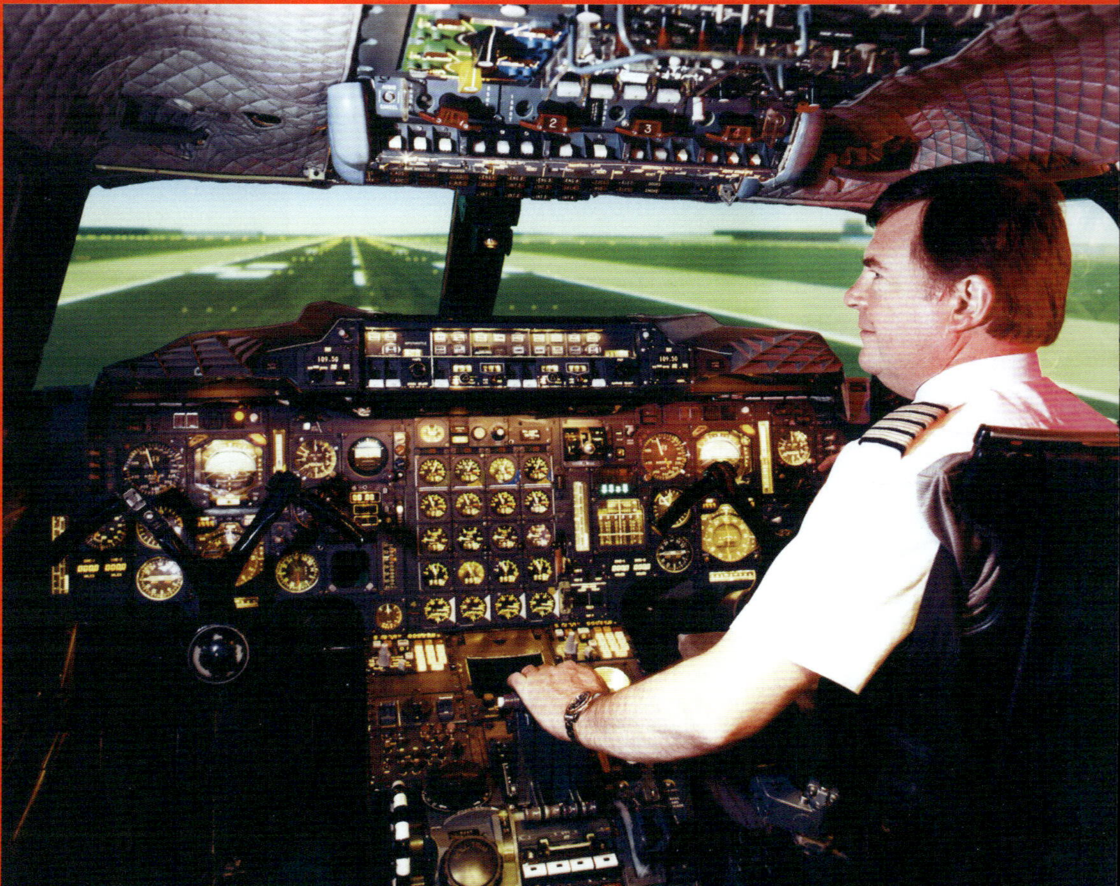

Captain Steve Wand modelling the very latest Rolex watch in 1994, which was used in an advertisement in the USA.

FLYING HIGH

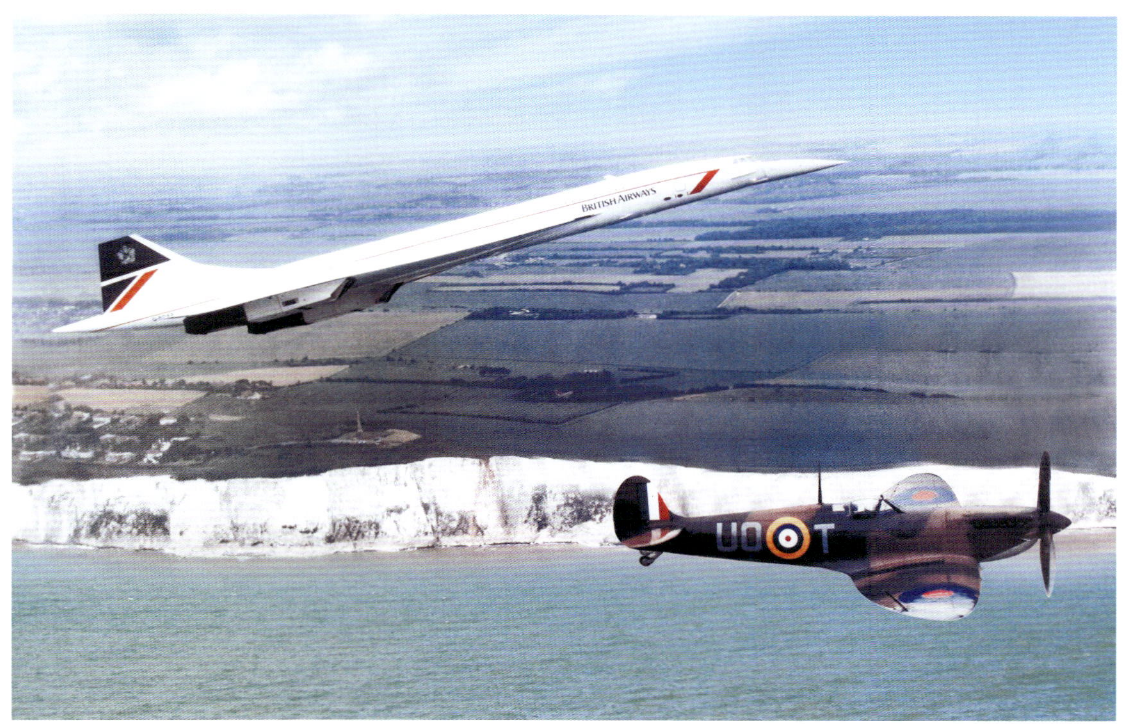

This photograph was shot on 26 March 1993 to celebrate the anniversary of the Battle of Britain. The air-to-air photography was shot with the white cliffs of Dover in the background. Captain Jock Lowe, at the controls of Concorde G-BOAA, said we had to fly as slow as possible, and the photograph shows Concorde at a very acute angle. The Spitfire P7350 was flying flat out, and finding it very difficult to keep pace with Concorde.

Concorde over Tower Bridge, London, 2003

Concorde would often be seen flying over London on her return homebound journey from New York. She flew daily, and would arrive at Heathrow at approximately 5.30 p.m. The flight time was three and a half hours. On 7 February 1996 Captain Leslie Scott with co-pilot Tim Orchard and flight engineer Rick Eades were recorded in the *Guinness Book of Records* for setting the fastest run time of two hours, fifty-two minutes and fifty-nine seconds from New York's JFK to London Heathrow Airport.

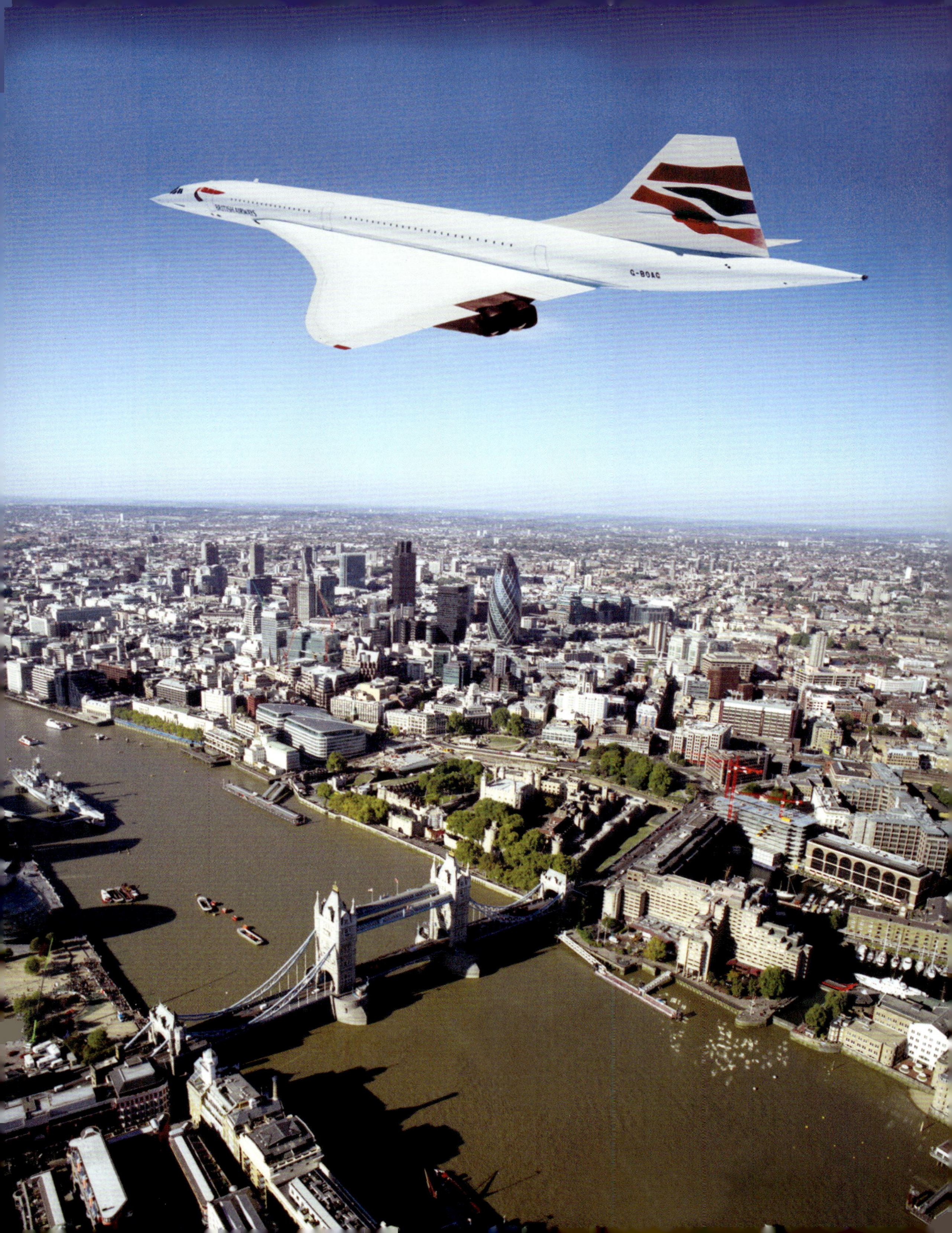
BRITISH AIRWAYS
G-BOAC

Concorde returns home late in the afternoon to a warm, sunny view of Windsor Castle beneath her; one can just see the royal standard letting us know that the Queen is in residence. The Queen often flew Concorde; her first flight with Prince Philip was in 1979 to Kuwait. Concorde was also a royal favourite of the Queen Mother and Princess Diana.

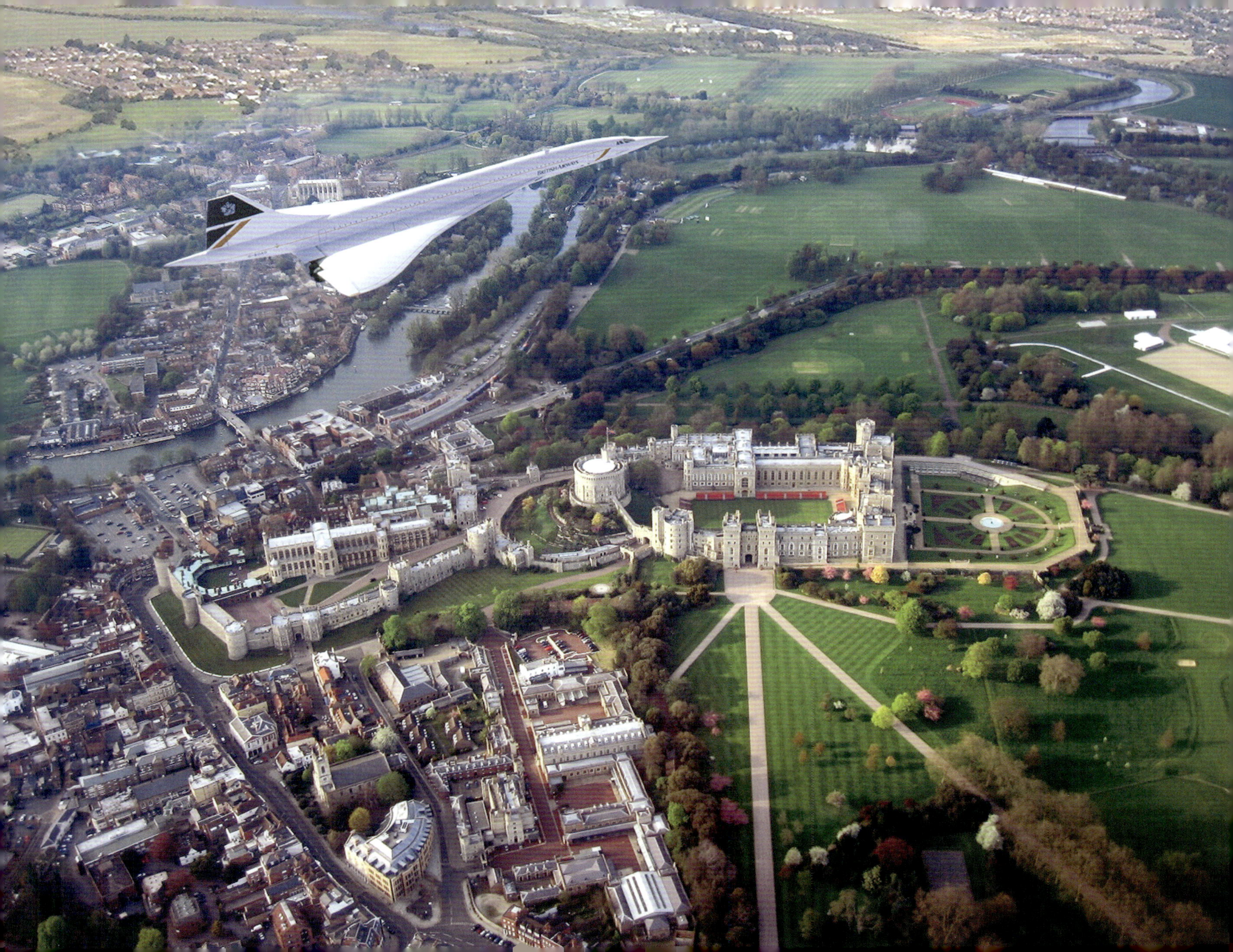

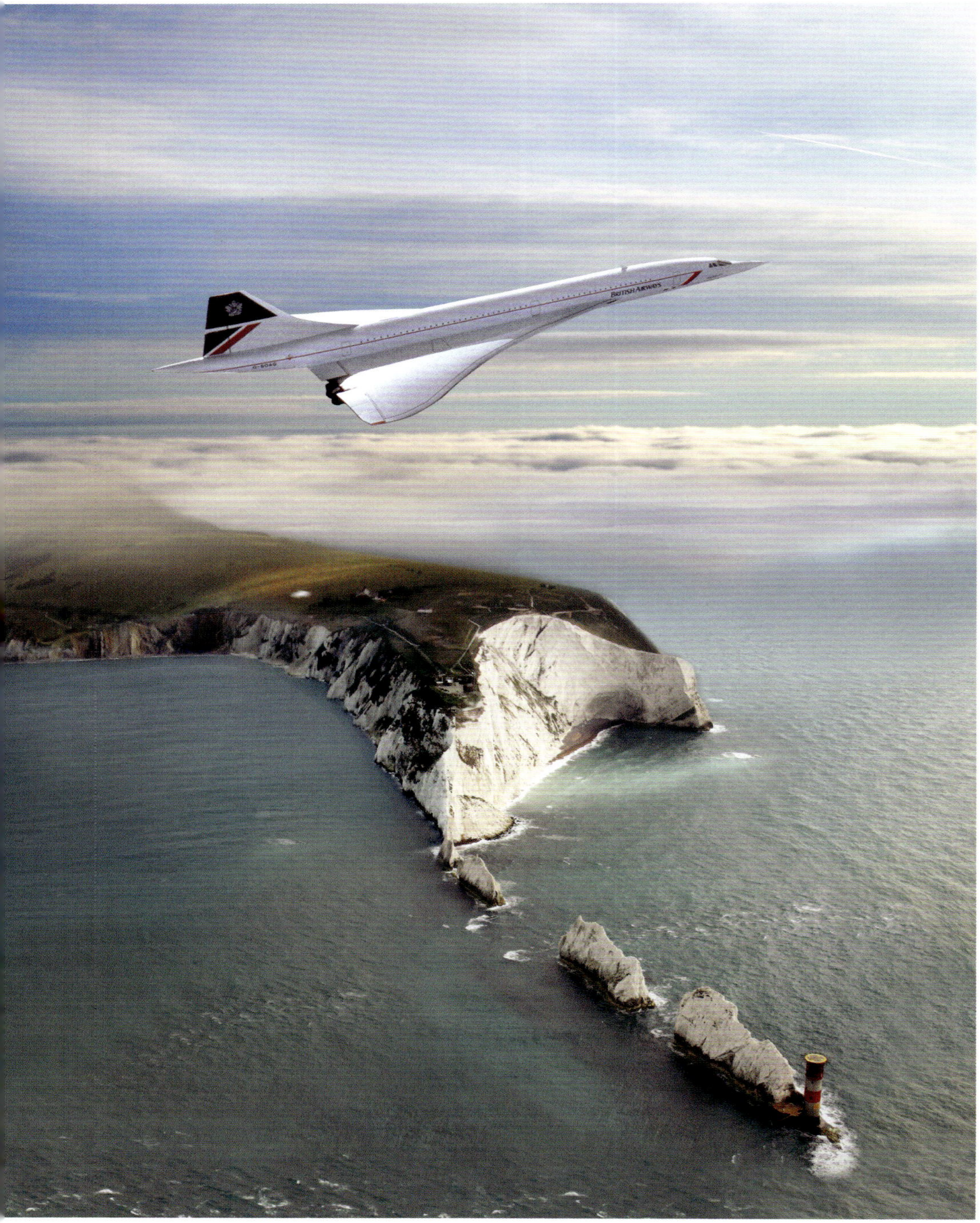

Concorde would often be seen flying over famous landmarks and here she is flying over The Needles, Isle of Wight, England. This picture highlights the beautiful delta wing of Concorde and her sleek 204ft-long fuselage, which is almost the same length as the 747 Boeing, against the The Needles' chalk white cliffs.

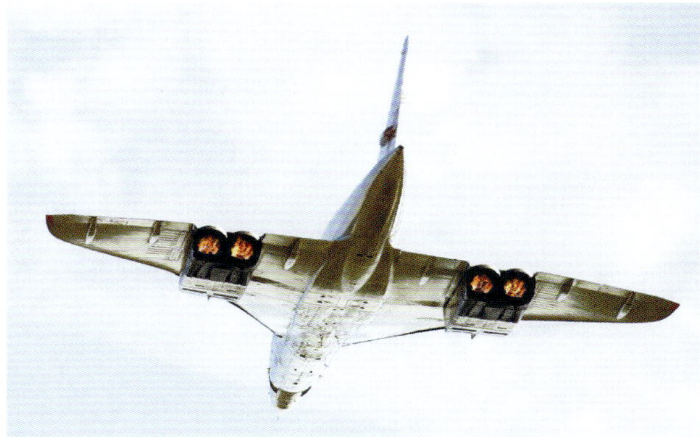

Once the air traffic control gives clearance for take-off, Concorde activates the reheat, better known as after-burners, and starts her acceleration from 0-250mph in less than forty seconds. She climbs away from the airfield and after a few minutes into flight they are turned off. The after-burners produce extra power whenever the transonic phase of the flight is required. The reheats are used to go through the sound barrier, and then at a speed of Mach 1.7. After this they are cut.

CHAPTER TWELVE

EPHEMERA

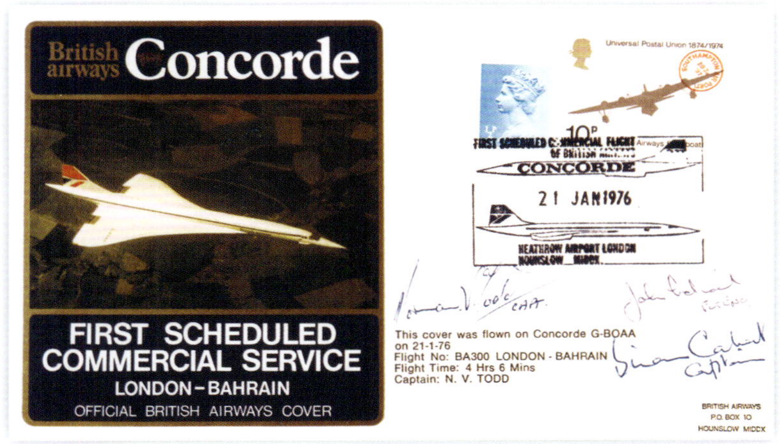

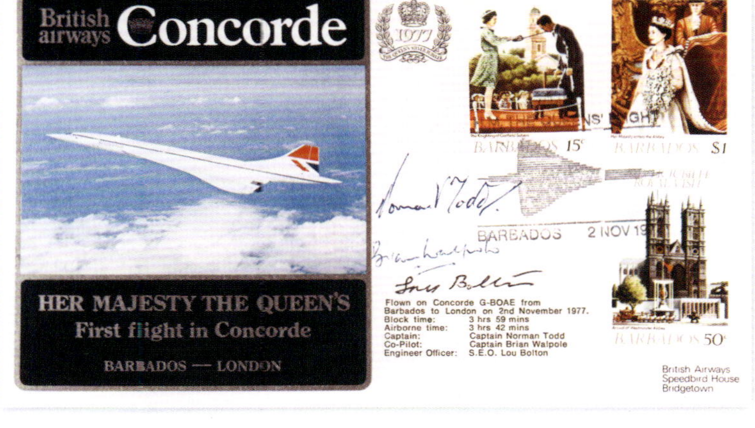

Commemorative covers from Concorde, signed by the captains who flew the aircraft.

- 21 January 1976: First scheduled commercial service London–Bahrain.

- 2 November 1977: Her Majesty the Queen's first flight in Concorde, Barbados–London, in the year of the Queen's Silver Jubilee.

- 22 November 1977: First scheduled commercial London–New York service.

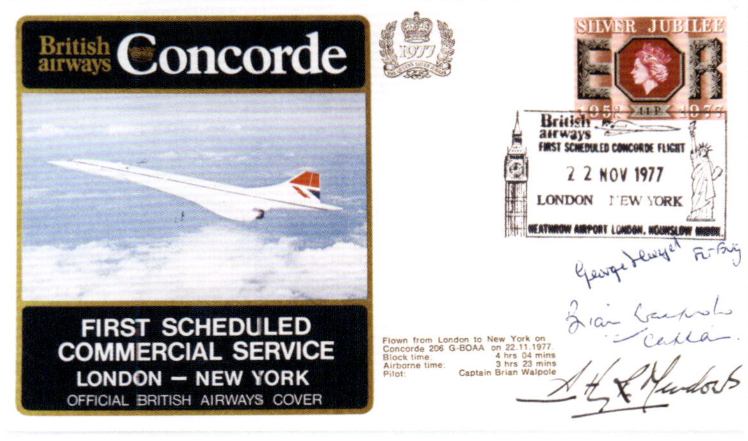

'One of life's great adventures has disappeared and the world is a poorer place. The Concorde was a magical fairy tale, proof of what man could achieve.'

Don Black, lyricist

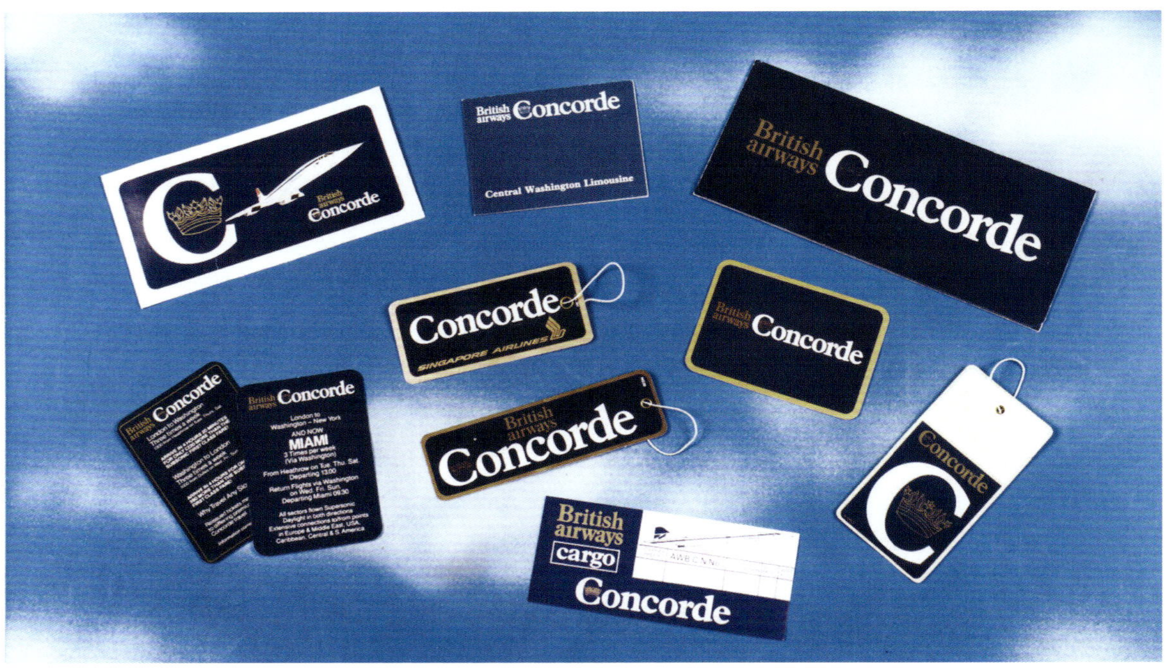

Ticketing, baggage tags and a timetable in the original Concorde crown logo, as well as a various selection of promotional gifts, all from 1976.

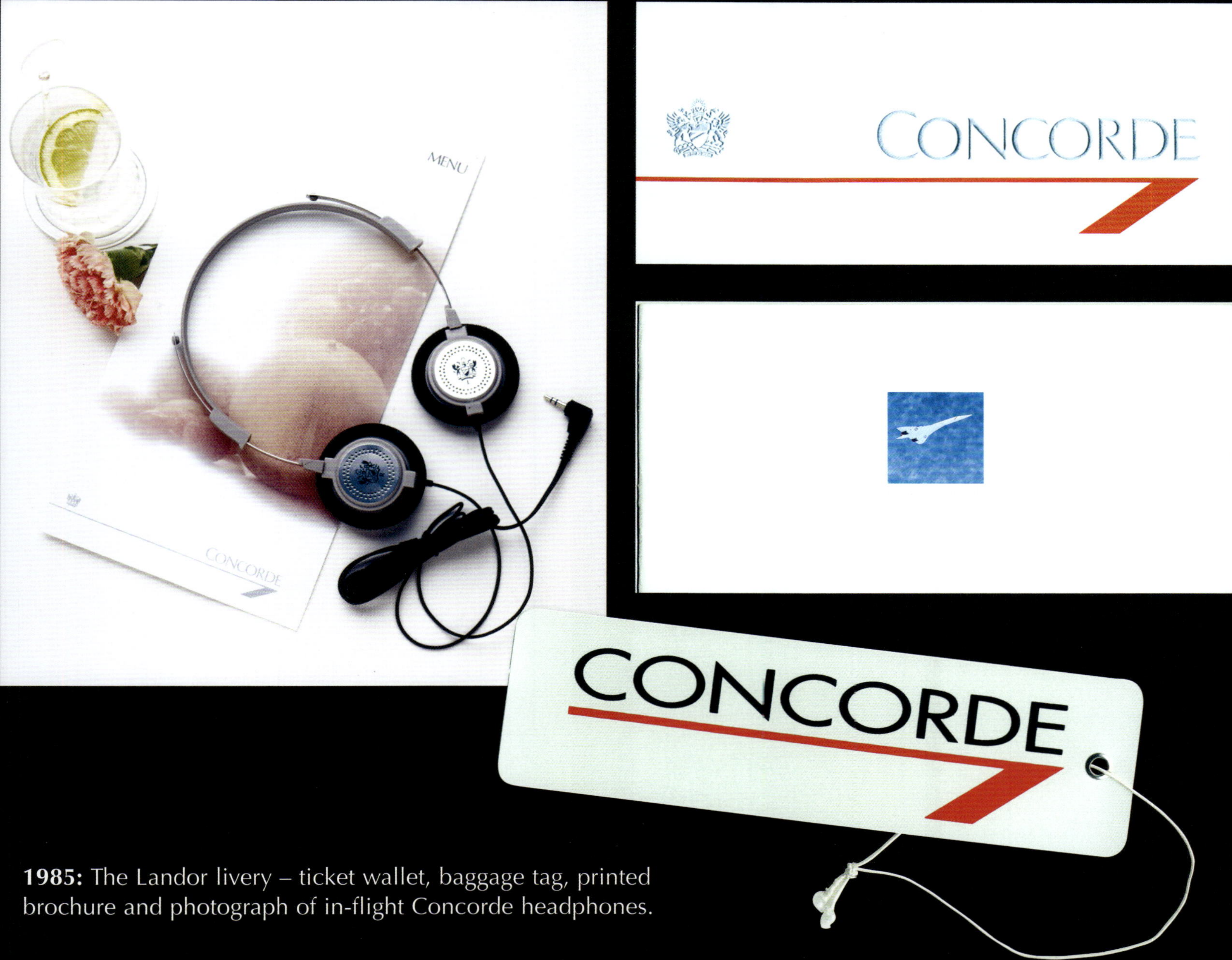

1985: The Landor livery – ticket wallet, baggage tag, printed brochure and photograph of in-flight Concorde headphones.

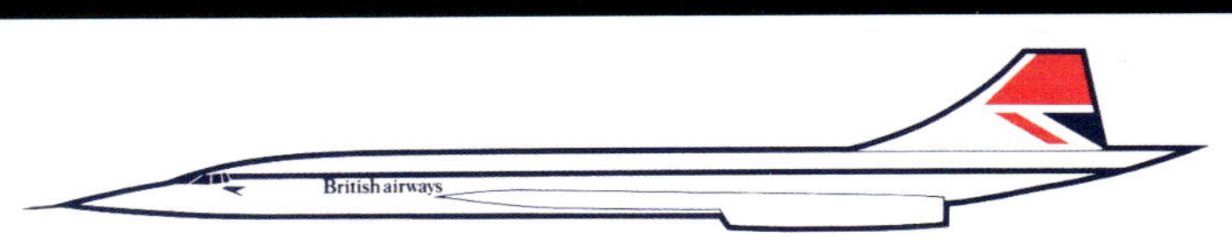

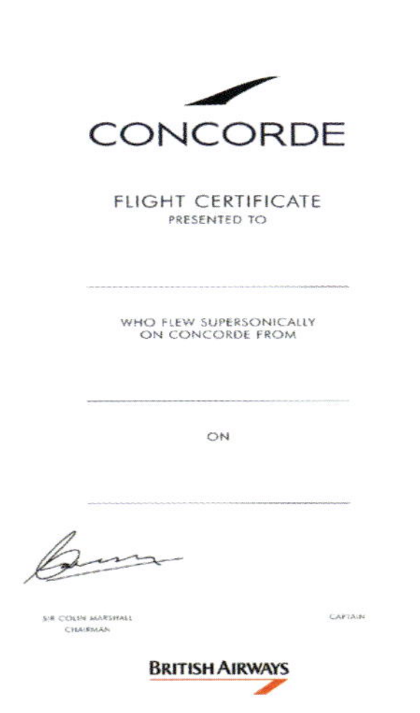

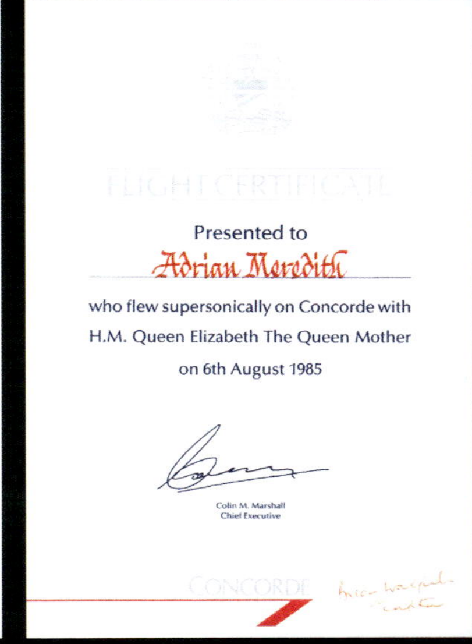

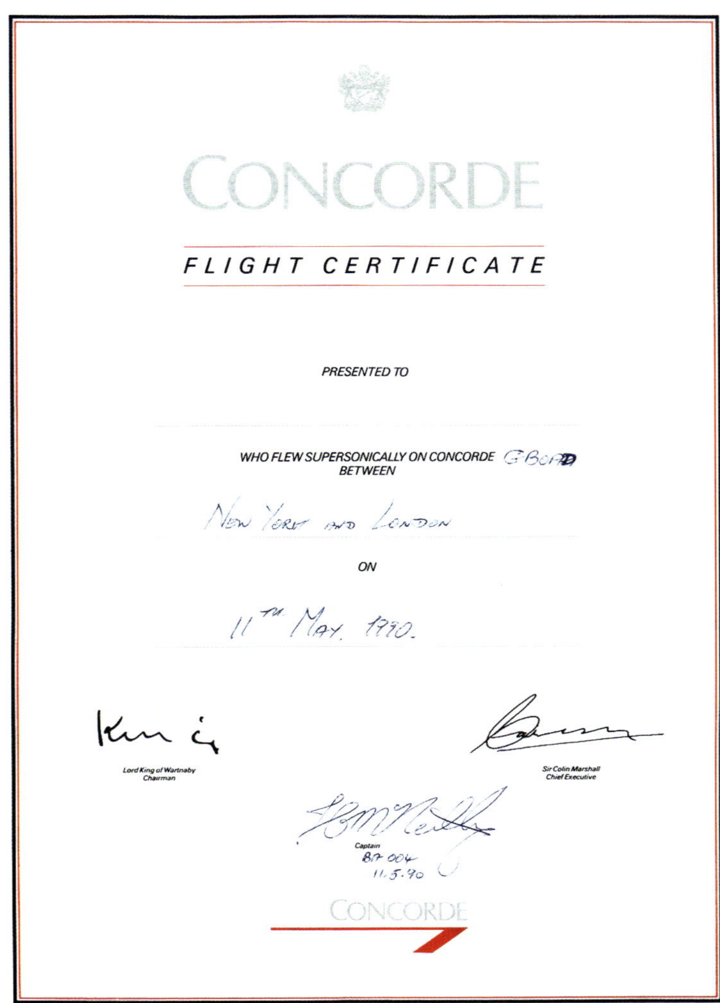

Every passenger that flew Concorde supersonically received a flight certificate that was signed by the flight crew. Here we can see a selection of different liveries. Every time the livery was changed, all marketing material was also changed.

'There's nothing quite like sitting on Concorde when you're taking off and they put on the full thrusters. It's the best thing on earth.'

Jodie Kidd, model

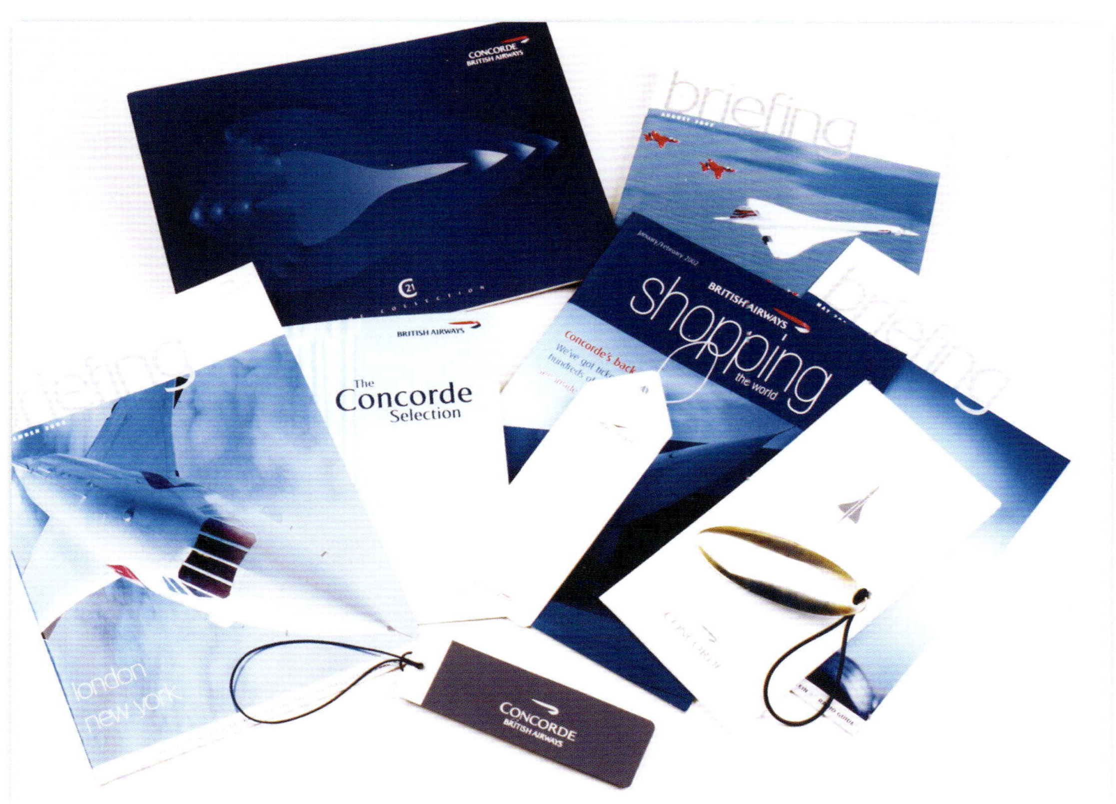

A selection of ticket wallets, baggage labels and in-flight printed material in the last Concorde livery designed by Newell and Sorrell, showing the new Speed Marque logo.

Aperitifs and Cocktails

Sweet and Dry Vermouth
Campari Soda
Americano . Negroni
Medium Dry Sherry
Dry Martini . Gin . Vodka
Bloody Mary . Old Fashioned . Manhattan
Sours – *Whisky . Gin . Brandy*
Gin Fizz

Highballs – *Whisky . Brandy . Gin . Rum*

Champagne Cocktail

Spirits

Whisky – *Scotch . Bourbon . Rye*
Gin
Vodka

Beers

Ale . Lager

Selection of Soft Drinks

Wines

Champagne
Laurent—Perrier Grand Siécle
*Presented in a bottle of unique shape used in time of the reign of Louis
XIV of France, this classic blend of three selected vintages of Champagne
epitomizes perfection. The Champagnes are selected from the best growths
of the Montagne des Reims and the Côtes des Blancs.*
or
Heidsieck Dry Monopole 1975
*Chosen from one of the leading Champagne houses of Reims, the 1975
vintage offer lightness and dryness with a pleasing firm bouquet.*

Red Bordeaux
Château Gruaud Larose 1974—St. Julien
*Château Gruaud Larose is a leading second growth château of St. Julien
and with 77 hectares under vine is one of the largest vineyards in this
commune. It constantly produces a powerful wine of great character and
longevity. The 1974 vintage is of good colour and character.*
or
Château la Dominique—St. Emilion
*This vineyard of some 44 acres under vine lies immediately to the north of
the famous Château Cheval Blanc and borders this classic estate.
The 1973 vintage is soft, well balanced with good colour.*

White Burgundy
Chablis
*The 1979 vintage of this famous white burgundy fully reflects its renowned
qualities of crispness, dryness and elegance.*
or
Meursault 1980
*This white wine from the Cote de Beaune is dry, fruity, smooth and
possesses a very subtle aroma. The 1980 vintage is light and delicate.*

Liqueurs

Remy Martin Napoleon Brandy
Drambuie . Cointreau . Coffee Liqueur
Fonseca Bin 27 Port

Jamaica Macanudo cigars

Aperitifs — Champagne

Canapés
Caviar, pâté de foie gras, parma ham and melon

Lunch
Déjeuner

Saumon fumé d'Ecosse
*Prime, new season Scotch smoked salmon with pinwheels of
buttered brown bread and a crown of lemon*

— ◦ —

Reléves assortis
*As a lighter alternative to the dishes featured below may we
suggest our classical selection of appetizing savouries which
include a crisp pastry case filled with sweetbreads à la financière,
glazed suprême of chicken, brochette of Cornish scallops with
scampi and bacon, salmon talmousse. Served with a light garnish of
mushrooms, asparagus spears and a cherry tomato*

Les trois filets
*Fillets of prime beef, lamb and veal, grilled to perfection and served
with cauliflower polonaise, buttered snow peas and cocotte potatoes*

Délice de turbot Aida
*Poached fillet of turbot served on a bed of spinach, coated with
creamy cheese and paprika sauce and glazed under the grill.
Served with cauliflower polonaise, buttered snow peas and
cocotte potatoes*

— ◦ —

Salade composée
Seasonal salad served with mustard flavoured vinaigrette dressing

— ◦ —

Choix de fromage
*A selection of French Coulommiers, English Stilton and
Cheddar cheese*

— ◦ —

Dessert
*Mango flavoured bavarois garnished with oranges and strawberries,
set on a bed of crushed raspberries*

— ◦ —

Café . Café sans caféine
*Coffee or caffeine free coffee, served with a selection of
home made chocolates*

One of the many Concorde menus from the '70s, and one of the very last menus from 2003. Concorde's sumptuous selections of the very highest-quality food and wines make for a tantalising, mouth-watering taste extravaganza.

Dinner

Canapés

Appetiser
Fresh prawn niçoise

Entrées
Roast guinea fowl and truffle stuffing, with
cep reduction and fondante potato

Lobster fish cakes with a light shellfish sauce

Grilled fillet of veal black pepper and lemon
butter, sauté mushroom mix, roasted sea salt
potatoes

Grilled artichoke, plum tomatoes, buffalo
Mozzarella on mixed leaves with balsamic
dressing

Dessert

Chocolate silk on a nut brittle base with
chocolate sauce

OR

Cheese

Old Pequlier, Mesulline goats cheese,
unpasteurised Dunshyre Blue

Selection of bread rolls

Coffee, decaffeinated coffee, a selection of tea
with chocolates

As an alternative to the full menu, we are
pleased to offer a selection of freshly made
sandwiches including smoked salmon and
cucumber on wholemeal bread, shaved
pastrami and American mustard on
wholemeal bread, Chicken salad on malted
bread

Wine List

We have great pleasure in introducing the
Concorde Cellar – a unique collection of fine
wines, specially chosen for Concorde,
from some of the finest vineyards in the
classic regions of Bordeaux, Burgundy and
Champagne. These wines have been
purchased, sometimes several years in
advance, and cellared until ready to drink.
The wines listed here are just a part of the
entire cellar – the rest are gently maturing at
the châteaux for your enjoyment
in years to come.

British Airways wine consultant is Jancis
Robinson M.W. Her expertise and knowledge
have been instrumental in the continued
success of the Concorde Cellar.

As a journalist Jancis Robinson was the first
person outside the wine trade to qualify as a
Master of Wine. Now she is the wine writer
for the Financial Times, editor of the Oxford
Companion to Wine and, with Hugh Johnson,
co-author of the latest edition of the World
Atlas of Wine. She is also an award winning
television presenter and today writes
principally for her website jancisrobinson.com
which has subscribers in more
than 25 countries.

This list features the wines chosen from the
Concorde Cellar for today's flight.

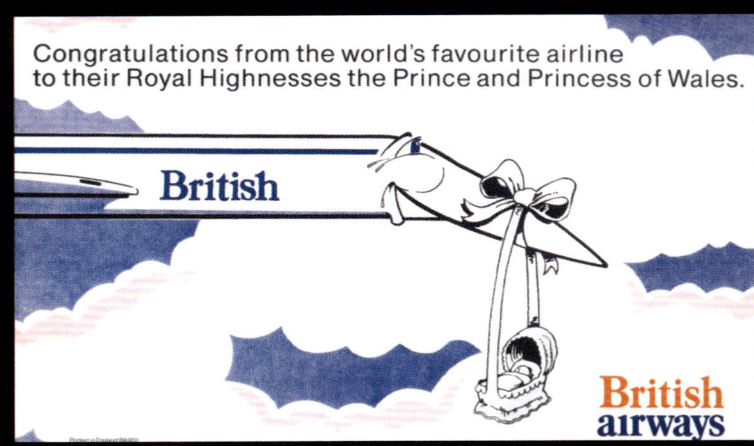

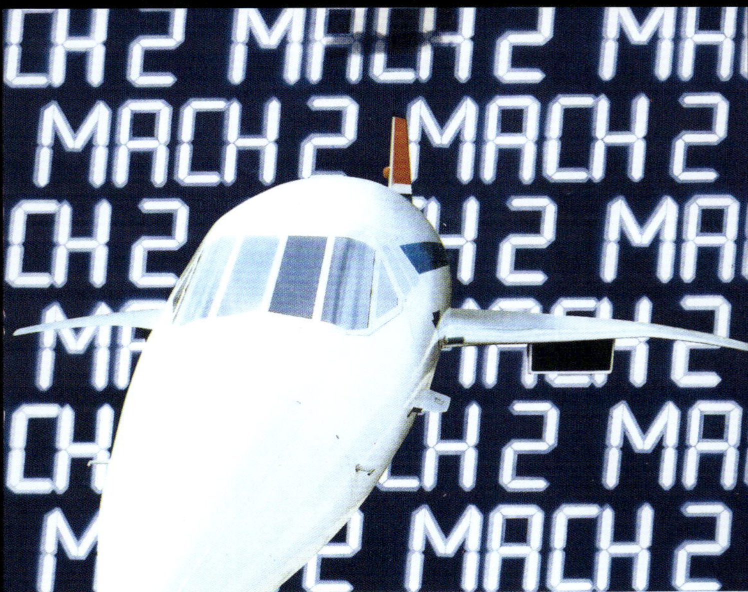

A commemorative plaque congratulating their Royal Highnesses the Prince and Princess of Wales on the birth of Prince Harry, who was born on 15 September 1984. This plaque was placed on the Concorde ticket desk.

In the 1970s advertising agency Foote Cone & Belding would make requests to produce images for advertising and media productions. This campaign shows one of my head-on shots of Concorde and advertising girl Roz Hanby, at the time the face of BA.

Opposite: PR studio shot with gloves, hat and scarf.

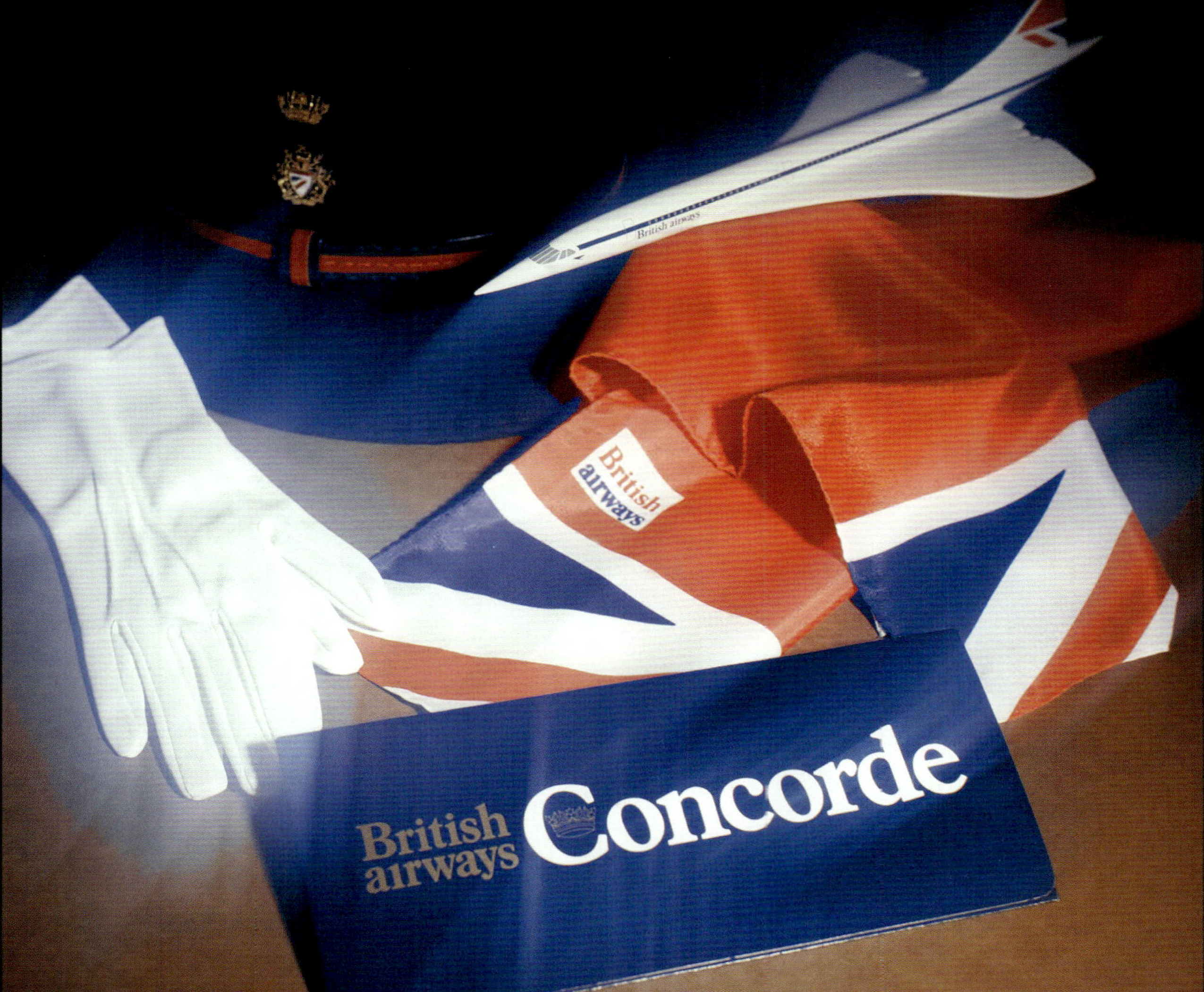
British airways
British airways
British airways Concorde

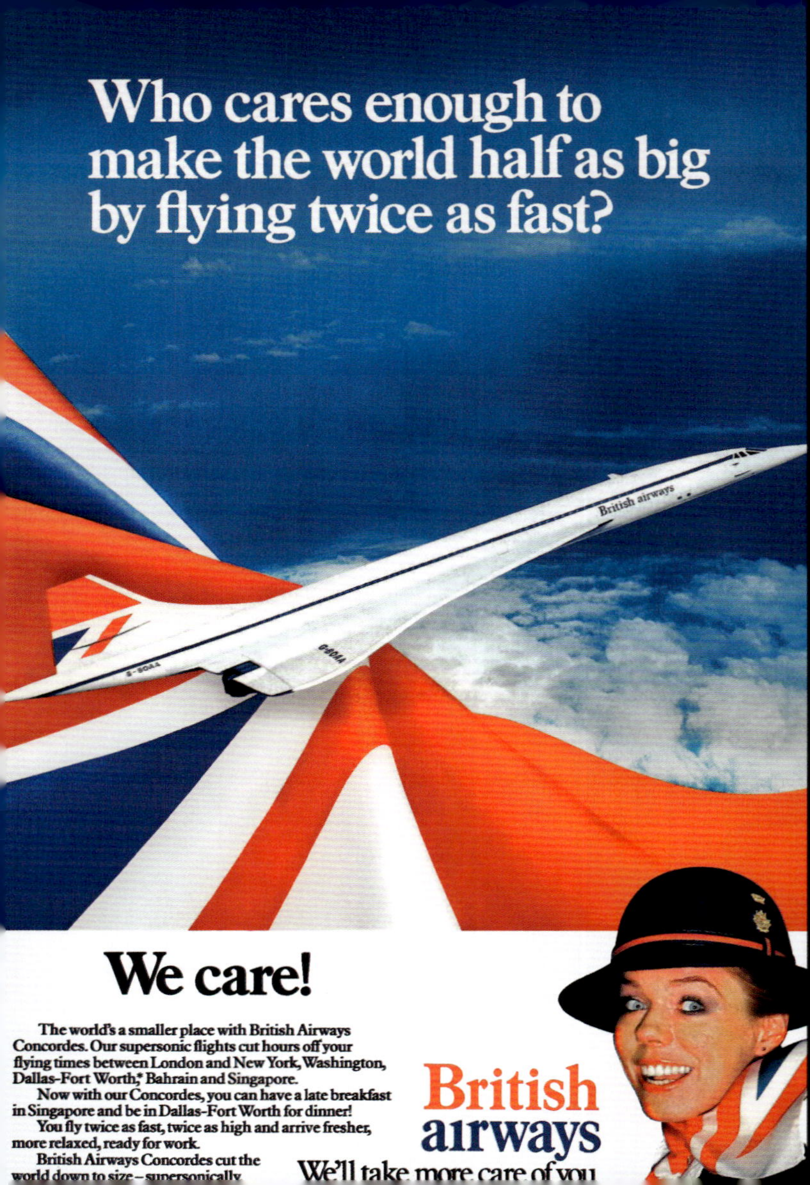

Who cares enough to make the world half as big by flying twice as fast?

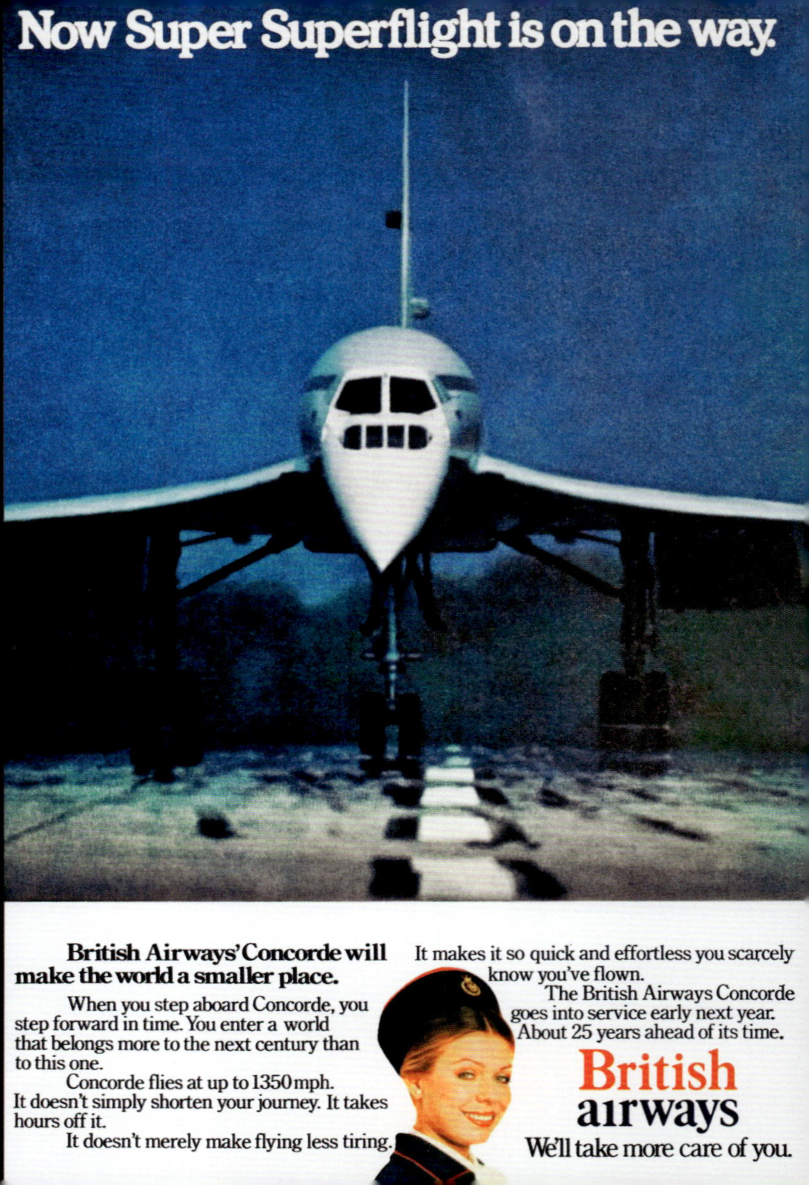

Now Super Superflight is on the way.

British airways

We care!

The world's a smaller place with British Airways Concordes. Our supersonic flights cut hours off your flying times between London and New York, Washington, Dallas-Fort Worth,* Bahrain and Singapore.

Now with our Concordes, you can have a late breakfast in Singapore and be in Dallas-Fort Worth for dinner!

You fly twice as fast, twice as high and arrive fresher, more relaxed, ready for work.

British Airways Concordes cut the world down to size – supersonically.

British airways

We'll take more care of you.

British Airways' Concorde will make the world a smaller place.

When you step aboard Concorde, you step forward in time. You enter a world that belongs more to the next century than to this one.

Concorde flies at up to 1350 mph. It doesn't simply shorten your journey. It takes hours off it.

It doesn't merely make flying less tiring.

It makes it so quick and effortless you scarcely know you've flown.

The British Airways Concorde goes into service early next year. About 25 years ahead of its time.

British airways

We'll take more care of you.

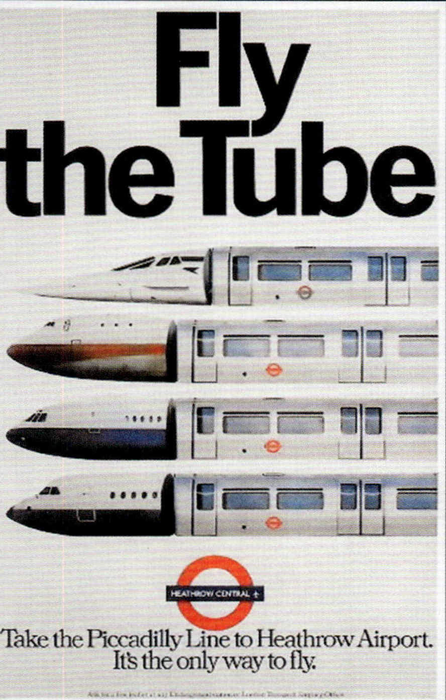

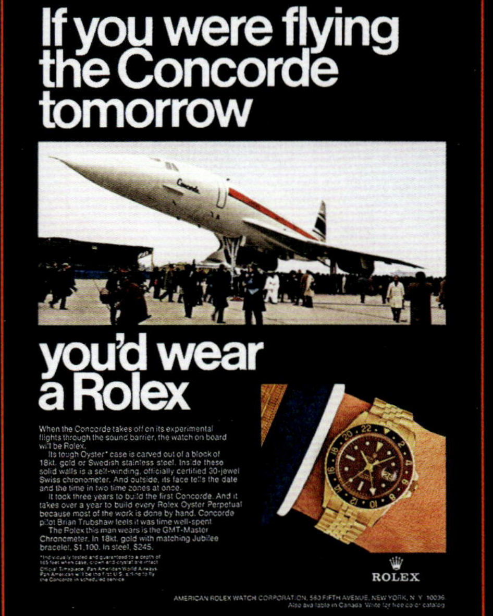

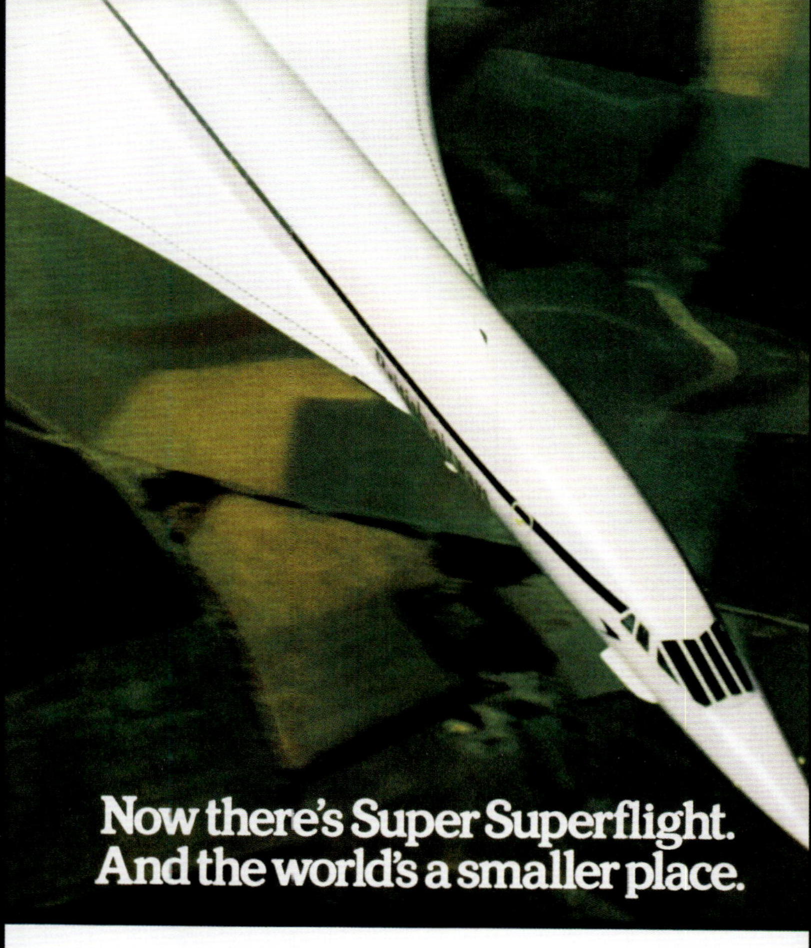

Now there's Super Superflight. And the world's a smaller place.

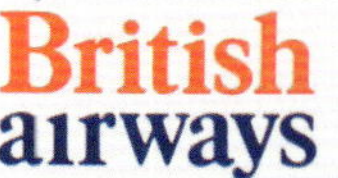

British Airways' Concorde goes into service.

When you step aboard Concorde, you step forward in time. You enter a world that belongs more to the next century than to this one.

Concorde cruises at 1350 mph. It doesn't simply shorten your journey. It takes hours off it.

It doesn't merely make flying less tiring. It makes it so quick and effortless you scarcely know you've flown.

The British Airways Concorde is now going into service. About 25 years ahead of its time.

British airways

We'll take more care of you

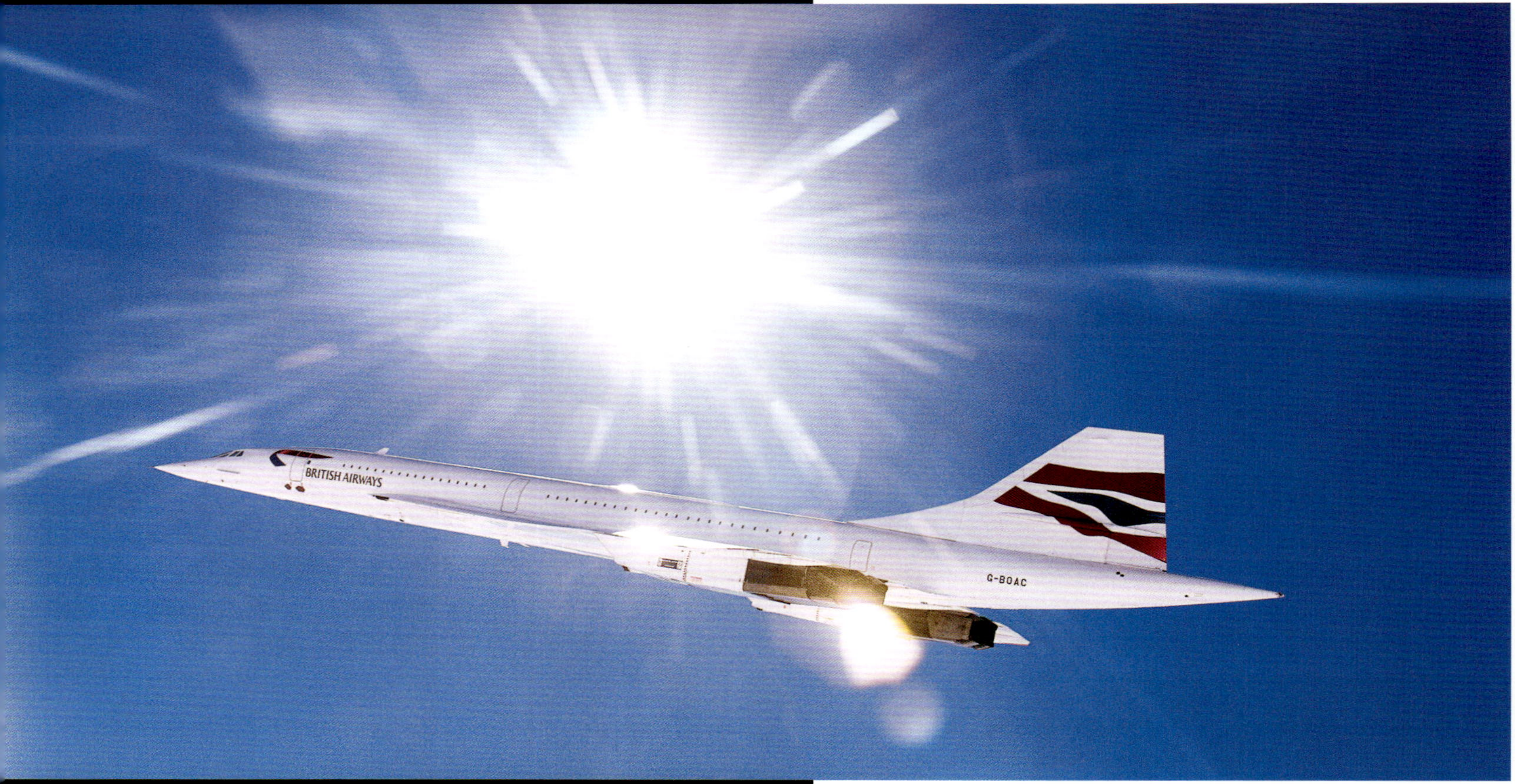

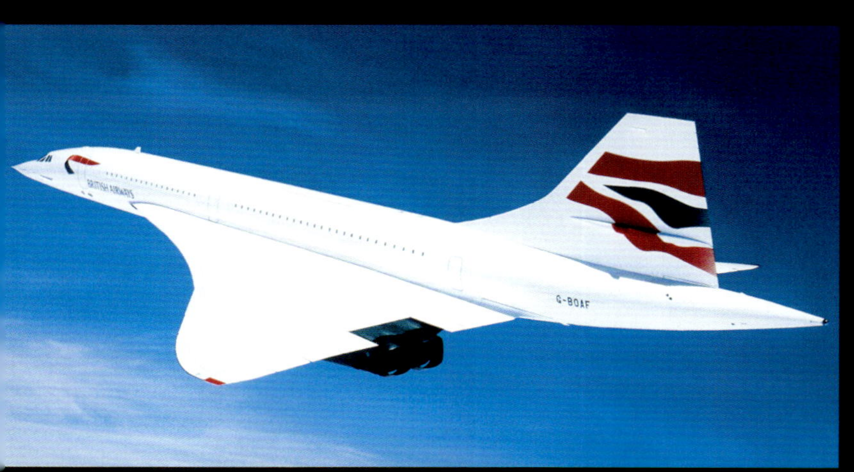

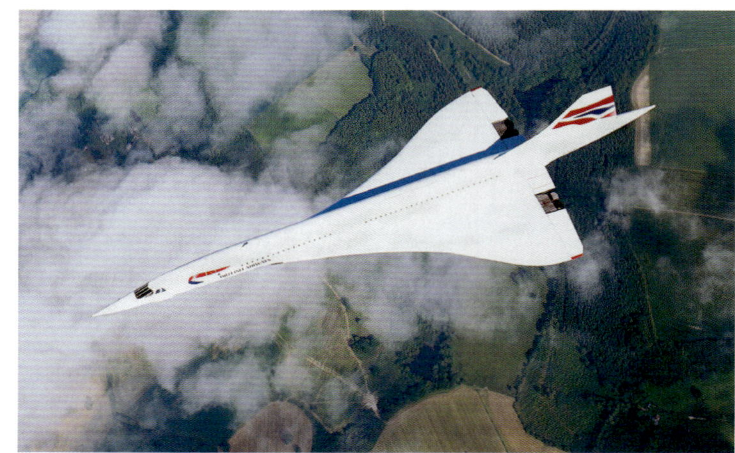

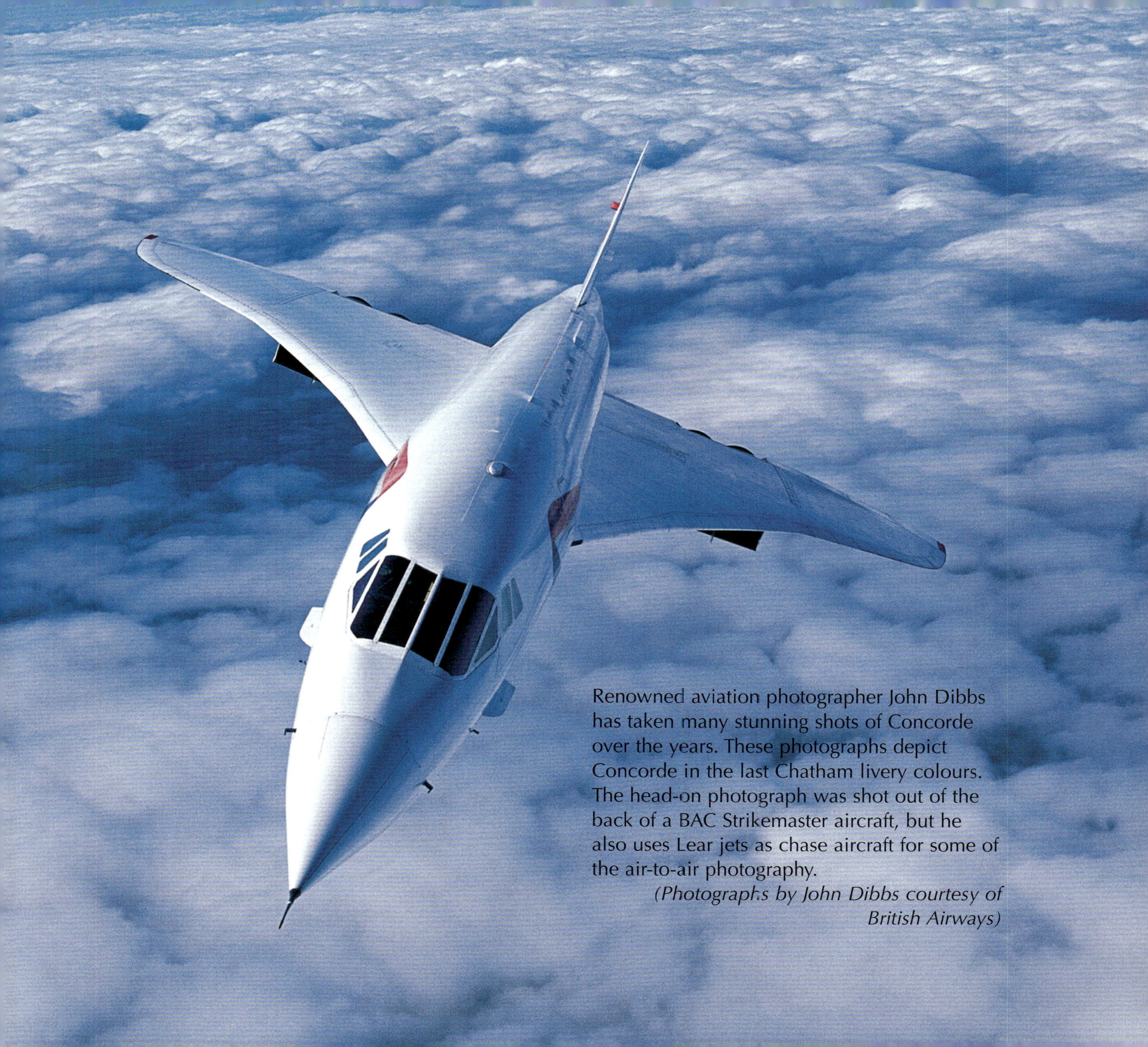

Renowned aviation photographer John Dibbs
has taken many stunning shots of Concorde
over the years. These photographs depict
Concorde in the last Chatham livery colours.
The head-on photograph was shot out of the
back of a BAC Strikemaster aircraft, but he
also uses Lear jets as chase aircraft for some of
the air-to-air photography.

*(Photographs by John Dibbs courtesy of
British Airways)*

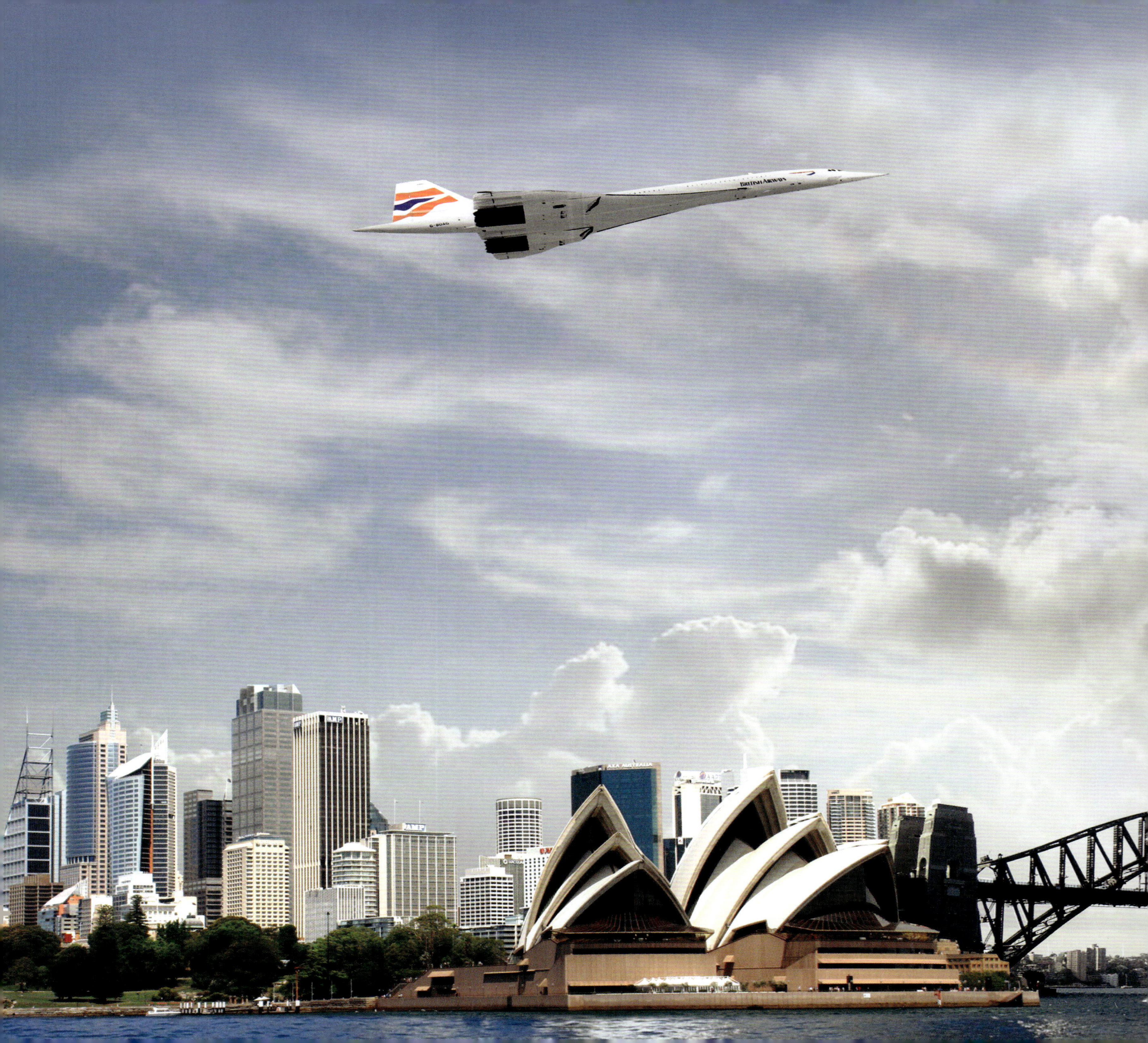

BRITISH AIRWAYS
G-BOAG

Champagne Flights

In 1981 British Airways started chartering the aircraft to a selection of different charter companies. This enabled people to experience Concorde to various destinations across the world. You could pay as little as £300 for a ninety-minute supersonic trip around the Bay of Biscay, or as much as £35,000 for a round-the-world trip visiting such places as Moscow, Cairo, Dubai, Hong Kong, Sidney, Beijing, Honolulu, Mexico City, Barbados and New York. Sometimes these trips would take up to twenty-eight days. Listed below are some of the most popular Concorde supersonic champagne flights:

- Christmas for Lapland. The Artic Circle and Reindeer Sleigh Rides
- Greenland, Icebergs in the Midnight Sun
- New Year's Eve Ball in Vienna
- Nice to see the Monaco Grand Prix
- Paris, returning on the *Orient Express*
- Jordan, to see Petra, the Rose Red City
- Cairo, the Pyramids, the Land of the Pharaohs
- New York, returning on the *QE2*
- Vienna, and the Vienna Opera House
- Delhi, India, the Taj Mahal
- Rio De Janeiro
- Istanbul, the City of Two Continents, The Magic Carpet Ride

A special thank you to my son Scott Meredith who has taken my Concorde photographs and put together a selection of tribute images to show Concorde flying over various iconic landmarks across the world. Being a graphic designer, Scott has also helped me immensely over the past five years to re-digitalise my original Concorde photographic works.

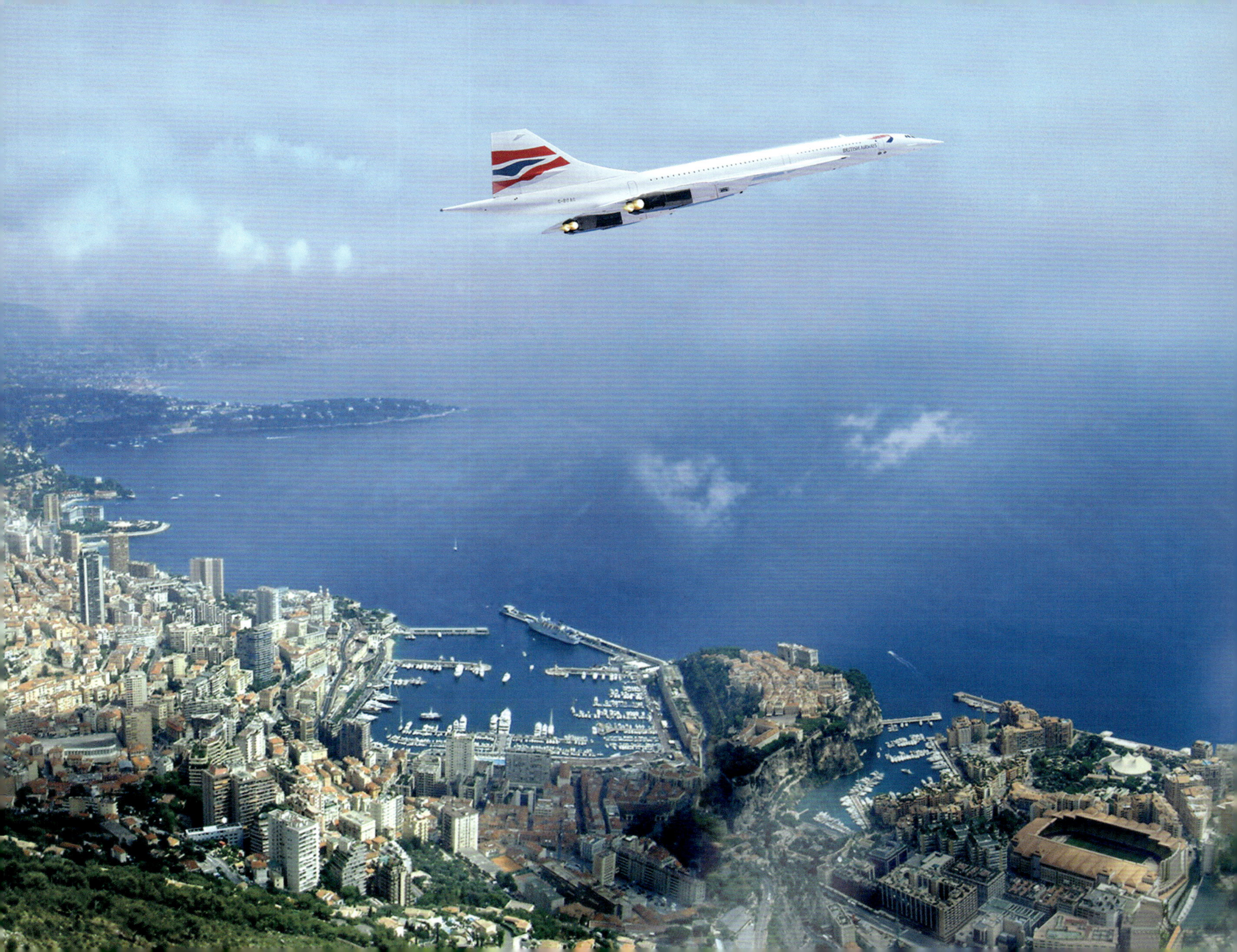

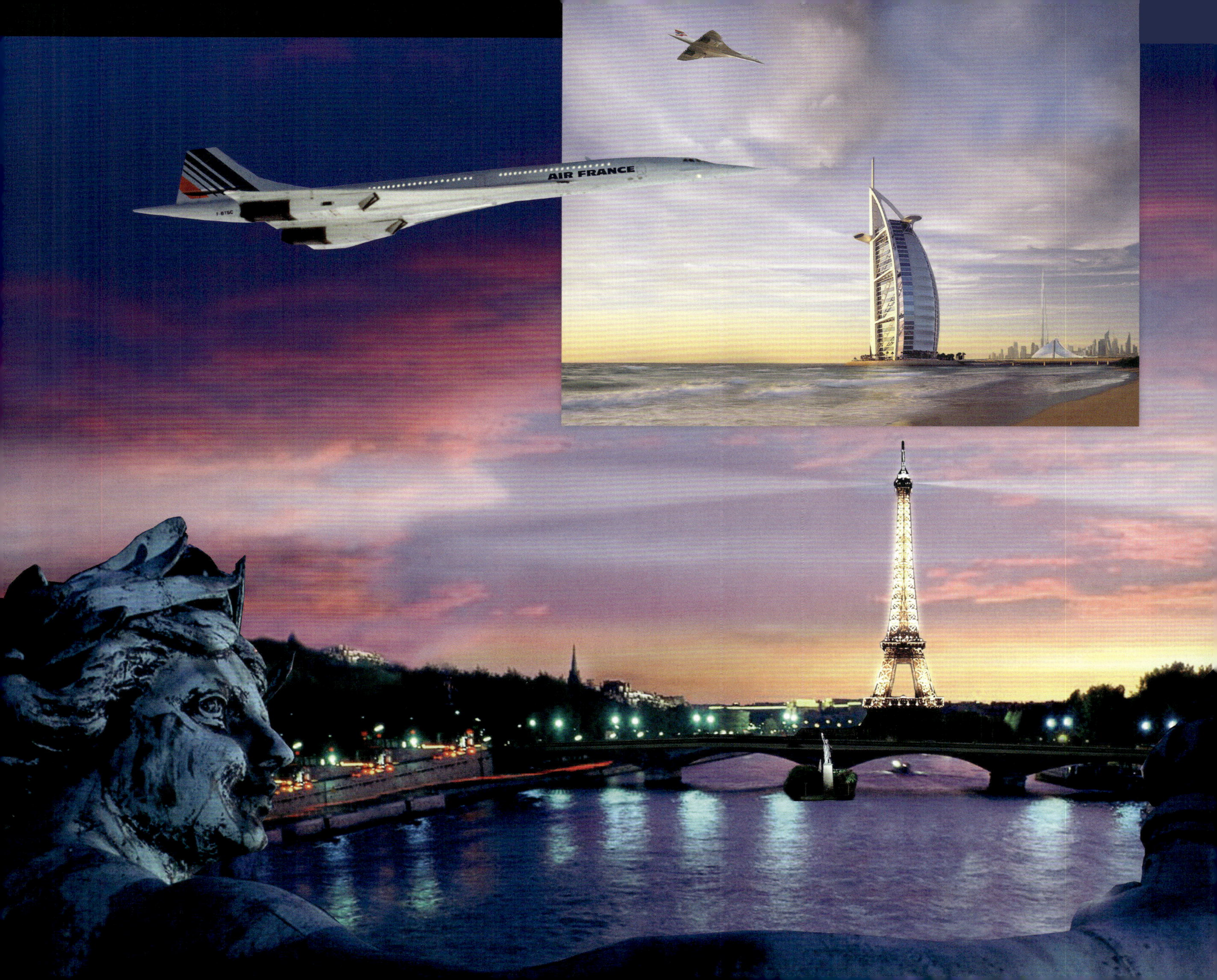
AIR FRANCE

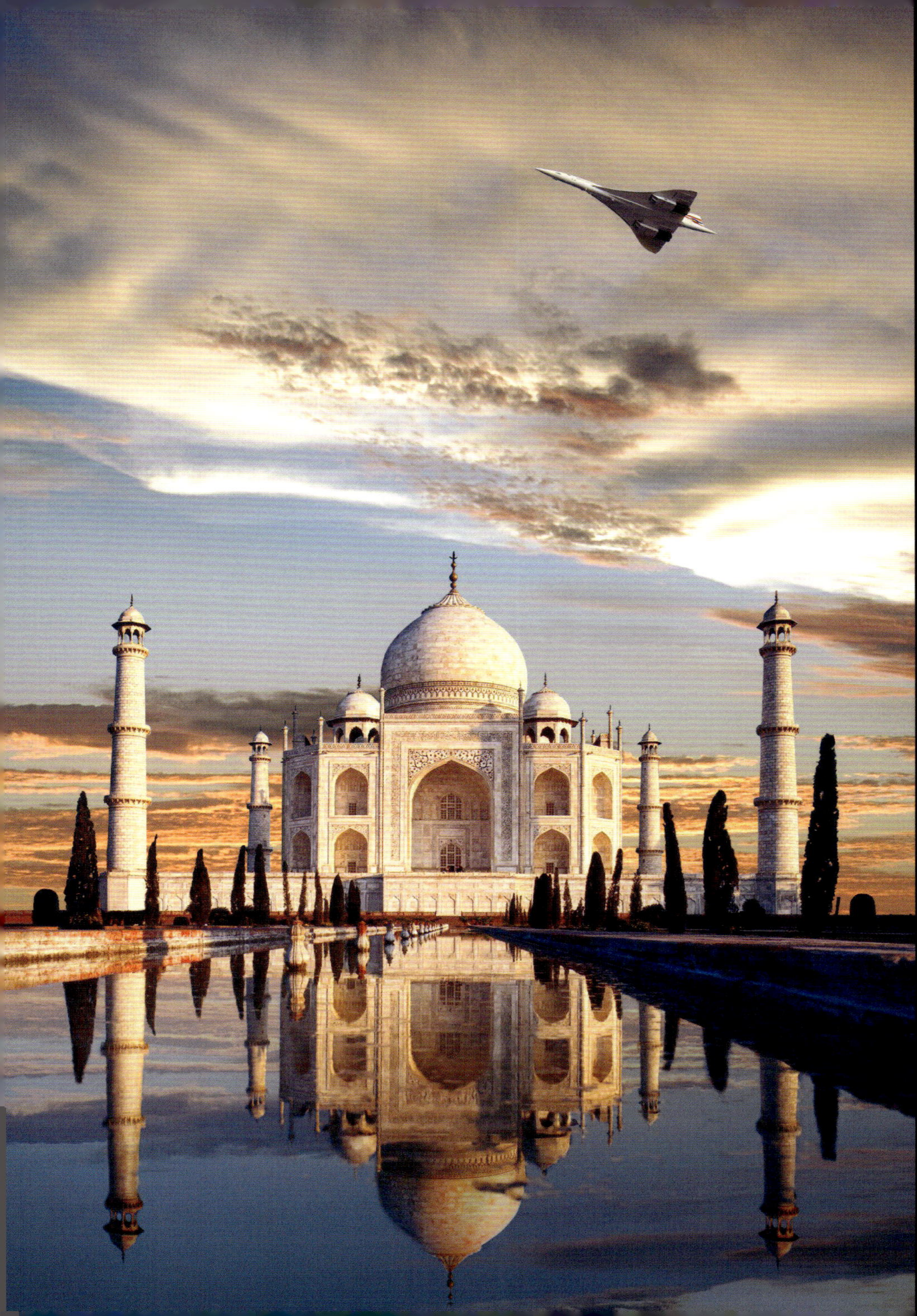

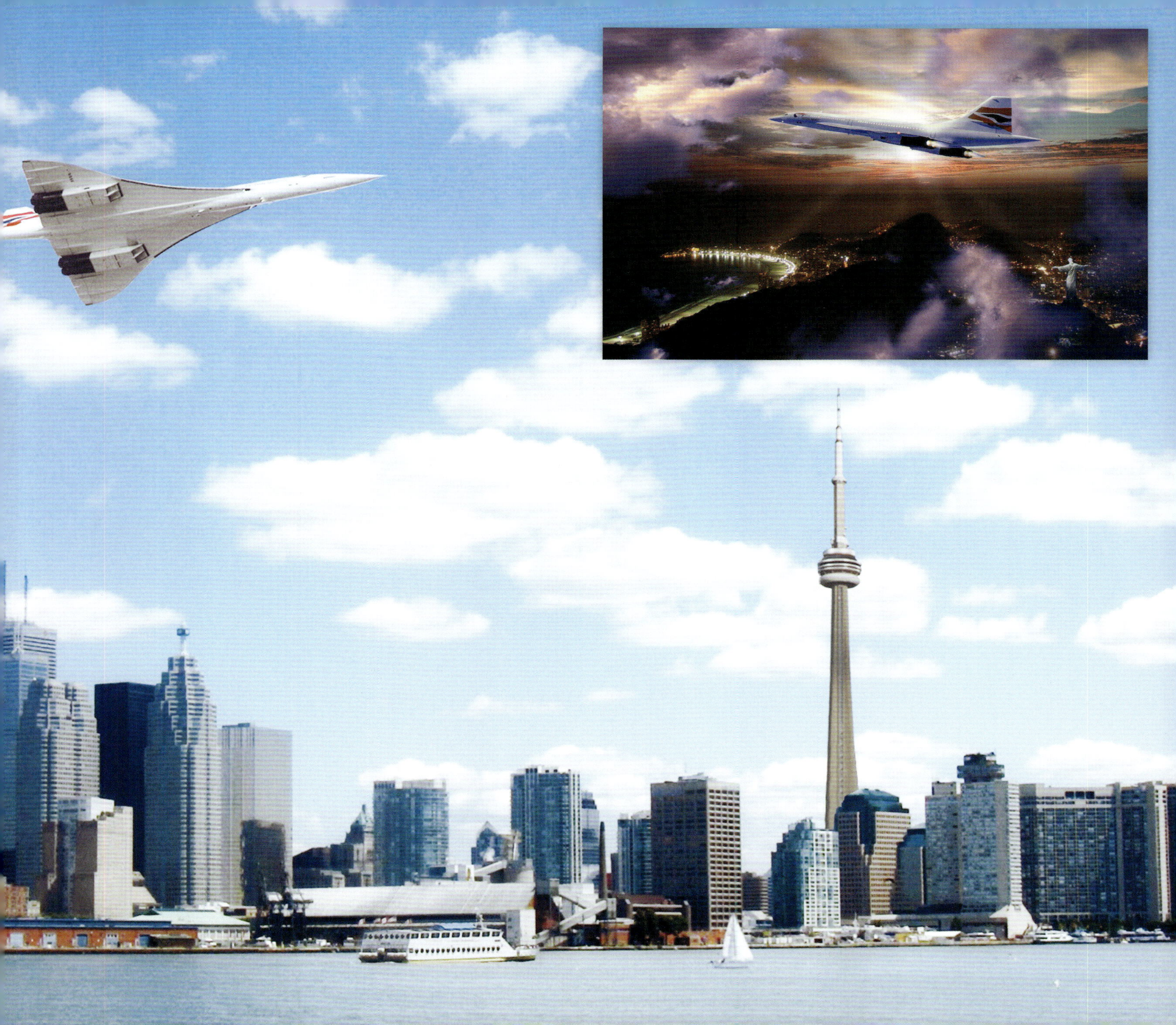

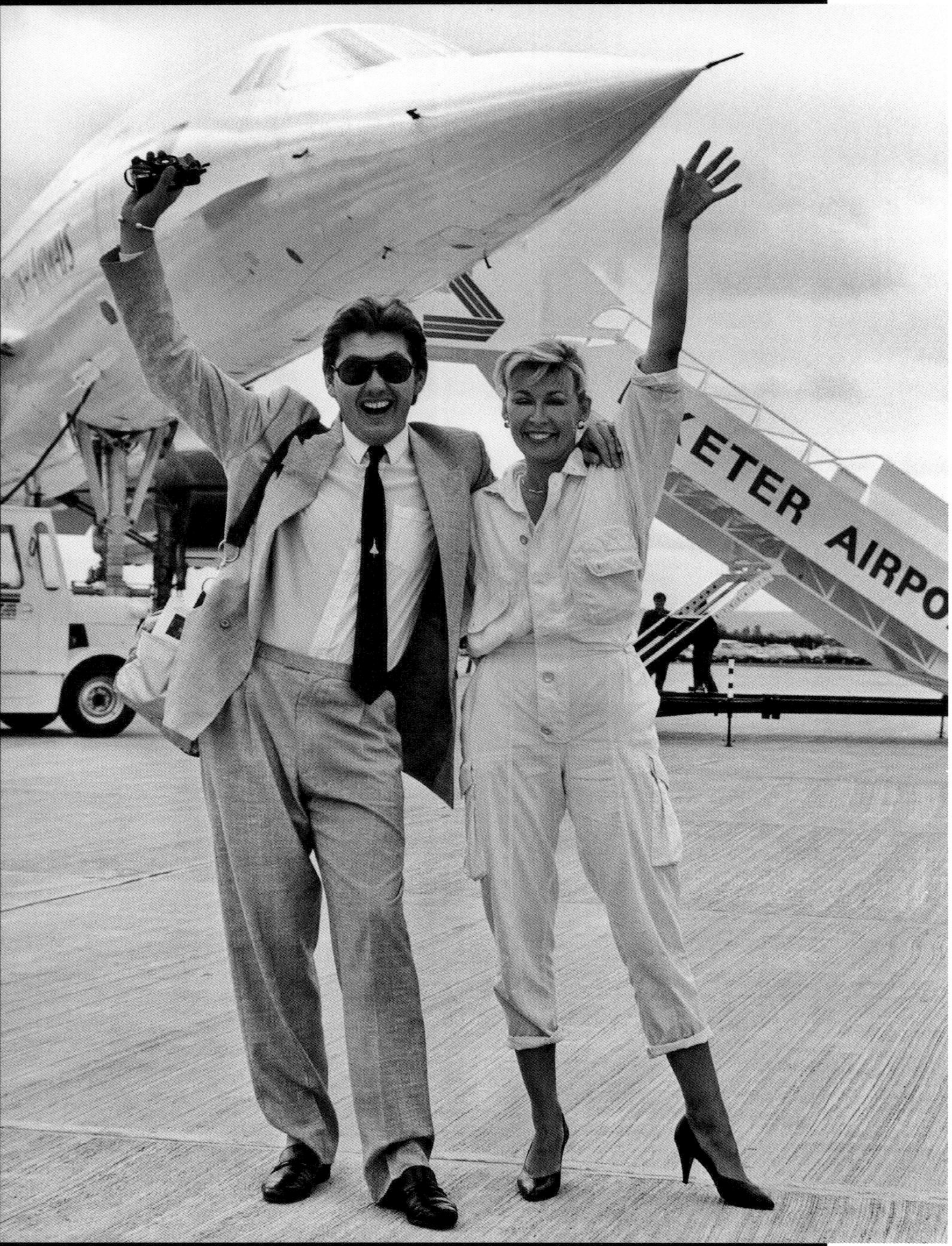

My wife Angela and I treated ourselves to a day out on a Concorde charter. After flying around the Bay of Biscay, we landed at Exeter Airport and then returned home to Heathrow, an experience we will never forget.

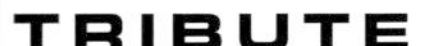

FINAL BOW

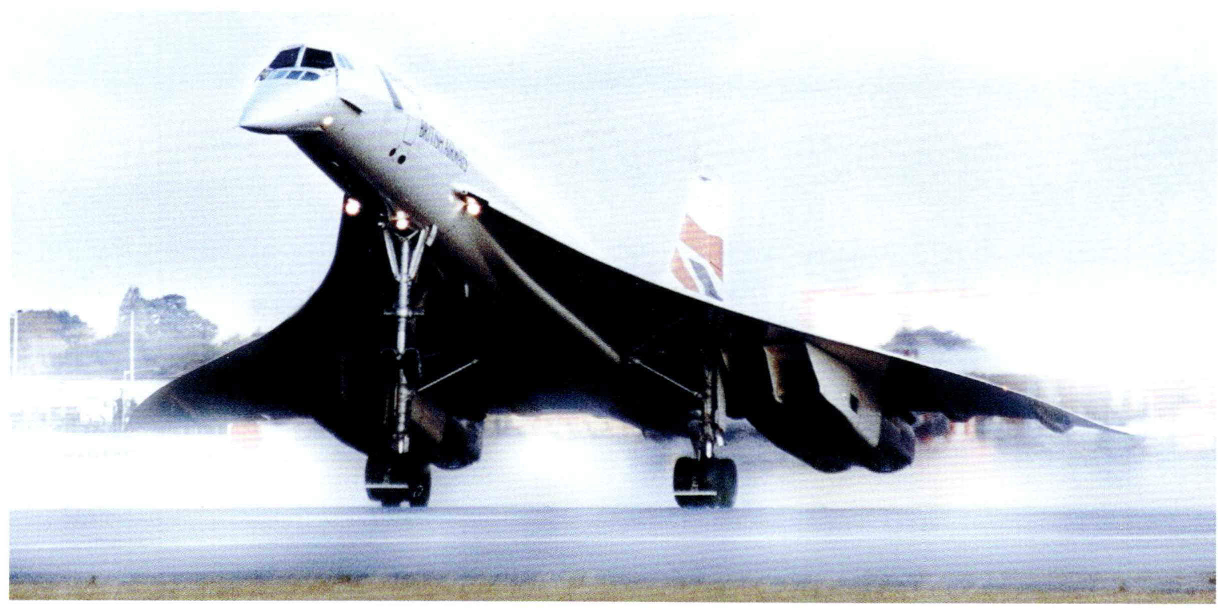

The supersonic legend takes her final bow and says her goodbyes to the world.

April 2003: shocking news, the message that no one wanted to hear – Concorde's retirement was announced. Amongst the 2.5 million passengers that she had carried, royalty, world leaders and some of the biggest names in the entertainment industry had all graced her seats. Within a week of the announcement all the seats on her final flights had been booked; there was a huge demand from the public in recognition of the passing of an iconic symbol. Concorde is the only commercial supersonic aircraft that has ever flown – now a symbol of advanced technical engineering was coming to an end. Concorde gave twenty-seven years of commercial service to the public and helped to raise millions of pounds for deserving charities.

(Photograph by Mike Bromfield/Adrian Meredith)

At the time there were rumours that Richard Branson had approached British Airways and offered £1 for each of the Concordes. As a publicity stunt, and without British Airways' knowledge, Virgin Airways draped the tail of the BA model of Concorde which stood on the main roundabout at the entrance to London Heathrow with the Virgin banner, and put Virgin Territory hoarding in front of it. Richard Branson dressed up as a buccaneer, with a stuffed parrot on his shoulder. BA was not amused.

Last three commercial landings at Heathrow, 24 October 2003

The first final flight to land at Heathrow, at 4.01 p.m., was from Edinburgh with 100 British Airways staff on board. G-BOAE was flown by Captain Les Brodie, Senior First Officer Paul Griffin and Senior Flight Engineer Trevor Norcott. It felt like a fantastic celebration party for many of the BA staff, rather than a final flight. It was better than the historic celebration when Concorde conquered the Atlantic supersonic, and Concorde arrived to bagpipes and a cheering crowd.

The next flight to land at 4.03 p.m., G-BOAF, was piloted by Captain Paul Douglas, Senior First Officer Mark Jealous and Senior Flight Engineer Pete Carrigan. This was a special VIP trip around the Bay of Biscay.

The historic flight BA 002 from New York's JFK was the very final commercial landing of Concorde. Piloted by Captain Mike Bannister, he summed up the mood when he expressed to the passengers: 'Concorde was a fabulous legend, born from dreams, built from vision, operated with pride by a family that loved her.' The landing time was 4.06 p.m. VIPs were amongst the passengers. The actress Joan Collins, a frequent flyer, said, 'The first time I ever flew Concorde, it was a bit like a white knuckle ride.' Other celebrities on board, such as Sir David Frost, had clocked up more than 500 trips. Also on the flight was supermodel Jodie Kidd, Christie Brinkley, ballerina Darcey Bussell, *Top Gear* presenter Jeremy Clarkson, and Formula One boss Bernie Ecclestone.

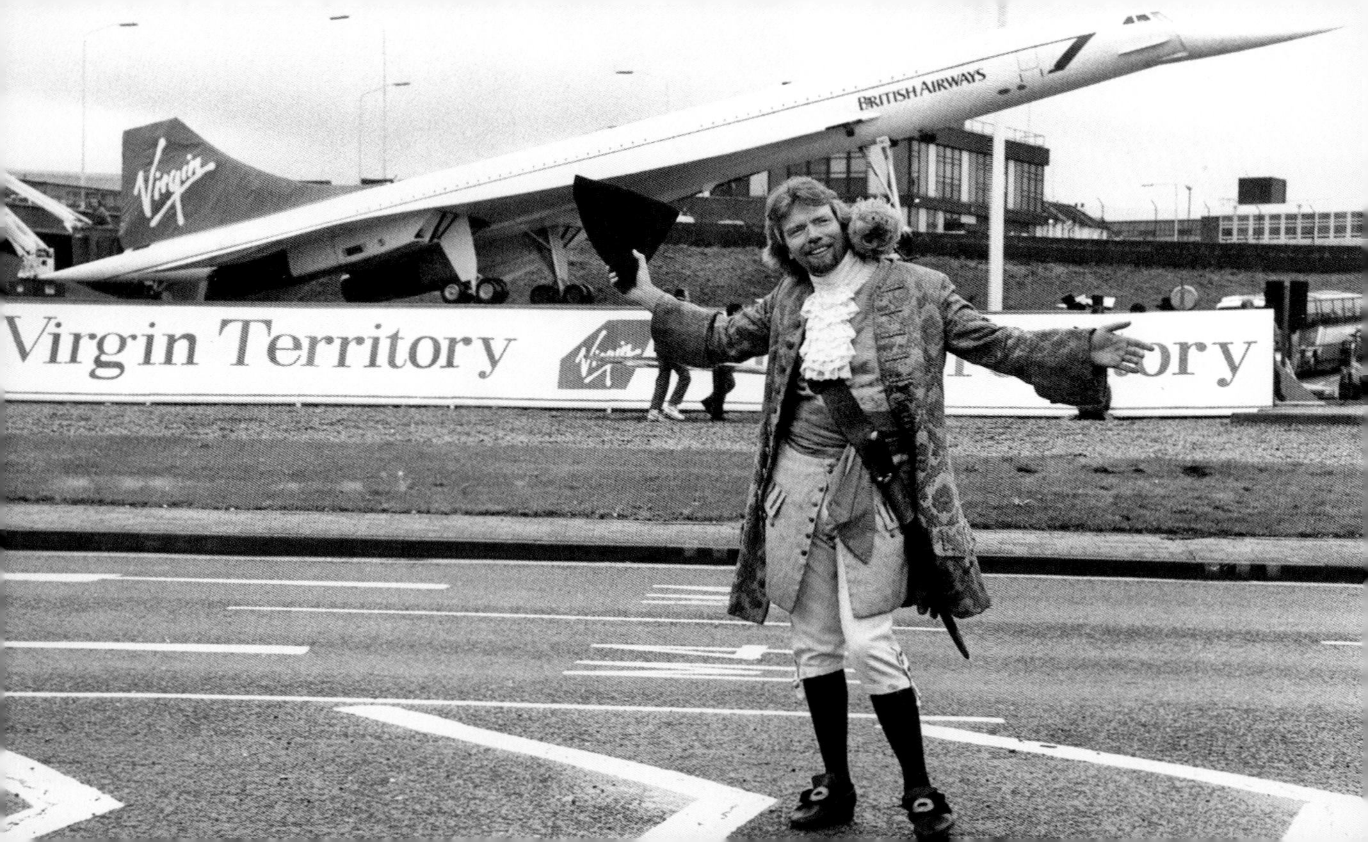

Virgin
BRITISH AIRWAYS
Virgin Territory

Concorde's final commercial take-off and last flight over London

Concorde G-BOAG BA 002's last commercial take-off from London Heathrow Airport to New York on 23 October 2003. Concorde measures 204ft in length and stretched between 6in and 10in during flight due to the heating of the airframe. Concorde took off at 250mph and cruised at around 1,350mph – more than twice the speed of sound – at an altitude of up to 60,000ft, with nine crew and 100 passengers. Concorde flew 50,000 flights and carried 2.5 million passengers, and 1 million bottles of champagne were consumed.

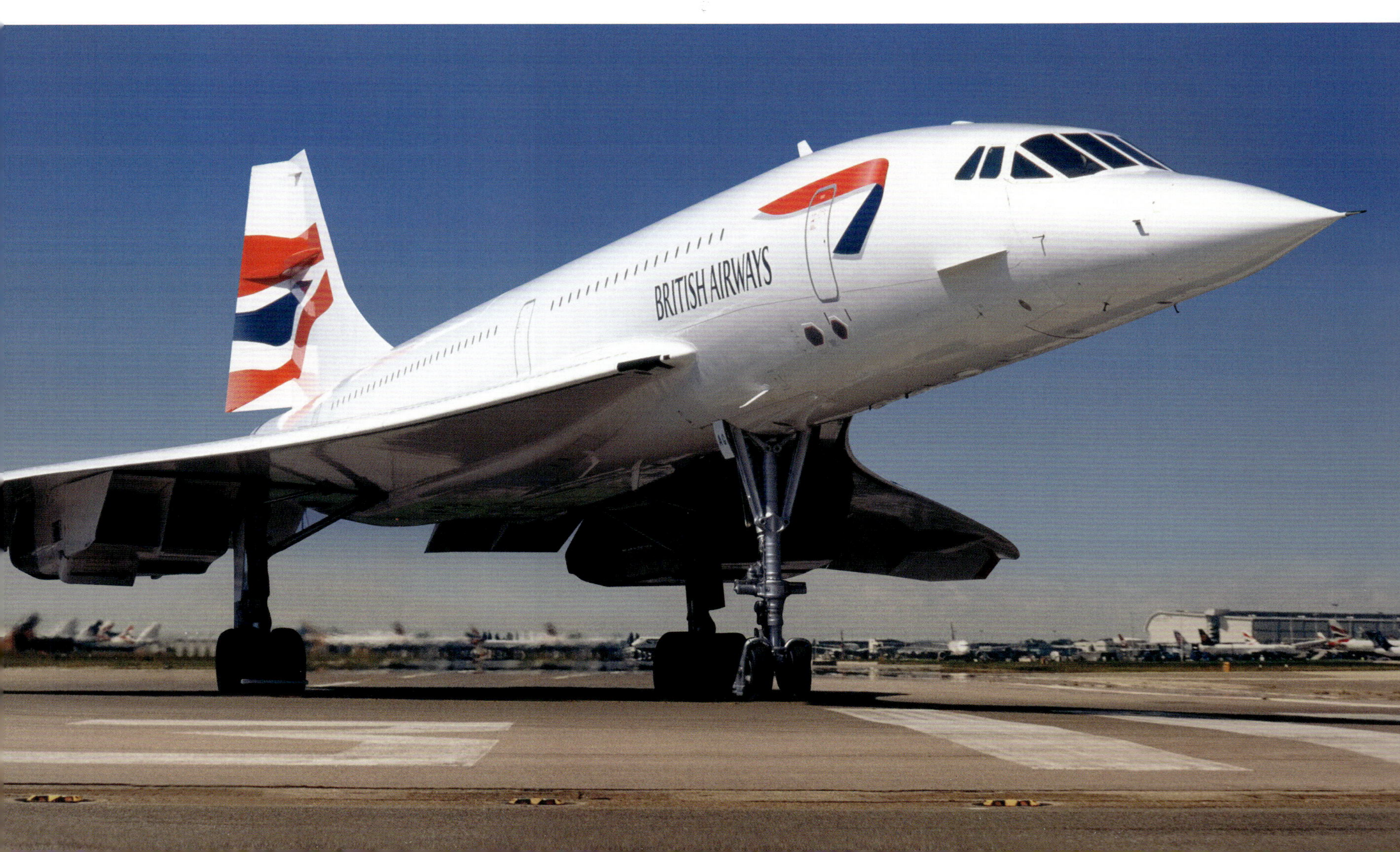

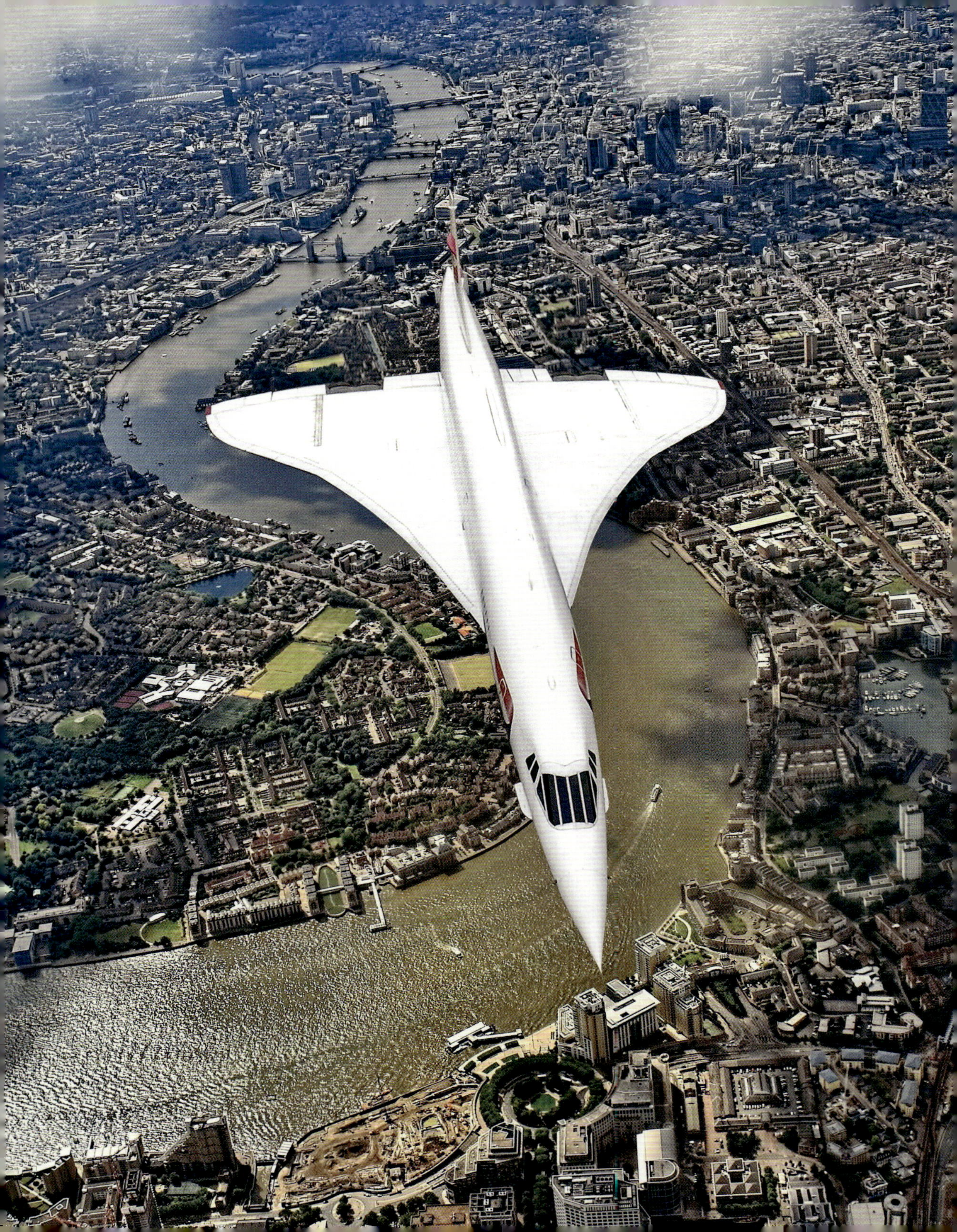

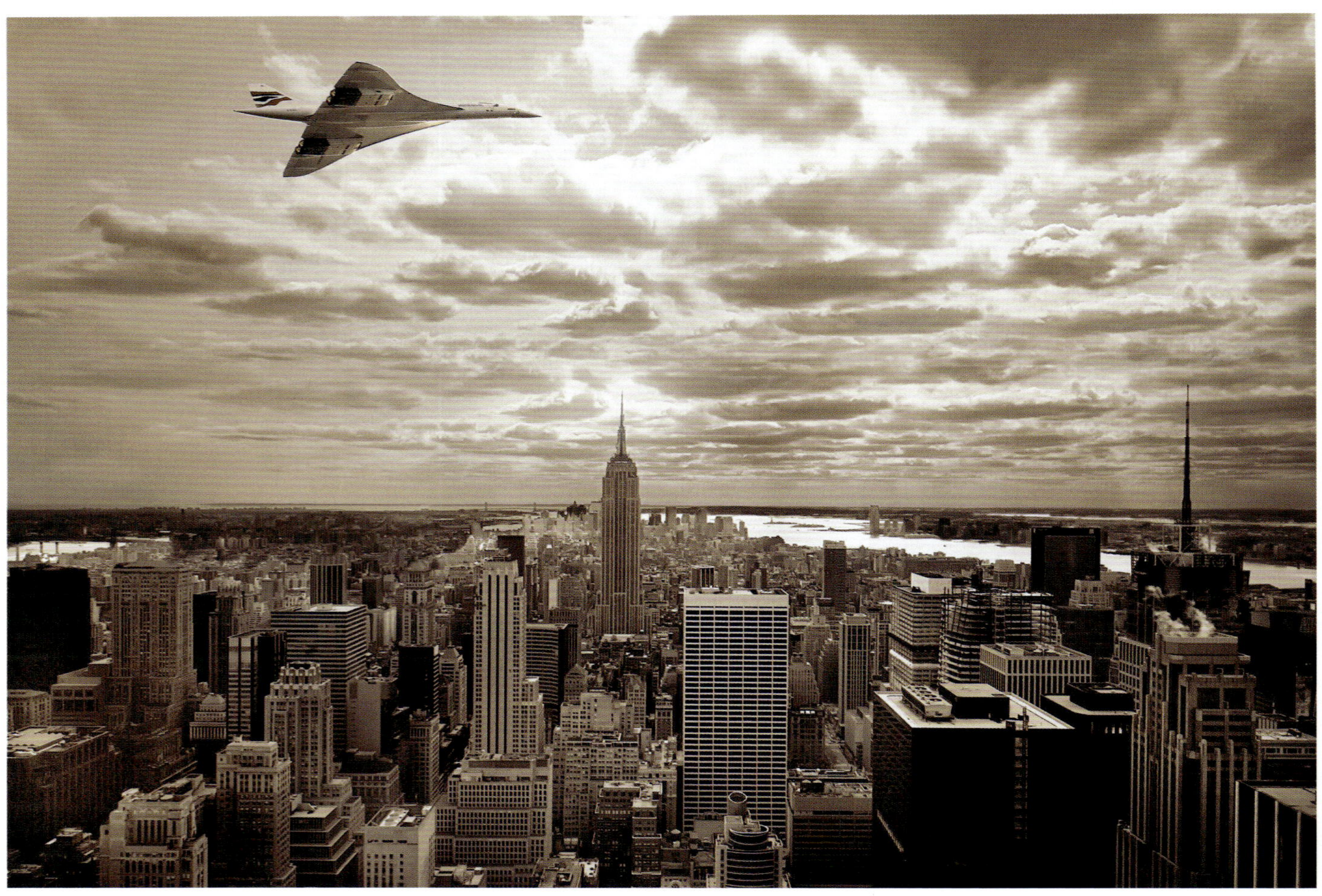

Last flight of Concorde over New York

British Airways Concorde Flight BA 001 made her first flight from London to New York on 22 November 1977, and from then a typical London to New York crossing would take a little less than three and a half hours. Concorde G-BOAG BA 002's final commercial flight from New York to London was on 24 October 2003, flown by Chief Concorde Pilot Mike Bannister, with SFO Jonathan Napier at the helm. I shot this photograph from the Chrysler Building with a very moody skyline.

Last flight to Seattle via New York

On 3 November 2003 British Airways Concorde G-BOAG headed to New York. Here she is flying out from New York for the last time en route to Seattle. This shot was taken late that evening from the other side of Brooklyn Bridge.

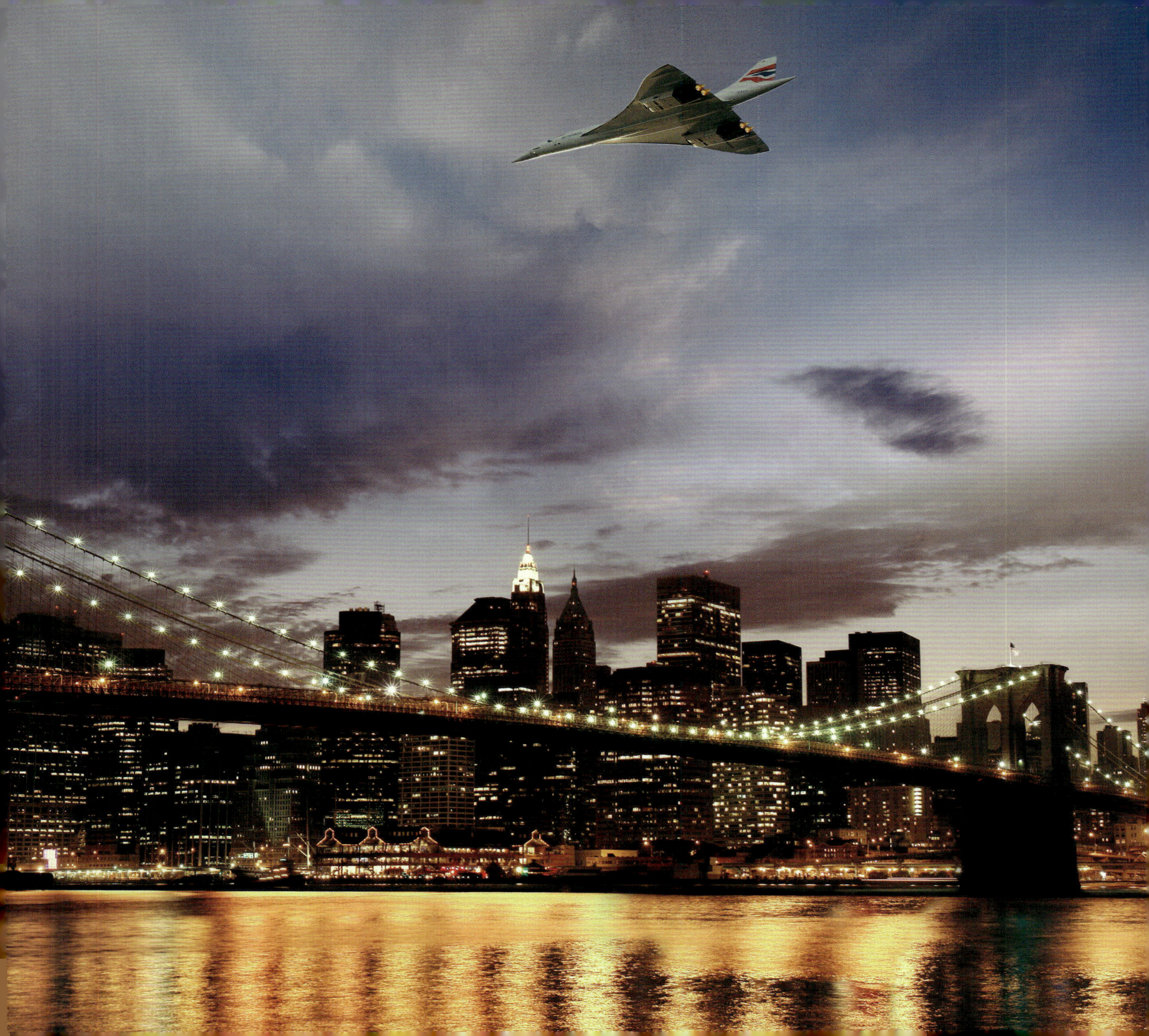

The last day line-up of three Concordes, 24 October 2003

On this historic day all three Concordes landed simultaneously, the flight crew opened the cockpit windows and waved the Union Jack flags, saluting a farewell to Heathrow. It was a bright, sunny day, and the sun was setting when all three Concordes were lined up for this historic photograph.

(Photograph by Mike Bromfield/Adrian Meredith)

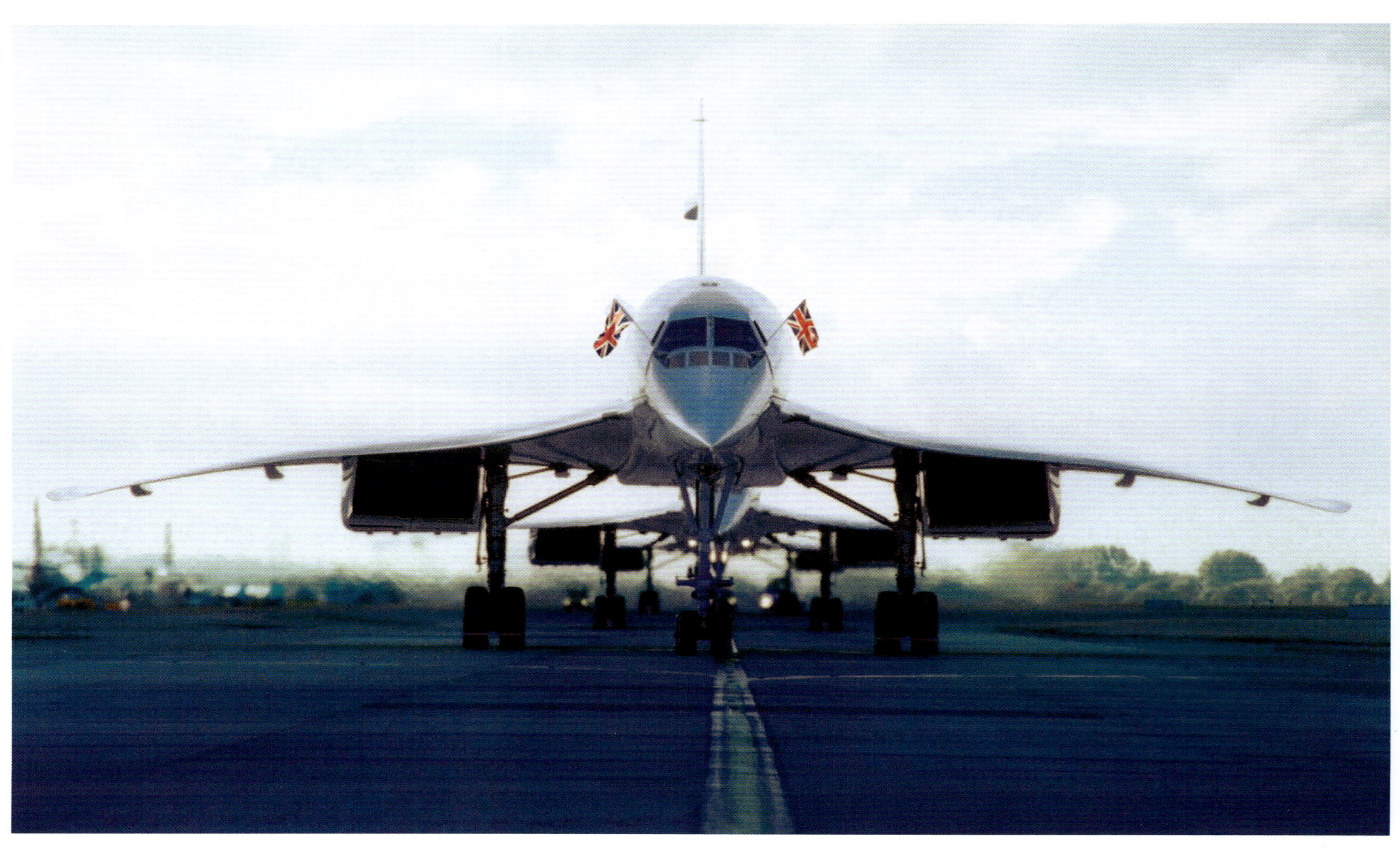

A supersonic turnout

Airport workers and British Airways staff turn out in their thousands to say goodbye. The crews were on a real high and the air was filled with mixed emotions.
(Photograph by Mike Bromfield/Adrian Meredith)

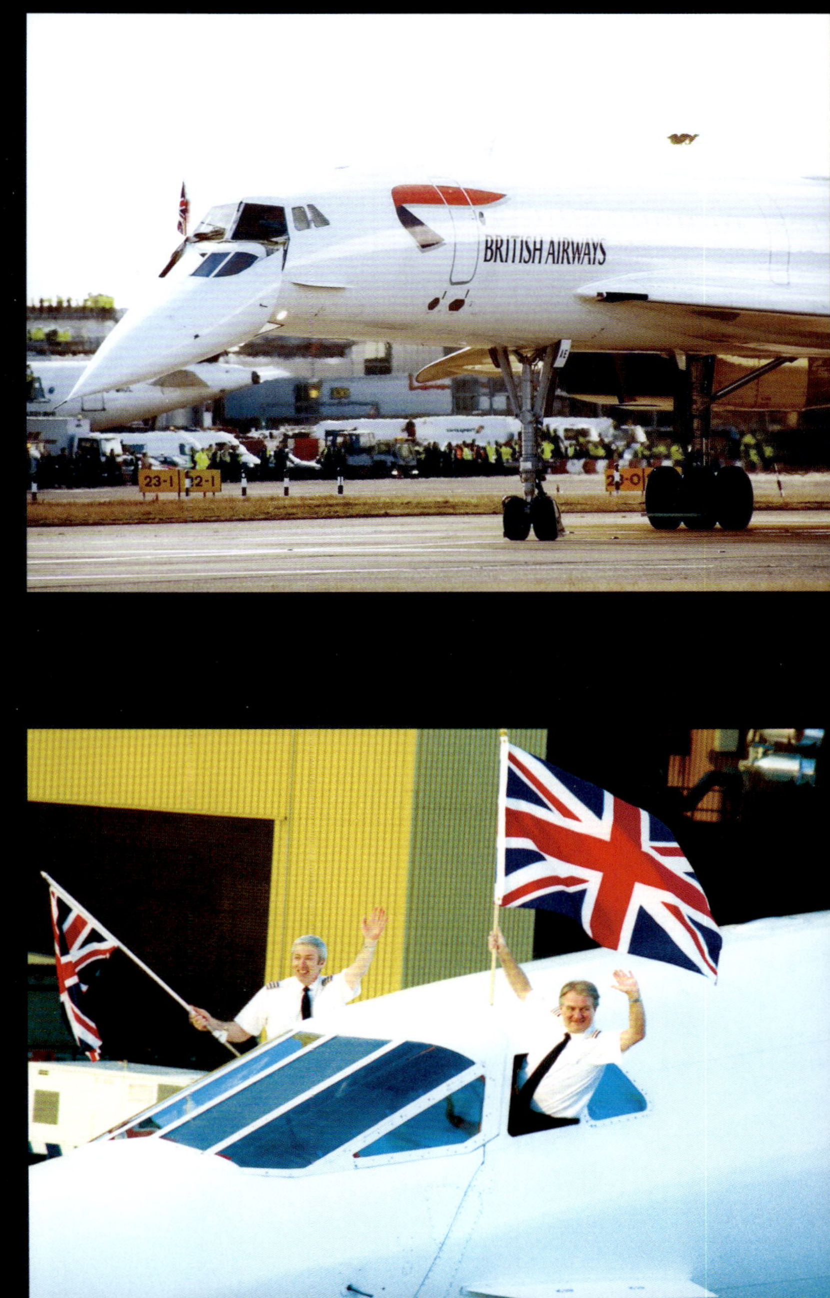

The historic final flight returning from JFK slowly taxied off the runway to the hangars. Captain Mike Bannister and First Officer Jonathan Napier greet the crowds of waiting staff and media by waving huge Union Jack flags out of the cockpit windows.

The world's media jostle for position

This photograph shows the five Concordes – one in the hangar, four on the tarmac. Special gantries had been erected to facilitate the press. We were all waiting to capture the celebrities and VIPs disembarking for the last time. The photographs show: Jeremy Clarkson, Sir David Frost, Joan Collins, Jodie Kidd, Christie Brinkley, Bernie Ecclestone and Darcey Bussell.

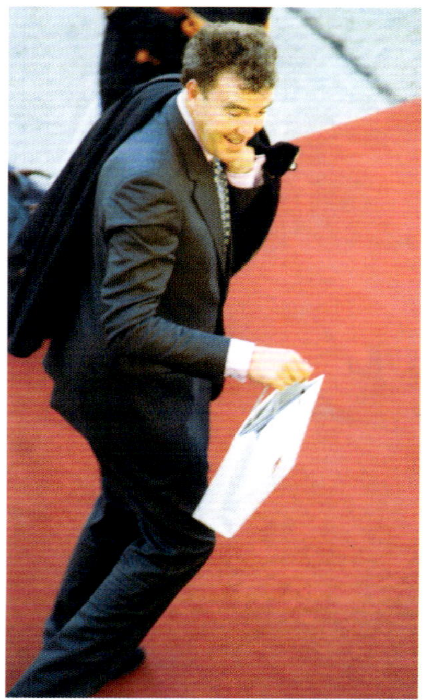
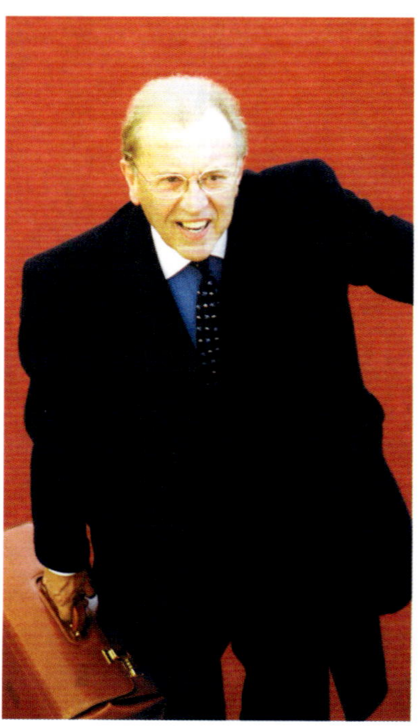
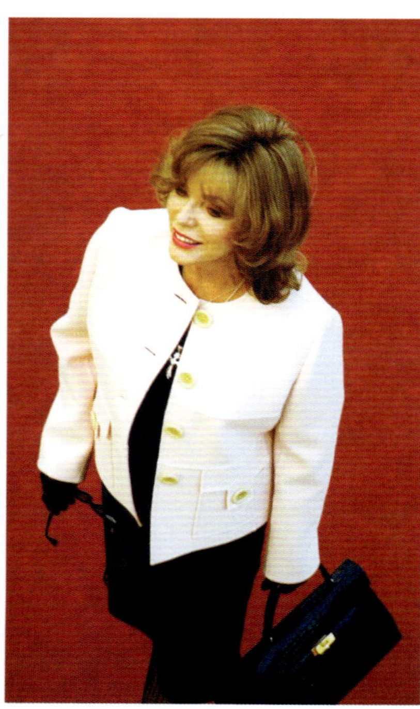
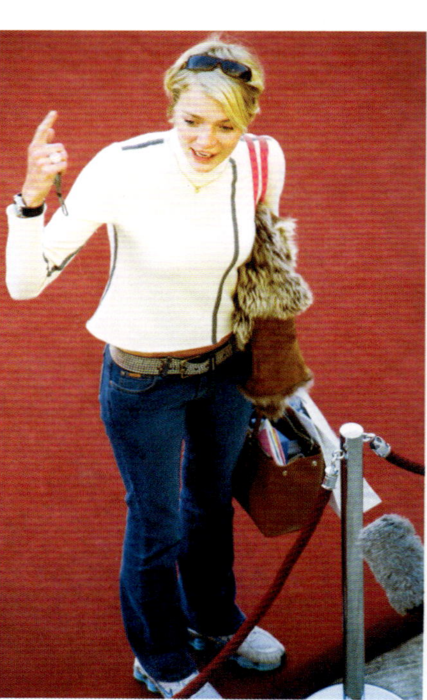

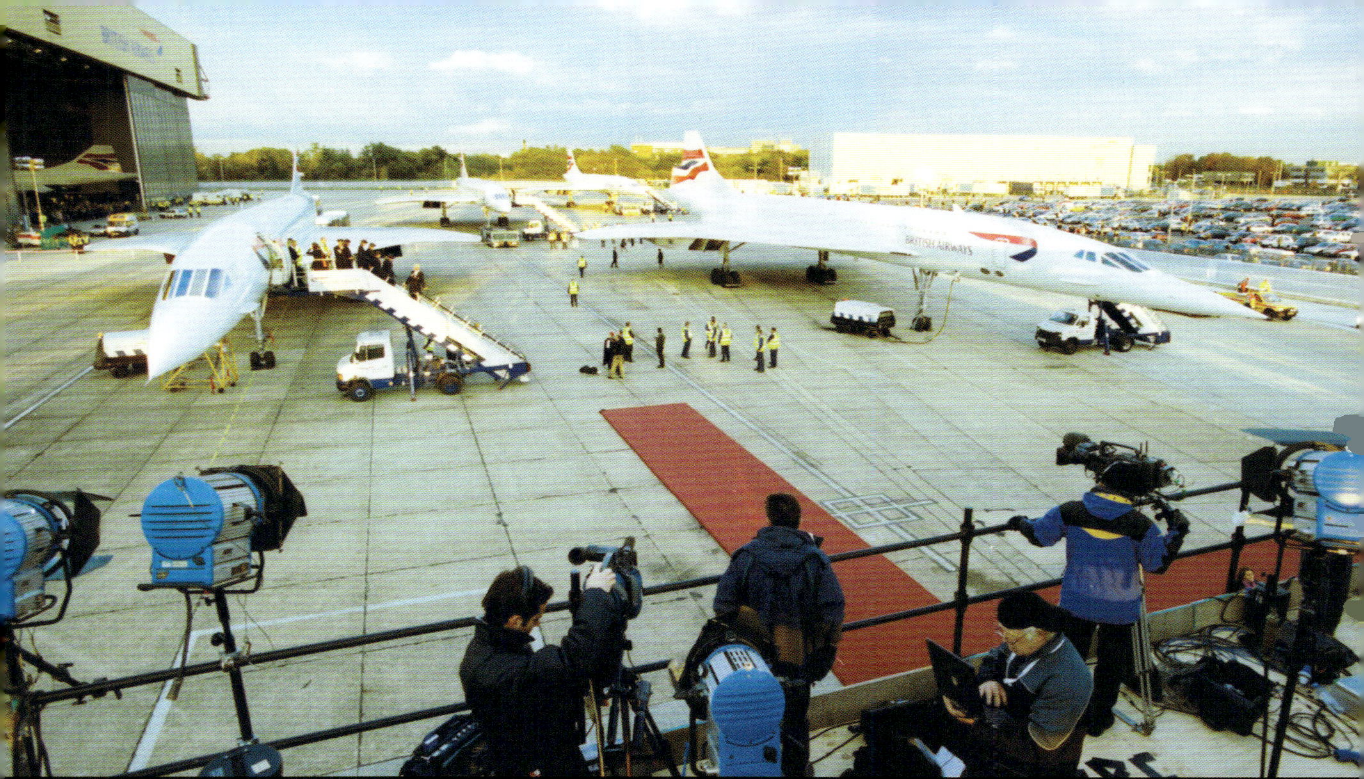

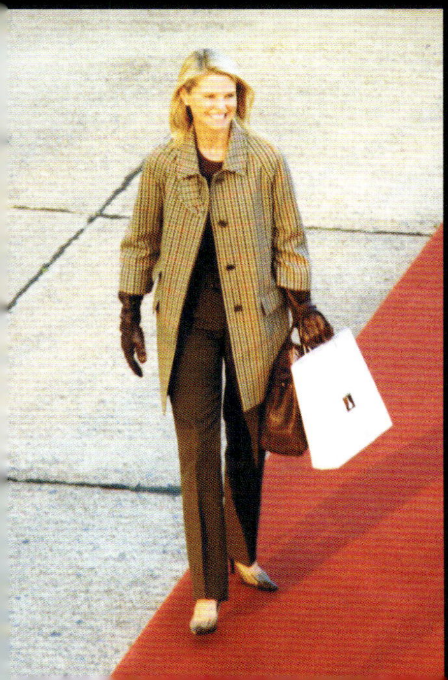

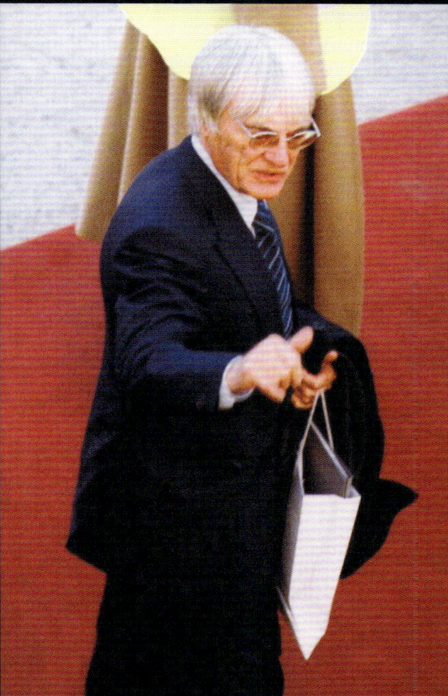

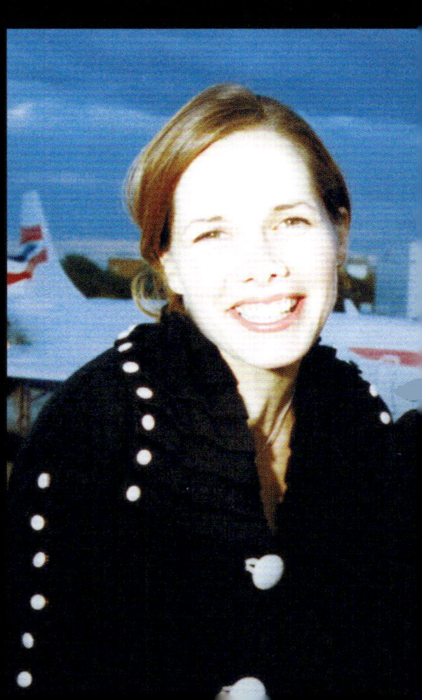

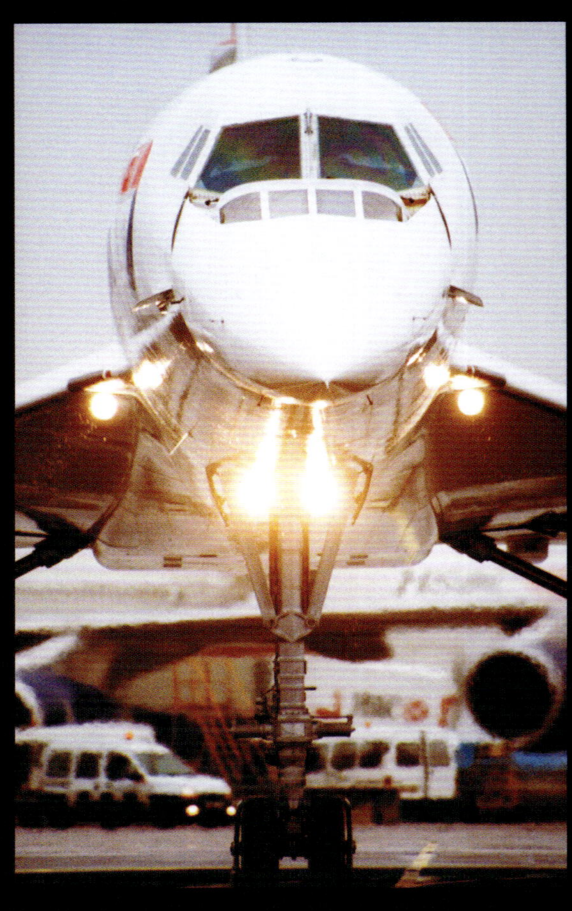

G-BOAE taxis for her final take-off to Barbados. A wet, gloomy day reflects the mood of the nation.

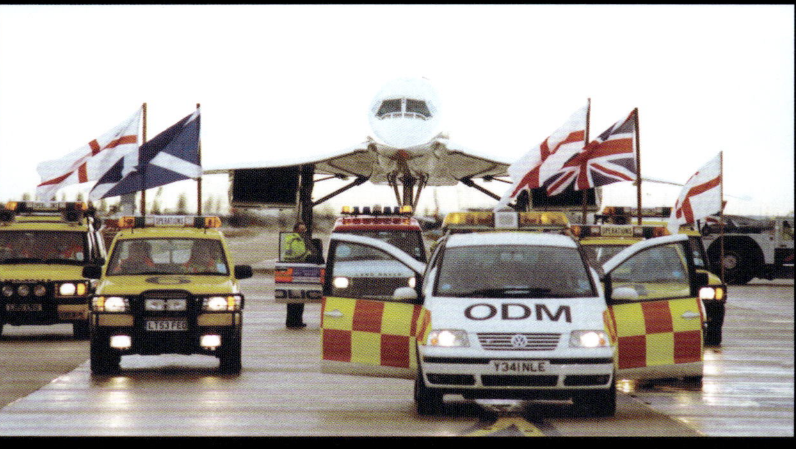

On 26 November 2003, G-BOAF taxies to the runway at London Heathrow for her final journey to Filton, Bristol. Many operations staff, police and BAA air traffic control turned out on a grey, wet November day to bid a farewell to the very last Concorde to leave London Heathrow. It was quite moving as everyone had made a very special effort and erected flags from their vehicles for a farewell tribute to Concorde.

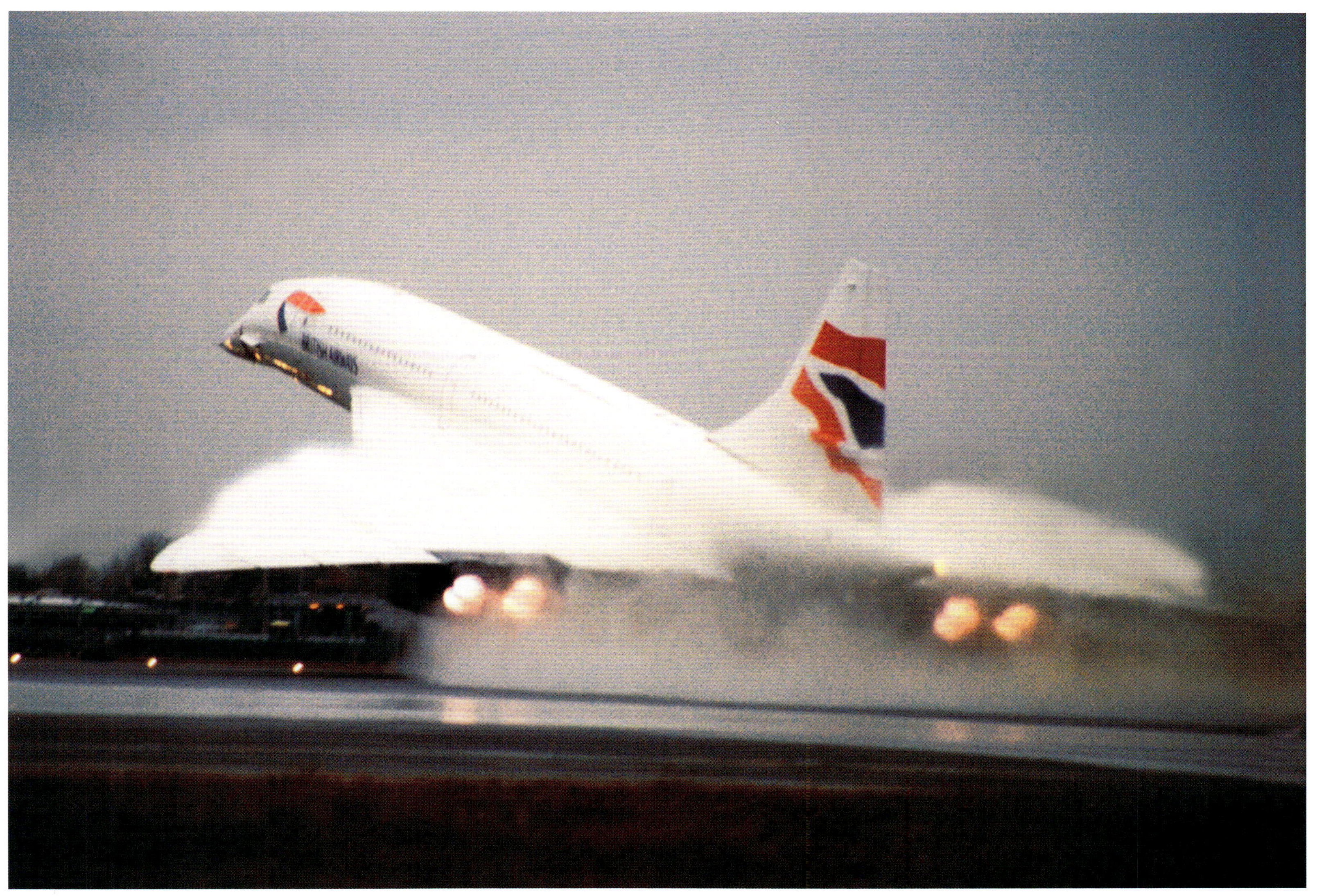

G-BOAE departed from Heathrow on 17 November 2003 on her final journey to Barbados. This Concorde is now displayed at Grantly Adams Airport, Barbados, to commemorate Concorde flights to this Caribbean island.

My photographer Mike Bromfield and the world's press were escorted to the edge of the runway to capture G-BOAF's final flight from Heathrow to Filton, the home of Concorde. While Mike was at Heathrow, I myself was at Filton waiting for the arrival of Concorde and her final landing. G-BOAF departed after 11 a.m. On her final tour she headed round the Bay of Biscay and continued her flight over Bristol for a final farewell. She was the last Concorde built, and the last of the Concordes to fly, and finally land, home at the place of her birth.

(Photograph by Mike Bromfield/Adrian Meredith)

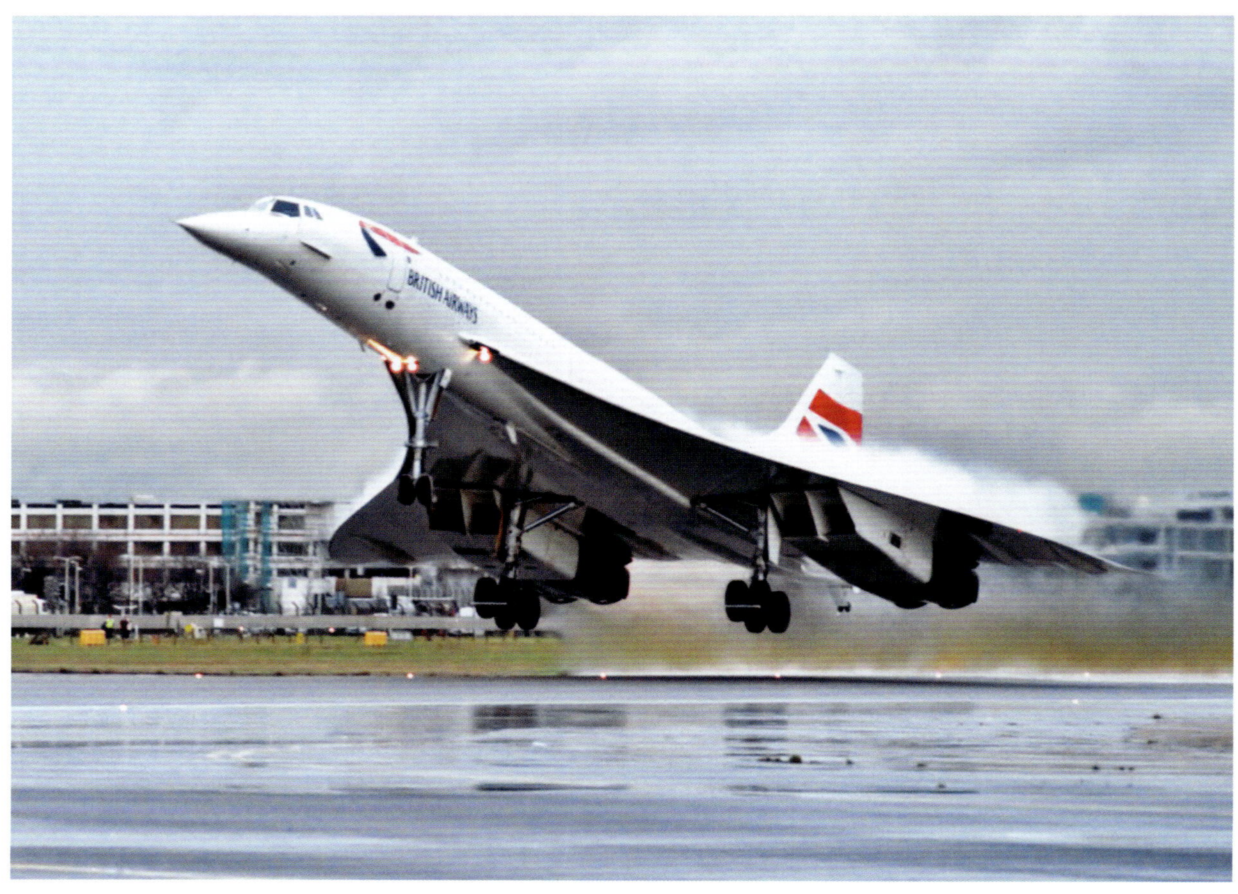

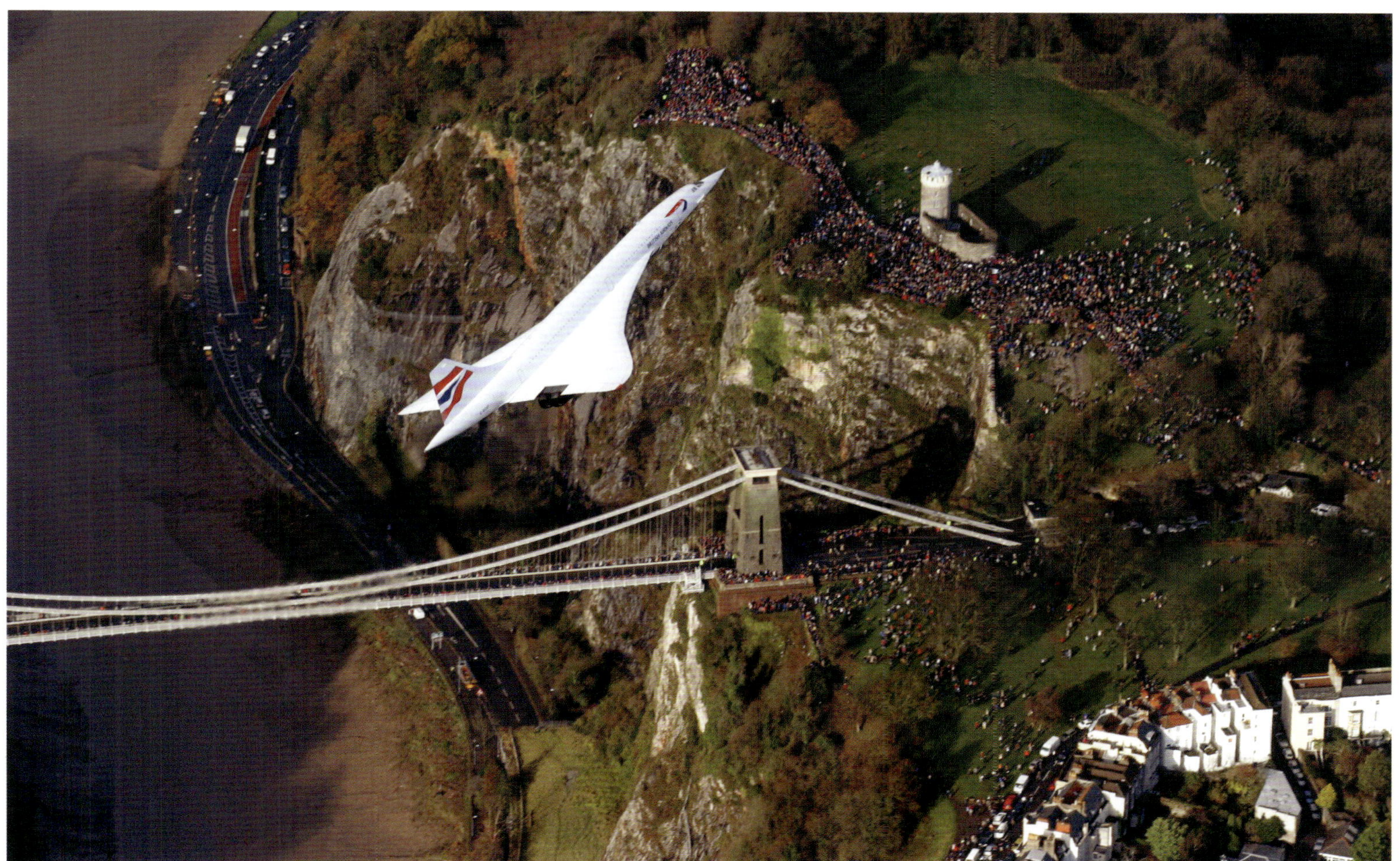

Final farewell from Bristol

Two technological wonders: G-BOAF photographed from a Bell Jet Ranger helicopter over Brunel's Clifton Suspension Bridge. Thousands gathered below to welcome her home to rest, an emotional occasion for both the workers and residents of Bristol, whose hearts hold a special place for Concorde. The shot captures crowds of well-wishers.

(Photograph by Lewis Whyld, South West News)

Technical genius and engineering came together at Filton, the home of Concorde. The aircraft was assembled here, whilst test flights were carried out at the Filton airfield base. She was presented to the world from here.

Captain Les Brodie was at the control for her final landing. Also on the flight deck were captains Mike Bannister, Paul Douglas and SFE Warren Hazelby.

This important occasion demanded special photographic equipment which was especially hired for the shoot. After the two-hour drive to Filton, two others and myself helped to mount the huge 1,000mm lens and camera onto the tripod, in preparation for the last landing. Around 30,000 waiting spectators waving flags filled the airfield and surrounding roads. Bristol residents loved Concorde; many have worked on the aircraft and have a special love affair with this superb plane. The mood was jubilant and very atmospheric; one could have cut the air with a knife as we all stood waiting in anticipation for the final roar of her engines. Weather conditions were mixed, one minute cloud, then rain, then sun – a typical November afternoon. Just before 1 p.m. we heard her engines. There were two fly-pasts, escorted by an RAF Spitfire as the lead plane, and the crowds roared with delight, flags waving. Finally we saw her come round for the final approach, and suddenly a cold front moved in rapidly. Clouds thickened, the temperature dropped dramatically, and a hailstone storm was upon us. Disaster struck: the plunge in temperature started to affect my camera – the auto focus froze and the batteries in the motor drive were on their last legs. It looked for a moment as if I was not going to be able to capture the last bit of history of Concorde. After what seemed hours the sun broke through the cloud and I managed to get the camera working, just before she touched down. A perfect landing shot, the back wheels made contact with a flurry of smoke from the runway, the reverse thrust was engaged, and a vortex of water spiralled under her wings: Concorde touched down for the very last time.

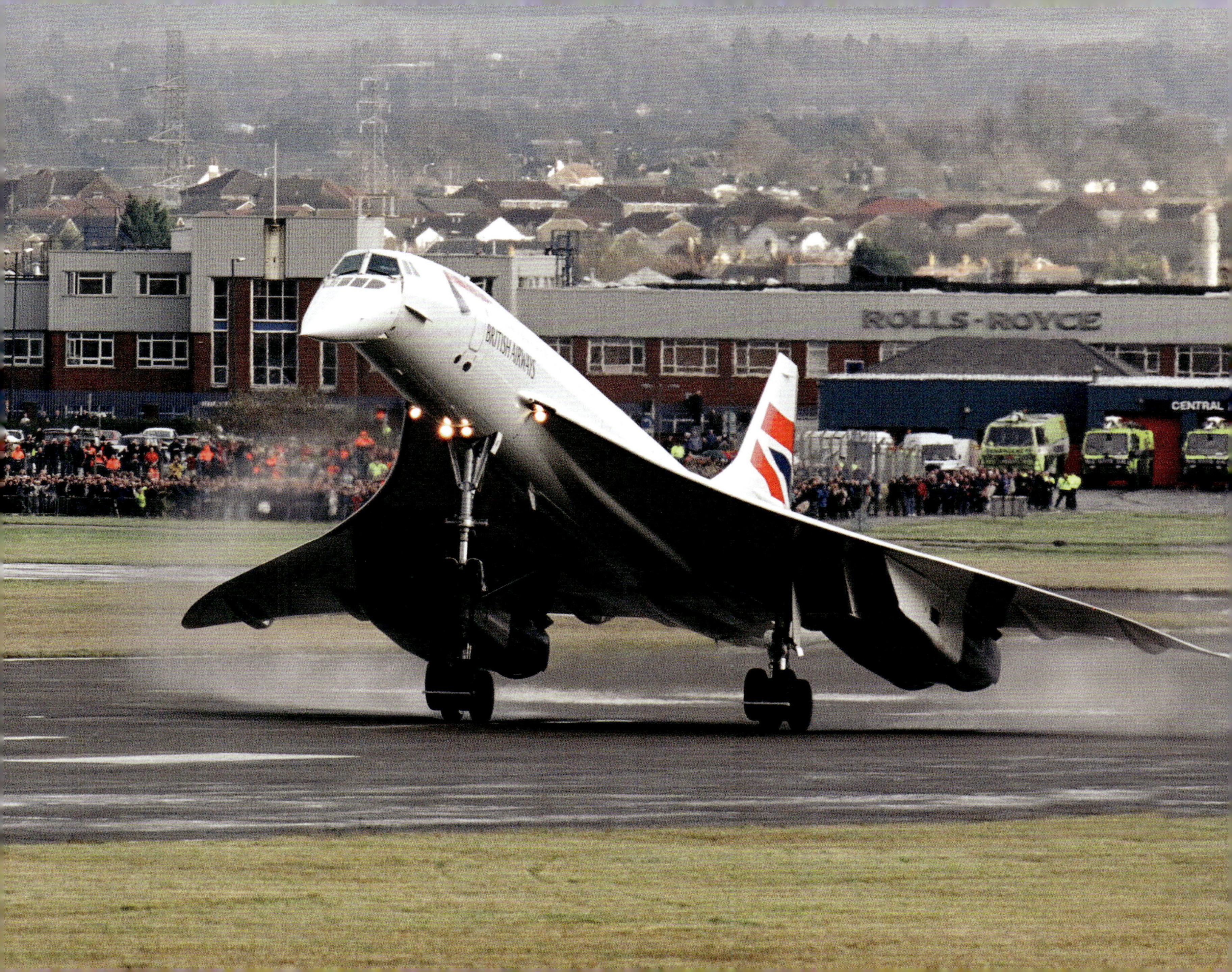

ROLLS-ROYCE
BRITISH AIRWAYS
CENTRAL

She landed, taxied to the end of the runway, and turned around to face the crowds. The cockpit windows were opened and the captains waved the Union Jack for one final time. True to tradition, they also had on board a very special VIP, as seen in the cockpit in this photograph: 'Pudsey Bear', the charity mascot for BBC Children in Need. Concorde has raised many thousands of pounds for this UK charity over the years.

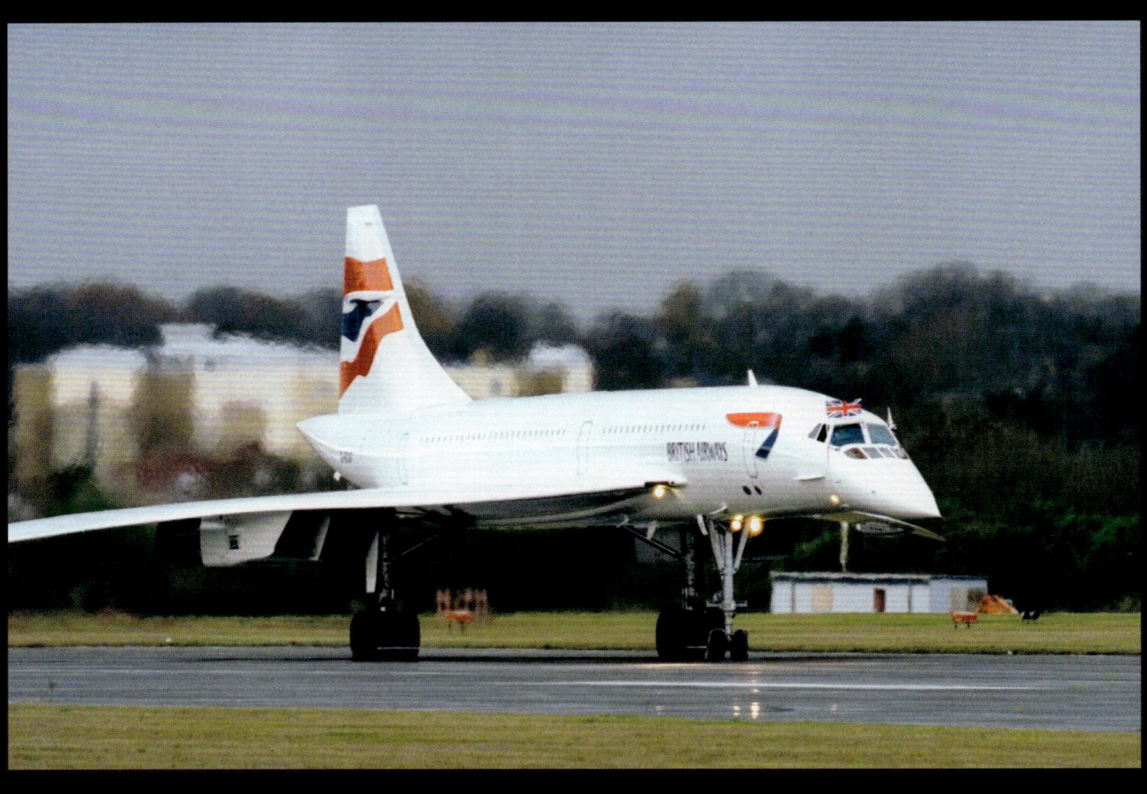

A royal welcome home

Concorde's retirement was celebrated by thousands of people waiting for her, cheering and waving flags, and amongst the special guests was HRH the Duke of York, who is pictured here with Captain Mike Bannister in the cockpit.

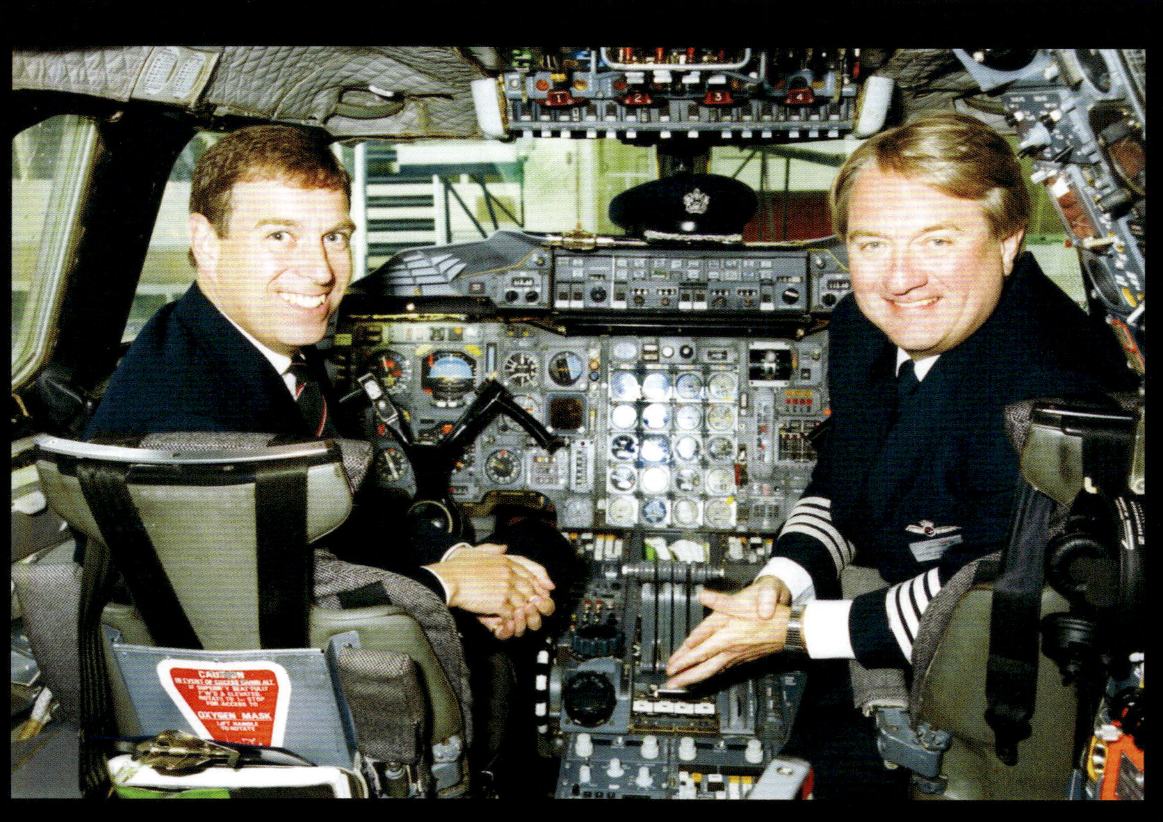

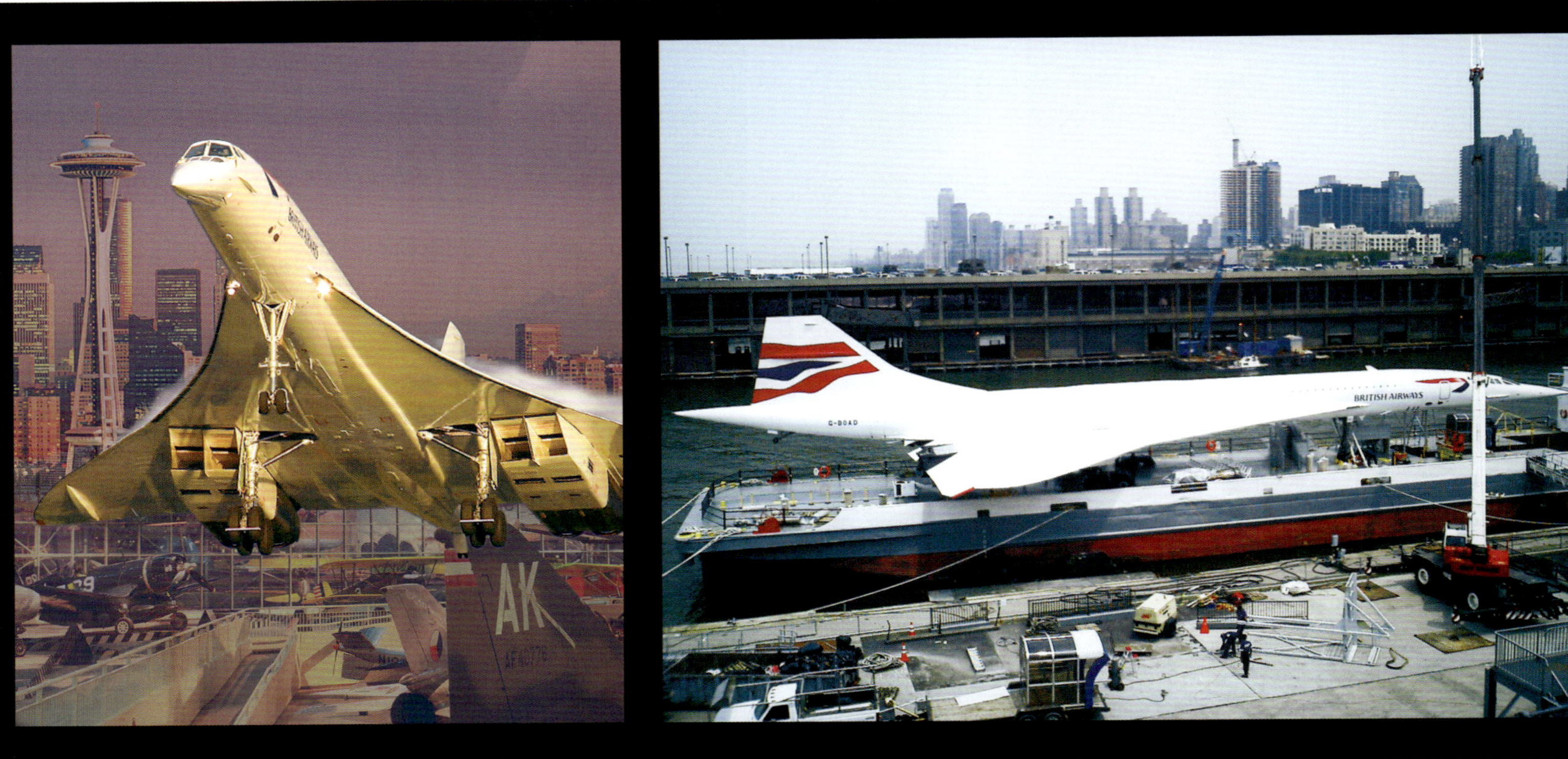

Last flight into Seattle, G-BOAG.

G-BOAD Intrepid Air and Space Museum.

CHAPTER FOURTEEN

THE FUTURE OF SUPERSONIC FLIGHT

The quest for supersonic speed without window-rattling sonic booms is spurring research by General Dynamics's Gulfstream, Boeing, Lockheed Martin, NASA and many others.

The efforts signal that the time may finally be nearing for corporate aircraft flying faster than sound, about 750mph (1,207km/h) at sea level. Technological leaps since Concorde's development in the 1960s are converging with the willingness of globe-trotting chief executives and celebrities to pay more for ever-bigger and longer-range jets. Given the amount of fuel you need to burn to achieve supersonic speeds, it's going to be expensive: 'When you're talking about a supersonic business jet, that begins to make more sense.'

The chief obstacle to supersonic flight is the same that bedevilled Concorde: the sonic boom. The US Federal Aviation Administration outlawed such flights by civilians over land in 1973 because of the noise, and other countries followed suit. NASA expects to start building a demonstrator plane in 2016 to show that disruptive booms can be minimised, and that jet may fly after 2020, according to supersonic research. This is great news for those who continue to dream of flights that cross continents and oceans in half the time it takes today. But will there be enough passengers willing to pay higher fares to fly more quickly?

However, not everyone is convinced that a return to supersonic passenger flight is just around the corner. Aviation experts, such as Chris Seymour of Ascend, are sceptical that there would be much progress before at least 2030: 'I think there are so many issues to be considered that I certainly can't see it happening in the next twenty years.'

Many aeronautical companies like Hyper Mach are looking at how to reach faster supersonic speeds, but there are still problems ahead: the latest research has found that there would be a need for a new type of fuel to propel the aircraft out of our atmosphere. This new fuel may take up to twenty years to develop. The company's Aircraft Sonic Star, with its new technology, will hope to fly at speeds of up to 2,500mph, around Mach 3.6, and fly an altitude of 60,000ft.

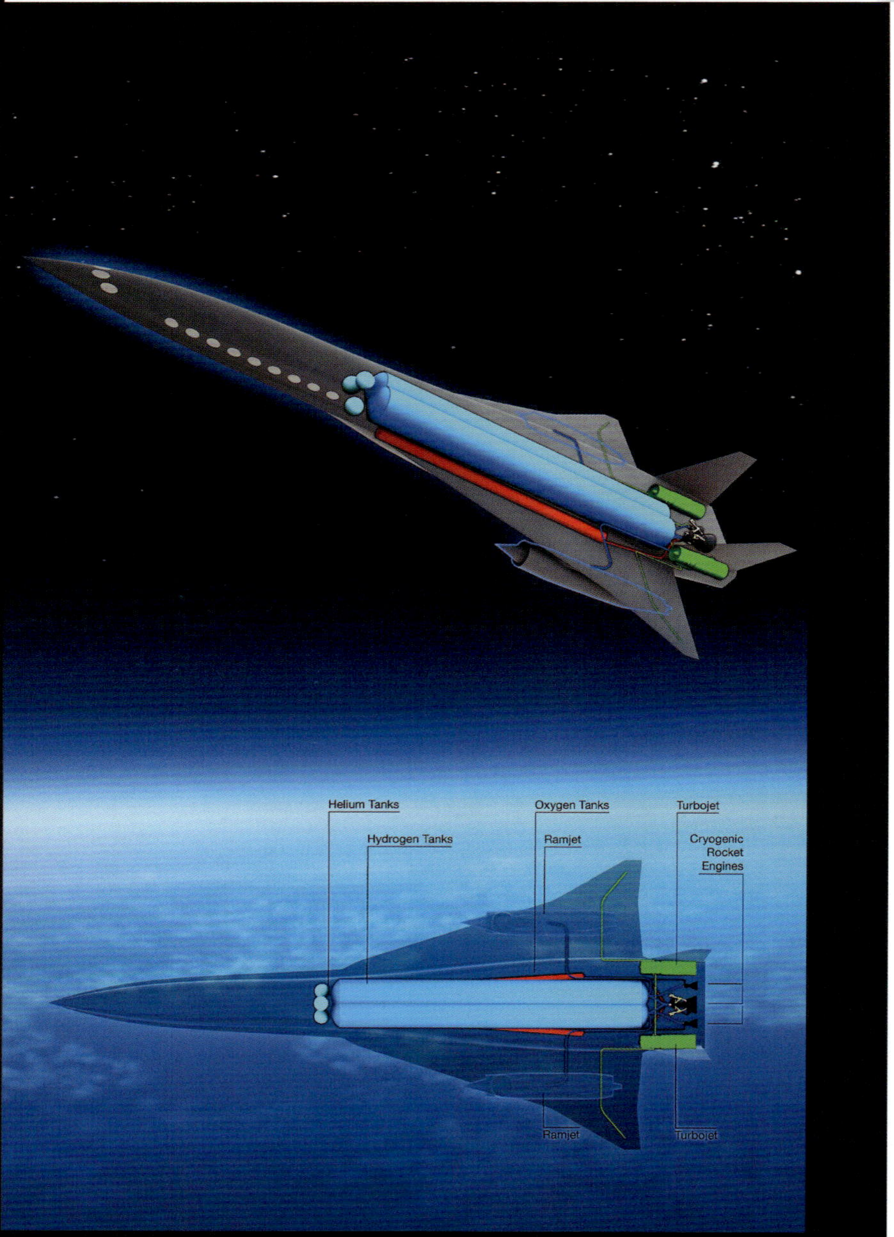

Hypersonic

I have read many articles on Hypersonic High Speed Travel, but the company EADS, the owners of Airbus, have said it's a long way off. It could take up to thirty years before we see their high-speed aircraft model ZEHST (Zero Emission High Speed Transport) take to the air.

It is believed that it could fly up to speeds of 3,000mph – four times the speed of sound – which would be fantastic; could you imagine flying from London to Tokyo in less than three hours? The aircraft would have to fly out of our atmosphere to achieve this, which would help with pollution and the noise from the sonic boom.

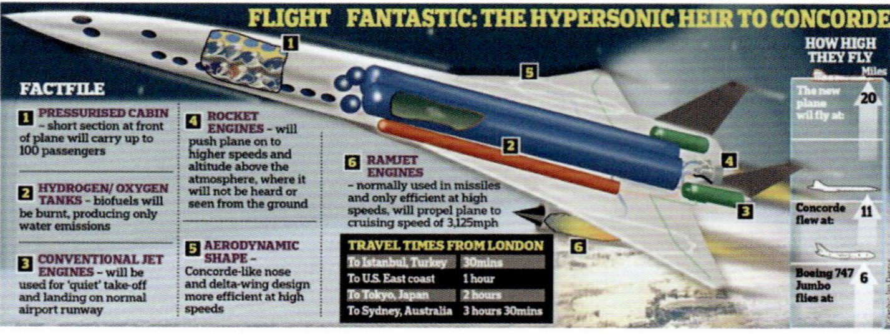

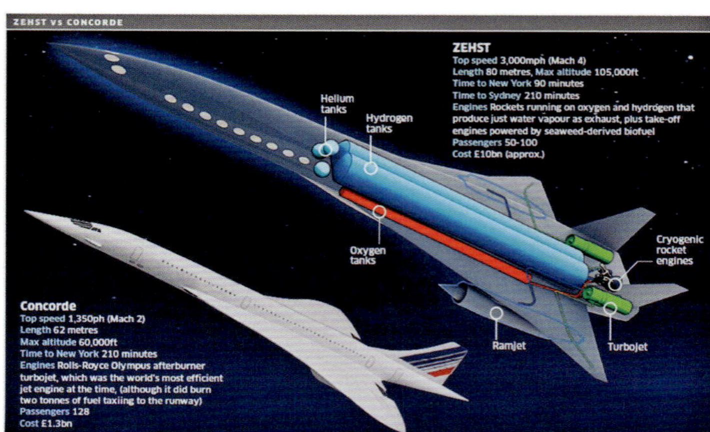

Virgin Galactic

The high deserts of New Mexico will house the operations centre for Virgin Galactic, called Spaceport America, once Sir Richard Branson's Virgin Galactic's routine flights begin in 2013. If you have a spare $200,000 you can be taken into orbit, 62 miles (100km) above sea level, which is defined as the edge of space.

The six passengers and two pilots will take off horizontally from the spaceport's 2.3-mile (3.7km) runway in a space plane that will likely have the ambiance of a trendy business jet. This craft is dubbed a spaceship and is slung beneath a double-fuselage carrier aircraft, *White Knight Two*, on take-off and for the flight's first couple of hours.

The real adventure begins after the two linked craft rise about 50,000ft (15km), at which point Spaceship Two will drop from its mounting, fire up its rocket motor, and go zooming upward into the heavens. Its passengers will then experience peak forces that are almost 4G – four times normal gravity and more than a ride up on the space Shuttle. However, for passengers on Spaceship Two, the push into their seats will last for just a minute or so. The feeling of acceleration will abruptly disappear when Spaceship Two's rocket motor shuts down, as the craft coasts upward through a broad arc that will give its occupants about four minutes of free fall, or 'weightlessness'.

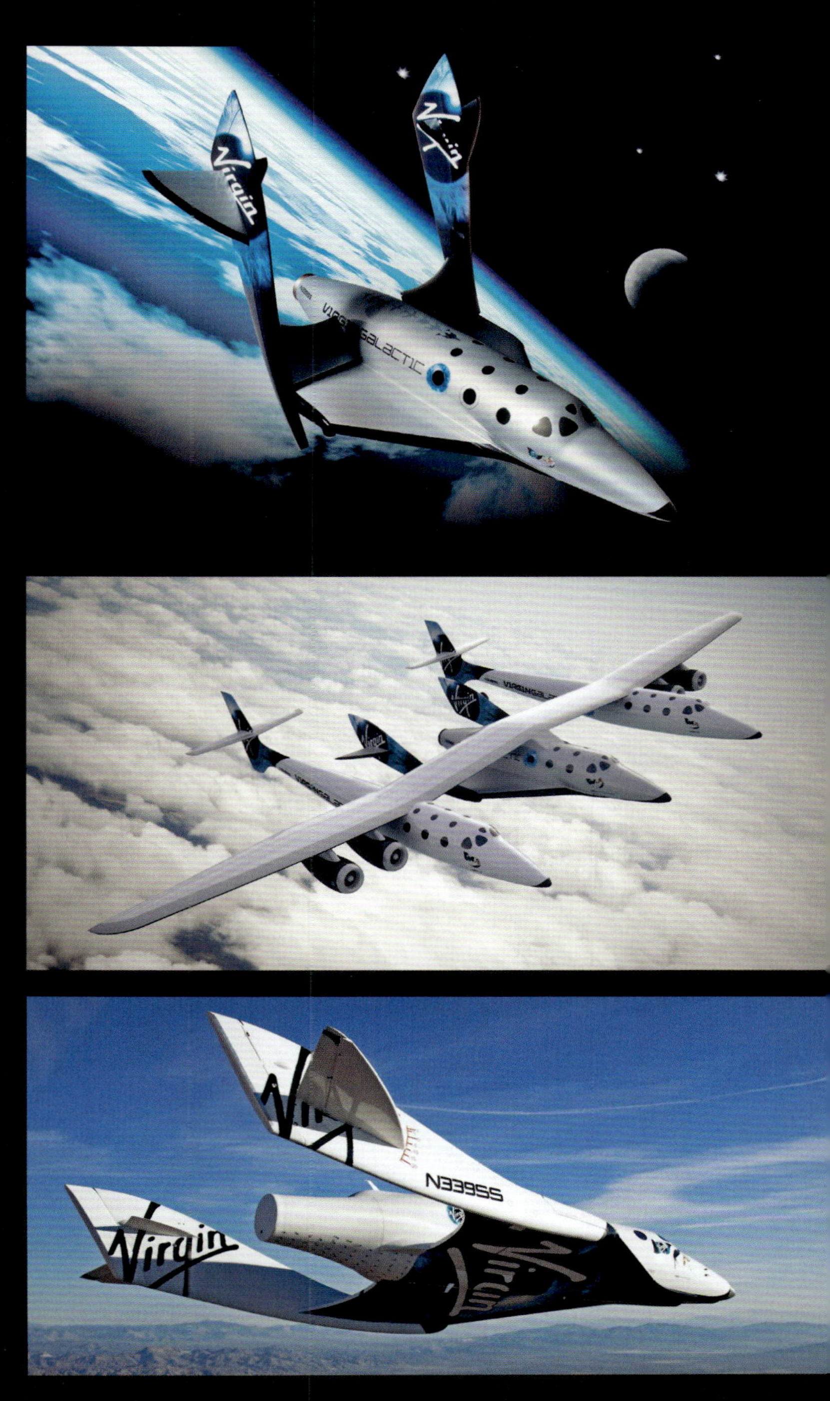

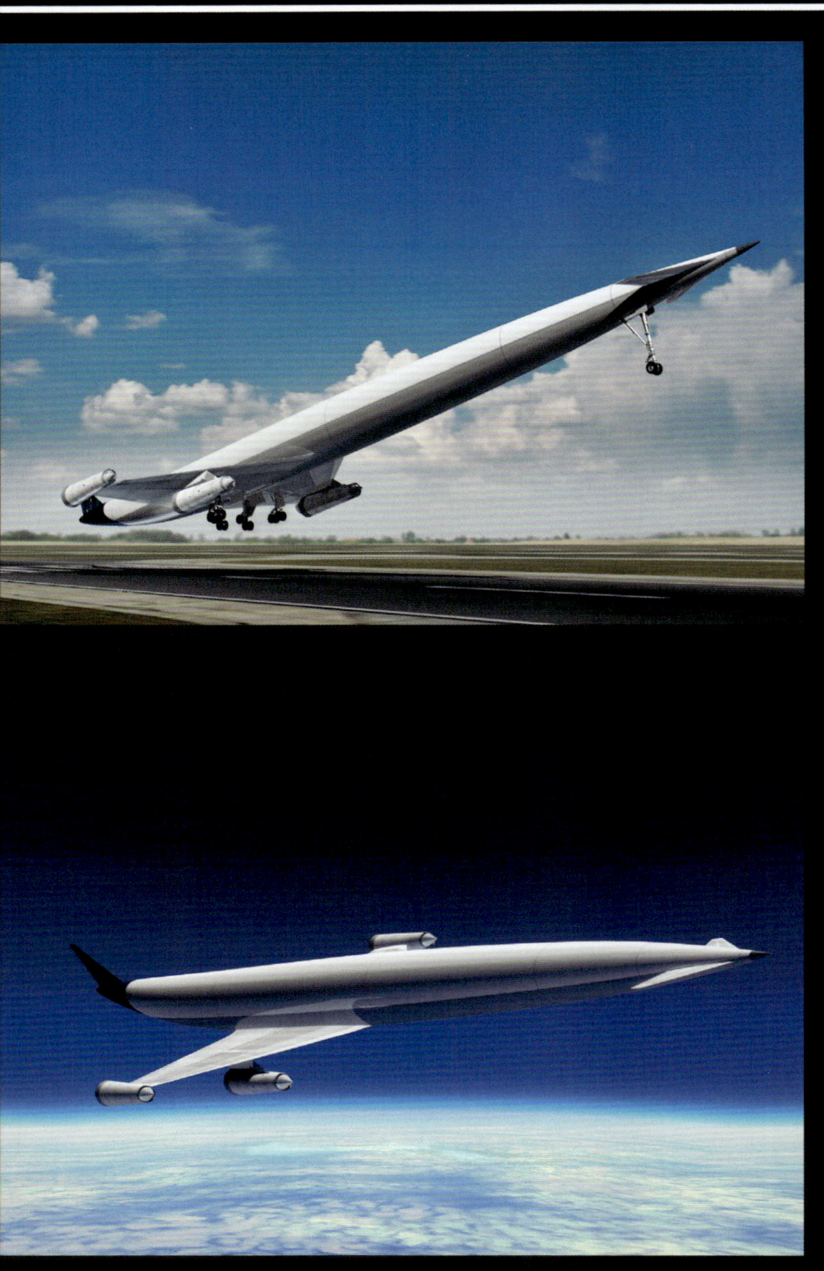

EADS Lapcat A2 Mach 5 Concept Aircraft

EADS Lapcat A2 Mach 5 with SABRE reaction engine technology can enable aircraft to cruise within the atmosphere at speeds of up to five times the speed of sound, for which the hypersonic aircraft with near antipodal range (12,427 miles/20,000km) is required. To achieve this range, liquid hydrogen fuel is required since the specific calorific energy of hydrocarbon fuels is too low.

The aim is to reduce long-distance flights to less than two to four hours. The vehicle is sized to carry 300 passengers.

Boeing and NASA Mach 4 Supersonic Aircraft

Teams led by Boeing and designers from Lockheed Martin, and funded through a NASA Research Announcement, came up with designs for two small supersonic airliners that would carry between thirty and eighty passengers, and could potentially enter service in the 2025 time frame.

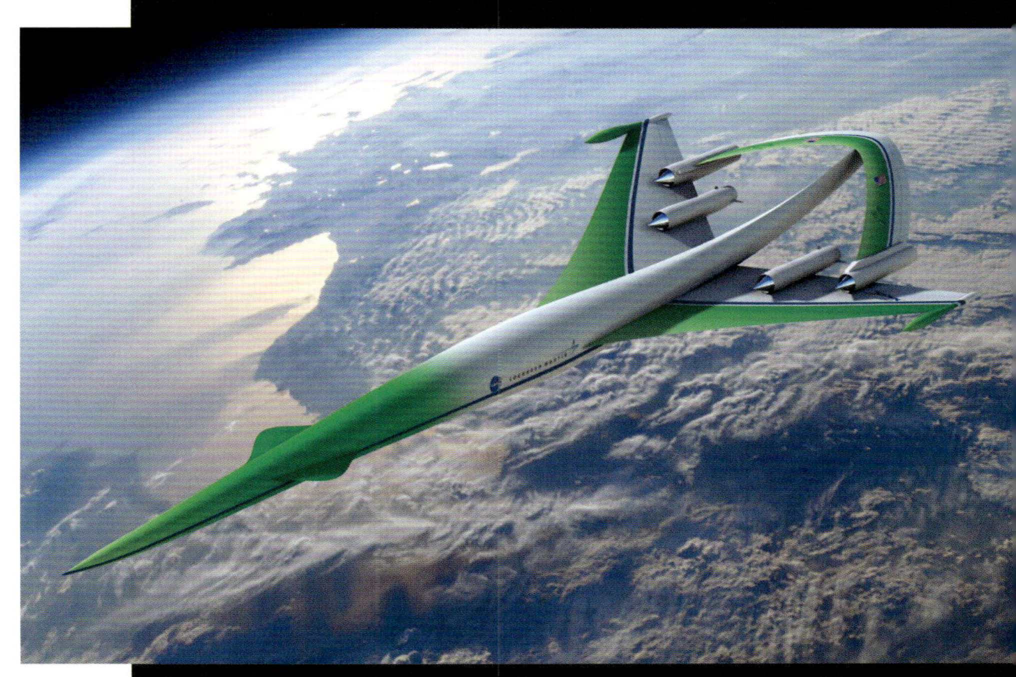

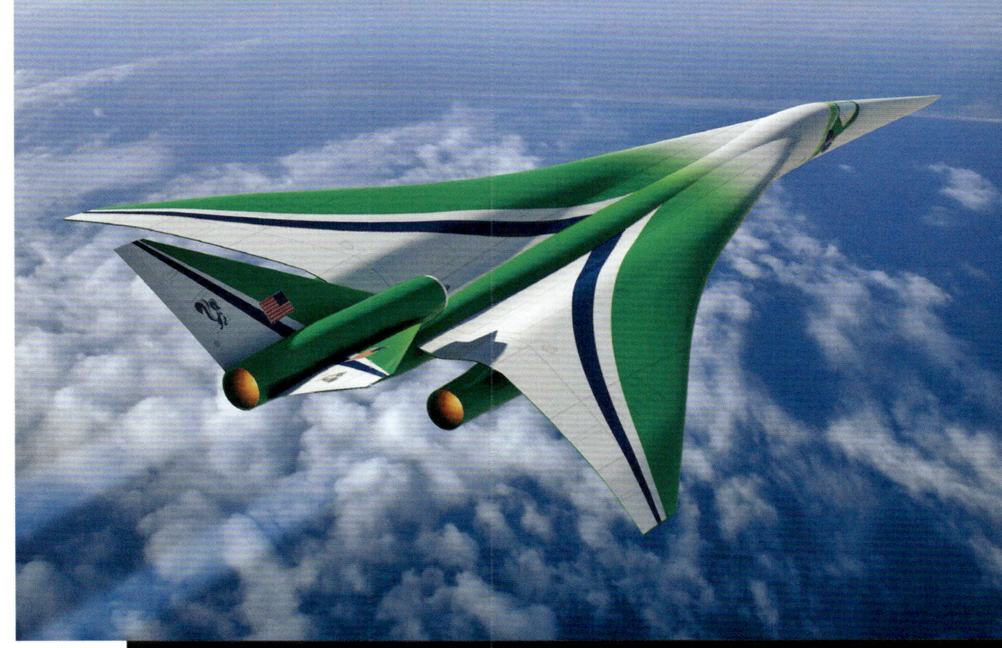

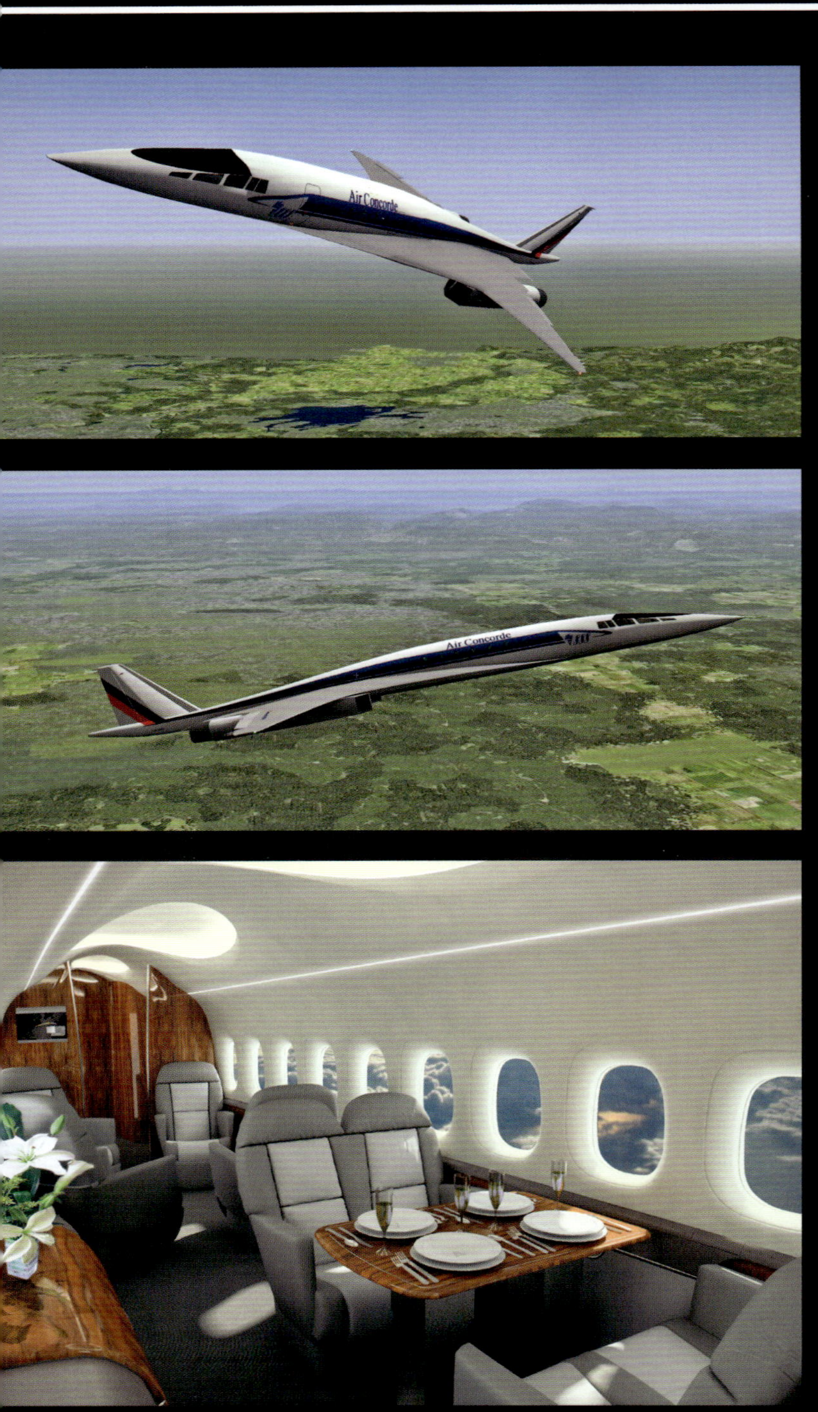

Air Concorde Tu-888

Andrey Tupolev (grandson of the founder of Tupolev Aviation) has said that the beautiful thing about the Tu-888 is that it's fast and small, with just two pilots and a maximum of ten passengers. Air Concorde will build twenty aircraft.

President Putin owns Tupolev, and he is supposedly the world's richest man; we are just waiting for him to give the green light. Tupolev has an incredible history with aviation technology; the company has a real love for Concorde and is looking forward to this new supersonic project. The aircraft will fly at speeds in excess of 1,336mph (2,150km/h), or Mach 2. They would have access to airspace above the 40,000ft ceiling, of approximately 60,000ft. The aircraft will comprise two Rolls-Royce engines, a Russian airframe, American avionics and the interior will most likely be designed by a British aviation interior design company.

APPENDIX 1

CONCORDE FACTS

Take-off speed: 250mph

Landing speed: 187mph

Cruising speed: Mach 2 1,350mph. Twice the speed of sound, up to 60,000ft

Range: 4,143 miles

Engines: four Rolls-Royce/SNECMA Olympus 593s, each producing 38,000lb thrust with reheat

Flight crew: two pilots, one flight engineer

Cabin crew: six

Seating: 100 seats, forty in the front cabin and sixty in the rear cabin

Capacity: 100 passengers and 2.5 tonnes of cargo

Length: 204ft long

Wingspan: 84ft wide

Height: 37ft high

Fuselage width: 9ft 6in

Fuel capacity: 26,286 imperial gallons (119,500 litres)

Fuel consumption: 5,638 imperial gallons per hour (25,629 litres)

Maximum take-off weight: 408,000lb (185 tonnes)

Landing gear: eight main wheels, two nose wheels, two tail wheels

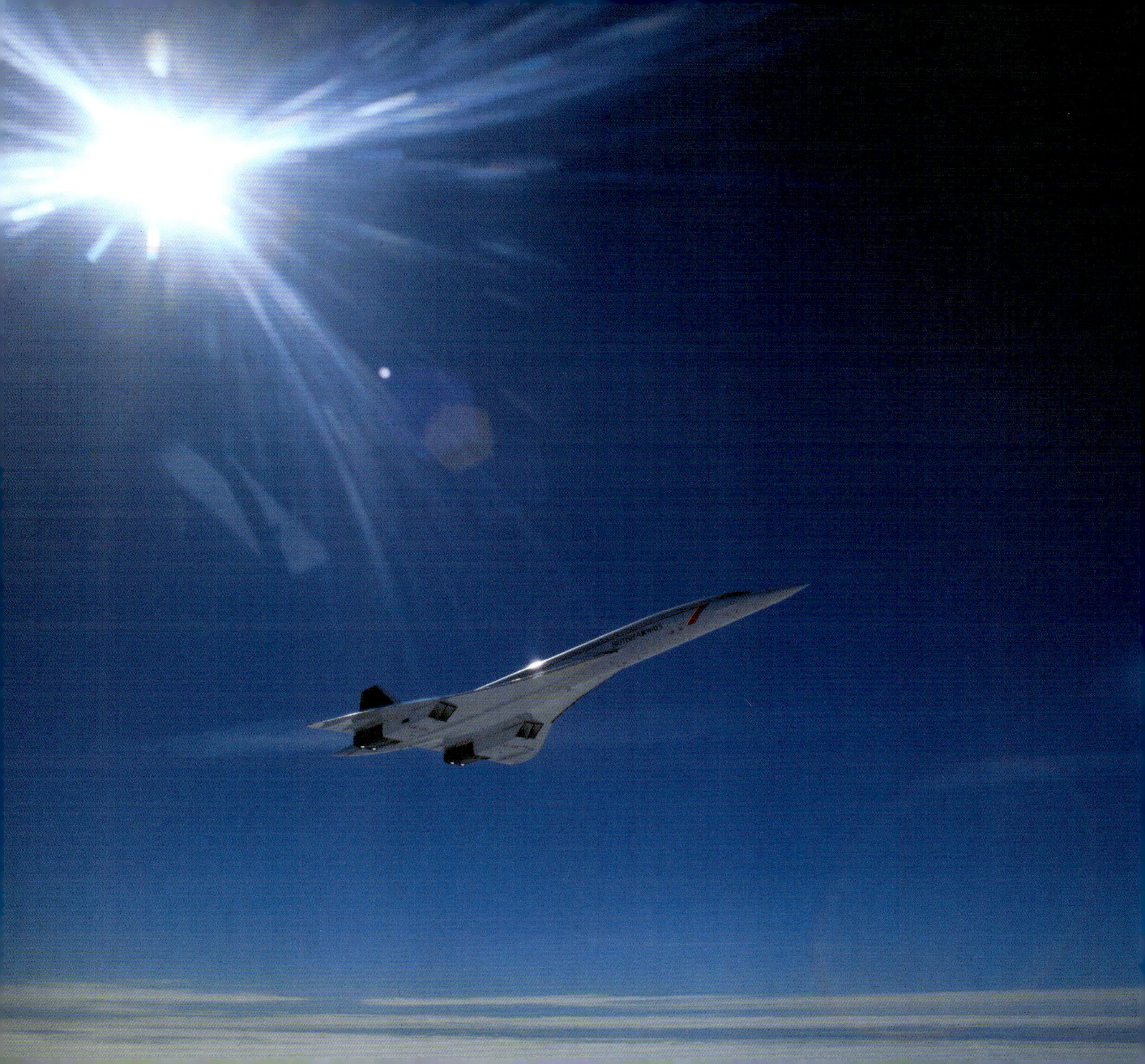

CONCORDE – WHERE YOU CAN SEE HER NOW

Concorde can be seen at these locations worldwide:

British Airways Concorde G-BOAA; last flew 12 August 2000

G-BOAA is now at the National Museum of Flight, East Fortune, Scotland.

Between 1976 and 2003 British Airways' Concordes operated close to 50,000 flights, clocked up more than 140,000 flying hours and travelled some 140 million miles.

Flight hours: 22,768

British Airways Concorde G-BOAB; last flew 15 August 2000

G-BOAB is still at British Airways Engineering Base, London Heathrow, and is looking for a permanent home.

Flight hours: 22,296

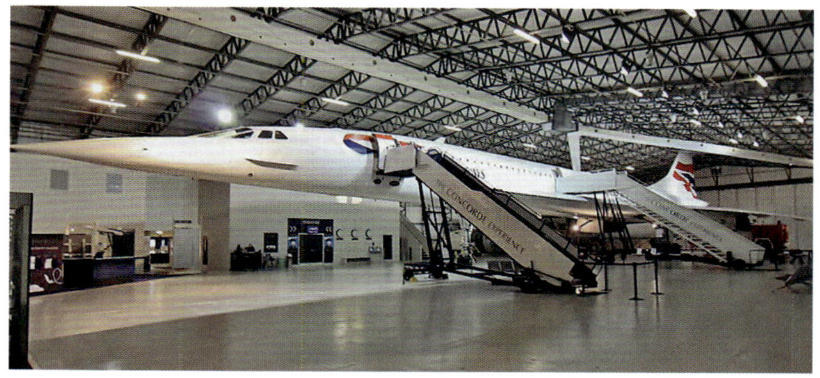

British Airways Concorde G-BOAA.

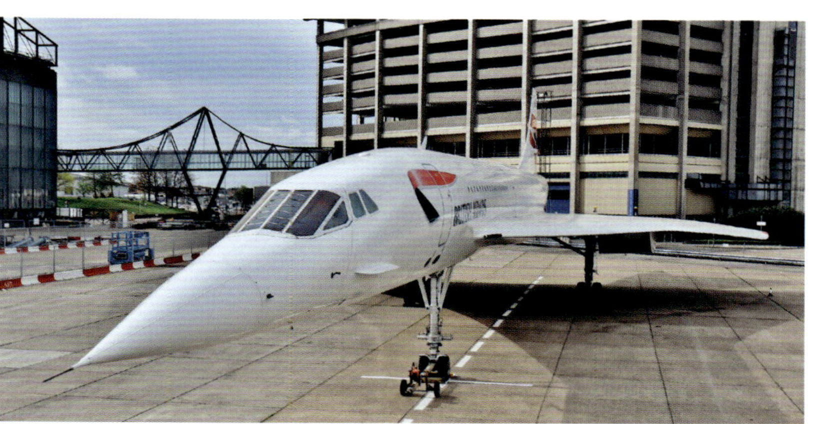

British Airways Concorde G-BOAB.

British Airways Concorde G-BOAC; last flew 31 October 2003

G-BOAC in her present location at Manchester Airport England.

Picture by Michael de Boer of the de Boer Company, who built the new hangar at Manchester.

Flight hours: 22,260

British Airways Concorde G-BOAD; last flew 10 November 2003

G-BOAD is now on the USS Intrepid*, which is at the Intrepid Sea Air and Space Museum in New York.*

Flight hours: 23,397

British Airways Concorde G-BOAE; last flew 17 November 2003

G-BOAE has now made her final home in Barbados' Grantley Adams International Airport.

Flight hours: 23,376

British Airways Concorde G-BOAF; last flew 26 November 2003

Alpha Foxtrot, simply known as 'Foxy', is now at Filton, Bristol, the home of Concorde, where the engineers, designers and everyone who helped develop and build Concorde worked.

Flight hours: 18,257

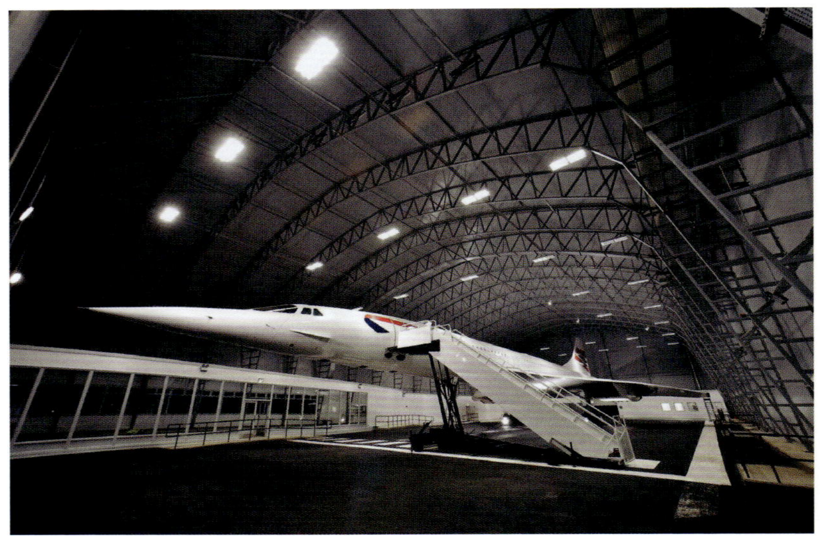

British Airways Concorde G-BOAC.

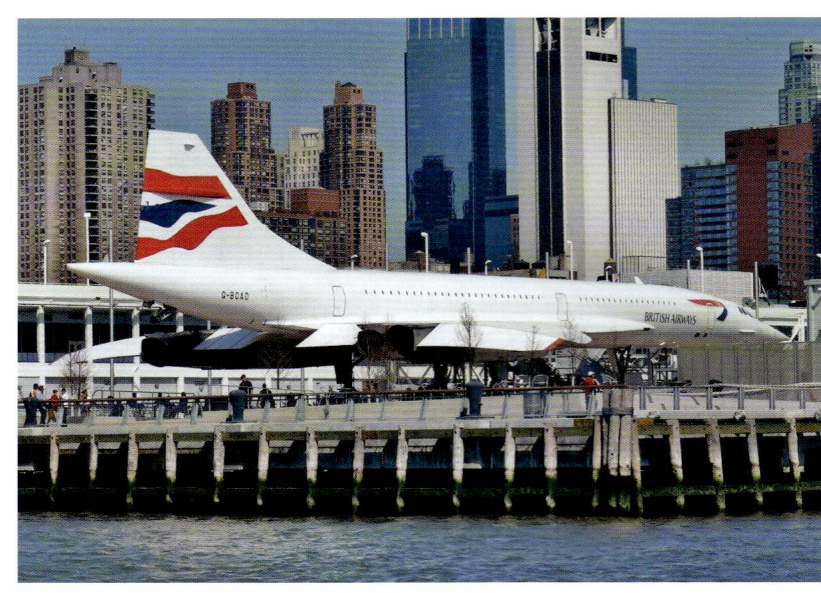

British Airways Concorde G-BOAD.

British Airways Concorde G-BOAG; last flew 5 November 2003

The registration code G-BOAG is referred to as 'Alpha Golf'. She is now at the Museum of Flight in Seattle.

She was first flown in April 1978 and delivered to British Airways in 1980. She had 5,600 take-offs and over 16,200 flight hours while in service. On 24 October 2003, on her way to the Museum of Flight, Alpha Golf set a New York City–Seattle speed record of three hours, fifty-five minutes and twelve seconds.

Flight hours: 16,239

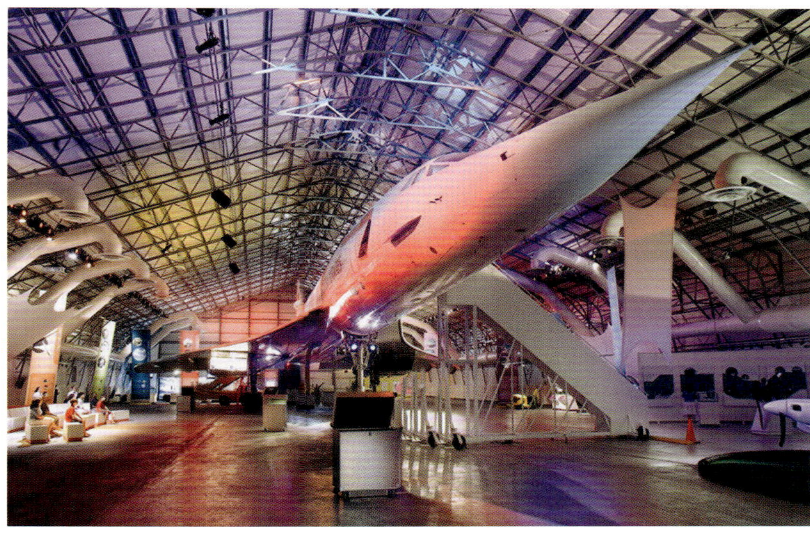

British Airways Concorde G-BOAE.

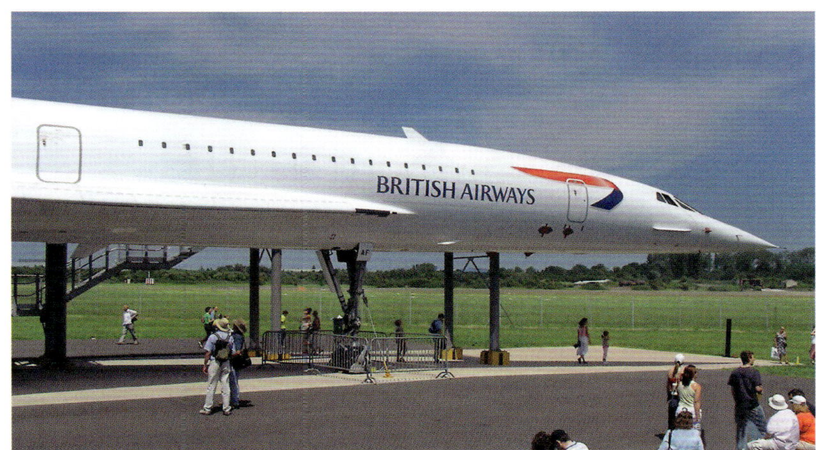

British Airways Concorde G-BOAF.

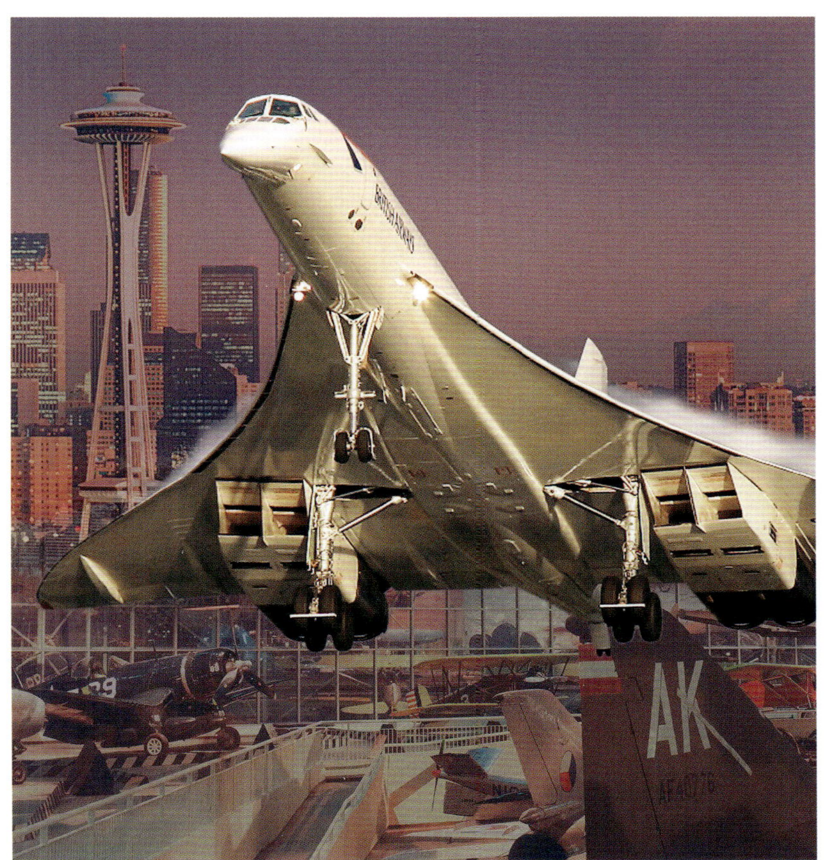

British Airways Concorde G-BOAG.

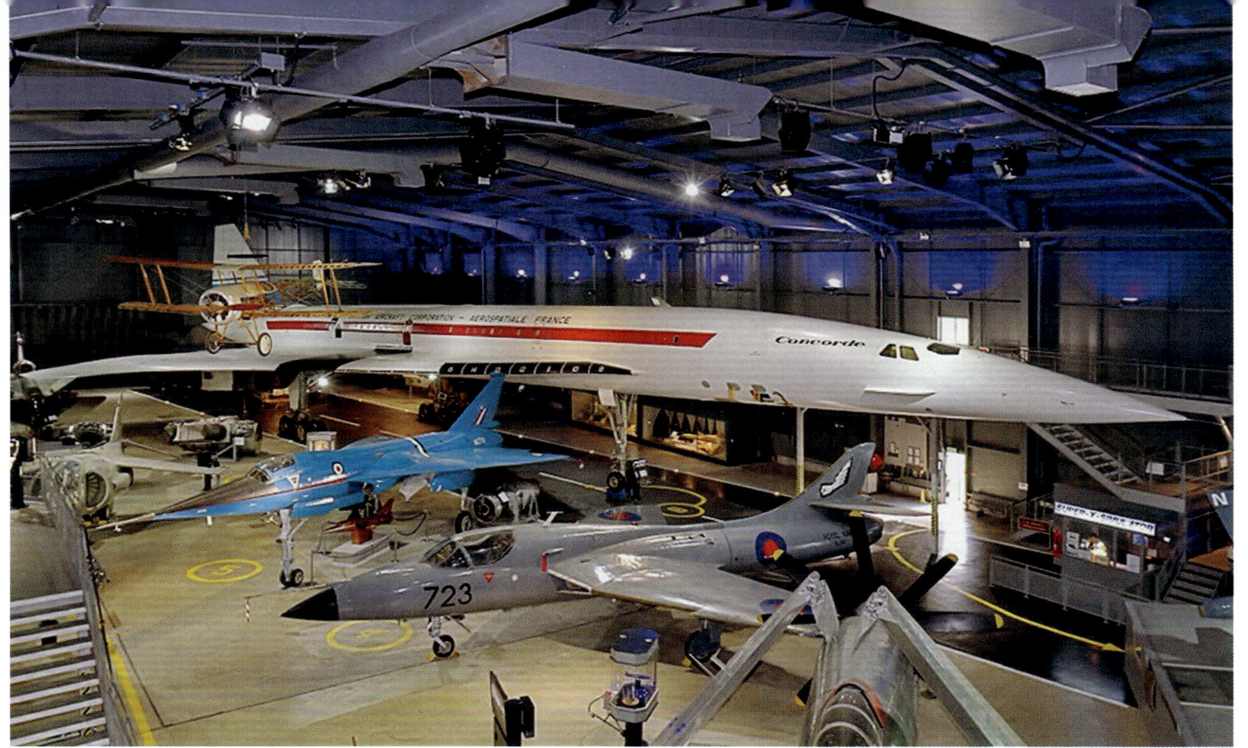

Concorde G-BSST 002 first took off in April 1969 and, following seven years of extensive supersonic testing, her last flight was made to the Fleet Air Arm Museum, Somerset, in July 1976, where she is preserved in one the museum's four exhibition halls.

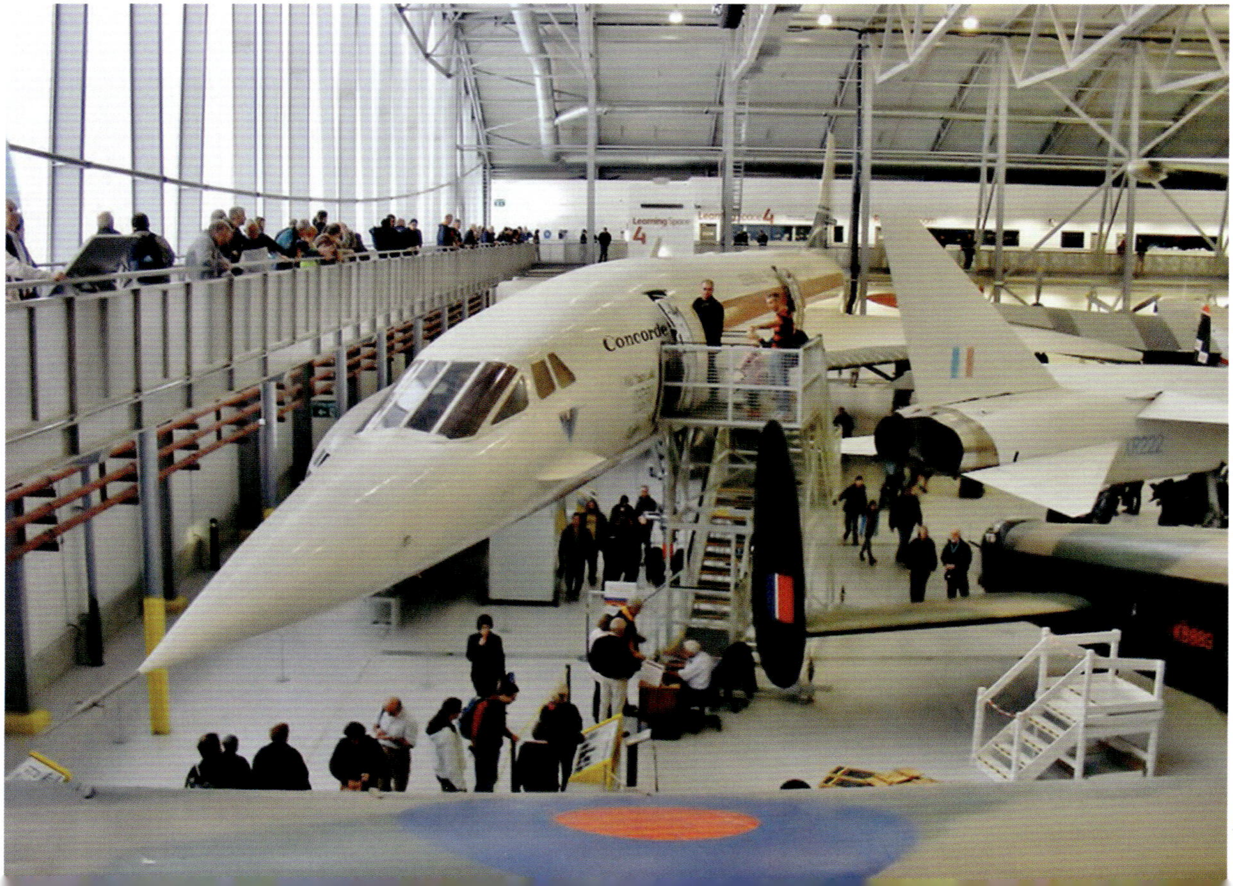

Concorde G-AXDN 01, a pre-production aircraft which achieved the highest speed of any Concorde, making a westwards transatlantic flight in two hours fifty-six minutes. She is now at the Imperial War Museum, Duxford, England.

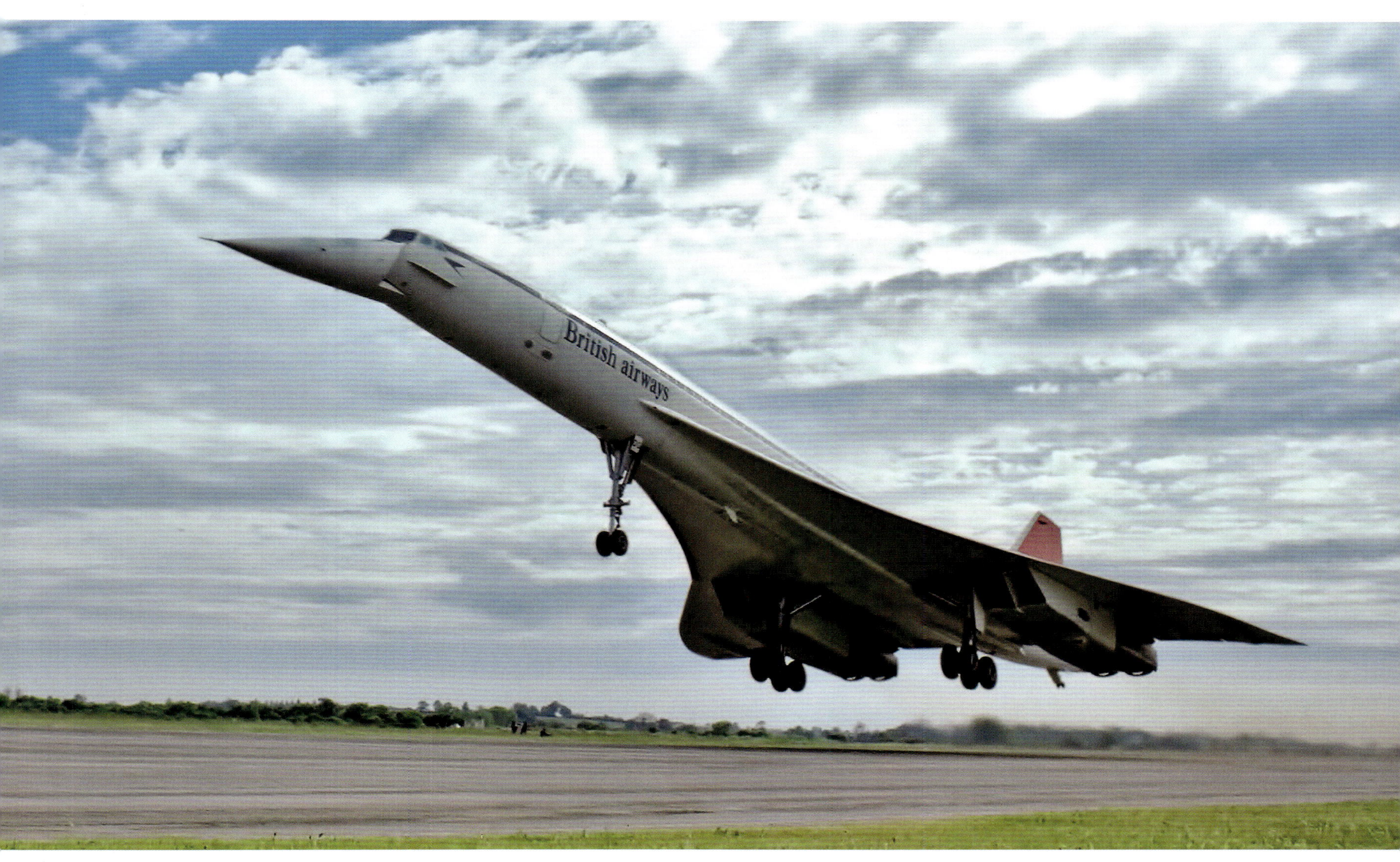

Concorde G-BBDG 202 first flew on 13 February 1974 from Filton to Fairford. Test flights took her to many destinations worldwide, but she only flew 1,282 hours. Her last flight was on 24 December 1981 and then she stayed at Filton until May 2004, when she was moved in sections by road to her new home at Brooklands Museum, Surrey. The project finished in July 2006 and was officially opened to the public by HRH Prince Michael of Kent.

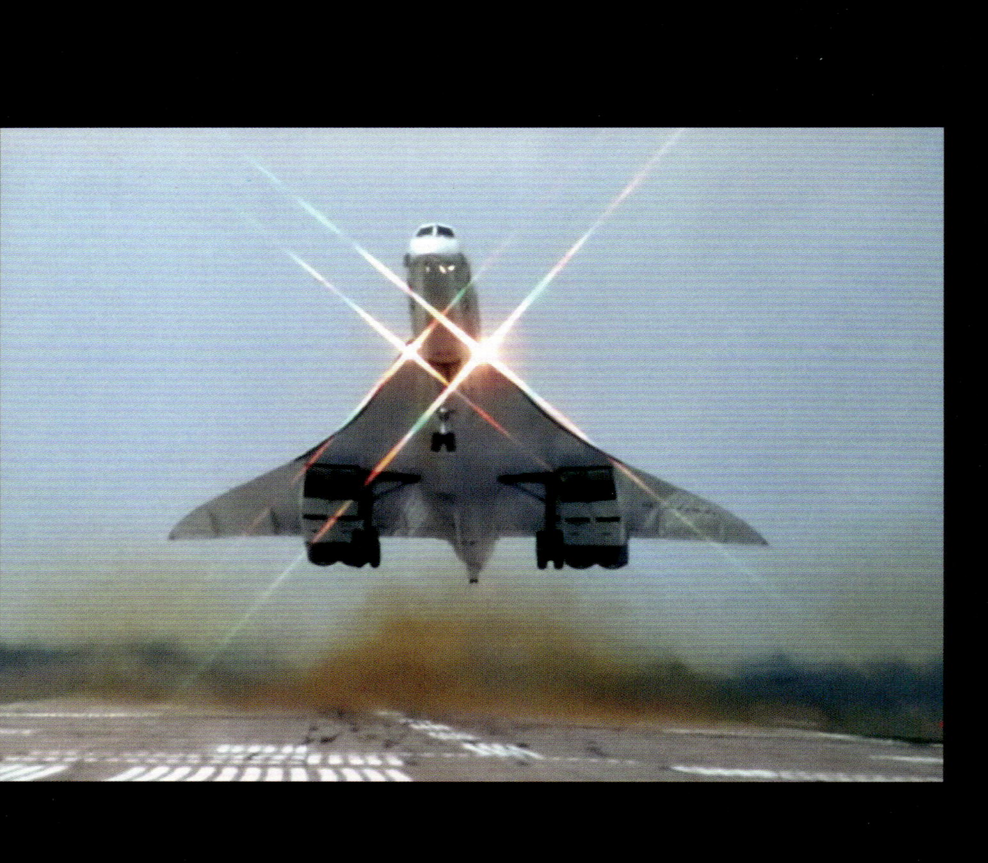